STUDIES IN HUMANISM

STUDIES

IN

HUMANISM

BY

F. C. S. SCHILLER, M.A., D.Sc.

FELLOW AND SENIOR TUTOR OF CORPUS CHRISTI COLLEGE, OXFORD

SECOND EDITION

GREENWOOD PRESS, PUBLISHERS
WESTPORT, CONNECTICUT

Originally published in 1912
by Macmillan and Co., Ltd., London

First Greenwood Reprinting 1970

SBN 8371-2812-9

TO

MY PUPILS

PAST PRESENT AND TO COME

PREFACE TO THE SECOND EDITION

THAT a new edition of these *Studies* (as also of *Humanism*) is called for is one out of many indications [1] that the Pragmatic Movement is gathering momentum and that Humanism has come to stay. Even the most obstinate conservatives are beginning to abandon their attitude of speechless indignation, and to admit that it constitutes an intelligible novelty, though they are not yet reconciled to it. But as it takes more than a day or a generation to undo the cumulative blunders of 2000 years of Intellectualism, it will probably remain a novelty for another century or two, until its applications have been fully worked out. Its rate of progress will depend on how soon the chief philosophic disciplines can be re-written in a Humanist spirit. As a foretaste of this necessary process the logical tradition has been systematically criticized in my *Formal Logic* (1912), and shown to be fundamentally inconsistent nonsense, as resting on an abstraction from meaning and oscillating between verbalism and ' psychology,' both of which it vainly tries to disavow. This puts *Humanism, Axioms as Postulates*, and these *Studies* into the position of prolegomena to a future Logic of Real Knowing. Even under the most favourable circumstances, however, years must elapse before this can

---

[1] To the writer it is, of course, peculiarly gratifying that these *Studies* have been translated into French (Paris, Alcan, 1909), and a selection from them and from *Humanism* into German (Leipzig, Klinkhardt, 1911).

appear ; so it seemed better to reprint these *Studies* with a minimum of alteration.

I must despair of cataloguing in this Preface the whole output of the Pragmatic Controversy. Much has been written since 1907 on both sides, but, mercifully, little that requires me to modify the views I had expressed. We have suffered, of course, an irreparable loss in the departure hence of the great initiator of the movement, William James, with his message but half told. The splendid series of his popular works, *Pragmatism* (1907), *A Pluralistic Universe* (1909), *The Meaning of Truth* (1909), *Some Problems of Philosophy* (1911), will live, but will always be somewhat too simple to be intelligible to the professorial mind, which finds them hard to 'categorize.' Lovers of thinking at first-hand, however, will enjoy them, and should not omit to read also H. V. Knox's article in the *Quarterly Review* (April 1909), Alfred Sidgwick's *Application of Logic* (1910), Dewey's *Influence of Darwin on Philosophy* (1910), and D. L. Murray's little primer of *Pragmatism* (1912).

OXFORD, *April* 1912.

PREFACE TO THE FIRST EDITION

OF the essays which compose this volume about half have appeared in various periodicals—*Mind,* the *Hibbert Journal,* the *Quarterly Review,* the *Fortnightly Review,* and the *Journal of Philosophy*—during the past three years. Additions have, however, grown so extensive that of the matter of the book not more than one-third, and that the less constructive part, can be said to have been in print before. That the form should still be discontinuous is due to the fact that the conditions under which I have had to work greatly hamper and delay the composition of a continuous treatise, and that it seemed imperative to deal more expeditiously with the chief strategic points of the philosophic situation. I hope, however, that the discontinuity of the form will not be found incompatible with an essential continuity of aim, argument, and interest. In all these respects the present *Studies* may most naturally be regarded as continuous with *Humanism* and *Axioms as Postulates,* without, however, ceasing to be independently intelligible. They have had to reflect the developments of philosophy and the progress of discussion, and this has rendered them, I fear, slightly more technical on the whole than *Humanism.* Nor can their main topic, the meaning of Truth, be made an altogether popular subject. On the other hand, they touch more fully than *Humanism* on subjects which are less exclusively technical, such as the nature of our freedom and the religious aspects of philosophy.

That in the contents construction should be somewhat largely mixed with controversy is in some respects regrettable. But whether one can avoid controversy depends largely on whether one's doctrines are allowed an opportunity of peaceful development. Also on what one has undertaken to do. And in this case the most harmless experiments in fog-dispelling have been treated as profanations of the most sacred mysteries. It is, however, quite true that the undertaking of the new philosophy may be regarded as in some ways the most stupendous in the history of thought. Heine, in a well-known passage, once declared the feats of the German Transcendentalists to have been more terrific than those of the French Revolutionaries, in that they decapitated a Deity and not a mere mortal king. But what was the Transcendental boldness of Kant, as described by Heine, when armed only with the 'Pure Reason,' and attended only by his 'faithful Lampe' and an umbrella, he ' stormed Heaven and put the whole garrison to the sword,' to the Transatlantic audacity of a Jacobin philosophy which is seriously suspected of penetrating into the 'supercelestial' heavens of the Pure Reason, and of there upsetting the centre of gravity of the Intelligible Universe, of dethroning the 'Higher Synthesis of the Devil and the Deity,' the Absolute, and of instituting a general ' *Götzendämmerung* ' of the Eternal Ideas ? Even its avowed aim of *humanizing* Truth, and bringing it back to earth from such altitudes, seems comparable with the Promethean sacrilege of the theft of fire. What wonder, then, that such transcelestial conflagrations should kindle burning questions on the earth, and be reflected in the heating of terrestrial tempers ?

But after all, the chief warrant for a polemical handling of these matters is its strict relevance. The new truths are most easily understood by contrast with the old perplexities, and the necessity of advancing in their direction is rendered most evident by the impossibility of advancing in any other.[1]

That the development of the new views, then, should have been so largely controversial, was probably in-

---

[1] Cp. pp. 73-4.

evitable.   It has been all the more rapid for that.   For
the intensity of intellectualistic prejudice and the intoler-
ance of Absolutism have compelled us to attack in sheer
self-defence, to press on our counter-statements in order to
engage the enemy along his whole front, and to hurry
every new argument into the line of battle as soon as it
became available.[1]

The result has been an unprecedented development
of converging novelties.   Within the past three or four
years (*i.e.* since the preface to *Humanism* was written)
there have appeared in the first place the important
Studies in Logical Theory by Prof. Dewey and his
coadjutors.   These, it is becoming more and more
evident, have dealt a death-blow, not only to the 'correspondence-with-reality' view of Truth, but also to all the
realisms and idealisms which involve it.   And so far no
absolutism has succeeded in dispensing with it.   Prof.
Dewey and his pupils have also contributed a number of
weighty and valuable papers and discussions to the philosophic periodicals (*Mind*, the *Journal of Philosophy*, and
the *Philosophical Review*).   Mr. C. S. Peirce's articles in the
Monist (1905) have shown that he has not disavowed the
great Pragmatic principle which he launched into the
world so unobtrusively nearly thirty years ago, and
seemed to leave so long without a father's care.   William
James's final metaphysic, on the other hand, is still in
the making.   But he has expounded and defended the
new views in a series of brilliant articles in the *Journal of
Philosophy* and in *Mind*.[2]   In England the literature of
the question has been critical rather than constructive.
In the forefront may be mentioned Mr. Henry Sturt's
Idola Theatri, a singularly lucid and readable study of
the genesis, development, and ailments of English Absolutism.   But the masterly (and unanswered) criticisms by
Capt. H. V. Knox and Mr. Alfred Sidgwick of the most

[1] Readers, however, who wish to avoid this controversial side as much as
possible, may be counselled to read Essays i., v., ii., iii., vii., xvi.-xx. in the
order indicated.

[2] *Journal of Philosophy*, I. Nos. 18, 20, 21, 25; II. Nos. 2, 5, 7, 9, 11;
III. No. 13.   *Mind*, N.S. Nos. 52 and 54.   (Now reprinted in *A Pluralistic
Universe*, *The Meaning of Truth*, and *Essays in Radical Empiricism*.)

essential foundations of absolutist metaphysics should not be forgotten.[1]   And lastly, Prof. Santayana's exquisite *Life of Reason* should be cited as a triumph, not only of literary form, but also of the Pragmatic Method in a mind which has espoused a metaphysic very different from that which in general Pragmatism favours.   For Prof. Santayana, though a pragmatist in epistemology, is a materialist in metaphysics.[2]

The new movement is also in evidence beyond the borders of the English-speaking world, either in its properly pragmatic forms or in their equivalents and analogues.   It is most marked perhaps in France, where it has the weighty support in philosophy of Prof. Bergson of the Collège de France, who has followed up the anti-intellectualism of his *Données immédiates de la Conscience* by his *Matière et Mémoire*, and in science of Prof. Henri Poincaré of the Institute, whose *La Science et l'Hypothèse* and *La Valeur de la Science* expound the pragmatic nature of the scientific procedures and assumptions with unsurpassable lucidity and grace.   He seems, indeed, as yet unwilling to go as far as some of the ultra-pragmatic followers of Prof. Bergson, *e.g.* MM. Leroy and Wilbois, and imposes some slight limitations on the pragmatic treatment of knowledge, on the ground that knowledge may be conceived as an end to which action is a means. But this perhaps only indicates that this pre-eminent man of science has not yet taken note of the work which has been done by philosophers in the English-writing world on the nature of the conception of Truth and the relation of the scientific endeavour to our total activity.   At any rate he goes quite far enough to make it clear that whoever henceforth wishes to uphold the traditional views of the nature of science, and particularly of mathematics, will have in the first place to confute Prof. Poincaré.

In Italy Florence boasts of a youthful, but extremely active and brilliant, band of avowed Pragmatists, whose

[1] *Mind*, N.S. Nos. 54 and 53.
[2] I have discussed the relations of his work to the Pragmatic movement in reviewing it for the *Hibbert Journal* (January and July 1906).

militant organ, the *Leonardo*, edited by Signor Giovanni Papini, is distinguished by a freedom and vigour of language which must frequently horrify the susceptibilities of academic coteries.   In Denmark Prof. Höffding is more than sympathetic, and the Royal Academy of Science has recently made the relations of Pragmatism and Criticism the subject for the international prize essay for which Schopenhauer once wrote his *Grundlage der Moral.*

In Germany alone the movement seems slow to take root *eo nomine.*   Nevertheless, there are a goodly number of analogous tendencies.   Professors Ostwald and Mach and their schools are the champions of a pragmatic view of science.   Various forms of 'Psychologism,' proceeding from the same considerations as those which have inspired the Anglo-American pragmatisms, disturb the old conceptions of Logic.   Among them Prof. Jerusalem's *Der kritische Idealismus und die reine Logik* is particularly noteworthy.   The 'school of Fries,' and conspicuously Dr. Julius Schultz, the author of the brilliant *Psychologie der Axiome*, excellently emphasize the postulation of axioms, though as their polemic against empiricism still presupposes the Humian conception of a passive experience, they prefer to call them *a priori*.[1]   The *humanistic* aspects of the movement find a close parallel in the writings of Prof. Eucken.   But on the whole Germany lags behind, largely because these various tendencies have not yet been connected or brought to a common focus. I have, however, reason to believe that this deficiency may soon be remedied.

What, meanwhile, is the situation in the camp of Intellectualism, which is still thronged with most of the philosophic notables ?   Although the technical journals have been full of controversial articles, and the interest excited has actually sent up the circulation of *Mind*, singularly little has been produced that rises above the merest misconception or misrepresentation ; and nothing to invalidate the new ideas.   Mr. F. H. Bradley has

[1] Cp. *Mind*, xv. p. 115.

exercised his great talents of philosophic caricature,[1] but a positive alternative to Pragmatism, in the shape of an intelligible, coherent doctrine of the nature of Truth, is still the great desideratum of Intellectualism.

The most noteworthy attempt, beyond doubt, to work out an intellectualistic ideal of Truth, which has proceeded from the Anglo-Hegelian school, is Mr. H. H. Joachim's recent *Nature of Truth*. But it may be doubted whether its merits will commend it to the school. For it ends in flat failure, and avowed scepticism, which is scientifically redeemed only by the fact that its outspokenness greatly facilitates the critic's task in laying his finger on the fundamental flaw of all Intellectualism. With the exception of Plato's *Theaetetus*, no book has, consequently, been of greater service to me in showing how fatal the *depersonalizing* of thought and the *dehumanizing* of Truth are to the possibility and intelligibility of knowledge, and how arbitrary and indefensible these abstractions really are.

It would seem, therefore, that the situation is rapidly clearing itself. On the one hand we have a new Method with inexhaustible possibilities of application to life and science, which, though it is not primarily metaphysical, contains also the promise of an infinity of valuable, and more or less valid, metaphysics : on the other, opposed to it on every point, an old metaphysic of tried and tested sterility, which is condemned to eternal failure by the fundamental perversity of its logical method. And now at last is light beginning to penetrate into its obscurities. It is becoming clear that Rationalism is not rational, and that 'reason' does not sanction its pretensions. Absolutism is ending as those who saw its essentially inhuman character foresaw that it must. In its 'Hegelian' as in its Bradleian form, it has yielded itself wholly up to Scepticism, and Mr. Bradley was evidently not a day too soon in comparing it to Jericho.[2] For its defences have crumbled into dust, without a regular siege, merely under the strain of attempts to man them. Its

---

[1] Cp. Essay iv.   [2] Cp. p. 119.

opponents really are not needed for their demolition ; they need merely record and applaud the work of self-destruction.

But that this process should provoke dissatisfaction and disintegration in the ranks of the absolutists is no wonder, nor that the signs of their confusion should be multiplying. No one seems to know, *e.g.*, what is to be done about the central point, the conception of Truth ; whether the ' correspondence-view ' is to be reaffirmed or abandoned, and in the former case, *how* it can be defended, or in the latter, *how* it can be discarded.[1] Nay, the voice of mutiny is beginning to be heard. The advice is openly given to the ' idealist ' host to shut up their Bradley and their Berkeley, and to open their Plato and their Hegel.[2] As regards Hegel this recommendation is not likely to be fruitful, because nothing will be found in him that bears on the situation : Plato, on the other hand, is likely to provide most salutary, but almost wholly penitential, reading. For I believe, these *Studies* will be found to fulfil a pledge given in *Humanism*,[3] and to show that Intellectualism may be confuted out of the mouth of its own founder and greatest exponent. For Plato had in fact perceived the final consequence of Intellectualism, viz. that to complete itself *it must dehumanize the Ideal and derealize the Real*, with superior clearness. His unwillingness either to avoid or to conceal this consequence is what has engendered the hopeless crux of the ' Platonic problem ' from his day to this, and from this difficulty no intellectualism can ever extricate itself. It may rail at humanity and try to dissolve human knowledge ; but the only real remedy lies in renouncing the abstractions on which it rests. Our only hope of understanding knowledge, our only chance of keeping philosophy alive by nourishing it with the realities of life, lies in going back from Plato to Protagoras, and ceasing to misunderstand the great teacher who discovered the Measure of man's Universe.

---

[1] Cp. Essays iv. § 7 ; vii. § 1 ; xx. § 2.

[2] *Mind*, N.S. No. 59, xv. p. 327.   [3] P. xvii.

I cannot conclude this Preface without recording my indebtedness to my friend Capt. H. V. Knox, who has read a large part of these *Studies* in proof and in manuscript, and with whom I have had the pleasure of discussing some of the knottiest points in the theory of knowledge. I have profited thereby to such an extent that I should find it hard to say how far some of the doctrines here enunciated were his or mine.

SILS MARIA, *September* 1906.

CONTENTS

I

THE DEFINITION OF PRAGMATISM AND HUMANISM

ARGUMENT

The need of definitions. I. Importance of the problem of Error. Truth as the evaluation of claims. The question begged and burked by Intellectualism. The value of the consequences as the Humanist test. Why 'true' consequences are 'practical' and 'good.' Impossibility of a 'purely intellectual' satisfaction. First definition of Pragmatism: *truths are logical values.* II. Necessity of 'verification' of truth by use or application ; the second definition, *the truth of an assertion depends on its application*; and the third, *the meaning of a rule lies in its application*; the fourth, *all meaning depends on purpose.* Its value as a protest against the divorce of logic from psychology. Fifth definition, *all mental life is purposive*, a protest against Naturalism, as is the sixth, *a systematic protest against ignoring the purposiveness of actual knowing.* No alien reality. Finally this leads to a seventh definition as a conscious application to logic of a teleological psychology, implying a voluntaristic metaphysic. III. Humanism as the spirit of Pragmatism, and like it a natural method, which will not mutilate experience. Its antagonism to pedantry. It includes Pragmatism, but is not necessitated by the latter, nor confined to epistemology. IV. Neither is as such a metaphysic, both are methods, metaphysical syntheses being merely personal. But both may be conceived metaphysically and have metaphysical affinities. Need of applying the pragmatic test to metaphysics.

REAL definitions are a standing difficulty for all who have to deal with them, whether as logicians or as scientists, and it is no wonder that dialectical philosophers fight very shy of them, prefer to manipulate their verbal imitations, and count themselves happy if they can get an analysis of the acquired meaning of a word to pass muster instead of a troublesome investigation of the behaviour of a thing. For a real definition, to be adequate, really involves a complete knowledge of the nature of the thing defined. And of what subject of scientific interest can we flatter ourselves to have complete knowledge?

The difficulty, moreover, of defining adequately is indefinitely increased when we have to deal with subjects of which our knowledge, or their nature, is rapidly developing, so that our definitions grow obsolete almost as fast as they are made. Nevertheless definitions of some sort are psychologically needed: we must know what things are, enough at least to know what we are discussing. It is just in the most progressive subjects that definitions are most needed to consolidate our acquisitions. In their absence the confusion of thought and the irrelevance of discussion may reach the most amazing proportions. And so it is the duty of those who labour at such subjects to avail themselves of every opportunity of explaining what they mean, to begin with, and never to weary of redefining their conceptions when the growth of knowledge has enlarged them, even though they may be aware that however assiduously they perform this duty, they will not escape misconception, nor, probably, misrepresentation. The best definitions to use in such circumstances, however, will be genetic ones, explaining how the matters defined have come into the ken of science, and there assumed the shape they have.

All these generalities apply with peculiar force to the fundamental conceptions of the new philosophy. The new ideas have simultaneously broken through the hard crust of academic convention in so many quarters, they can be approached in such a multitude of ways, they radiate into so many possibilities of application, that their promoters run some risk of failing to combine their labours, while their opponents may be pardoned for losing their tempers as well as their heads amid the profusion of unco-ordinated movements which the lack of formal definition is calculated to encourage.

Even provisional definitions of Pragmatism and Humanism, therefore, will possess some value, if they succeed in pointing out their central conceptions.

I

The serious student, I dare not say of formal logic, but of the cognitive procedures of the human intelligence, whenever he approaches the theory of actual knowing, at once finds himself confronted with the problem of error.[1] All 'logical propositions,' as he calls them, make the same audacious claim upon him. They all claim to be 'true' without reservations or regard for the claims of others. And yet, of course, unless he shuts his eyes to all but the most 'formal' view of 'truth,' he knows that the vast majority of these propositions are nothing but specious impostors. They are not really 'true,' and actual science has to disallow their claim. The logician, therefore, must take account of this rejection of claims, of this selection of the really 'true' from among apparent 'truths.' In constituting his science, therefore, he has to condemn as 'false' as well as to recognize as 'true,' *i.e.* to evaluate claims to truth.

The question therefore is—How does he effect this? How does he discriminate between propositions which claim to be true, but are not, and claims to truth which are good, and may be shown to be valid? How, that is, are valid truths distinguished from mere claims which may turn out to be false? These questions are inevitable, and no theory of knowledge which fails to answer them has any claim on our respect. It avows an incompleteness which is as disgraceful as it is inconvenient.

Now from the standpoint of rationalistic intellectualism there is no real answer to these questions, because

---

[1] Contrast with this the putting of the question in an absolutist logic, *e.g.* Mr. Joachim's instructive *Nature of Truth*, which I had not seen when this was written. Mr. Joachim begins at the opposite end with 'the Ideal,' and avoids the consideration of Error as long as he can. But when he does come to it, he is completely worsted, and his system is wrecked. Thus the difference between the Absolutist and the Humanist theory lies chiefly in the standpoint ; the facts are the same on either view. The question, in fact, resolves itself into this, whether or not 'Logic' is concerned with *human* thought. This the humanist affirms, while the absolutist is under the disadvantage of not daring to deny it *wholly*. Hence the incoherence and inevitable collapse of his theory. Cp. Essay ii. §§ 16-17.

a priori inspection cannot determine the value of a claim, and experience is needed to decide whether it is good or not.[1]   Hence the obscurity, ambiguity, and shiftiness, the general impotence and unreality, of the traditional logic is largely a consequence of its incapacity to deal with this difficulty.   For how can you devise any practicable method of evaluating 'truths,' if you decline (1) to allow practical applications and the consequences of the working out of claims to affect their validity, if you decline (2) to recognize any intermediate stage in the making of truth between the mere claim and a completed ideal of absolute truth, and if, moreover, (3) you seek to burke the whole question of the *formation* of ideals by assuming that prior to all experience and experiment there exists one immutable ideal towards which all claims *must* converge?

Pragmatism, on the other hand, essays to trace out the actual 'making of truth,'[2] the actual ways in which discriminations between the true and the false are effected, and derives from these its generalizations about the method of determining the nature of truth.   It is from such empirical observations that it derives its doctrine

---

[1] The complete failure of intellectualism to apprehend even the most obvious aims of Pragmatism is amusingly illustrated by Mr. Bradley's fulminations against us on the ground that we cannot possibly distinguish between a random claim and an established truth.   He pontifically declares (*Mind*, xiii. p. 322) that "the Personal Idealist . . . if he understood his own doctrine must hold any end, however perverted, to be rational, if I insist on it personally, and any idea, however mad, to be the truth, if only some one will have it so."   Again, on p. 329, he ludicrously represents us as holding that "I can make and I can unmake fact and truth at my caprice, and every vagary of mine becomes the nature of things.   This insane doctrine is what consistency demands," but Mr. Bradley graciously concedes that "I cannot attribute it even to the protagonist of Personal Idealism."   Of course if there is one subject which pragmatist logicians may be said to have made their own from the days of Protagoras downwards, it is that of the evaluation of individual claims and their gradual transformation into 'objective' truths (cp. Essay ii. § 5).   Intellectualists, on the other hand, have ever steadfastly refused to consider the discrepancies arising from the existence of psychological variations in human valuations (cp. p. 30), or lastly preferred to attribute to 'the human,' or even to 'the absolute,' mind whatever idiosyncrasies they discovered in themselves.   Thus inquiry into the actual making of truth has been tabooed, the most important questions have been begged, and both the extent and the limitations of the 'common' world of intersubjective social agreement have been left an unaccountable mystery, sometimes further aggravated by the metaphysical postulation of a superhuman mind conceived as 'common' to all human minds, but really incompetent to enter into relation with any of them, and *a fortiori* incapable of accounting for their individual differences.

[2] Cp. Essay vii.

that when an assertion claims truth, *its consequences are always used to test its claim.* In other words, what follows from its truth for any human interest, and more particularly and in the first place, for the interest with which it is directly concerned, is what established its *real* truth and validity. This is the famous ' Principle of Peirce,' which ought to be regarded as the greatest truism, if it had not pleased Intellectualism to take it as the greatest paradox. But that only showed, perhaps, how completely intellectualist traditions could blind philosophers to the simplest facts of cognition. For there was no intrinsic reason why even the extremest intellectualism should have denied that the difference between the truth and the falsehood of an assertion must show itself in some visible, observable way, or that two theories which led to precisely the same practical consequences could be different only in words

Human interest, then, is vital to the existence of truth : to say that a truth has consequences and that what has none is meaningless, means that it has a bearing upon some human interest. Its 'consequences' must be consequences *to* some one engaged on a real problem *for* some purpose. If it is clearly grasped that the 'truth' with which we are concerned is truth *for man* and that the 'consequences' are human too, it is, however, superfluous to add either (1) that the consequences must be *practical*, or (2) that they must be *good*,[1] in order to distinguish this view sharply from that of rationalism.

For (1) all consequences are 'practical,' sooner or later, in the sense of affecting our action. Even where

---

[1] In *Mind*, xiv. N.S. No. 54, p. 236, I tried to draw a distinction between a narrower and a wider 'pragmatism,' of which I attributed only the former to Mr. Peirce. In this I was following James's distinction between the positions that 'truths should have practical consequences,' and that they 'consist in their consequences,' and that these must be 'good.' Of these he seemed to attribute only the former to Mr. Peirce, and denominated the latter Humanism. But Humanism seems to me to go further still, and not to be restricted to the one question of 'truth.' If, as Mr. Peirce has privately assured me, he had from the first perceived the full consequences of his dictum, the formulation of the whole pragmatic principle must be ascribed to him. But he has also exhibited extensive inability to follow the later developments, and now calls his own specific form of Pragmatism, 'pragmaticism.' See *Monist*, xv. 2.

they do not immediately alter the course of events, they alter our own nature, and cause its actions to be different, and thus lead to different operations on the world.

Similarly (2) if an assertion is to be valuable, and therefore 'true,' its consequences must be 'good.' They can only test the truth it claims by forwarding or baffling the interest, by satisfying or thwarting the purpose, which led to the making of the assertion. If they do the one, the assertion is 'good,' and *pro tanto* 'true'; if they do the other, it is 'bad' and 'false.' For whatever arouses an interest or forwards an end is judged to be (so far) 'good,' whatever baffles or thwarts is judged to be 'bad.' If, therefore, the consequences of an assertion turn out to be in this way 'good,' it is valuable for our purposes, and, provisionally at least, establishes itself as 'true'; if they are bad, we reject it as useless and account it 'false,' and search for something that satisfies our purpose better, or in extreme cases accept it as a provisional truth concerning a reality we are determined to unmake. Thus the predicates 'true' and 'false' are nothing in the end but indications of logical value, and *as values* akin to and comparable with the values predicated in ethical and æsthetical judgments, which present similar problems of the validation of claims.[1]

The reason, therefore, why truth is said to depend on its consequences is simply this, that if we do not imagine truths to exist immutably and *a priori* in a supercelestial world, and to descend magically into a passively recipient soul, as rationalists since Plato have continually tried to hold,[2] they must come into being by winning our acceptance. And what rational mode of verification can any one suggest other than this testing by their consequences?

Of course the special nature of the testing depends on the subject-matter, and the nature of the 'experiments' which are in this way made in mathematics, in ethics, in physics, in religion, may seem very diverse superficially. But there is no reason to set up a peculiar process of

[1] Essay v. § 3.   [2] Cp. Essay ii. §§ 15, 16.

verification for the satisfying of a 'purely intellectual' interest, different in kind from the rest, superior in dignity, and autocratic in authority. For (1) there is no pure intellect. If 'pure intellect' does not imply a gross blunder in psychology, and this is probably what it too often meant until the conception was challenged, it means an abstraction, an intellect conceived as void of function, as not applied to any actual problem, as satisfying no purpose. Such an intellect of course would be absurd. Or is it possibly conceived as having the end of amusing its possessor? As achieving this end it may claim somewhat more regard, but apart from its value as exercise, the mere play of the intellect, which is meant for serious work, does not seem intrinsically venerable; it is certainly just as liable to abuse as any other game. And (2) if we exclude morbid or frivolous excesses, the actual functioning of the intellect, even in what are called its most 'purely intellectual' forms, is only intelligible by reference to human ends and values.

All testing of 'truth,' therefore, is fundamentally alike. It is always an appeal to something beyond the original claim. It always implies an experiment. It always involves a *risk* of failure as well as a prospect of success. And it always ends in a valuation. As Prof. Mach has said:[1] "knowledge and error flow from the self-same psychic sources; the issue alone can discriminate between them." We arrive, therefore, at our first definition of Pragmatism as the doctrine that (1) *truths are logical values*, and as the method which systematically tests claims to truth in accordance with this principle.

II

It is easily apparent that it directly follows from this definition of truth that all 'truths' must be verified to

---

[1] *Erkenntnis und Irrtum*, p. 114. The German word '*Erfolg*,' translated 'issue,' covers both 'consequence' and 'success': it is, in fact, one of many words by which language spontaneously testifies to the pragmatic nature of thought. Cp. 'fact'—'made,' 'true'—'trow'—'trust,' 'false'—'fail,' 'verify,' 'come true,' 'object' = 'aim,' 'judgment' = 'decision'; and in German '*wirklich*'—'*wirken*,' '*wahr*'—'*bewähren*,' '*Wahrnehmung*,' '*Tatsache*,' etc.

be properly true. A 'truth' which will not (or cannot) submit to verification is not yet a truth at all. Its truth is at best potential, its meaning is null or unintelligible, or at most conjectural and dependent on an unfulfilled condition. On its entry into the world of existence a truth-claim has merely commended itself (perhaps provisionally) to its maker. To become really true it has to be tested, and it is tested by being *applied*. Only when this is done, only that is when it is *used*, can it be determined what it really means, and what conditions it must fulfil to be really true. Hence all real truths must have shown themselves to be useful ; they must have been applied to some problem of actual knowing, by usefulness in which they were tested and verified.

Hence we arrive at a second formulation of the pragmatic principle, on which Mr. Alfred Sidgwick has justly laid such stress,[1] viz. that (2) *the 'truth' of an assertion depends on its application.* Or, in other words, 'abstract' truths are not fully truths at all. They are truths out of use, unemployed, craving for incarnation in the concrete. It is only in their actual operations upon the world of immediate experience that they cast off their callous ambiguity, that they mean, and live, and show their power. Now in ordinary life men of ordinary intelligence are quite aware of this. They recognize that truth depends very essentially upon context, on who says what, to whom, why, and under what circumstances ; they know also that the point of a principle lies in the application thereof, and that it is very hazardous to guide oneself by abstract maxims with a doctrinaire disregard of the peculiarities of the case. The man of science similarly, for all the world-embracing sweep of his generalizations, for all his laudations of inexorable 'law,' is perfectly aware that his theoretic anticipations always stand in need of confirmation in fact, and that if this fails his 'laws' are falsified. They are not true, unless they 'come true.'

The intellectualist philosopher alone has blinded him-

---

[1] *The Application of Logic*, p. 272, and ch. ix. § 43.

self to these simple facts.   He has dreamt a wondrous dream of a truth that shall be absolutely true, self-testing, and self-dependent, icily exercising an unrestricted sway over a submissive world, whose adoration it requites with no services, and scouting as blasphemy all allusion to use or application.   But he cannot point to any truth which realizes his ideal.[1]   Even the abstract truths of arithmetic, upon which alone he seems to rest his case, now that the invention of metageometries has shown the 'truth of geometry' to involve also the question of its application, derive their truth from their application to experience. The abstract statement, *e.g.* that "two and two make four," is always incomplete.   We need to know to what 'twos' and 'fours' the dictum is applied.   It would not be true of lions and lambs, nor of drops of water, nor of pleasures and pains.   The range of application of the abstract truth, therefore, is quite limited.   And conceivably it might be so restricted that the truth would become inapplicable to the outer world altogether.   Nay, though states of consciousness could always be counted, so long as succession was experienced, it is impossible to see how it could be true to an eternal consciousness.   The gods, as Aristotle would have said, seeing that they cannot count, can have no arithmetic.

In short, truths must be used to become true, and (in the end) to stay true.   They are also *meant* to be used. They are rules for action.   And a rule that is not applied, and remains abstract, rules nothing, and means nothing. Hence we may, once more following Mr. Alfred Sidgwick, regard it as the essence of the pragmatic method that (3) *the meaning of a rule lies in its application.*   It rules, that is, and is true, within a definite sphere of application which has been marked out by experiment.

Perhaps, however, it is possible to state the pragmatic character of truth still more incisively by laying it down that ultimately (4) *all meaning depends on purpose.*   This formulation grows naturally out of the last two.   The making of an assertion, the application of an alleged

[1] Cp. Essay ii. §§ 16-18.

truth to the experience which tests it, can only occur in the context of and in connexion with some purpose, which defines the nature of the whole ideal experiment.

The dependence of meaning on purpose is beginning to be somewhat extensively recognized, though hardly as yet what havoc this principle must work among the abstractions of intellectualist logic. For it is one of the most distinctive ways in which the pragmatic view of truth can be enunciated, and guards against two of the chief failings of Intellectualism. It contains an implicit protest against the abstraction of logic from psychology : for purpose is as clearly a psychological conception as meaning is professedly a logical one.[1] And it negatives the notion that truth can depend on how things would appear to an all-embracing, or 'absolute,' mind. For such a mind could have no purpose. It could not, that is, select part of its content as an object of special interest to be operated on or aimed at.[2] In human minds, on the other hand, meaning is always selective and purposive.

It is, in fact, a biological function, intimately related to the welfare of the organism. Biologically speaking, the whole mind, of which the intellect forms part, may be conceived as a typically human instrument for effecting adaptations, which has survived and developed by showing itself possessed of an efficacy superior to the devices adopted by other animals. Hence the most essential feature of Pragmatism may well seem its insistence on the fact that (5) *all mental life is purposive.* This insistence in reality embodies the pragmatic protest against naturalism, and as such ought to receive the cordial support of rationalistic idealisms. But it has just been shown that absolutist idealisms have their own difficulties with the conception of purpose, and besides, it is an open secret that they have for the most part long ago reduced the 'spiritual nature of reality' to a mere form, and retired from the struggle against naturalism.[3] A 'spiritual nature of reality' which accepts all the naturalistic negations of

---

[1] See Essay iii. § 9.   [2] Cp. Essay ix. § 5.
[3] Cp. Essay xii. § 5.

human activity and freedom, and leaves no room for any of the characteristic procedures and aspirations of the human spirit, is a more dangerous foe to man's spiritual ambitions than the most downright materialism.

Pragmatism, therefore, must enter its protest against both the extremes that have so nearly met. It must constitute itself into (6) *a systematic protest against all ignoring of the purposiveness of actual knowing*, alike whether it is abstracted from for the sake of the imaginary 'pure' or 'absolute' reason of the rationalists, or eliminated for the sake of an equally imaginary 'pure mechanism' of the materialists. It must insist on the permeation of all actual knowing by interests, purposes, desires, emotions, ends, goods, postulations, choices, etc., and deny that even those doctrines which vociferate their abhorrence of such things are really able to dispense with them. For the human reason is ever gloriously human, even when most it tries to disavow its nature, and to misconceive itself. It mercifully interposes an impenetrable veil between us and any truth or reality which is wholly alien to our nature. The efforts, therefore, of those who ignore the nature of the instruments they use must ever fail, and fail the more flagrantly the more strenuously they persist in thinking to the end.

If, however, we have the courage and perseverance to persist in thinking to the end, *i.e.* to form a metaphysic, it is likely that we should arrive at some sort of Voluntarism. For Voluntarism is the metaphysic which most easily accords and harmonizes with the experience of activity with which all our thinking and all our living seem to overflow. Metaphysics, however, are in a manner luxuries. Men can live quite well without a conscious metaphysic, and the systems even of the most metaphysical are hardly ever quite consistent, or fully thought out. Pragmatism, moreover, is not a metaphysic, though it may, somewhat definitely, point to one. It is really something far more precious, viz. an epistemological method which really describes the facts of actual knowing.

But though it is only a method in the field of logic, it may well confess to its affinities for congenial views in other sciences. It prides itself on its close connexion with psychology. But it clearly takes for granted that the psychology with which it is allied has recognized the reality of purposes. And so it can be conceived as a special application to the sphere of logic of standpoints and methods which extend far beyond its borders. So conceived we may describe it as (7) *a conscious application to epistemology (or logic) of a teleological psychology, which implies, ultimately, a voluntaristic metaphysic.*

These seven formulations of the essence of Pragmatism look, doubtless, very different in words ; but they are nevertheless very genuinely equivalent. For they are closely connected, and the 'essence,' like the 'definition,' of a thing is relative to the point of view from which it is regarded.[1] And the problems raised by Pragmatism are so central that it has points of contact with almost every line of philosophical inquiry, and so is capable of being defined by its relation to this. What is really important, however, is not this or that formulation, but the spirit in which it approaches, and the method by which it examines, its problems. The method we have observed ; it is empirical, teleological, and concrete. Its spirit is a bigger thing, which may fitly be denominated Humanism.

III

Humanism is really in itself the simplest of philosophic standpoints ; it is merely the perception that the philosophic problem concerns human beings striving to comprehend a world of human experience by the resources of human minds. Not even Pragmatism could be simpler or nearer to an obvious truism of cognitive method. For if man may not presume his own nature in his reasonings about his experience, wherewith, pray, shall he reason ? What prospect has he of comprehending a radically alien

---

[1] Cp. *Formal Logic*, pp. 53-4.

universe? And yet not even Pragmatism has been more bitterly assailed than the great principle that man is the measure of his experience, and so an ineradicable factor in any world he experiences. The Protagorean principle may sometimes seem paradoxical to the uninstructed, because they think it leaves out of account the 'independence' of the 'external' world. But this is mere misunderstanding. Humanism has no quarrel with the assumptions of common-sense realism ; it does not deny what is popularly described as the 'external' world. It has far too much respect for the pragmatic value of conceptions which *de facto* work far better than those of the metaphysics which despise and try to supersede them. It insists only that the 'external world' of realism is still dependent on human experience, and perhaps ventures to add also that the data of human experience are not completely used up in the construction of a real external world.[1] Moreover, its assailants are not realists, though, for the purpose of such attacks, they may masquerade as such.[2]

The truth is rather that Humanism gives offence, not because it leaves out, but because it leaves in. It leaves in a great deal intellectualism would like to leave out, a great deal it has no use for, which it would like to extirpate, or at least to keep out of its sight. But Humanism will not assent to the mutilations and expurgations of human nature which have become customary barbarisms in the initiation ceremonies of too many philosophic schools. It demands that man's integral nature shall be used as the whole premiss which philosophy must argue from wholeheartedly, that man's complete satisfaction shall be the conclusion philosophy must aim at, that philosophy shall not cut itself loose from the real problems of life by making initial abstractions which are false, and would not be admirable, even if they were true. Hence it insists on *leaving in* the whole rich luxuriance of individual minds, instead of compressing them all into a single type of 'mind,' feigned to be one and immutable ; it leaves in also the psychological

[1] Cp. Essay xx. § 14.　　[2] Cp. Essay xx. § 4.

wealth of every human mind and the complexities of its interests, emotions, volitions, aspirations. By so doing it sacrifices no doubt much illusory simplicity in abstract formulas, but it appreciates and explains vast masses of what before had had to be slurred over as unintelligible fact.[1]

The dislike of Humanism, therefore, is psychological in origin. It arises from the nature of certain human minds who have become too enamoured of the artificial simplifications, or too accustomed to the self-inflicted mutilations, and the self-imposed torments, whereby they hope to merit absorption in absolute truth. These ascetics of the intellectual world must steadfastly oppose the free indulgence in all human powers, the liberty of moving, of improving, of making, of manipulating, which Humanism vindicates for man, and substitutes for the old ideal of an inactive contemplation of a static truth. It is no wonder that the Simeons Stylitæ of the old order, hoisted aloft each on the pillar of his metaphysical 'system,' resent the disturbance of their restful solitude, 'alone with the Alone,' by the hoots of intrusive motor-cars; that the Saint Antonys of the deserts of Pure Thought are infuriated by their conversion into serviceable golf-links; and that the Juggernaut Car of the Absolute gets fewer and fewer votaries to prostrate themselves beneath its wheels every time it is rolled out of the recesses of its sanctuary—for when man has grown conscious of his powers he will prefer even to chance an encounter with a useful machine to being run over by a useless 'deity.'

The active life of man is continuously being transformed by the progress of modern science, by the knowledge which is power. But not so the 'knowledge' which is 'contemplation,' which postpones the test of action, and struggles to evade it. Unfortunately, it is hard to modernize the academic life, and it is this life which is the fountain-head of intellectualism. Academic life naturally tends to produce a certain intellectualistic bias, and to

[1] Contrast Mr. Joachim's *Nature of Truth* throughout, especially pp. 167-8, and compare Essay ii. § 16.

select the natures which incline to it. Intellectualism, therefore, in some form will always be a congenial philosophy which is true to the academic life.

Genuine whole-hearted Humanism, on the other hand, is a singularly difficult attitude to sustain in an academic atmosphere ; for the tendencies of the whole mode of life are unceasingly against it. If Protagoras had been a university professor, he would hardly have discovered Humanism ; he would more likely have constructed a Nephelococcygia of a system that laid claim to absolute, universal, and eternal truth, or spent his life in overthrowing the discrepant, but no less presumptuous, systems of his colleagues. Fortunately he lived before universities had been invented to regulate, and quench, the thirst for knowledge ; he had to earn his living by the voluntary gratitude for instructions which could justify themselves only in his pupils' lives ; and so he had to be human and practical, and to take the chill of pedantry off his discourses.

Just because Humanism, then, is true to the larger life of man it must be in some measure false to the artificially secluded studies of a 'seat of learning' ; and its acceptance by an academic personage must always mean a triumph over the obvious temptation to idealize and adore the narrownesses of his actual life. However much it exalts the function of man in general, it may always be taken to hint a certain disparagement of the academic man. It needs a certain magnanimity, in short, in a professor to avow himself a Humanist.

Thorough Humanists, therefore, will always be somewhat rare in academic circles. There will always be many who will not be able to avoid convincing themselves of the truth of a method which works like the pragmatic one (and indeed in another twenty years pragmatic convictions will be practically universal), without being able to overcome the intellectualistic influences of their nature and their mode of life. Such persons will be psychologically incapacitated to advance in the path which leads from Pragmatism to Humanism.

Yet this advance is in a manner logical as well as psychological. For those whose nature predisposes them towards it will find it reasonable and satisfying, and when they have reached the Humanist position and reflect upon the expansion of Pragmatism which it involves, there will seem to be a 'logical' connexion. Pragmatism will seem a special application of Humanism to the theory of knowledge. But Humanism will seem more universal. It will seem to be possessed of a method which is applicable universally, to ethics, to æsthetics, to metaphysics, to theology, to every concern of man, as well as to the theory of knowledge.

Yet there will be no 'logical' compulsion. Here, as always when we come to the important choices of life, we must be free to stop at the lower level, if we are to be free to advance to the higher. We can stop at the epistemological level of Pragmatism (just as we can stop short of philosophy on the scientific plane, and of science on the plane of ordinary life), accepting Pragmatism indeed as the method and analysis of our cognitive procedure, but without seeking to generalize it, or to turn it into a metaphysic. Indeed if our interest is not keen in life as a whole, we are very likely to do something of the kind.

IV

What, then, shall be said of metaphysics? As Pragmatism and Humanism have been defined, neither of them necessitates a metaphysic.[1] Both are methods; the one

---

[1] Hence the criticism to which both have frequently been subjected on the ground that they were not metaphysically complete philosophies (*e.g.* by Dr. S. H. Mellone in *Mind*, xiv. pp. 507-529) involves a certain misconstruction. I can refer the curious to a (rather myl) humanist metaphysic in *Riddles of the Sphinx* (new ed. 1910). But the essay on 'Axioms as Postulates' in *Personal Idealism* was epistemological throughout ; so were the pragmatic parts of *Humanism*. 'Activity and Substance' does indeed contain some metaphysical construction, but it is not distinctively pragmatic. When, therefore, Dr. Mellone (*l.c.* p. 528) ascribes to me the assumption of an absolute chaos as the *prius* of experience, condemns it as unthinkable, and finally complains of feeling a 'collapse' when "this incredible metaphysical dogma is suddenly transformed into a methodological postulate," he has made his difficulty by construing my epistemology as metaphysics. Antecedently this misinterpretation would never have seemed

restricted to the special problem of knowing, the other more widely applicable. And herein lies their value ; for methods are necessities of scientific progress, and therefore indispensable. Metaphysics, on the other hand, are really luxuries, personal indulgences that may be conceded to a lifelong devotion to science, but of no coercive objective validity. For there is an immense discrepancy between the ideal claims of metaphysics and the actual facts. By definition metaphysics is (*i.e.* tries to be) the science of the final synthesis of *all* the data of our experience. But *de facto* these data are (1) insufficient, and (2) individual. Hence (1) the metaphysical synthesis is lacking in cogency : it is imaginative and conjectural. It is the ideal completion of an image of reality which is rough-hewn and fragmentary ; it is the reconstruction of a *torso*. Whoever therefore prefers to remain within the bounds of actual knowledge, is entitled to refrain from pledging himself to a metaphysic. He may recognize any realities, he may employ any conceptions and methods, he finds necessary or expedient, without affirming their ultimate validity.

(2) And so those whose spirits crave for an ideal

---

possible to me, and so I thought it unnecessary to insert a warning against it. But that several able critics have fallen into this error shows the extent of the confusion of thought induced by the deliberate blurring of the boundaries between logic and metaphysics which we owe to Hegelizing philosophers. If, however, Dr. Mellone will do me the honour of re-reading my doctrine as purely epistemological, he will see that both the difficulty and the ' collapse ' were in his own preconceptions. In itself the conception of knowledge as developing by the progressive determination of a relatively indeterminate and plastic ' matter ' never pretended to be more than an analysis of knowledge. It does indeed point to the conceptual limit of a ' first matter ' in which as yet no determinations have been acquired, but it does not affirm its positive existence, and it is quite conceivable (1) that our analysis may be brought up against some irreducible datum of fact, and (2) that it should never actually get back to the metaphysical origin of things. Anyhow, the question of the proper metaphysical interpretation of the conceptions used in pragmatic epistemology was not raised. Epistemologically, however, the conception of a determinable plastic ' matter ' seems useful enough as descriptive of our knowing, and as innocent and at least as valid as the Aristotelian notion that knowledge always arises out of pre-existent knowledge. Of course such notions get into difficulties when we try to extract from them accounts of the absolute origin of knowledge. But is it so sure that absolute origins can ever be traced ? They are certainly not to be had for the asking. For they always seem to involve a demand for the derivation of something out of nothing. And I am not aware that any theory has up to date answered these questions. But I am hopeful that Humanist metaphysics will not be so wildly irrelevant to actual life as in the past metaphysical attempts have mostly been.

completion and confirmation of knowledge by a meta-physical construction must abate their pretensions. They must renounce the pretence of building what is universal, and eternal, and objective, and compulsory, and ' valid for intelligence as such.' In view of the actual facts, does it not argue an abysmal conceit and stupendous ignorance of the history of thought to cherish the delusion that of all philosophies one's own alone was destined to win general acceptance *ipsissimis verbis*, or even to be reflected, undimmed and unmodified, in any second soul ? Every metaphysic, in point of fact, works up into its structure large masses of subjective material which is individual, and drawn from its author's personal experience. It always takes its final form from an idiosyncrasy.

And, furthermore, this is quite as it should be. If it really is the duty of metaphysics to leave out nothing, to undo abstractions, to aspire to the whole of experience, it *must* have this personal tinge. For a man's personal life must contribute largely to his data, and his idiosyn-crasy must colour and pervade whatever he experiences. It is surely the most sinister and fatal of abstractions to abstract from the variety of individual minds, in order to postulate a universal substance in which personal life is obliterated, because one is too ignorant or indolent to cope with its exuberance. Two men, therefore, with different fortunes, histories, and temperaments, *ought not* to arrive at the same metaphysic, nor can they do so honestly ; each should react *individually* on the food for thought which *his personal life* affords, and the resulting differences *ought not* to be set aside as void of ultimate significance. Nor is it true or relevant to reply that to admit this means intellectual anarchy. What it means is something quite as distasteful to the absolutist temper, viz. tolera-tion, mutual respect, and practical co-operation.

It means also that we should deign to see facts as they are. For in point of fact, the protest against the tyrannous demand for rigid uniformity is in a sense superfluous. No two men ever really think (and still less feel) alike, even when they profess allegiance to the

self-same formulas.   Nor does the universe appear to
contain the psychological machinery by which such
uniformity could be secured.   In short, despite all
bigotry, a philosophy is always in the last resort the
theory of *a* life, and not of life in general or in the
abstract.

But though Pragmatism and Humanism are only
methods in themselves, it should not be forgotten (1) that
methods may be turned into metaphysics by accepting them
as ultimate.   Whosoever is wholly satisfied by a method
may adopt it as his metaphysic, just as he may adopt
the working conceptions of a science.   Both Pragmatism
and Humanism, therefore, may be held as metaphysics :
this will induce no difference in their doctrines, but only
in the attitude towards them.

(2) Methods may have metaphysical affinities.   Thus
our last definition of Pragmatism conceived it as derivative
from a voluntarist metaphysic.   Humanism, similarly,
may be affiliated to metaphysical personalism.

(3) Methods may *point*, more or less definitely, to
certain metaphysical conclusions.   Thus Pragmatism may
be taken to point to the ultimate reality of human
activity and freedom,[1] to the plasticity and incompleteness
of reality,[2] to the reality of the world-process 'in time,'
and so forth.   Humanism, in addition, may point to the
personality of whatever cosmic principle we can postulate as ultimate, and to its kinship and sympathy with
man.

Clearly, therefore, there is no reason to apprehend
that the growth of the new methods of philosophizing
will introduce monotonous uniformity into the annals of
philosophy.   'Systems' of philosophy will abound as
before, and will be as various as ever.   But they will
probably be more brilliant in their colouring, and more
attractive in their form.   For they will certainly have to
be put forward, and acknowledged, as works of art that
bear the impress of a unique and individual soul.   Such
has always been their nature, but when this is frankly

[1] Cp. Essay xviii.   [2] Cp. Essay xix.

recognized, we shall grow more tolerant and more appreciative. Only we shall probably be less impressed, and therefore less tormented, than now, by unclear thinking and bad writing which try to intimidate us by laying claim to absolute validity. Such 'metaphysics' we shall gently put aside.

It is clear, therefore, that Metaphysic also must henceforth submit its pretensions to the pragmatic test. It will not be valued any longer because of the magniloquent obscurity with which it speaks of unfathomable mysteries which have no real concern with human life, or because it paints fancy pictures which mean nothing to any but their painters. It will henceforth have to test all its assumptions by their working, and above all to test the assumption that 'intellectual satisfaction' is something too sacred to be analysed or understood. It will have to verify its conjectures by propounding doctrines which can be acted on, and tested by their consequences. And that not merely in an individual way. For subjective value any philosophy must of course have—for its inventor. But a valid metaphysic must make good its claims by greater usefulness than that. It need not show itself 'cogent' to all, but it must make itself acceptable to reasonable men, willing to give a trial to its general principles.

Such a valid metaphysic does not exist at present. But there is no reason why it should not come into being. It can be built up piecemeal bit by bit, by the discovery that truths which have been found useful in the sciences may be advantageously taken as ultimate, and combined into a more and more harmonious system. The opposite procedure, that of jumping to some vast uncomprehended generality by an *a priori* intuition,[1] and then finding that it does not connect up with real life, is neither scientifically tolerable, nor emotionally edifying

[1] It matters not at all what that intuition is. Whether we proclaim that All is 'Matter,' or 'Spirit,' or 'God,' we have said nothing, until we have made clear what 'God,' 'Spirit,' and 'Matter' *are in their application to our actual experience*, and wherein one practically differs from, and excels, the other. But it is just at this point that intuitions are wont to fail their votaries, and to leave them descanting idly on the superiority of one synonym of 'the blessed word Mesopotamia' over the others.

in the end.   All experience hitherto has proved it a delusion.   The procedure of a valid metaphysical construction must be essentially 'inductive,' and gradual in its development.   For a perfect and complete metaphysic is an ideal defined only by approximation, and attainable only by the perfecting of life.   For it would be the theory of such a perfect life, which no one as yet is contriving to live.

II

FROM PLATO TO PROTAGORAS[1]

ARGUMENT

§ 1. The value of classical studies and their relation to a ' liberal' education.
§ 2. The paradox of Greek thought—its development from science to
theology. Philosophic pantheism obvious, but anti-scientific. Why did
the Greek gods preserve their personality? § 3. The genesis of Science.
Anaximander's 'Darwinism.' Why so little experimentation? § 4.
The great Sophistic movement humanistic, but not therefore anti-
scientific. § 5. Protagoras's great discovery. Is the *individual* man
the measure of all things? The transition from 'men' to 'man,' from
subjective to objective truth. Protagoras's speech in the *Theaetetus*.
Its humanism is not scepticism, nor has Plato refuted it, or understood
it. § 6. Plato's anti-empirical bias leads to misconstruction of Protagoras and Heraclitus, and ultimately ruins Greek science. § 7. Plato's
genius and personality. § 8. The scientific importance and anti-scientific
influence of the Ideal Theory. § 9. The difficulty of formulating it.
Had Plato *two* theories? The 'later theory of Ideas' criticized. It
does *not* remove the difficulties of the 'earlier.' § 10. The unity of
Plato's theory defended. § 11. Its primary aspect is the logical, and
this too is the source of its metaphysical embarrassments. § 12. The
Idea as Plato's solution of the predication problem, and as the mediation
between Heraclitus and Parmenides. Ideas as 'systems' and as
necessarily connected *inter se*. § 13. The culmination of the Ideal
system in the Idea of Good, a teleological postulate. Its degeneration
into an abstract unity under mathematical analogies. § 14. Plato's
misconception of the Idea's relation to perception leads to a reduction
of the sensible to a 'non-existent,' and an impossibility of knowing it.
His confusion of ethical with epistemological 'sensationalism.' § 15.
From this epistemological dualism arises the metaphysical chasm between
the Real and the Sensible. It is at bottom a collapse of intellectualistic
logic. § 16. The 'transcendence' of the Idea as its translation into
metaphysics. Plato well aware of its failure, but unable to remedy it
with his notion of the Concept. Platonism has *two* worlds only from
its critics' standpoint, but relapses into Eleaticism. On which side of
' Plato's chasm' should we stand? Aristotle's inability to extricate himself.
§ 17. The functional nature of the concept not perceived by Plato or
his followers. His two mistakes : abstraction (1) from personality ; (2)

---

[1] §§ 2-9 of this essay are a considerably expanded form of part of an article
which appeared in the *Quarterly Review* for January 1906.

from the growth of truth.   Concepts are not immutable unless they are cut loose from human knowing, and then they become useless, because inapplicable to our knowing.   Human concepts grow and are not 'eternal.' But ideal knowledge is defined as something humanly unattainable. Intellectualism is less clear-sighted Platonism. § 18. 'Back to Plato,' therefore, *and* from Plato to Protagoras, lest knowledge be dehumanized.

§ 1. AN essay on Greek Philosophy should nowadays be prefaced by an excursus on classical education— desperate as its vindication may appear. For the only thing which can justify our continued preoccupation with the past as the staple procedure of a 'liberal' education is that the past should *not* be studied entirely for its own sake, *i.e.* in a merely historical spirit. This latter notion is one which never stands in need of support : academic pedantry may always be trusted to champion it. A host of specialists is ever eager to exaggerate the modicum of truth which it conceals, and it is notorious that if only the specialists are allowed to have their way, they will not only ruin every system of education ever devised, but will themselves become so triumphantly unintelligible and illiterate, as to render indigestible and innutritious every science and every study society has endowed them to cultivate. It is probably by this senseless policy of insisting (falsely) on the uselessness of knowledge in order to arouse intellectual interests in the young, that these same sages have fostered the 'deficient interest in the things of the mind,' which they are wont to deplore. Human indolence does indeed naturally shrink from the labour of learning, but there would probably be far less ground for complaint, if the victims of their educational prejudices were allowed to learn how knowledge is the most useful and salutary of all things, and shown the uses even of the staple methods. Nay, if the pedagogical value of interest were more extensively exploited, even the optimistic dictum of Aristotle that 'all men by nature desire knowledge' might cease to seem a pathetic paradox.

Such a policy, moreover, would afford far less nutriment to the 'sordid utilitarianism,' which it is so customary and so hypocritical to denounce, than the working of our

actual institutions.   For inasmuch as it is not considered
legitimate to lay stress on the intrinsic usefulness of knowing, on the value of language as our means of communicating with each other, on the value of science as our
means of controlling the world, on the value of philosophy
as our means of controlling ourselves, extraneous motives
of a far baser kind have to be supplied to arouse the
interest which sets in motion the wheels of our educational machinery.   All the talk about the nobility of a disinterested pursuit of learning is almost wholly cant.   In
point of fact 'liberal education' in England at the present
day is *liberally endowed* ; it rests not on the legendary 'love
of knowledge for its own sake,' but on the twin pillars of
Commercialism and Competition, buttressed perhaps in
some few cases by the additional support of snobbishness.
These two major motives have been combined in the crafty
device of 'scholarships,' awarded on the results of competi-
tive examination, and their operation on the minds alike
of parents and of children is practically irresistible.   This
coarsely and artificially utilitarian system extends from the
preparatory school right through the public schools and
universities, gathering momentum as it rises, until finally,
in the great Civil Service examination, the reward of
successful competition is an honourable career for life !
Surely such inducements would be sufficient to sustain
any amount of nonsense ; they would render useful, and
therefore interesting (at all events *pro tem.*), the silliest
subtleties, the most abstruse absurdities which an ex-
aminer's intelligence may have succeeded in excogitating !
If the advocates of 'useless knowledge' had not sternly
suppressed their ('useless'?) sense of humour, they would
surely wear a perpetual Roman augur's smile at the
exquisite figure which our 'liberal' studies cut, so long
as, *e.g.* in the Oxford 'School' of 'Humaner Letters'
three-fourths, and in that of 'Pure' Mathematics practically all, of the students are paid anything between thirty
and two hundred pounds *per annum* to tolerate and to
abate their vaunted 'uselessness.'

The natural and true way of making a classical education really 'liberal' is not to bolster it up with scholarships and prizes, but to make it as intrinsically useful as possible as a means of appreciating language, that indispensable instrument of human thought and intercourse, of developing the power of using it, and of bracing and expanding the mind by training it to trace the interesting and instructive connexions and contrasts which exist between ancient and modern civilization. It is, moreover, to its efficiency in performing these very functions that the Oxford School of *Literae Humaniores* owes its actual value as an educational instrument. As a training school of a 'disinterested' interest in knowledge it is a complete and utter failure; as a mode of mental training its success and survival is a marvel, more particularly to those who are in a position to appreciate the constant struggle to preserve its value, and are aware of the perils which continually beset its existence.

§ 2. The above considerations must form my apology for venturing upon a sketch of some important points in the history of Greek thought which have hitherto been neglected, or, perhaps, were not visible from the standpoints hitherto adopted. Their discussion will display a certain unity, owing to the fact that they may all be grouped around the problems presented by the genesis, the growth, the arrest, and the decline of Greek science, and their outcome will be to exhibit Plato as the great fountain-head of intellectualism, his victory over Protagoras as the great clog upon science, his failure to give a true account of the function of the Concept and of the nature of Truth, as the secret canker vitiating all philosophy, and a return to the frankly human view of knowledge advocated by Protagoras as the surest guarantee of philosophic progress.

Let us begin, then, by observing that the paradoxical character of Greek genius shows itself also in the course of Greek thought; for in Greece the development of thought reverses the direction taken in all other nations. It begins, apparently, where the others end, and it ends where the others begin. Broadly viewed, the movement of Greek thought is from science to theology, or rather theosophy ; elsewhere it starts from theology and struggles towards science. The emancipation from theological pre-occupations with which the scientific philosophy of the Ionians appears to have started, is an extraordinary and unique phenomenon. In Egypt, in Babylonia, in India, reflection never frees itself from the fascinations of religious speculation.

The religious independence of Greek thought, therefore, is utterly unparalleled. It is, moreover, psychologically unnatural. The natural development of a polytheistic religion when transformed by reflexion is not into science, but into philosophic pantheism. The interest in the problem of life arises in a religious context; what more natural, therefore, than that the answers given should be couched in the familiar religious terms ? The more so that these answers look easy and seem adequate. It is easy enough for thought to fuse the multitude of discrepant deities, the ἀμενηνὰ κάρηνα of imperfectly personified gods, into one vast power which pervades the universe, πολλῶν ὀνομάτων μορφὴ μία. This process is typically shown in the evolution of Hindu thought. And pantheism is not only easy, but also specious. At the various stages of its development it seems capable of satisfying all man's spiritual needs ; to the end it satisfies *one* craving of, perhaps the most reflective, souls. Whoever conceives religion as nothing more than an emotional appreciation of the unity of the universe may rest content with pantheism, and even derive from its obliteration of all differences the most delirious satisfaction. Whoever demands more, such as, *e.g.*, a moral order and a guiding and sympathizing personality, will ultimately fail to get it from any theory which equates God with the totality of being.

But a mighty effort at clear and persistent thinking is needed to perceive these limitations ; and, scientifically at first, pantheism seems adequate enough. It needs a very clear grasp of the nature of science to perceive that the One is as useless scientifically as it is morally, because a principle which explains everything, whether it be called ' God ' or ' the devil,' or conceived as the ' higher synthesis '

of both, really explains nothing. If, however, we seem
to ourselves to have reached the conviction that the one
thing really worth the toil of knowing is that all is
'Brahma,' or 'the Absolute,' and that plurality is but
phenomenal illusion, why should we trouble laboriously
to unravel the intricate web of a multitude of partial
processes, to study the relations of a multitude of partial
beings, as if they were real and important and independent,
and as if anything they could do or suffer could in any
wise affect the absolute and immutable truth of the one
reality ?   Pantheism, therefore, is prejudicial to science ;
and Greece was fitted to become the birthplace of science
by the fortunate circumstance that in Greece alone philosophic pantheism was developed too late to destroy all
the germs of scientific progress.   It makes its appearance,
indeed, in the Eleatic philosophy, significantly enough dis-
guising its anti-scientific bias in the delightfully stimulating
paradoxes of Zeno ; but its sterilizing influence could never
overpower the original Greek tendency to pry unceasingly
into every fact that an infinitely various world presented.

We may, therefore, regard the non-religious and non-
pantheistic character of early Greek philosophy as connected with the genesis of science, and also connect these
anomalies with the striking uniqueness of all the really
important things in history.   Science, like civilization, has
only been invented once.   Monotheism arises similarly
through an anomaly of religious development which, elsewhere than in Judæa, reached unity only by sacrificing
personality.   A similar refusal to give up the personality
of the divine probably underlies the failure of philosophic
reflection to transform Greek popular religion into a pantheism.   But in Greece the motives for this refusal were
certainly different.   The philosophers could not effect a
unification of Olympus, because the personality of the
gods was strong enough to resist the merger.   But this
personality did not rest on moral or intellectual conceptions ; it was essentially an *æsthetic* or artistic thing.
The clearness and intensity with which the Greeks conceived their gods under definitely sensuous shapes is one

of the earliest and most distinctive features of their religion. Homer already could use the divine shapes as standards for the description of human beings. Agamemnon, he once tells us (*Iliad*, ii. 478-9), went to battle with head and eyes like thunder-loving Zeus, with a waist like Ares, and a chest like Poseidon.

Thus the gods possessed an artistic, humanly beautiful personality, uncorrupted by the unæsthetic symbolism which encumbers Hindu deities with superfluous limbs. And we may be sure that, as Greek sculpture developed its glories, it would become less and less plausible to confound Apollo with Ares, or Athene with Aphrodite. If, therefore, the philosophers had ever attempted to interpret the gods into a unity, they would have found that Zeus, for example, was so essentially the god with hyacinthine locks that it was absurd to transfigure him into a cosmic unity. To do them justice, they never seriously attempted it ; they were glad enough that the lack of organization of the popular cults and the non-existence of a professional priesthood permitted them to pursue their scientific researches with only nominal and ritual concessions to the established forms of divine worship.

§ 3. Science, therefore, owes its genesis to a curious and unique emancipation from the pressure of religious problems, and this dominance of the scientific interest in the early Greek philosophy is well brought out in Prof. Gomperz's admirable *Greek Thinkers*. In dealing with the whole of pre-Platonic philosophy the historian is, however, woefully hampered by the fragmentary condition of his material. He has to reconstruct systems of thought out of scanty references and more or less casual quotations in later writers, who are usually biassed, and often careless or incompetent. The palæontologist's task in reconstructing fossils from a tooth or a bone is child's-play in comparison ; for the bones, at least, of *Pithecanthropus erectus* (the Missing Link) cannot lie, while in Greece the Cretans had many rivals.

At times, therefore, the process of writing a history of

early Greek philosophy rather resembles that of making
bricks without clay out of the scattered straws of a dubious
tradition.   At others we get singularly suggestive but
ambiguous glimpses, which suggest alternative interpretations, between which it is impossible to decide.   For
example, our accounts of Anaximander's doctrine are so
wretchedly inadequate that we may please ourselves as
to how far we believe him to have carried his anticipations of Darwinism.   If we choose to suppose that the
tatters of his reasoning, which their very quaintness has
preserved, were merely childish guesses of an infant science,
we shall regard these anticipations merely as coincidences.
If, on the other hand, we note the singular acuteness of
the observations, and the cogency of the reasoning which
they still display, there is little to hinder us from hailing
him as the scientific discoverer of organic evolution.
Gomperz inclines rather to the former view, but he might
have changed his opinion if he had noted how clearly
and completely Anaximander anticipated the argument
for evolution from the helplessness of the human infant,
by which an American Spencerian, John Fiske, gained
great glory.[1]   Our record runs as follows:[2]—" Further,
he says that man originally was generated from animals
of a different kind, seeing that other animals are quickly
able to manage for themselves, whereas man alone
requires protracted nursing.   Wherefore he could not
as such originally have been preserved."   How could
the case be put more concisely or scientifically?

   The scientific promise of the Ionian philosophy is so
great that it becomes a legitimate perplexity to account
for the fact that it was so imperfectly fulfilled, and that,
after making steady progress for three centuries, science
should begin to languish shortly after Aristotle had
codified knowledge and apparently provided the sciences
with a firm platform for more extensive operations.   It
is part of the same puzzle that the Greeks, though, as
Prof. Gomperz is careful to notice, they undoubtedly ex-

[1] *Outlines of Cosmic Philosophy*, ii. 343.
[2] Plutarch Strom. 2, *Doxogr.* 579, 17.

perimented,[1] never did so systematically, and that, in
spite of their devotion to mathematics and enthusiasm
for ‘ measure,’ they never had recourse to exact measurements nor constructed instruments of precision.   Why, a
modern is disposed to wonder, when it had been perceived
that ‘ all things flow,’ was not the next question, ‘ at what
rate ? ’   Why, when it had been laid down that ‘ man is
the measure of all things,’ was not the next question,
‘ How, then, does he measure ? ’   It is idle to suggest that
the Greeks lacked instruments.   Had they wished to experiment they would have constructed them.

We believe that it is possible to point out some, at
least, of the influences which conduced to the disappoint-
ing end of Greek philosophy.   Experimentation demands
manual dexterity and familiarity with mechanisms, as well
as ingenuity.   In a slave-holding society, however, anything savouring of manual training is despised as illiberal
and ‘ banausic.’   ‘ No gentleman,’ Plutarch naïvely tells
us, ‘ however much he may delight in the Olympian
Zeus or the Argive Hera, would like to have been their
sculptor, a Phidias or a Polyclitus.’   Whence we may
infer the depth of the contempt for experiment entertained by a nobleman of Plato’s distinction.

§ 4.   The rise of Sophistry is sometimes regarded as
another reason for the progressive alienation from science
exhibited by Greek thought.   And there is perhaps a
certain measure of truth in this.   The natural acuteness
of the Greek mind and the great practical value of forensic
and political speechifying no doubt tended to an over-
development of dialectical habits of thought.   As Prof.
Gomperz says :[2] “ The preference for dialectic expressed
here and elsewhere in Plato bespeaks an intellectual attitude which is almost the opposite of that of modern
science.   For him all that is given in experience counts
as a hindrance and a barrier to be broken through : *we*
are learning to content ourselves more and more with
what is so given.”   But, as his example shows, it would
be most unjust to render the Sophists responsible for this.

[1] *Greek Thinkers*, i. 291.   [2] *Loc. cit.* iii. 88.

The great humanistic movement of the fifth century B.C.,
of which they were the leaders, is now beginning to
be appreciated at its true value.   Gomperz, following
Grote, points out that the source of the whole development lay in the political situation.   The rise of democracies
rendered a higher education and a power of public speaking a *sine qua non* of political influence, and—what
acted probably as a still stronger incentive—of the safety
of the life and property, particularly of the wealthier
classes.   The Sophists, 'half professors, half journalists,'
or as one might perhaps say with a still closer approximation to modern conditions, ' university extension lectures
hampered by no university,' professed to supply this
great requisite of practical success.   Their professional
success attests the solid value of their instructions.   It
seems almost incredible that an age in which it was
deemed revolutionary to be educated, and monstrous to
have to pay your teachers, when it had not yet become
a fashionable pastime to go to college, when pupils were
allowed and encouraged to appraise their professors' instructions at their spiritual value and to remunerate them
accordingly,[1] should have been the Golden Age of the
teaching profession, in which *rara temporum felicitate*
' Sophists ' could grow rich by intellectual labour.
Yet Plato's glowing descriptions of the numbers and
enthusiasm of the youths who flocked to hear the great
Sophists are too embittered by envy to be suspected of
exaggeration.   The fact, moreover, was that the Sophists
had discovered for their pupils a way both to honour
and to safety.   As Gomperz tersely puts it (i. 417), in
so litigious and quarrelsome a place as Athens their
function was analogous to that of ' professors of fencing
in a community where the duel is an established institu-
tion.'   Nowadays the rich no longer become lawyers :
they hire them.   But the lucrative profession of the law
had not yet been invented.

The result was a great development of rhetoric and
dialectic, to which, it may be noted, Socrates (whom it

---

[1] An astonishing custom of Protagoras.

is quite unhistorical to oppose to the Sophists [1]) appears to have contributed the invention of the art of cross-examination, which Plato, when it suits him, denounces as 'eristic.' Naturally, however, this sophistic education was not popular with those who were too poor or too niggardly to avail themselves of it, *i.e.* with the extreme democrats and the old conservatives ; it was new, and it seemed to bestow an unfair and undemocratic advantage on those who had enjoyed it. Further reasons for the bad name acquired by the Sophists are to be found in the jealous polemic directed by the philosophers (especially by Plato) against rival teachers and in what Prof. Gomperz calls 'the caprice of language' (i. 422). This, however, is more properly an accident in the history of logic. When the Sophists first began to reflect on reasoning they had to make logic along with rhetoric and grammar. They naturally fell into many errors, which their successors gradually corrected. And so what was of value in their logical researches came to be appropriated by later logicians (Plato and, above all, Aristotle), while their crude failures clung to them and engendered the mistaken impression that 'Sophists' were men foolish enough to specialize in *bad* reasoning.

§ 5. Intrinsically, then, there was no reason why this great intellectual movement should have injured scientific interests. It ought more properly to have broadened its basis by adding the psychological and moral inquiries, the sciences of man, to those of nature ; and perhaps there actually was a chance of events taking this course if only

---

[1] In Plato's dialogues he converses with them on amicable and familiar terms. In Aristophanes he is actually selected as their representative, largely, no doubt, by reason of his well-known ugliness and the aid his physiognomy afforded to a comic mask, while the nature of the conservative prejudices is revealed by the pursuits for which he is derided ; they are scientific rather than philosophic, and nowadays, *e.g.*, an entomologist who had measured the length of a flea's leap would be listened to with respect, and perhaps quoted in *Tit-Bits*. The fact, again, that his conversations were probably too rambling and unsystematic to earn money can just as little be held to constitute an essential difference between Socrates and the Sophists, as the fact that Socrates was an amateur who neglected his duties (as a sculptor and a husband and a father) in order to teach, while the Sophists were professional teachers who, apparently, fulfilled theirs. In short, as Socrates had not started a regular philosophic school like Plato and Aristotle, there was no reason for any antagonism between him and the Sophists on account of the struggle for pupils.

the great idea of Protagoras, the greatest of the Sophists, had been scientifically interpreted and properly elaborated. His famous dictum that ' man is the measure of all things ' must be ranked even above the Delphic ' Know thyself,' as compressing the largest quantum of vital meaning into the most compact form.

It must be admitted, of course, that we do not know its exact context and scope, and so can interpret it in various ways. But, however we understand it, it is most important and suggestive, and, *in every way but one*, it is a fundamental truth. That one way, of course, is Plato's, and of it more anon. It might have proved impossible to refute his version of Protagoras, if it had not lapsed into discrepancies within itself. Even as it stands it is plausible enough to have mostly been accepted without cavil, and even those who realized the danger of accepting Plato's polemics without a large grain of salt have been beguiled by it. It is needless, however, with Gomperz, to adopt the expedient of denying the plain application of the words to the individual, and to insist that ' man ' in the dictum must be understood generically. This would render the dictum as tame as Plato rendered it nonsensical. Nor does it follow that Plato's rendering is authentic. Indeed, we take it that the extraordinary value and suggestiveness of Protagoras's dictum largely reside in the conciseness which has led to these divergent interpretations.

Their great mistake is that each should lay claim to exclude the other. For this procedure, however, there is neither logical nor linguistic warrant. Protagoras may well have chosen an ambiguous form in order to indicate both the subjective and the objective factor in human knowledge and the problem of their connexion. Initially, no doubt, his dictum emphasizes the subjective factor. And this is most important. For whatever appears to each that really *is*—to him. And *also to others*, in so far as they have to deal with him and his ideas. Hallucinations, illusions, whims, individual preferences and private judgments, idiosyncrasies of every kind, *are* real, and woe betide any thinker or manager of men who fancies that he can ignore them with impunity ! It is a fact, more-over, that individuals are infinitely different, and that the more carefully they are studied the less true does it seem to lump them all together. To have been the first to have an inkling of all this was Protagoras's great achieve-ment, for the sake of which science owes him an eternal debt of gratitude.

The subjective interpretation, therefore, of the dictum embodies a great scientific truth ; and it is astonishing that this should have been ignored in order to denounce it as subversive of all truth, especially by thinkers who, starting uncritically from the opposite assumption, have themselves completely failed to develop a coherent theory of truth. Surely was there no occasion to conceive it as denying what it did not state directly, the objectivity of truth, and to assume Protagoras to have been unaware of this. The fact that a man makes a great discovery does not necessarily deprive him of all common sense. And that there *is* objective truth, in some sense 'common' to mankind, is a matter of common notoriety. The difficulty about ' objective truth ' lies, not in observing the fact, but in devising a philosophic theory of its pos-sibility ; and concerning this philosophers are still at variance. That reality for us is relative to our faculties is likewise a clear truth which must be assumed even in questioning it.

Man, therefore, is the measure also in the generic sense of man ; and it is very unlikely that Protagoras should have overlooked these obvious facts. Nor had he any motive to ignore them. It is most likely, therefore, that he would placidly have accepted the truisms which are commonly urged against him. His Humanism was wide enough to embrace both 'man' and 'men,' and it could include the former because it had included the latter.

There only remains, therefore, the question of what is the connexion between the two senses in which the dictum is true. What, in other words, is the transition from subjective truth for the individual to objective truth for all ? That we must pass from the one to the other, and succeed in doing so, is obvious ; but how we do so forms a very pretty problem.   And to any scientifically disposed mind it should have been clear that here was a splendid subject for research, *e.g.* along the lines since taken by modern psychological experiment.   Conceived, therefore, in a scientific spirit, the Protagorean dictum yields great openings for science.

But is there any reason to suppose that Protagoras himself conceived it so, and had formed any ideas as to how objective truth arose?   Constructively the tolerant humaneness of his temper (even in Plato's account), his ' strictly empirical method,' [1] and the caution and candour implied in his complaint (for which he suffered martyrdom),[2] that he had never been able to obtain trustworthy information about the gods, almost entitles us to answer both these questions in the affirmative.

But much more direct evidence can be extracted from Plato's own polemic.   In the *Theaetetus* (166-8) Protagoras is represented as replying, that though one man's perceptions could not be *truer* than another man's they might yet be *better*.   So far, therefore, from admitting that on his theory men, pigs, and dog-headed baboons must all alike and equally be the measure of all things, the Platonic ' Protagoras' very lucidly explains that the wise man is he who, when something appears amiss and is ' bad' to any one, is able to alter it so as to make it appear to be ' good' to him instead, and to bring him from a bad to a better state of mind.   In other words, he is represented as recognizing *distinctions of value* among the individual perceptions to all of which ' reality' is conceded.

And not only that.   There are distinct traces in that marvellous speech on behalf of Protagoras of other doctrines to which attention has only been recalled in the last few years.   (1) It is plainly hinted throughout that the attain-

---

[1] Gomperz, i. 455.

[2] A fact which, like the similar cases of Anaxagoras and Aristotle, E. Caird appears to have forgotten when he says, in his *Evolution of Theology in the Greek Philosophers* (i. p. 44), that Socrates was "the only martyr of philosophy in the ancient world, the only man who can be said to have suffered for the freedom of thought."   What rendered the case of Socrates different in its issue was merely his obstinate refusal to go into exile.

ment of wisdom is not a matter of idle speculation, but of *altering reality*, within oneself and without. (2) There are repeated protests against the dialectical spirit which argues solely from the customary uses of words, and un-critically accepts verbal 'contradictions,' as if they proved more than the incompleteness of the human knowledge which has been embodied in the words. And (3) in one or two passages (167 A, 168 A) the point, though some-what obscured in the Platonic statement, seems genuinely to be a repudiation of the intellectualistic trick of repre-senting all moral shortcomings as defects of intelligence. The diseased man, 'Protagoras' protests, is not merely 'uninstructed'; he has to experience a change of heart. Nor is education merely intellectual instruction ; it is the making of a new man and the getting rid of an old self. These hints are all of a tantalizing brevity, but they evince a depth of moral insight with which nothing else in the orthodox Greek ethics, corrupted as they were by intel-lectualism and enervated by æstheticism, can at all compare. And they very distinctly savour of the moral fervour of St. Paul.

The doctrine as a whole, however, is perfectly clear, rational, and consistent. It differs from that of modern Humanism, apparently, only in the terminological point that 'true' and 'false' are not regarded as values essentially cognate with 'good' and 'bad,' or, in other words, that they are used primarily of the individual claims to cog-nitive value rather than of their subsequent recognition. But this is a secondary divergence, if such it is. It is quite possible that Protagoras already perceived the 'ambiguity of truth,'[1] and that his distinction has merely been blurred in the Platonic statement, which is clearly in-complete. As regards the necessity of altering reality, and of connecting this process with the making of truth, and the impossibility of reducing evil to ignorance, Protagorean and Neo-Protagorean Humanism would appear to be at one.

The only question, therefore, that remains is, how far this whole doctrine can be transferred from the Platonic

[1] Cf. Essay v.

to the historical Protagoras, and as in the similar case of the Platonic 'Socrates,' complete cogency cannot be attained by arguments on this point. The historic Socrates wrote nothing ; the *magnum opus* of the historic Protagoras, his book on *Truth*, has been destroyed. It began too incisively with a declaration that its subject was logic, not theology ; so the Athenians set the hangman to burn it. If any copies escaped him—as is improbable because their owners, though pupils of Protagoras, would be in sympathy with the oligarchs who persecuted him—they soon perished of neglect during the long reign of Platonic intellectualism. And so the combined bigotries of vulgar piety and dogmatic philosophy have deprived us of what was probably one of the great monuments of Greek genius.

Nevertheless, it seems extremely probable, on internal evidence, that the ' defence of Protagoras,' so far as it goes, embodies genuine doctrines of his, greatly curtailed, no doubt, and perhaps somewhat mangled in the reproduction. For the reason, mainly, that Plato manifestly has not understood its argument at all. Nowhere else does he betray the slightest suspicion of the doctrine that the nature of truth is essentially dependent upon the 'alteration' of reality. Had he examined it, he could not only have concluded his *Theaetetus* with less negative results, but would have transformed his whole view of knowledge. Nowhere else does he perceive the radical vice of the intellectualistic analysis of wickedness as ignorance. To the end he retained his faith in the dialectical play with concepts as the method of penetrating to the secret of the universe. And, most significantly of all, the recognition by ' Protagoras ' of distinctions of value in perceptions is treated as wholly non-existent or unintelligible. Not only does Plato fail to see that it is a complete answer to the trivial objections and shallow gibes of his ' Socrates,' not only does he fail to answer it, but he feels that he must divert attention from the plea of ' Protagoras ' by recourse to the most artistically brilliant digressions. The whole subsequent course of the discussion shows that he had not the faintest idea of the

scope and significance of the argument he had stated. It
is clear that if he had grasped the meaning of his ' Protagoras,' the whole argument of his *Theaetetus* would have
had to proceed and end differently. It seems incredible,
therefore, that Plato should have invented a distinction
which he did not know how to handle, and it remains
that he was really candid enough to reproduce genuine
contentions of Protagoras.

If, then, this doctrine that truth is a valuation, and to be
discriminated from ' error ' as ' good ' from ' bad,' can really
be attributed to Protagoras, it is easy for us to see how it
might provide him with the means of passing from subjective
to objective judgments in a perfectly valid and scientific
manner. For if there is a mass of subjective judgments
varying in value, there must ensue a selection of the more
valuable and serviceable, which will, in consequence, survive and constitute growing bodies of objective truth,
shared and agreed upon by practically all. It is highly
probable that the general agreement about sense perceptions has actually been brought about by a process of
this sort ;[1] and it is still possible to observe how society
establishes an ' objective ' order by coercing or cajoling
those who incline to divergent judgments in moral or
æsthetic matters. And, though no doubt Protagoras
himself could not have put the point as clearly as the
discovery of natural selection enables us to do, it seems
probable that he saw, at least, the beginnings of the very
real connexion between the two meanings of his dictum.

§ 6. Plato's interpretation, therefore, of the Protagorean
dictum is merely a trick of his anti-empiricist polemic,
and it may be very closely paralleled by similar charges
which have been brought against modern revivals of
Protagoreanism, and are not likely similarly to prevail
only because they cannot command the services of a
Plato and an executioner. To say that ' man is the
measure of all things ' necessarily conducts to subjectivism
and to scepticism is simply not true.

The truth is rather that the way to scepticism lies

[1] Cp. pp. 316-20.

through a *denial* of this dictum.   To a mind, then, desirous
of scientific knowledge the dictum should be fertile only
of a multitude of instructive observations and experiments.
Unfortunately this was not the spirit in which it was
received.   A spirit of dialectical refutation cared nothing
for the varieties of physical endowment and of psychical
reaction ; it took no interest in the problems and methods
of scientific measurement.   The question ' If man is the
measure, then how do we manage to measure?' was not
raised.   What was raised was the unfair, untrue, and
uninstructive cry, 'then knowledge becomes impossible!'
The levity with which this outcry rises to the lips of *a
priori* metaphysicians is as extraordinary as the vitreous-
ness of the abodes which ultimately house their own convictions.   It has often been remarked that the 'deceptions'
and 'contradictions' of the senses, which, to the ancients,
provided only texts for sceptical lamentation and excuses
for taking refuge in 'suprasensible' Ideas (which were
really nothing more than the acquired meanings of words),
have yielded to modern energy valuable starting-points
for scientific inquiries.   To the dialectical temper the fact
that a stimulus may feel both hot and cold simultaneously
is merely a contradiction ; to the scientific temper it gives a
clue to the discovery of the 'cold' and 'hot' spots of cutaneous
sensibility.   Similarly such notions as 'solid solutions,' 'liquid
crystals,' invisible 'light,' divisible 'atoms,' 'unconscious'
mental life, seem mere foolishness until we realize that the
work of science is not to avoid verbal contradiction, but to
frame conceptions by which we can control the facts.

Another parallel is afforded by the treatment of
Heraclitus's great discovery of the universality of process
or change.   It too was taken to mean that knowledge
was impossible, as if, forsooth, men were usually altered
beyond recognition overnight, and rivers changed their
courses daily.   If the Greeks, instead of indolently contenting themselves with a qualitative enunciation of its truth,
had attempted a quantitative estimation of the universal
process, they might have anticipated some of the
most signal triumphs of modern science ; and, it may be

added, they would speedily have convinced themselves of
the practical innocuousness of the Flux, and perhaps even
have learnt, from the impossibility of any but relative
determinations, that practical limitations and a relation to
practical application are inherent in the very nature of
truth, and that the pretensions of 'ideals' which cannot
be applied, and can only condemn all human experience
as unintelligible, prove nothing but the ludicrous falsity of
such ideals. But this assumes that they wanted to know
and were willing to view these doctrines in a scientific
spirit. And this is just where they lamentably failed.

§ 7. That the Hellenic will to know scientifically gave
out at this point is a fact which must certainly be connected
most vitally with the appearance of the stupendous genius
whom history knows only by his nickname, Plato. This
extraordinary man was equally great as a writer and as
a thinker. He was at once a poet and a philosopher, a
prophet and a professor, an initiator and an imitator, a
theologian and a sceptic ; and he excelled in all these
parts. Regarded from the literary side he is admirable
as a parodist, as a maker of stories and inventor of fairy-
tales, as a delineator of character, as a critic, as a dissector
of arguments. Regarded as a thinker, he maintains in
equipoise the most contrary excellences. One hardly
knows whether to admire more the grandeur of his constructions, or the subtlety of his criticisms, the compre-
hensive sweep of his 'synoptic' view, or the patience
which descends into the minutest details. Regarded as
a wit, he was capable of the most reckless raillery, the
most savage satire, the gentlest humour, and a *persiflage*
so graceful, that Aristophanes compared with him seems
coarsely farcical ; and yet in his serious moods he could
reach heights of solemnity in which the slightest hint of
comedy would seem a profanation. In spite, or perhaps
by reason, of a life-long devotion to philosophy, he never
scrupled to deride the pretensions of philosophers. The
most devoted of disciples, he yet became the most potent
of masters. One of the world's great artists, he was yet
one of the most puritanical of the censors of art. The

idealizing apologist of erotic passion, he was also the most austere of moralists and the eulogist of asceticism. A typical intellectualist, he was also intensely emotional. By birth a man of quality, he yet knew how to withdraw from the world of fashion without offending it ; an abstainer from political life, he was yet the most inspiring of radical reformers ; by turns a counsellor of princes and a recluse in the groves of Academe.

It is plain that no great man has laid upon the world a harder task in imposing on it ‘the duty of understanding him’ ; and it is no wonder that posterity has but imperfectly succeeded. We read his writings, preserved for us in far more perfect shape than those of any other ancient thinker, and are plunged in unending perplexities as to their meaning. We listen to the comments of one of his immediate pupils, and doubt whether, after eighteen years of intimacy, Aristotle’s genius has comprehended Plato’s. We flatter ourselves that we should understand him better if we knew more facts about the historical order of his works and the circumstances which evoked them, and hope by the minutest tabulation of his tricks of style to extort the secrets of their history. But Plato was master of so many styles, and could parody himself with such consummate ease, that it is no wonder that the conclusions of ‘stylometry’ are dubious, and hardly compatible with any coherent view of Plato’s philosophic development. Moreover, even if we knew the facts we now desiderate, it is quite probable that our perplexities would only recur in subtler forms. For they ultimately spring from the personality of their author.

The core of the Platonic problem is Plato’s personality, a personality whose diversity and many-sidedness is the delight of his readers and the despair of his critics. How can the clumsy canons of a formal criticism ever determine what degree of seriousness and literality attaches to any of his statements, and how far its meaning should be modified by a touch of irony, of humour, of satire, of imagination ? The simplest even of Platonic myths is infinitely baffling. Who will undertake to expound its meaning fully, to determine where precisely its formal teaching melts into its imaginative setting, how much of its detail was premeditated, how much of it the spontaneous outgrowth of the fairy tale ? What again of the dialogue form? What at any point is the working compromise between the dogmatic and the dramatic interest by which the course of the proceedings is determined ? No one, assuredly, who has ever tried so far to enter into Plato's spirit as to imitate his literary methods, will delude himself into thinking that these questions are ever likely to be answered with exactness. Plato's personality is far too rich for the precise analysis all pedants love.

And yet, perhaps, we may observe a conspicuous gap even in the far-extended spectrum of this giant soul. It seems incapable of vibrating in response to the enlightenment of mere empiric fact ; and this defect has had tremendous consequences. For similarly constituted souls are common ; and Plato has become their greatest spokesman. Yet the pathetic futility of apriorism appears again in this, that ultimately the whole world is empirical and all that therein is. However, therefore, we may try to hedge round portions of it against the intrusions of the unexpected, the very facts that our hedges can withstand intruders, that we desire to keep them in repair, and that all this will continue to be true, are as empirical as the greatest brute of a fact against which our reason sought protection. Of what value, then, are *a priori* guarantees, if the continuance of their applicability to experience, and of their own apriority are both empirical, and can *not* be guaranteed ?

§ 8. We must affirm, therefore, that Plato's anti-empirical bias renders him profoundly anti-scientific, and that his influence has always, openly or subtly, counteracted and thwarted the scientific impulse, or at least diverted it into unprofitable channels. The potency of this influence may best be gauged by observing how completely Plato's greatest pupil, Aristotle, has fallen under his spell. For if ever there was a typically scientific mind it was Aristotle's. That he should revolt against his master was inevitable for many reasons. That he should assail the citadel of Plato's power, the theory of the 'Ideas,' in which Plato had hypostasized and deified the instruments of scientific research and uplifted them beyond the reach of human criticism, evinced a sound strategic instinct. But in the end his spirit also proved unable to escape out of the magic circle of conceptual realism, which he renders more prosaic without making it more consistent or more adequate to the conduct of life. Indeed his analytic sharpness, by exaggerating into opposition the rivalry between practical and theoretic interests, which Plato had sought to reconcile in too intellectualist a fashion, probably contributed, much against his intentions, an essential motive to that alienation from scientific endeavour which marks the decline and fall of Greek philosophy.

It has already been suggested that the theory of Ideas was the fountain-head whence flowed Plato's baleful influence on the growth of knowledge. This influence it would be hard to overrate. The cognitive function of the Concept, which Socrates (if we conceive ourselves to have any really authentic information about his doctrine) may perhaps be said to have discovered, was so exalted and exaggerated by Plato that it became the subtlest and most dangerous of obstacles to the attainment of the end it is its proper function to subserve. And so, wherever there is hypostasization and idolatry of concepts, and wherever these interpose between the mind and things, wherever they lead to disparagement of immediate experience, wherever the stubborn rigidity of prejudice refuses to adapt itself to the changes of reality, wherever the delusive answers of an *a priori* dialectic leave unanswered questions of inductive research, wherever words lure and delude, stupefy and paralyse, there Truth is sacrificed to Plato, even by barbarians who have never heard his name. The Ideal Theory resembles a stranger torpedo-ray than that to which Plato in the *Meno* likens Socrates. Itself one of the great achievements of the human intellect, it both electrifies the mind with brilliant vistas of suprasensible dominion for the soul, and yet numbs and paralyses some of its highest functions. For it deludes us into thinking that man was made for Ideas, to behold and contemplate them for ever, and not Ideas for man and by man, to serve the ends of action.

§ 9. Not the least extraordinary fact about this wondrous theory is that, strictly speaking, we do not even know what precisely it was. The culminating point of conceptual Idealism has always been screened by impenetrable clouds from the gaze of the faithful as of the profane, and the former have always had to accept a ' myth ' in lieu of the final revelation of truth absolute. The justification of this assertion is necessarily somewhat technical, but will go far to initiate us into the secret of Plato's fascination.

That there is some ground for doubting whether any one really knows what exactly the Ideal Theory was, may be perceived when we ask *how many* Ideal Theories Plato really had. For it seems impossible to trace a single consistent view throughout his writings ; and in the course of fifty or sixty years of authorship even a strenuous denier of the Flux may change his views. It is plain, moreover, that new problems, new difficulties, new methods, and new points of view sprang up in Plato's mind, though it is usually hard to determine how far they modified his earlier convictions. The critics, however, agree that the Ideal Theory is not one, but several, and that an earlier may be distinguished from a later form thereof.

The earlier theory, as described, *e.g.* by Zeller, forms the typical or Standard Platonism to which the others are referred. It is extracted mainly from the *Meno*, the *Phaedrus*, the *Phaedo*, and the *Republic*, and is certainly the most picturesque and fascinating form of conceptual Idealism. It describes the true home of the soul in a suprasensible supercelestial world of True Being, where pure, incorporeal, and without passions, it leads a holy, blessed, and eternal life, contemplating the beauty and

excellent harmony of the Ideas, the indivisible and immutable archetypes of the fleeting phenomena that flow
in multitudinous confusion before our dazzled senses.
Thence it is driven (by some inscrutable necessity) to
make periodical descents into the perishable world of
Sense, which is not truly real, but is saved from utter
unreality by its relation to the Ideas in which it can
mysteriously 'participate.' To know such a world, but
for the Ideas, would be impossible, and to know is really
to *remember* these.

The weak point in this theory lies in the difficulty of
conceiving the connexion between the Ideal world and
the phenomenal, *i.e.* the precise nature of 'participation.'
That in some sense Plato felt this weakness is brilliantly
attested by the incisive criticism he inflicts on what
seems to be his own theory in the *Parmenides.* On the
strength of this it is commonly supposed that Plato must
have altered his views ; and the evolution of his 'later
theory of Ideas' is thought to be traceable in a series of
critical and 'dialectical' dialogues, which include also the
Theaetetus, the *Sophist*, and the *Politicus.*

The puzzle, however, is to find the theory in its developed
form. It must lurk either in what are regarded as his
latest works, the *Laws*, the *Philebus*, and the *Timaeus*, or
in the oral lectures, of which Aristotle's *Metaphysics* give
a very obscure and polemical account. But the search
through the *Laws* and the *Philebus* yields little that is
enlightening, while the *Timaeus* is so mythical in form
that it is hard—or fatally easy—to find anything therein.
Nevertheless a 'later theory of Ideas' has been extracted
or constructed. Its distinguishing marks are, the substitu-
tion of an ideal exemplar ($\pi\alpha\rho\acute{\alpha}\delta\epsilon\iota\gamma\mu\alpha$), which is copied
or imitated by the sensible, for the discarded notion of
'participation' ($\mu\acute{\epsilon}\theta\epsilon\xi\iota\varsigma$); the restriction of Ideas to
'natural kinds'; the reduction of 'not-being' to differ-
ence ; and the recognition of an efficacy or spiritual
activity in the Ideas, which converts them into efficient
causes.

Unfortunately this 'later theory of Ideas' is by no

means well authenticated. The external evidence is dead against it. Aristotle also has a notion of a 'later' Platonic theory. But he represents his aging master, not as soaring to an absolute idealism, but as sinking into childish habits of pythagoreanizing. Gomperz points out [1] that this is confirmed by the growing importance of mathematics shown in the creative operations of the *Timaeus*, and in the educational methods of the *Laws*, in which they wholly take the place of 'dialectic.' For the restriction of Ideas to 'natural kinds' some Aristotelian support may, it is true, be invoked. But is it not unfortunate for this aspect of the 'later theory of Ideas' that in the *Parmenides* this very procedure should be derided as a youthful error? And we shall presently see reason to doubt whether it is an improvement. In any case, Aristotle's account of Platonism does not at all square with the theory of a substantially altered 'later' theory. The theory he mainly combats is the old one; and he parades all the old objections of the *Parmenides* without a doubt of their complete relevance,[2] nay, with an air of having invented them himself.[3] But to suppose that Aristotle misunderstood Plato's fundamental doctrine is a monstrous assumption, And, we may add, a futile one.

[1] *L.c.* iii. 246-47.

[2] His objection that the Ideas are not efficient causes would be particularly curious and inept, if Plato had adhered to the alleged discovery of the *Sophist* (247 E) that substance is activity, and had thereby anticipated Aristotle's own conception of ἐνέργεια. But the context shows that Plato had not overcome the antithesis of motion and rest, and the whole passage is only one of those which express his inability to unite the human and the Ideal. Cp. § 17.

[3] If we can put the *Parmenides* so late as 360 B.C., it is just possible that he did. For we can then read this puzzling dialogue as an attempt by Plato to abate the conceit of his obstreperous pupil by narrating a fictitious parallel to an existing situation in the form of a discussion between the venerable 'Parmenides' and the youthful 'Socrates.' In the self-criticism of 'Parmenides' which follows, depths of metaphysics are sounded which are intended to make the objections to the Ideas seem shallow, and to show that their author still retains his mastery, while an earlier 'Aristotle' is satirically made to give his later name sake a lesson in manners by prettily and amiably answering just what is required, because, forsooth, he is too 'young' to raise vexatious objections. But the dates seem a serious obstacle. For even if it be supposed that the genius of Aristotle at twenty-four was capable of propounding posers which the genius of Plato could not cope with, this dating of the *Parmenides* would leave only a dozen years of Plato's life for the composition of all his later dialogues. And after all, if neither Plato nor his school had ever answered the objections of the *Parmenides*, Aristotle had a perfect right to reiterate them.

For it makes out Aristotle to have been either a fool, if he could not understand it, or a knave, if he knowingly misrepresented it.   Or rather, in this case, he would have been a fool as well as a knave, if he supposed that his iniquitous procedure could escape exposure at the hands of Plato's other pupils.

The 'later theory of Ideas' appeals essentially to internal evidence.   But here also its case is none too strong.   Gomperz, who is a friendly critic and accepts the order of the Platonic dialogues which the theory demands, has to call attention to the persistence of phrases characteristic of the 'earlier' theory, even in the *Timaeus*.   And Dr. Horn boldly challenges the fashionable placing of the 'dialectical' dialogues *after* the *Republic*.[1]   Far from agreeing with Gomperz (iii. 357) that the latest of them, the *Statesman*, is "manifestly the bridge leading from the *Republic* to the *Laws*," he argues forcibly that it is quite a preliminary sketch, which would have been pointless after the *Republic*.   The logical point involved when the same author treats the same subject twice with more and less fulness clearly does not admit of absolute decision.   The later version may be either an elaboration of an earlier sketch or a succinct reference to a fuller treatment. It is fallacious also to assume that, because a theory has been remodelled, it has been improved.   So here. Even Gomperz, who believes in a 'later' theory, but holds that it did not answer the *Parmenides*, and amounted really to "consigning the Ideas to a sphere of dignified repose in conferring upon them divine rank," [2] has to admit that in some respects its transformation was retrograde.[3]

This possibility is the less negligible because the 'later theory of Ideas' comes out very badly under logical examination.   Its advocates seem unable to show us how it escapes from the dilemmas of the *Parmenides*.   How does the suggestion that the Ideas are models for sensible phenomena to 'imitate,' bridge the dualistic chasm between the worlds of 'reality' and of 'appearance'?   If 'Ideas'

[1] *Platonstudien*, ii. 379 foll.   [2] *L.c.* iii. 181.   [3] *L.c.* iii. 173.

and 'things' are different in essence and unrelated in function, how can they be so connected that the things can take cognizance enough of the Ideas to imitate them? In the *Timaeus* Plato escapes the difficulty by the divine fiat of his Demiurge; but this expedient the modern 'friends of the Ideas' would certainly condemn as 'mythical.' The question is the more urgent because somewhere or other it reappears in all systems of conceptual Idealism.[1]

Moreover, it would seem that this later version of the Ideas is fatal to their *logical* function. If phenomena become intelligible only by being subsumed under concepts, there *must* be Ideas of whatever can be predicated, of relations and of artefacts, of hair and dirt and evil, of doubleness and if-ness; their restriction to 'natural kinds,' despite its *metaphysical* attractiveness, is a gross *logical* inconsequence. And that a desire to justify the procedures of predication and to explain the nature of knowledge was one of the main motives of the Ideal Theory seems undeniable, although Plato does not make this as explicit as its metaphysical aspect. Nor can we be wrong in thinking that he intended it to be logically,[2] as well as metaphysically, a *via media* between Eleaticism and Heracliteanism, both of which seemed to him to render significant assertion incomprehensible. But to serve this logical purpose the Ideas *had* to be conceived after the fashion of his 'earlier' theory. They had to be single, stable, self-identical predicates common (*i.e.* applicable) to an infinite plurality of particulars. They had to live in a world apart in order to transcend the flux that would otherwise have swamped them. They had to have communion *inter se*, in order that the connexions of our predications might be absolutely validated by conforming to those of their eternal archetypes. They had to be immutable; for how else could truth be absolute?

Whatever the difficulties, therefore, which they might seem to involve, they could not be disavowed without,

[1] Cp. p. 177.   [2] Especially in the *Theaetetus*.

in Plato's way of thinking, abolishing the very notion of
truth and all knowledge of reality.   It is quite probable,
therefore, that, despite the candour of the *Parmenides*, he
never really surrendered to criticism, and that all the
objections he encountered only seemed to him to proceed
from a failure to reach his standpoint, and to argue logical
incapacity to grasp the cogency of the grounds on which
his theory reposed.   And in a manner he was right.
The logical cohesion of the fabric of his thought was such,
that no one, who had once attributed to concepts a reality
superior to that of the phenomena they interpret, could
question it without succumbing ultimately to the very
difficulties brought against himself.

§ 10. If, therefore, we desire to account both for
Plato's self-criticism in the *Parmenides*, and the reiteration
of its arguments, almost in so many words, by Aristotle,
and yet to retain the belief that Plato's Ideal Theory was
one of the great landmarks in the history of thought, and
that its author never quite abandoned it, what shall we
do ?   We shall have, certainly, to discard the notion of
diminishing our difficulties by doubling the Ideal Theories,
which have to be grasped, expounded, and defended
against substantially the same objections.   By trying to
extract *two* theories from Plato we only complicate the
situation with the problem of their relation and that of
Plato's psychological development ; and we sacrifice the
unity of Platonism.

Let us try rather to understand thoroughly the one
theory which indubitably is in Plato.   It may then
appear that it leaves no real room for any other.   We
may then perceive that it forms the soul of Plato's
thought, which is neither abandoned, nor altered, nor improved in any points which can be treated as essential,
but persists substantially the same throughout.   Not
that, of course, Plato may not have varied at different
times the emphasis and attention bestowed on its various
aspects ; but the truth is, that it could not be really
altered without renouncing what seemed to Plato the most
essential of truths, and that so, however clearly he had

perceived its difficulties, he was equally unable to remedy them or to remodel it. Plato was perfectly aware of his difficulties, but unable to remove them; because he was aware also that they were directly connected with what most he valued in his theory. But it is just in this that his greatness appears; his critics and successors, from Aristotle downwards, have perceived his difficulties, but not their own; they do not perceive, that is, that their own conception of knowledge is at bottom Plato's, that the difficulties are common to them and him, and that there is no escape from them except by a complete abandonment of Plato's intellectualistic pre-supposition, and a thorough correction of his fundamental error as to the functioning of concepts. So their gibes recoil upon their own heads, and their imperfectly thought-out theories of knowledge either stop short of these ultimate difficulties, or, if they reach them, wreck themselves on the same rock, and in the same helpless and inevitable way as Plato's; while they periodically raise the cry of 'back to Plato,' without perceiving that Plato can teach them nothing if they are not willing to take to heart the lesson of his failure. In short, the grounds of Plato's embarrassments are also those of his success; but to prove this, it is necessary to hark back much farther than Platonic criticism is wont to go, namely, to the beginnings of the Ideal Theory, and to examine its deepest roots.

§ 11. Broadly considered, the Ideal Theory has two main aspects, the one metaphysical or ontological, the other logical. It is, on the one hand, Plato's account of the true and ultimate reality, and on the other, his account of the problem of thought, and his solution of 'the predication puzzle,' as to how S can be P. Of these two aspects we have already noted (§ 9) that the first has been made more prominent by Plato's readers, rather than by Plato himself. Men are more interested to arrive at ultimate reality than careful to scrutinize the logical soundness of the steps by which they hope to reach it. Yet, from a scientific standpoint, it is probably the

logical aspect of the Ideal Theory which is more worthy
of admiration ; and it will also prove to be more fundamental. For the metaphysical difficulties of Platonism,
which have attracted such widespread attention, are
really secondary ; they arise from deeper logical difficulties
which have been hardly noticed. Hence the *impasse* in
which the Ideal Theory ends; hence the perplexities about
its meaning, and that of the whole Platonic problem ;
hence, too, the predestined failure of attempts to repair
the metaphysic of Platonism without rectifying its logic.

Plato could not cure his metaphysical troubles
because he could not disavow their logical foundations.
He could not disavow these foundations because of his
conception of the Concept, to renounce which seemed to
him to revert to intellectual chaos ; and rather than
provoke this, he was content to recognize a final in-
explicability in his theory of reality.   After all it might
seem better to retain an important and valuable truth,
while honestly avowing its shortcomings, than to reject
it wholly because it was not complete.   Such an attitude
is natural and pardonable ; it only becomes indefensible,
if the theory which has to own to final failure originally
claimed a completeness which it cannot reach.

§ 12. Without, therefore, attempting to fathom the
vicissitudes of Plato's psychological development, which
were doubtless many though not necessarily recorded in
his writings, we may follow the logical order of his train
of thought, and see how it conducted him to his final crux.

It seemed evident to Plato that his philosophic predecessors had left knowledge in an impossible position.
Neither the ' Flux ' of Heraclitus, nor the one ' Being ' of
the Eleatics, admitted of significant assertion.   In the one
case predication was rendered meaningless ; how could it
be asserted that ' S *is* P ' ?   If neither S nor P remain
identical for two moments together, how can it be truer
to say that S *is* P than that S *is not* P?   Nay, if both
are in a continual flux, if S is for ever passing into *not-S*,
and P into *not-P*, how can any assertion mean anything
at all?   The Eleatic alternative is no better.   It so

emphasizes the identity and unity of Being as to exclude all difference ; it cannot be asserted that *S is P*, but only that *S is S*, and necessarily incapable of 'becoming' *P*. But is not this to restrict truth to idle tautologies, and to invalidate the very form of judgment ?

To Plato, as he meditated on this problem, salvation seemed to lie in the Concept, which seemed to mediate between and to reconcile the logical demands of the antagonistic metaphysics. The philosophical discovery of the Concept's function is, perhaps, to be credited to Socrates, but it is not probable that he had used it as the basis for a complete *Weltanschauung*. The Socratic Concept was still used merely in its natural 'pragmatic' way, as the ideal unity whereby the human mind classifies and controls the confusing and confused multitude of particulars, and orders its experience. It was thus essentially an instrument of human cognition ; but it may be doubted whether Socrates had recognized its fundamental importance for logic.

Plato was immensely struck with the Concept's apparent character as a unity in plurality. Here was a 'one' which apparently controlled a 'many,' which obediently *meant* nothing but the 'one' they exemplified ; a 'one' which pervaded, instead of excluding a 'many,' and stood related to them, and yet stood aloof, *i.e.* was not affected by them nor merged in the flux of sense ; a 'one,' therefore, which could form the stable centre for a fixed scheme of classification, whereby the fleeting flux of indefinite and infinite perceptions could be measured and apprehended. The Concept thus became the principle of permanence and knowableness, opposed to change and ignorance, as well as the principle of unity. In so far as anything could be said really to *be*, and really to be known, it was by predicating some concept of it. The '*is*' of predication was different in kind from the '*becomes*' of sense-perception ; but it was the meaning of the latter and the solution of its mystery.

The more he meditated on the nature of the Concept, the clearer it seemed to Plato that it supplied the remedy for the defects of both his predecessors. By it the Heraclitean flux of sense was arrested, and provided with a stable standard of reference, and thereby rendered intelligible. By it was vindicated not only the independence, but the reality of thought—nay, its superior reality, as against the turbulent confusion of the senses. By it, again, was rendered intelligible the rigid unity of the Eleatic One, which now became flexible and adaptable to the world ; for the ' Idea ' could be predicated of the flux without losing its unity and identity.

Nay, more, what was true of each Idea in its relation to its particulars was *a fortiori* true of the Ideas in their relation to each other. The World of Ideas formed a system of interrelated concepts, the fixed relations of which could be made to guarantee the truth of the predications which reproduced this order. Thus the undifferentiated unity of Eleaticism was expanded and articulated into a well-knit system of perfectly knowable Ideas.

Plato, in short, had discovered the function of the Concept in the organization of experience. He had become aware of 'the ideal network,' by means of which we fish out of the swirl of events what is of value for our life. Nor had he discovered this *by halves*. It seems impossible to suppose that he had first discovered the existence of Ideas, and then realized the need of connecting them into a system, and thereupon improved his former theory. For no first-rate philosopher could have discovered the one without at once inferring the other. The systematic character of the Ideas is implicit from the first in the assertion of the Idea as the ' one ' in the ' many,' as the unity pervading the flow of perceptions. Each concept, that is, is a scheme, or rubric, or pigeon-hole, for the organization and control of a stream of particulars. It is, in short, a system. It is equally manifest that these systems are parts of larger ones. Concepts are manifestly related to each other. They congregate into sciences, and the study of these easily points to the conception of an Ideal which will completely unify our conceptual world.

Accordingly, it is not in the least surprising that the dialogue which is usually conceived as the culminating point of the 'earlier' theory of Ideas, the wonderful *Republic*, should already contain in principle the chief points elaborated in the 'later' theory, or that in it Plato should unequivocally recognize the systematic character of the Ideas and the need for their unification by an ultimate Ideal. The mutual participation in one another of the Ideas (κοινωνία εἰδῶν), which is introduced as a familiar notion in 476 A, is just as essential and integral a postulate of the Ideal Theory as the 'participation' of the Sensible in the Idea. For it would be of no use to be able to predicate Ideas of sensible things, if Ideas could not be predicated of one another. Such 'participation' is also a necessary presupposition of the Ideal of the 'Idea of Good,' by which Plato puts the coping-stone on his theory of knowledge. This grand conception is so simple, and has been so often misinterpreted, that we may devote a section to the elucidation of its 'mystery.'

§ 13. The 'Idea of Good,' in its actual functioning, is Plato's substitute for 'God,' the Prime Cause of all Goodness, Beauty, Knowableness, and True Being in the world. But it is exalted to this supreme position by gradual steps which it is possible to trace, and to which the clue lies in an exact translation of the Greek. Its exact meaning is 'the Concept of End.' So translating it we see at once that it represents not only the ideal of unification of knowledge, but also (what is quite as important) the absorption into Platonism of Anaxagoras's conception of Purposive Reason (Νοῦς), as the cosmic principle of order and discrimination, or, as we should say, selection. It demands, that is, not only that knowledge shall be unified and ordered, but that its order shall be *teleological*, 'rational' and 'good.' A complete explanation of the world must be in terms of 'ends,' and not of 'causes'; the principle of cosmic order must be assimilated to the procedure of human reason and to human recognitions of moral values. It is, in short, *the postulate of a complete teleological explanation of the universe.*

Now Plato was quite well aware that this was a postulate which in the existing state of the sciences it was impossible to satisfy. When the time comes for 'Socrates' in the *Republic* (532 E) to expound to 'Glaucon' the actual nature of the process whereby the teleological deduction of everything real and intelligible is to be demonstrated, he simply declares that he cannot, because the latter has not studied mathematics far enough. This obviously means that *Plato* cannot tell *us*, because *Science* is not sufficiently advanced. But Plato thought that the discovery of the secret of the universe was not far off; hence the ardour with which he subsequently devoted himself to the pursuit of the sciences, which in his time were most advanced, which seemed most plainly *a priori* and 'independent of experience,' and appeared to illustrate most lucidly both the 'participation' of Ideas in one another and their fixed ordering by a superior principle, viz. the mathematical. Do we not see how, *e.g.* in arithmetic, the numbers stand in fixed and intelligible relations to one another, and are yet pervaded and systematized by the nature of the unit? What wonder, then, that when Plato essayed to expound the nature of the Good and its relation to the universe, his lectures should grow, as we are told, so clogged with abstruse mathematics as to drive away the throngs which had been attracted by their title? What wonder, again, that the Good should insensibly degenerate again into the One, and that a bare, formal, intellectual unity should take the place of the purposive harmony which the Ideal of the Good had at first demanded? For it was most unfortunate to try to illustrate the content of the Supreme Purpose from mathematics. These sciences, no doubt, are ultimately purposive structures, and admirably illustrate the systematic character of knowledge; but superficially their procedure is not teleological at all. To reduce the Good, therefore, to a mere demand for a formal unity, verbally implicit in the notion of a universe, was to stultify the whole conception.

§ 14. Plato had discovered the function of the Concept, and constructed the Ideal of perfect knowledge. But his

Theory of Ideas overshot the mark in losing sight of the Concept's instrumental character. Consequently he proceeded to misconceive (1) its relation to perception, and (2) the real nature of the Concept itself.

(1) He had perceived that concepts colligated and classified percepts, which are 'known' by such conceptual classifications. He perceived also that this 'knowing,' however completely it may satisfy our immediate interest, never exhausts the *potential* significance of percepts. However many 'Ideas' are predicated of a percept, it still admits of further predications (should any one need to make them). What this really proves is the excellence of an instrument which cannot be worn out by use.

But Plato took it as a defect. Not in the *concept, however, but in the percept.* It meant that the percept was such as to elude the grasp of thought. It was too impermanent, too various, too unstable, too indefinable, to be fully known, to be really knowable. Whatever you might say it was, it was always something else as well ; it was always turning into an 'other.' The perceptual was always changing, that is, always 'becoming'; and 'becoming' set reason at defiance. It could only be thought as an unintelligible union of 'not being' with 'being.' Hence the perceptual world was stained with an ineradicable taint ; it did not possess true being, nor the permanence which that entailed. It was vitiated through and through by a 'non-existent,' a μὴ ὄν, which rendered it impermanent, and imperfect, and individual, and in general accounted for the flux of sense.

It followed that the Sensible was not strictly to be known. Knowledge is only of universals, 'Ideas'; that which eludes the universal, the infinite particularity of the 'this,' 'here,' and 'now,' is strictly unknowable. Science takes no account of the differences between one man and another ;[1] demonstration stops with the least general 'law' (which, however, is still a universal) ;[2] there can be no definition of the individual. True knowledge, there-

---

[1] *Theaetetus,* 209. Cp. *Essay,* iii. § 18.
[2] Cp. *Rep.* 511 B., and *Essay,* vi. §§ 3, 4.

fore, is wholly conceptual, and essentially independent of
'sense,' even though for unreal beings, wallowing in the
obscurities of the phenomenal, it may have to be
perceived, and extracted from a 'this-here-now.'

An easy fusion, further, of the ethical with the epistemological meaning of 'living by the senses,' here forms
a natural starting-point for a moral development of the
Ideas as Ideals, which made the Platonic disparagement
of the world of sense a basis for asceticism and a
jumping-off place to a 'heaven' of pure thought, which
assuredly no individual souls could have attained.[1]

§ 15. The question which naturally arises at this
point is why any one should look any further for the
source of the Platonic χωρισμός, the 'transcendence' or
'hypostasization' of the Platonic Ideas.   The metaphysical
dualism of the Ideal Theory is plainly implicit in its
epistemological dualism.   The dualistic chasm between
the Real and the Phenomenal is merely the translation
into ontological language, the application to the metaphysical problem, of the dualistic antithesis between
'thought' and 'sensation,' 'knowledge' and 'opinion,'
merely a consequence of a formulation of an ideal of
knowledge which had abstracted from personality and
ignored individuality, and so had constitutionally incapacitated itself from understanding actual knowing.

The Platonic Idea has emancipated itself from man;
it has become so 'independent' as to have lost all intrinsic
connexion with human knowing; it has soared to so
'supercelestial' an Empyrean that human effort and
human aspiration can no longer follow it.   Consequently
when it revisits the terrestrial scene, it 'descends into the
Cave,' and demeans itself by consorting with man, whose
whole life, with its interests, individuality, and impermanence, it must heartily despise.   For the 'Ideal'
Theory of knowledge has no intrinsic connexion with
human life; man for it is an encumbrance to be over-

---

[1] Whether, however, Plato himself perceived the incompatibility of individual
immortality with his theory of knowledge is doubtful.   His arguments, as Teich-
müller has shown, never 'prove' more than the immortality of soul as a principle; but he may have taken the plurality of souls for granted empirically.

come, and not a master to be served. The connexion which appears to exist between the two is intrinsically unintelligible, because they are not really related ; it is impossible to explain how man can rise to the contemplation of eternal truth, or why the Idea should descend to distort itself in human thoughts. And what is the relation of the Ideal archetype to its human ' copies ' is the greatest unintelligibility of all. To shirk this question by merely remarking that all the copies are imperfect is plainly insufficient. For this does not explain the various sorts and degrees of inadequacy with which human ideas are afflicted, nor account for their occurrence in the place and at the time they occur. And since *ex hypothesi* the ideal Idea is never realized on earth, it cannot be appealed to to discriminate between a ' true ' idea and a ' false,' between one man's idea, and one man's ideal, and another man's : the whole notion of the eternal Idea is, in short, devoid of application.

§ 16. If, however, undismayed by this logical collapse, we proceed to translate the theory into metaphysics, we inevitably reach the results on which the charge of dualism is commonly based.

The Ideas are the true Reality which exists eternally in absolute self-sufficing independence (αὐτὸ καθ' αὑτὸ ἀεὶ ὄν): sensible things, which ' somehow ' are debased unintelligible ' copies ' of them, are not truly real. Human ideas (' opinions ') are in general at a still lower level of imitation (εἰκασία) ; yet the philosopher can ' somehow ' rise to a vision of the true Ideas, and, when he does so, he grasps reality, and his ideas are rendered true because they predicate the eternal relations of the absolute Ideas.

This is all the metaphysical version of the Ideal Theory comes to, the substance of Platonic metaphysics. Only Plato, being a poet, translates the ' somehow ' into brilliantly pictorial imagery and the most gorgeous ' myths.' His modern imitators, who are not poets, can eke out this jejune ' somehow ' only by pseudo-religious homilies on the necessary limitations of human knowledge, and the presumption of trying to understand wholly what is avowedly a theory of absolute truth ; but it is a moot point whether they perceive the grotesque contradiction between the claims and the achievements of their theory.[1] There is no reason to suppose, however, that Plato himself was, even transiently, deceived. Even without the *Parmenides*, the variegated metaphors with which he else- where describes the relation which is null, the connexion which is impossible, between the Ideal and the Sensible, the Real and the inexplicable unreality of the Apparent, between Absolute Truth and absolutely incomprehensible Error, should convince us that his language was intended to be pictorial. It does not really matter whether the Sensible is said to ' participate ' in the Real, or to ' imitate ' it, or to ' copy ' it as an archetypal model. It does not really matter whether ' the world of Ideas ' is situated in ' a heavenly place ' or in ' supercelestial space,' whether human knowledge is derived from ' recollections ' of pre- natal visions, or elicited from potentialities of eternal truth inherent in the mind, whether human souls are one or many, incarnated or reincarnated, composed of mortal or immortal ' parts,' or both ; in every case the real diffi- culty is one and the same. The descent from the Ideal is an unmediated, incomprehensible Fall, a submergence of the Real in a Flux of Illusion. So long as this Fall is unexplained, Plato has rescued knowledge from the Flux only by getting it into a fix.

It is quite superfluous, therefore, to indict Plato's meta- physic for its failure ' to derive the Sensible,' to connect the Real with the Transcendent, to bridge the chasm

---

[1] Prof. J. S. Mackenzie in *Mind*, N.S. xv. No. 59, must surely be ironical. For after advocating what he calls his ' old idealism ' (which, as attenuated in his statement, becomes indiscernible from realistic monism) on the ground that " the theory seems to make the universe intelligible to us, and we cannot think of any alternative theory that does " (p. 323), and alleging that this is " the only ultimate kind of proof that can be given," he goes on to say that " it would be absurd to expect any system of Idealism to show the rationality of the universe in such a sense as this," *i.e.* by a teleological explanation of particular events and physical processes, such as *Plato himself demanded* in the *Phaedo* ! And finally it turns out that even so ' Idealism ' cannot fulfil the duty to which it has restricted itself, and he will " by no means affirm that it can, in this present life, become com- pletely intelligible to us " (p. 328). Truly, an amazing confession from a theory which demanded acceptance on the ground of its unique ability to render the world completely intelligible ! Cp. also Mr. Bradley in *Mind*, No. 74, and my comments in No. 76.

between the Ideal and the Human. *Habemus confitentem reum* ; Plato himself has admitted and deplored the fact, far more completely and compactly, and in far finer language than any of his critics and successors.[1] Plato has anticipated all their difficulties, objections, and suggestions for a cure—the problem of the 'transcendence' or 'independence' of the Idea—Aristotle's 'third man,' *i.e.* the infinite series of impotent mediators between the Idea and the sensible thing—the problem of the unity of an Idea which is exemplified in and distributed among infinite particulars—the objection to recognizing eternal Ideas of everything that can be named or invented—the nullity of a thought which neither is nor can be thought by any one—the vain device of an absolute thinker to retain in thought the Ideas not in human use [2]—the fatal divorce between human and Ideal truth—the unknowableness of the latter and its unconcern about the former—the incapacity of the Divine, just because it is divine, to know the human—all these were familiar to Plato as consequences of his theory.

But it is fallacious to argue that, because he recognized these difficulties, he was able or willing to remove them. He appears to have regarded them as the price which had to be paid for the Ideal Theory. And he never refuses to pay the price. All that in the *Parmenides* (135 C) he has to set against the objections he has enumerated is, that if the Ideas are abandoned, knowledge is impossible ; and this remark is significantly put into the mouth of 'Parmenides,' who has just made havoc of the 'Socratic' theory. If the price seems to us stupendous, and the gain incommensurate, we should at least reflect that the cost of an (approximately) consistent intellectualism has not been reduced since Plato's day, and that, even with all its difficulties, Plato might well remain convinced of the fundamental value of his theory.

For after all was not all knowledge, in the true sense, still manifestly conceptual? Were not Ideas, and

[1] Cp. especially *Parmenides*, 131-4.
[2] For this would seem to be implied in the 'thinking Ideas' of *Parm.* 132 C.

nothing but Ideas, used in all predication? Was not
that which is not 'Idea' incapable of being thought, or
expressed, or understood? Nay, in the end, what but
an Idea could be predicated as existent, *i.e.* could *be*
at all? All this was true and important, and less
specious theories have often been upheld on feebler
grounds.

What, then, of the charge that Plato has wantonly and
vainly duplicated the real world by his Ideal world? It
is simply not true that he has asserted the existence of
two real worlds, of which one is superfluous. He has
asserted only *one* real world, viz. the Ideal world, just as
he has asserted only one form of true 'knowledge,'
viz. that of concepts. He has had to admit, indeed, that
besides the real world there appears to exist also a world of
sense, which is a world of illusion, and can be perceived,
but is not to be rendered fully intelligible even by the Ideas
which pervade it. But his metaphysic is no more really
dualistic than that of the Eleatics. Parmenides also had
described a 'way of opinion' to deal with the sensible world
which 'somehow' coexisted with the Absolute One. Plato's
account is essentially the same, with two improvements. He
has articulated the One into a system of Ideas ; and he
has suggested that though the illusion is incomprehensible, we can yet in a way comprehend why it should,
and that it must, be so. For we can understand that if
reasoning as such inevitably predicates Ideas, a rational
deduction of what is not Idea is inconceivable. Thus the
very existence of the non-existent is to be grasped only
by 'a spurious reasoning.'

And yet it was most natural that the Platonic doctrine
should be, at once and persistently, misunderstood. The
truth of Plato's theory is evident only to those who can
see with Plato's eye and from Plato's point of view. His
doctrine must appear as an assertion of *two* real worlds
once we presume the initial reality of our phenomenal
world of sense. To view it in this way at once renders the
Ideal world a *second* world, which claims *superior* reality,
but is ludicrously unable to make good its claim, because

it fails to establish any real connexion with the primary reality of the world it essays to control.

But this interpretation is false to Plato's thought. Plato had never admitted the primary reality of our phenomenal world. On the contrary, he had denounced it as tainted with unreality. For Plato, therefore, Platonism is a *one-world* view; its dualism lies not in metaphysics, but in epistemology.

For Aristotle, his unknown predecessors (answered in the *Parmenides*), and his successors, it is no doubt a *two-world* view, split by a metaphysical chasm between the two worlds.

It all depends, therefore, on the standpoint. The true Platonic standpoint assumes the reality of the Ideal, and starts with it, but is unable to get down to the human world. The Aristotelian standpoint, which is that of common-sense, assumes the reality of the human world, starts with that, comes to the brink of the same chasm from the opposite side, and is, of course, unable to leap across it to the Ideal. There is not really any difference of opinion about the actual facts of the situation: both sides come to the same gap, and are stopped by it.

The sole question is as to which is our proper standpoint. Now this question might be argued with endless subtlety; for on the one hand absolute truth would seem to be visible only from the Ideal standpoint; on the other human truth would seem to be that proper to man. What, however, cuts the discussion short is the simple fact that *before a man can maintain the Ideal standpoint it must be reached from the human by a man.* And if man can attain it, he ought to be able to leave it again. If, therefore, it appears that there is no road back to the human from the Ideal, it clearly cannot have been reached by valid means. So what Plato has forgotten is the deduction of his standpoint. He must have jumped to his Ideal standpoint. Once he got to it, all went swimmingly, until the time came for a return to earth; then he found he could not return, but without understanding why. Accordingly all he can say is that the Ideal world is certainly real, that the world of sense is not, and that if the Ideas are denied, thinking must stop, because all predication uses concepts. Now all these things, which are in a manner true, he says unweariedly from first to last. That his attitude has seemed perplexing and obscure is wholly due to his critics' lack of perception. They have not penetrated into the depths of Plato's problem, nor seen that the real difficulty springs from his conception of knowledge.

And so they have actually thought themselves entitled to scorn Plato's metaphysic while submissively accepting his notion of the Concept! But this is no way of breaking Plato's spell ; and the resulting failures to solve his problem, nay, to avoid repeating his confessions of embarrassment, in almost the same words, are distinctly humorous. Aristotle's devices, for example, for avoiding the transcendence of the Idea seem deliciously naïve. He declares that, of course, 'universals' must be conceived as immanent in their 'particulars' ; but how this can be, he is quite unable to explain. He protests (rightly enough) that individual substances are primary reality, and that universals are only 'second substances' ; but for lack of insight into the instrumental function of the latter, his theory of knowledge ends in the unresolved contradiction that, since knowledge is essentially of universals, the metaphysical order is epistemologically impossible, and individuals, which in metaphysics are ultimate reality, in epistemology are as such unknowable! It thereupon seems only a secondary mishap that after all his denunciations of Platonic χωρισμός he should have to make his own νοῦς something χωριστόν, or to postulate the transcendence of his deity, who is really quite as much dissevered from the universe as the Platonic Idea, and can act on it only by the magic of the world's desire for his perfect 'form.'

As for Plato's followers, whose name is legion, their labour has been that of Danaids. They have been trying to carry the waters of truth in Plato's conceptual sieve, without so much as perceiving that the vessel leaked.

And this, at least, Plato may claim to have perceived, even though he was at a loss for means to stop the leakages of truth through the holes in his conception of the Concept.

§ 17. For the only real escape from his embarrassments lay in a direction in which he could not and would not look for it, viz. in a radical recognition of the functional and instrumental nature of the Concept. But this would have involved a rehabilitation of the senses and of immediate experience, and a complete remodelling of Plato's conceptions of Truth and Reality. Even if by some strange chance he had caught a glimpse of this way out, he would have averted his eyes from the impious spectacle. The view that concepts are not unalterable and only relatively constant (like mere material things), being essentially tools slowly fashioned by a practical intelligence for the mastery of its experience, whose value and truth reside in their application to the particular cases of their use, and not in their timeless validity nor in their suprasensible *otium cum dignitate* in a transcendent realm of abstractions, would have seemed to him as paradoxical and monstrous and unsatisfying as it still does to his belated followers. Yet it is this notion of Truth, this insight into the function of Ideas, which the working of Science has slowly brought to light, after many centuries of incessant and by no means always successful warfare against the glamour of the gorgeous castles which Platonism has erected in and out of the air.

There had been a couple of huge mistakes in Plato's conception of the Concept's function: (1) The initial abstraction from its human side was really illegitimate ; and so (2) no provision had been made for the *growth* of truth.

(1) Because in ordinary cases our reasoning can often abstract from the personal peculiarities of this man or that, it does not follow that we can abstract from *all* men, and dehumanize truth as a whole. Because we make truth what may be, roughly, called 'independent,' it does not follow that it can be absolutely so, or that it

is logically irrelevant that *we make* it so *for certain purposes* of our own. In point of fact, the whole depersonalizing or dehumanizing of truth (and of reality) must be conceived, and limited, pragmatically. It is a procedure which is useful, and works for certain limited purposes ; but it breaks down woefully and irretrievably when it is conceived as ultimate. ' Pure Reason,' defecated of all human interests, can assert its rationality as little as its existence.

(2) One of the chief characteristics of human truth is its progressiveness. It is essentially a thing that must grow and develop through stages subsequently known as ' errors.' Ideal truth, on the other hand, is conceived as inerrant, and as fixed and immutable in its perfection. When, therefore, Platonism abstracted from the human side of knowing, it implicitly rejected also the conception of a growth of knowledge. To render such growth conceivable, concepts must *not* be conceived as rigid, but as improvable and adjustable to new conditions. It is here that *a priori* dogmatism fails. Its fallacy does not lie in its deductive procedure, but in its tacit assumption that *the conceptions it argues from are final and not to be revised.* But for this assumption, a ' contradiction' might only prove that the conceptions used were insufficient for their work. And if there is always this alternative inference from an apparent case of contradictory conceptions, how can the intellectualist belief in a purely formal criterion of truth, which regards it as mere self-consistency, be sustained, or the pragmatic appeal to consequences be averted ?

The Platonic Ideas illustrate this situation admirably. Plato had perceived that stable concepts were needed for significant assertion and profitable inquiry. But (as in the similar cases of the ' independence' of ' reality,' and of ' truth ') this stability was not conceived pragmatically, *i.e.* as the amount and sort of stability which concepts need to fulfil their actual function. It was cut loose from human knowing, and taken as absolute. Concepts thereby became immutable. But if our concepts are immutable, our knowledge cannot grow. Conversely, if our knowledge grows, our concepts cannot be immutable. If, therefore, there are immutable concepts, they cannot, at any rate, be ours. They are different in kind, and so cannot explain human knowledge. The inability, in short, of the Platonic Idea to descend to earth is inherent in its construction.

If, without realizing this fundamental divorce between the Ideal and the human, into which Platonism has been beguiled, we try to adjust the Platonic Idea to the growth of knowledge, we at once evolve a tissue of absurdities.

(1) If the Ideal World is to remain connected with ours, and to be affected by our judgments, it would follow that any change in our world would have to be reflected in the Ideal. Every time any one hit upon a new predication which could sustain its claim to truth, every time a new reality, say a motor car, was made or generated, or an old one, say a dodo, became extinct, there would have to ensue a responsive readjustment in the eternal system of Ideas. But would not this destroy its eternity, and effectively include it in the sphere of the Sensible? How could Ideas, thus subject to Becoming, thus perfected in time, any longer function as representative of timeless 'Being'?

(2) But even if a Becoming of the Ideas were admitted, it would not explain the Becoming of the Sensible. The Ideal Bed may be, as we are told in the *Republic* (596), the eternal reality, of which all real beds are imperfect copies ; but how does it assist or explain the genesis of the latter? Humanly speaking, beds were invented by men, in response to human needs, by the practical exercise of their intelligence for the manipulation of reality, at a definite stage in the history of man's progress. But what had eternal Ideas to do with any part of this history? How can the eternal nature of the Ideal Bed account for the time, or the place, or the material, or the inventor of the first construction of beds, or for their subsequent improvements, and the consequent expansion in our notions of what an ideal bed requires?

Shall we assert that the Ideal Bed, *e.g.* had spiral springs all along, because the best beds now possess them, or deny this, because in Plato's time such modern improvements had not been thought of?

(3) If, on the other hand, we rigidly maintain the transcendence of the Ideal, we must lose connexion with human knowing. The latter becomes a self-directing process which Pure Reason cannot sanction or understand, while Ideal Truth becomes the meaningless monopoly of Gods who, as Plato said, *cannot* know the human.[1] How clearly Plato himself had seen this objection is attested also by a remarkable passage in the *Sophist* (247-9), which points out that knowledge of the Ideas implies an interaction between them and us, and so their alteration, and thereby a sacrifice of their independence, absoluteness, and immutability. In return, they are promised motion, life, soul, intelligence, and purposive reason : but what of their stability? Plato can see a way to reconcile these conflicting postulations as little as in the *Parmenides* ; he leaves the contradiction unresolved.

It is easy, of course, to say that he ought on no account to have put up with it. He ought to have adopted the more tolerable alternative ; he ought to have upheld at all costs the relevance of the Ideas to human knowing ; he ought to have taken account of the growth of knowledge ; he ought to have sacrificed the eternity and immutability of truth.

It is easy for us to say this, because we can realize that the concepts we use are continuously changing as our knowledge grows, though more slowly than our percepts, and that immutability is neither a fact nor a necessity. We can see, indeed, that so far from postulating immutability, our concepts could not perform their functions if they did not change. We are thus compelled to conceive any 'absolute' truth which is relevant to actual knowing as nothing more than, as it were, *humanly absolute, i.e.* as an ideal for us, which we are

[1] *Parmenides*, 134 E.

really making and realizing, and which must, for that very reason, *not* be eternally accomplished.

But Plato could not see this.[1] He could not see his way to changing his notion of the Concept without demolishing knowledge. He could see no way of combining the purity of knowledge *per se* with its attainment *by us*. He could not see that the constancy of a concept predicated, need be no greater than suffices to express the purpose and convey the meaning of a judgment. He could not see this, because the purpose was just part of that Protagorean humanism, which he had interpreted and repudiated as scepticism.

But though he did not see this, he saw far more than his successors. The whole intellectualist theory of knowledge is a washed-out replica of Platonism, inferior in design, execution, vividness of colouring, and above all in significance. For the clearness with which Plato had pointed to the flaw of his theory ought to have suggested the need for a thorough re-examination of the function of the Concept. In point of fact it did nothing of the kind. The later intellectualists hardly realized how completely they were dependent on Plato for the foundations on which they built ; they hardly ever penetrated to the fundamental difficulties of their common theory.

§ 18. To us at last the way is clear. We must conceive the Concept as an instrument of human knowledge, and its nature as relative to, and revealed in, its use, and therefore to be discovered by attentive study of actual knowing, and not by meditation and dialectical

---

[1] Prof. J. A. Stewart has, however, propounded (in *Plato's Doctrine of Ideas*) a brilliant and original theory that the so-called 'Socratic' dialogues, so far from being scientifically negligible, are really essential to the complete statement of the Ideal Theory, and should be taken as exemplifying *the function of the Concept in use*, and as supplementing the account of the *abstract* concept given in the dogmatic dialogues, on which alone the traditional descriptions of Platonism have been based. If this attractive theory can be substantiated in detail, the current estimates of Plato will have to be profoundly modified, and we also can no longer treat him as a complete intellectualist. He could be charged only with a failure to make clear the logical connexion between his two types of dialogue, and to emphasize the vital importance of the functional view of the Concept. Even on the most favourable interpretation, however, we can hardly ascribe to him a full perception of the fact that the whole meaning of concepts depends on their use and application.

'criticism' of abstracted and unmeaning 'forms of thought.' Let us go back to Plato, by all means; but let us go back, not with the intention of repeating his mistake and painfully plunging into the 'chasm' he has made, but in order to correct his initial error. But to do this we must return from Plato to Protagoras. We must abandon the attempt to dehumanize knowledge, to attribute to it an 'independence' of human purposes, an 'absoluteness' which divorces it from life, an 'eternity' which is unrelated to time.

Or rather, if we wish to retain these hallowed terms, we must construe them pragmatically. 'Independence' must not be construed as a denial of connexion with human life, but as a description of the selective valuation which discriminates some more precious contents in human experience from others of inferior value. 'Absoluteness' must designate the ideal of complete adequacy for every human purpose, while the 'eternity' of truth must mean its applicability at whatever time we will.

But to follow up the promise of these novel courses, we must start once more, with Protagoras, from the personal judgments of individuals, and study their developments, the ways in which they originate under the promptings of complex psychic forces, the ways in which they are combined into systems, and are verified, and claim and secure 'objective' validity, and engender the final ideal of an independence and absoluteness which are so easily misinterpreted into a nullification of the processes that generated them. We must radically disabuse our minds of the notion that Humanism means Subjectivism, or Subjectivism Scepticism.

That Subjectivism need not coincide with Scepticism is apparent from the fact that even the extremest Solipsism need not doubt its own sufficiency. In point of fact, it is Intellectualism which passes into Scepticism: it engenders Scepticism so soon as the breakdown of its impossible demands becomes evident to those who cannot bear to part with it.

As for Subjectivism, no Protagorean would admit the

charge. He would not admit that in starting with the individual he had also committed himself to finish up with him. In knowing, also, the beginning and the end of man's career lie far asunder. And he sees, of course, that of the individual judgments made only a small percentage are ever recognized as valid. But he observes also that every one has a strong interest to get his claims validated. Truth is one of the very few objects of human desire of which no one desires the exclusive rights.[1] For if it could win no recognition, it would so far not work, and so fail to be 'true.' It is easy to see, therefore, that beings who live socially must speedily accumulate large bodies of what they take to be 'objective' truth, and that such truth must, on the whole, involve and facilitate salutary adjustments of action. In point of fact, the great social problem is not how to control the individual and to secure conformity with existing valuations, but how to secure and promote the individual variations which initiate improvements.

The two supreme maxims of Hellenic wisdom, *Know thyself*, and *Man is the Measure*, therefore, are not in conflict with each other, nor with the facts of life, and their prosperous manipulation. They yield, at any rate, a better guidance and a saner inspiration for man than the unattainable phantom of an Ideal which exists eternally, immutably, and absolutely for itself.

---

[1] Cp. *Humanism*, p. 58.

III

THE RELATIONS OF LOGIC AND
PSYCHOLOGY[1]

ARGUMENT

§ 1. Humanism as logical 'psychologism.' § 2. It is beneficial to a Logic which has lapsed into scepticism, because it has abstracted from actual knowing. § 3. Definition of Psychology as a descriptive science of concrete mental process. It can recognize cognitive values and claims, though § 4 Logic must evaluate them, and thus arises out of Psychology. Impossibility of forbidding it to describe cognitive processes. § 5. Definition of Logic, a normative science arising out of the existence of *false* claims. § 6. Interdependence of the two sciences. The risks of abstracting from any psychical fact. § 7. (1) Thinking depends essentially on psychological processes, such as interest, purpose, emotion, and satisfaction. § 8. (2) The fundamental 'logical' conceptions, 'necessity,' 'certainty,' 'self-evidence,' 'truth' are primarily psychical facts. 'Logical' certainty due to the extension of potential beyond actual purpose in thinking. § 9. (3) The fundamental 'logical' operations have psychological aspects. *E.g.* the postulate of '*identity.*' *Meaning* dependent on context and purpose. The actual meaning *vs.* the meaning *per se.* The problem of understanding. The 'logical' abstractions as to meaning dangerous and false. *Judgment* an intimately personal affair, which cannot be depersonalized, and is naturally

---

[1] The necessity of treating this subject from a Humanist point of view is evident. It was borne in upon me with peculiar force by two circumstances. The first was that the excellent articles on 'Pragmatism *versus* Absolutism,' by Prof. R. F. A. Hoernle in *Mind* (xiv. N.S. Nos. 55 and 56), seemed to imply a serious misapprehension of the conception of Psychology which we are bound to entertain. Such misapprehension, however, is so natural, so long as no formal treatment of the interrelations of Logic and Psychology is in print, that it seemed imperative to attempt its removal.

Secondly, being called upon to start a discussion before the Aristotelian Society, in which Professor Bosanquet and Dr. Hastings Rashdall also participated, I selected the question whether Logic can abstract from the psychological conditions of thinking. The discussion which ensued will be found in the Society's *Proceedings* for 1905-6, and though it was rather at cross purposes, and on the whole illustrates only the difficulty philosophers have in understanding one another, it enabled me to realize what a radical difference exists between the Humanist and the intellectualist conceptions of these sciences. It seemed helpful, therefore, to discuss these conceptions, and so this essay is based in part on the 'symposium' of the Aristotelian Society.

related to questions and postulates. § 10. Can even desire be abstracted from? A case of postulatory reasoning examined. § 11. As meaning always depends on context, and context on personality, is Logic entitled to abstract from the knower's personality? § 12. The anti-psychological standpoint of intellectualist logic. Its assumptions. (1) 'Pure,' and (2) 'independent' thought. (3) 'Depersonalization.' (4) The separation of thinking from 'willing' and 'feeling.' § 13. Is its standpoint descriptive or normative? or both and either? § 14. Incompetence of Logic for psychological description: its unjust encroachment on psychology and result, § 15, the stultification of psychology and the suicide of logic, *teste* Prof. Bosanquet. § 16. The great abstraction which ruins logic. § 17. 'Depersonalization' involves abstraction from error, which must yet be acknowledged to exist. Mr. Joachim's confessions. Hence § 18 the complete breakdown of intellectualist logic, owing to a separation of the ideal and the human which renders both meaningless. This is Plato's old error, in the *Theaetetus*. § 19. The remedy is to refrain from *dehumanizing* knowledge, by (1) *etherealizing* it, *i.e.* abstracting from its *application*, and (2) *depersonalizing* it, *i.e.* abstracting from the knower's purpose.

§ 1. IT will, probably, be conceded by all philosophers that the sciences are all (in some sense) connected with one another, and that the precise way in which their connexion is conceived will depend on the way we conceive the sciences themselves. Nor will it be disputed that since the definitions of a growing science must to some extent change with the growth of our knowledge of the data of that science, the relations of such sciences to each other cannot be immutable. Consequently it may be inferred with some confidence that the Humanist movement must have introduced some modifications and novelties into our conceptions of Logic and of Psychology, and of their relations to each other. This has, indeed, been pretty widely recognized. In Germany, for example, the analogous tendencies are commonly described, as 'Psychologism,' and if 'Psychologism' means a demand that the psychical facts of our cognitive functioning shall no longer be treated as irrelevant to Logic, it is clear, both that Humanism is Psychologism, and that the demand itself is thoroughly legitimate, and not to be dismissed with a mere *non possumus*. For when Humanism demands that philosophy shall start from, and satisfy, the whole man in his full concreteness, and not exclusively concern itself with a sort of elegant extract, a highly perfumed and sophisticated 'essence' of man, dubbed 'the rational intelligence,' there is certainly included in its demand a much greater respect for the actual procedures of human cognition and a much less easy-going acceptance of petrified conventions than the traditional Logic will find at all convenient.

§ 2. Yet a sincere attempt to comply with the demands made upon it, whether in the name of Psychology or of Humanity, would do Logic no harm. Nay, it might even prove its salvation. For its present condition is anything but prosperous. It has lapsed into an impotent scepticism, which is irremediable so long as it cannot, or will not, emancipate itself from intellectualistic presuppositions which render actual knowing inherently 'irrational.' So it has been forced practically to abandon the attempt to account for knowing. It has been driven to represent the processes by which *de facto* knowledge is increased as logically invalid. Predication has become for it a puzzle, inference a paradox, proof an impossibility,[1] discovery a wonder, change a contradiction, temporal succession incompatible with Science (which all the while is busily engaged with predicting the future!), individuality an irrelevance, experience an impertinence, sensation a piece of unmeaning nonsense, thinking 'extra-logical,' and so forth and so on. After delivering itself of these valuable 'criticisms' of our ordinary cognitive procedures, it has retired into an 'ideal' world of its own invention, out of space, out of time, out of sight (and almost out of mind!), where it employs its ample leisure with studying 'types' that never lived on land or sea, and constructing a *hortus siccus* of 'forms,' and compiling unworkable 'systems,' and concocting unrealizable 'ideals,' of 'Thought,' all of which have about as much relation to actual knowing and to human truth as the man in the moon! But even in its suprasensible asylum the Erinyes of the Reality it has abandoned and betrayed pursue it; it cannot manipulate to its satisfaction even the figments and phantoms of the imaginary world which haunt it.

---

[1] See Prof. Case's article on 'Logic' in the *Encyclopedia Britannica* (10th ed. xx. 338) for a lucid exposition of this situation, with some excellent comments.

Its 'forms' do not afford it æsthetic satisfaction ; its 'types' are broken before ever they are used ; its 'systems' will not hold together ; its 'ideals' decline to be harmonious. In vain does it cry out to metaphysics to save it from imminent collapse into the abyss of scepticism ; its cognate metaphysics have abundant troubles of their own, and are even more hopelessly involved in morasses that border the brink of the pit ; they find, moreover, *all* the sciences beset by similar distresses, and can vouchsafe no answer save that the Real, at all events, does not appear, nor can what appears be real.

In such a desperate plight it is surely not unbecoming to approach the logician with the suggestion that his troubles may be largely of his own making, that possibly his conception of Logic is at fault and capable of amendment, and gently to point out to him that after all what he originally undertook to do, but has now apparently quite forgotten, was to provide a reasoned theory of actual knowing, that the existence of such actual knowing is an empirical fact which is not abolished by his failure to understand it, that this fact constitutes his datum and his *raison d'être*, that he may as well accept it as the touchstone of his theories, and that it is the 'ideals of thought' which must be accounted wrong if they cannot be rendered compatible with the facts which formed their basis. He may at least be called upon to consider the possibility that, if he consents to start from actual knowing, and refrains from welcoming 'ideals' until they have been authenticated by their connexion with the facts and verified by their working *when applied*, he may reach an altogether more profitable and effective conception of Logic than that which is falling to pieces.

§ 3. Let us make bold, then, to re-define our sciences and to re-conceive their relations.

And first of all let us consider the wider and lower of these sciences, to wit Psychology. Without concerning ourselves with the questions as to how far Psychology is, or may be, experimental or explanatory, and even as to how far its descriptions should be 'functional' rather than 'structural,' as not affecting our present purpose, we may most conveniently conceive it at present as a *descriptive* science, whose aim is the description of mental process as such. It is implied in this, and hardly in need of explicit statement, that the mental processes of individual minds are intended. For we cannot experience or observe mental processes in any other way. Still it is worth noting that, in this implication, Psychology gives us a certain guarantee that it will do justice to the concreteness of the actual human soul ; so far, at least, as the necessary abstraction of its standpoint consequent on the limitation of its purpose permits it to do.

The definition we have adopted clearly assigns to Psychology a very extensive field of operations—practically the whole realm of direct experience.   It recognizes *a psychological side also to everything that can be known*, inasmuch as everything known to exist must be connected with our experience, and known by a psychical process. In so far as any real is known, a process of experiencing is involved in it, and this process appertains to the science of Psychology.   Thus all physical objects and questions become psychological, so soon as we ask how they can be experienced, and whether the psychical process of experiencing them warrants our claiming for them an 'objective reality.'   In some cases, as *e.g.* with regard to the existence of sea-serpents, N-rays, and ghosts, the question about the 'reality' of these objects is really one as to whether the psychological treatment does not exhaust their significance, or whether the psychical processes are such as to justify our interpreting them as indicative of 'objective reality.'

Now among mental processes those which may be called 'cognitive' are very common and predominant, and therefore the description of cognitive process will properly fall into the province of Psychology.   It stands to reason, moreover, that it must be described as it occurs, and without arbitrary attempts at reserving some of its aspects for the exclusive consideration of another science.   Now, as cognitive process is naturally productive of 'knowledge,' and valuable as such, it follows that cognitive values are properly subject to psychological description. Mental Life is, naturally and in point of fact, packed with values ethical, æsthetical, and cognitive ('logical'), of which it is the vehicle.[1] It is the plain duty, therefore, of Psychology to record this fact, and to describe these values. Cognitive values, as psychical occurrences, are facts for Psychology. It is their specific character which subsequently renders them subjects for Logic. Their specific character is that they are *claims to truth*, and employ the predicates 'true' and 'false'; precisely as *e.g.* ethical judgments use the predicates 'right' and 'wrong.'

The special value, however, of these specific valuations and their functions in the organization of Life form no part of the purpose of Psychology. Having a merely descriptive purpose, it is content to record all values merely as made, and as facts. Thus it is psychologically relevant to recognize that the predication of 'true' and 'false' occurs, and that what A judges 'true,' B may judge to be 'false.' But it is psychologically indifferent that A is a much *better* judge than B. Psychology, that is, does not seek to *evaluate* these claims, to decide which is really 'right,' or what is really 'true'; still less to frame generalizations as to how in general claims are to be sustained, and humanly valid judgments to be attained. All processes of immanently and reciprocally criticizing, systematizing, harmonizing, and utilizing the claims actually made fall as such without its purpose: they are the business of Logic.

§ 4. The relation of the two sciences to cognitive process, and to each other, is thus quite simple. Yet it has been woefully misunderstood. Thus it is commonly asserted that Psychology does not recognize values, nor Logic care about psychical existence. Yet if so, how could values enter human minds, and how could truths ever become facts?[2]

---

[1] Cp. *Humanism*, p. 163.

[2] No one, probably, has given greater currency to this fallacious notion than Mr. Bradley, by the sharp contrast he drew in his *Logic* (ch. i. *e.g.* pp. 7, 8, and p. 526) between the validity of the 'idea' (=concept) and the psychical existence of the 'idea' (=mental image). It has, unfortunately, not been as extensively

Still more extraordinary is the assumption that Psychology is not to describe values. Yet this assumption is made without the least consciousness of its monstrosity, and without the slightest attempt to defend it, as if it were self-evident, by writers of repute. Dr. Hastings Rashdall gravely assures us that "the Psychologist . . . knows nothing of the truth or falsity of judgments."[1] And even Prof. Hoernle takes it for granted[2] that "truth, in fact, is not an object of inquiry to Psychology at all. That certain of the mental processes which it studies have the further character of being[3] true or false, is, for Psychology, an accident," and infers that "this inability to deal with validity seems to beset all psychologies alike." This arbitrary restriction on the functions of Psychology is no doubt in the interest of an impracticable conception of Logic, which instinctively seeks to reduce Psychology to an equal or greater futility ; but we, assuredly, can have no reason to accept it.

For us the function of Logic develops continuously, rationally, and without antagonism, out of that of Psychology. Cognitive values and claims to truth exist as empirical facts. If they were all indefeasible, congruous, and compatible with each other, as, *e.g.* my having

---

recognized that his remark in *Appearance and Reality* (p. 51), that "it is not wholly true that 'ideas are not what they mean,' for if their meaning is not psychical fact, I should like to know how and where it exists," is, *inter alia*, a scornful self-correction.

Prof. Bosanquet (*Logic*, i. p. 5) declares that "in considering an idea as a psychical occurrence we abstract from its meaning" ; but *ibid.* ii. p. 16 *n.*, he advocates the remarkable doctrine that "when psychical images come to be employed for the sake of a meaning which they convey, *they ex hypothesi* are not treated as fact. And their meaning is not itself a psychical fact, but is an intellectual activity which can only enter into fact by being used to qualify reality." This is sufficiently oracular, and it would be interesting to hear the reasons *why* Psychology should be debarred from recognizing 'intellectual activities' as psychical facts.

[1] *Arist. Soc. Proc.*, 1905-6, p. 249.
[2] *Mind*, xiv. p. 473.
[3] This should be '*claiming to be*' ; for no one supposes that Psychology is concerned with the *decision* between conflicting claims to truth. Whether what claims to be true really *is* true, is admittedly left to Logic. Here, however, it seems to be argued that because Psychology cannot *decide* between claims, it may not even *register* them, nor describe cognitive values. I fear that Prof. Hoernle throughout has not steered quite clear of the confusion between *claim* (psychological fact) and *validation* (logical fact), which so effectively vitiates the intellectualistic theories of truth. For the distinction see Essay v., especially § 1.

a toothache is compatible with your not having one, there would be no ground for a further science. But in point of fact *false* claims to truth are commoner than valid ones, and they not only conflict with 'the truth,' but also with each other, so that the problem of *Error* cries out for further treatment.

§ 5. There is need, therefore, for a discipline which will evaluate these claims, and try to determine the various degrees of validity and trustworthiness which may be assigned to them. *Logic* is the traditional name for the science which undertakes this function. It may be defined as *the systematic evaluation of actual knowing*. It is a normative science, because it not only records defects, but prescribes remedies ; it reflects on the claims actually made, and prescribes methods for their evaluation. But its normative function arises quite naturally out of our actual procedures, when we observe that some cognitive processes are in fact more valuable than others, and select the more valuable among conflicting claims. Thus the need for Logic, its genesis and its procedures, all seem to be essentially empirical, and it is quite conceivable that no special science of Logic should ever have arisen. If all claims were *ipso facto* true and valid, if we had never been confronted with conflicting claims or driven by our 'errors' to rescind our first assertions, what need were there for Logic ? Our attention would never be called to the problem of values, our primary attributions would stand, and no superior science would be devised to adjudicate between conflicting judgments.

As it is, the natural process has to be regulated and controlled, and so falls a prey to *two* sciences. The same cognitive values occur twice over, first in Psychology as so many facts, then in Logic, as subjects for critical evaluation. Nor is it difficult to understand how two sciences can work over the same ground : they cultivate it with a different purpose, and so raise different crops.

§ 6. It is manifest, moreover, that the two sciences must work together hand in glove. Logic requires trustworthy descriptions of cognitive happenings before it can evaluate

them with safety ; for these it should be able to rely on
the co operation of Psychology. In other words, the
collection and preparation of the material which the
logician proposes to use is essentially a psychological
function, alike whether it is performed by a psychologist
who bears in mind the need of Logic and the needs of
Logic, or whether the logician is enough of a psychologist
to do it for himself. In the latter case he resembles a
painter who, like those of old, makes and mixes his own
colours ; the logician, on the other hand, who proposes to
dispense with the aid of Psychology is like a painter who
will not use anything so gross as colours wherewithal to
paint his ' ideal ' pictures.

Thus Logic and Psychology, though perfectly distinct,
are perfectly inseparable. It is, moreover, because they
are so intimately related that they must be so sharply
distinguished, and because they have been so clearly distinguished that they can be so closely connected. It is
hardly possible to exaggerate the intimacy of their
relations. Nothing psychological can be affirmed *a priori*
to be irrelevant to Logic. The logician, no doubt, from
motives of practical convenience or necessity, often abstracts
provisionally from trivial characteristics of the actual psychic
process ; but, except in cases where he has learnt from experience what features are unessential and may safely be
neglected, he always takes a certain risk in so doing.
Now this risk may be fatal to the validity of his argument,
and in any case impairs its theoretical exactness. The
formal logician, therefore, can never, as such, claim to be
the *final* judge of the value of any argument. He can
never by his ' rules ' preclude the examination of its
' material ' worth ; however formally perfect the syllogism
which expresses it, a fatal flaw may lurk in its actual
application ; however grotesque its formal fallacy, a road
to the truth may be barred by its rejection. If he is wise,
therefore, he will not magnify his office of reminding
reasoners of what they are about, and of how far their
reasonings are attaining the ends they aim at. Thus the
burden of proof, at any rate, lies on those who affirm that

the logician may assume the irrelevance of any psychic fact.

Nay, more. One never can tell whether the proper answer to a 'logical' claim does not lie in the psychological domain, and take the form of a psychological explanation. Thus a claim to have discovered the secret of the universe is not usually met by a 'logical' refutation, but by an inquiry into the assertor's 'state of mind,' and the revelations of mystic ecstasies are treated as exhibitions of mental pathology. We know, in short, that it is folly to reason with the mentally deranged, and that, even in dealing with the sane, it is usually more effective to *persuade* than to *convince*.

We may take it, therefore, that the logician's ignoring of Psychology, and abstracting from the psychical concomitants of actual thinking, can only be very hazardous affairs, which must be understood to be strictly conditioned and limited by the requirements of his temporary purpose. When the logician really knows what he is about he does not intend them to be more than provisional, nor dream of transcending human experience by their aid. Unfortunately, however, this simple situation has been misapprehended so long, and so profoundly, that it is imperative to set forth in greater detail the thoroughgoing dependence of Logic on psychological assistance. We shall do well, therefore, to show (1) that without processes which are admittedly psychological the occurrence of cognition, and even of thinking, is impossible ; (2) that all the processes, which are regarded as essentially and peculiarly 'logical,' have a well-marked psychological side to them, and that their logical treatment develops continuously out of their psychological nature.

(1) All actual thinking appears to be inherently conditioned throughout by processes which even the most grasping logician must conceive as specifically psychological. It is difficult to see, therefore, on what principle logic has any business to ignore them, and to claim to be 'independent' of what must influence its own structures in every fibre. At any rate the *onus*

probandi would seem to lie on those who affirm that these correlated and interpenetrating processes do not influence each other, and that, therefore, their psychical nature may be treated as logically irrelevant. Without, however, standing on ceremony, let us show by actual examples that our thinking depends for its very existence on the presence in it of (*a*) interest, (*b*) purpose, (*c*) emotion, (*d*) satisfaction, and that the word ' thought ' would cease to convey any meaning if these were really and rigidly abstracted from.

(*a*) Where can we discover anything deserving of the name of thought which is not actuated by psychological interest ? To affirm this, moreover, seems merely a truism. It is merely to deny that thinking is a mechanical process like, *e.g.* gravitation. It is to assert that the processes during which the course of consciousness comes nearest to being a purposeless flux of mental images are most remote from cognition. It is to deny that thinking proceeds without a motive and without an aim, and to assert that, in proportion as interest grows more disciplined and concentrated, thought becomes more vigorous and more definitely purposive.

The only way of contesting our inference would seem to be to affirm that the specifically logical interest is *sui generis*, and not to be confounded with the common herd of its psychological congeners.[1] This contention, however, we must regard as merely an arbitrary fiat. It is merely a refusal to let Psychology describe all interests as such. And this refusal can only be prompted by ulterior motives. Moreover, even if the allegiance this special interest owes to Logic exempted it from psychological description, it could do so only *qua* its *specific* nature. *As an interest* it would still fall into the province

---

[1] This I take to be the meaning of Prof. Bosanquet's remarks in *Arist. Soc. Proc.* 1905-6, p. 238. He insists that it can either be " adequately investigated within the bounds of logic proper," so as to leave nothing for " a further scrutiny of these phenomena as purely psychical disturbances," or that the common psychological element can make no specific difference in the logical interest. But how, as a logician, is he to know all this ? And how if the psychologists dispute this claim ? He is setting up as a judge in a case to which he is a party.

of the science which describes the *generic* nature of interests. Lastly, a Humanist Logic can recognize no reasons for relegating the cognitive interest to a world apart, as if it were unconcerned with life and dissociated from personality. On all these grounds, then, we must repudiate the claim that a thought which depends on interest can be independent of Psychology.

(*b*) Purpose may be conceived as a concentration of interest, and thinking must be conceived as essentially purposive, and as the more consciously so, the more efficient it grows. Whenever Logic, therefore, seeks to represent the actual nature of thinking, it can never treat of 'the meaning' of propositions in the abstract. It must note that the meaning depends on the use, and the use on the user's purpose. Now this purpose is primarily a question of psychical fact, which admits of being psychologically determined, and which no theory can safely ignore. If we attribute to logical rules a sort of inherent validity, a sort of discarnate existence apart from their application to cases of actual thinking, we reduce them to phantoms as futile as they are unintelligible.

(*c*) Emotion accompanies actual cognition as a shadow does light. Even so unexciting an operation as counting has an emotional tone. The effect of this emotional tone seems to be various, but may be salutary ; we can often observe how love and hate inspire men with an insight to which the fish-like eye of cold indifference could never penetrate. It need not be denied, however, that in some people and in some forms it may have a hurtful effect on the value of the cognitive results. But this must be shown, and cannot be assumed, in any given case. Nor is its alleged hurtfulness a reason for denying the existence of this emotional bias, except to those who are very far gone in that application of 'Christian Science' to philosophy which declares all evil to be 'appearance.' Our only chance of counteracting emotional bias, moreover, lies in admitting its existence.

(*d*) If a feeling of satisfaction did not occur in cognitive processes the attainment of truth would not be felt to

have value. In point of fact such satisfactions super-
vene on every step in reasoning. Without them, logical
' necessity,' ' cogency,' and ' insight ' would become meaningless words.

It seems clear, therefore, that without these psychological conditions which have been mentioned, thinking
disappears, and with it, presumably, Logic.[1] They cannot, therefore, be dispensed with. Purpose, interest, desire,
emotion, satisfaction, are more essential to thinking than
steam is to a steam-engine.

§ 8. (2) The most fundamental conceptions of Logic,
like 'necessity,' 'certainty,' 'self-evidence,' 'truth,' 'meaning,'
are primarily descriptions of processes which are psychical
facts. They are inseparably accompanied by specific
psychical feelings. What is called their ' strictly logical '
sense is *continuous with* their psychological senses, and
whenever this connexion is really broken off, its meaning
simply disappears. This need not here be set forth at
length. The logician's embarrassments in discriminating
' logical ' from ' psychological ' necessity [2] and self-evidence
are well known. It is also beginning to be clear that
he had not, until the pragmatic controversy arose, ever
seriously considered what was the nature of truth-pre-
dication as a psychic process.

But the conception of ' certainty ' is often considered
the essential differentia of logical thought, and, therefore,
may deserve a brief discussion. Every one, of course,
would have to admit that all ' certainty ' in its actual
occurrence was accompanied by a psychical feeling of
certainty in various degrees of intensity. An appeal
might, however, be made to the distinction of ' logical '
and ' psychological ' certainty. Psychological certainty,
we commonly say, is ' subjective,' and exists for individuals ; ' logical ' certainty is ' objective,' and imposed
on intelligence as such. Again, psychological certainty
may set in long before logical proof is complete, often

[1] Some symbolic logicians, however, seem to regard thinking, *i.e.* judging
and inferring, as so inherently psychological as to be extra-logical. Cp. *Formal
Logic*, p. 377.
[2] Cp. *Personal Idealism*, p. 70 *n.*

long before it ought; and conversely our psychological stupidity may rebel against mathematically demonstrated truths. From these current distinctions the logician is apt to infer that psychological and logical certainty have really nothing to do with each other and ought not to be confused. But if this be true, why are they both called by the same name? Surely, if logicians wished to keep them apart and could afford to do so, they could label them differently. That they have not done so is a strong presumption that it is impracticable.

Indeed, the truth would seem to be, (a) that if the *feeling* of certainty is eliminated the word becomes unmeaning, and (b) that 'logical' is quite continuous with psychological certainty. The notion of 'logical' certainty arises from the extension of potential beyond actual purpose in thinking. We actually stop at the point at which we psychologically are satisfied and willing to accept a claim to truth as good; but we can sometimes conceive ulterior purposes which would require further confirmation, and other minds that would be satisfied less easily. This engenders the ideal of a complete 'logical' proof transcending that which is good enough for us, and capable of compelling the assent of all intelligences. But even if it could be attained, its certainty would still be psychological, as certainly psychological as is our capacity to project the ideal. Both are dependent on the actual powers of individual minds. Thus for the moment mathematical demonstration seems to satisfy the logical ideal of most intellectualist logicians, and is praised as absolutely certain. But that they think it so is merely psychical fact. For the reason simply is that so far they do not seem to have psychologically conceived the thought of varying the postulates on which such demonstration rests. If they had recognized the hypothetical basis of mathematical certainty, they could conceive something more 'certain.'

§ 9. The fundamental logical operations, like meaning, conceiving, discriminating, identifying, judging, inferring, all have psychological aspects, and could not come about by 'pure' thought. I have suggested elsewhere[1] that logical identity is always a postulate. It should be stated as that '*what I will shall mean the same, is (so far) the same.*' And by 'the same' I do not mean *indistinguishable* (though this criterion too rests on a psychological property) as Mr. Bradley does in what he considers "the indisputable basis of all reasoning," the axiom that "*what seems the same is the same,*" which he himself calls "a monstrous assumption."[2] Logical identity emphatically does not rest on an easy acquiescence in appearances or psychical carelessness about noticing differences. It is a conscious act of purposive thinking, performed *in spite of observed differences.* 'The same' means a *claim* that for our purposes these differences may be ignored, and the two terms treated alike.

The principle, therefore, is not mere psychological fact, carrying no logical consequences. Nor certainly is it a mere tautology, 'A is A.' It is ultimately one of the devices we have hit upon for dealing with our experience. As such it may be supposed to have passed through an experimental stage as a mere postulate ; and even now a certain risk remains inherent in its use. That there shall be identity we have good grounds for insisting, but our claim that any A is A may often be frustrated. That therefore every attempted 'identification' should come true, would be the experience only of an omnipotent being, whose volitions the course of events could never contravene. Only to such a being (if such can be conceived) would it be self-evidently, invariably, and 'necessarily' true that 'A is A'; in our human thinking the identities we select may prove to be mistaken. Thus the validity of the principle in the abstract in no wise guarantees its validity in its actual use, or its application to any particular case. But on the whole the principle is valuable enough for us to ascribe our failures, not to its inapplicability to our world, but to our own stupidity in selecting the 'wrong' identities.

---

[1] *Personal Idealism*, pp. 94-104. *Formal Logic*, ch. x. §§ 8, 10.
[2] *Principles of Logic*, p. 264.

Meaning is a psychical fact which should have great interest for Psychology.   It is also a fundamental function for Logic.   But unfortunately intellectualist logicians, by abstracting too easily from its concrete nature as a psychical process, have involved the whole subject in confusion and completely obscured the problem of understanding.

As we saw in Essay i. § 2, meaning depends upon purpose, *i.e.* upon *context*, as the purpose lies in the context.   Now that context is of logical importance is, in a manner, recognized.   But this recognition takes the form of asserting that the meaning (and truth) of an assertion depends on the totality of knowledge ; and this at once rules out *human* knowledge.   For as we cannot know this totality, if meaning depends on this, it is impossible. This interpretation of context, however, is quite false. Meaning is not in the first instance logical at all, but psychological.   It is primarily a question of what the person who made the assertion *actually meant*.   And as, of course, *the whole of his concrete personality* went to the making of the assertion, and contributed to his actual meaning, a case must be made out for its mutilation by 'Logic.'   The next question is the problem of the 'understanding' or transference of the meaning.   We have to discover not merely what the assertor meant, but also how he was understood.   The inherent difficulty of this problem, to which since the days of Gorgias 'Logic' has paid little heed, lies in this that practically meaning must be transferred by verbal symbols, and conveyed in 'propositions.'   But such propositions must always be ambiguous.   They *may* mean whatever they can be used to mean.   They are blank forms to be filled up with concrete meanings according to requirements.   They afford, therefore, no security that the meaning which they are *taken* as conveying is identical with that which they were *intended* to convey.   Until we have assured ourselves of this, it is vain to discuss 'the meaning' of the assertion, or to attempt its logical evaluation.   Consequently the logical treatment of meaning is *meaning-*

less, until these psychological preliminaries have been settled.

What now is the way in which these matters have been treated by 'Logic'? It has made a series of monstrous abstractions, which break down as soon as they are applied to the facts of actual knowing.

(1) It has abstracted from context, *i.e.* from the *actual* context in which the assertion was made and tried to convey its meaning, as being psychological and irrelevant. This is a gigantic blunder, after which it is vain to seek to provide for the 'logical' relevance of context. For the 'logical' context never recovers its full concreteness, and so can never guarantee to 'Logic' a knowledge of the actual meaning. (2) It has framed the abstraction of 'the logical meaning' of the assertion, which it has usually conceived also as existing *per se* and independently of human assertors, and taken it for granted that it could be used as the standard to which to refer the meanings meant and understood. But in actual knowing 'the meaning' is *the* problem. It is not what we may presume, but what we must discover. It is an ideal to be reached, and not a presupposition to be started from. It does not exist; it has to be made—by mutual understanding. Moreover, for the reasons given above, the abstract 'meaning *per se*' of the assertion reduces itself in practice to the *average meaning* of a form of words which will *probably* be used in a certain sense, but may be used in any sense in which any one can convey (or try to convey) *his* meaning. 'The meaning,' therefore, *is infinitely ambiguous.*[1] And hence to operate with it is always hazardous and often false. (3) In abstracting from the assertor's actual meaning, 'Logic' always runs the risk of excluding the real point. For this may lie in some of the 'irrelevant' psychical details of the actual meaning, whose essence may not lie in its plain surface meaning, but in some subtle innuendo.

---

[1] Thus the assertion 'Smith is red-haired' has as many 'meanings' as there are past, actual, and potential 'Smiths,' of whom it can be (truly or falsely) predicated, and occasions on which it can be made.

Moreover, even where 'the logical meaning' does not miss the real point, it nearly always fails to convey the *whole* meaning. For the actual meaning is fully concrete, and contains much more than it conveys, and infinitely more than 'the logical meaning' of the form of words. The latter, therefore, is always something *less* than what was actually meant, and fails to express it fully. For the appropriateness of an assertion always depends in some degree on the personality of the assertor and the particularity of the occasion. (4) 'Logic,' in abstracting from the psychological problem, has burked the whole question of the communication of meaning. It has assumed that there is *only one* meaning with which it need concern itself, and that every one must understand it. In point of fact, there are usually two or more meanings concerned in every question. For the assertor commonly fails to convey his meaning, or his whole meaning, and his assertion is taken in a meaning different from that in which it was meant. There are, in consequence, at least as many 'meanings' as parties to the discussion, and the 'logic' which is concerned only about 'the meaning' is troubling about the non-existent. Whereas if it were recognized that what is called 'the meaning' is an indication, but not a guarantee, of the real meaning, and that the meaning understood may not be that intended, we should take more care to secure a real identity of meaning before beginning to dispute, and so the chances are that many 'logical questions' would never arise.

(5) Lastly, 'Logic' has assumed not only that 'the meaning' of an assertion can be ascertained without regard to the psychological facts, but also that it can be quite dissociated from the personality of its assertor. It becomes, consequently, a matter of indifference whether it was made by A or by B, nay even whether or not it was (or could be) made by any one. Whoever made it, 'it' is equally true, even though A was a fool or a crank asserting it at random, and B a great authority who knows the subject. Our common-sense accordingly pro-

tests against this paradox, and urges that the status of the assertor must make a difference to the assertion. And the practice of science would seem to bear this out. The logical value of an assertion is constantly treated as conditioned by the qualifications of its author. If these are adequate, it is received with respect; if they are nil, it is treated as scientifically null and disregarded. Thus dozens of sailors have sighted sea-serpents, but the testimony of the two competent naturalists on the *Valhalla* is far more likely to shake the incredulity of zoologists.[1] On the other hand, when Prof. Curie reported the extraordinary and unparalleled properties of radium, his assertions were at once accepted. The solution of the paradox lies of course in the falsity of the assertion that when two persons ‘say the same thing’ (i.e. *use the same form of words*) they make the same assertion. They really make *two* assertions, which may (or may not) subsequently be made to coincide and identified with the (usual) meaning of the proposition they use. But they *need not mean* the same thing, nor understand alike. They will probably make the assertion on different grounds, and will certainly have different motives and aims. What *their* assertion means will vary accordingly. And so will its logical value, which here plainly shows itself as dependent on psychological circumstances. Why then should ‘Logic’ stubbornly blind itself to these facts, and insist on cutting meaning loose from its psychological roots, and on confounding in its abstract ‘forms’ cases which all actual knowing must discriminate? The practical convenience and rough adequacy of the easy-going convention that ‘the meaning’ may be taken as identical with the meanings meant and understood, is surely no defence *an intellectualistic logical theory* can plead against the charge of false abstraction and inadequate analysis.

As regards judging, it may suffice to suggest that ‘the judgment’ is as dangerous an abstraction as ‘the meaning’ which is ascribed to it. For what is called *one*

---

[1] Cp. *Nature*, No. 1914, p. 202.

is usually *many*. It follows, moreover, from our last discussion both that every judgment, in its actual use, is an
intimately personal affair, and that its personal aspects
often have (and always may have) important bearings on
its logical value. No judgment could come into being,
even in the world of thought, if some individual mind
were not impelled by its total psychical contents and
history to affirm it upon some suitable occasion, and to
stake its fortunes on this personal affirmation. And even
after it has come into being, its logical status is still
vitally dependent on its relations to the minds which
entertain it. The judgment, therefore, essentially presupposes a mind, a motive, and a purpose. To 'depersonalize' it is to do violence to its concrete nature. Similarly,
its 'objective validity' is not a question of the interrelation
of absolute static truths in a supercelestial sphere. It
depends on its adaptation to our world and its congruous-
ness with the opinions and aims of others. Hence every
recognition of a judgment by others is a social problem,
often of a very complicated character.

To bring out the unreality of the logician's conception
of Judgment, we may note also that 'Logic' is always
held to exclude the evaluation of questions and com-
mands. And yet are not postulates often the basis of
our reasonings, and are not all real judgments the implicit
or explicit answers to a question? Does any sane person
knowingly argue about what is universally admitted?
Ought it not to be truly 'illogical,' then, to sever the
connexion between things which belong so closely together?
To confine Logic to categorical statements in the indicative mood, is to abstract at one blow from the sense and
actual use of judgments. Contrast with this an intellectualist view of the question's function. Prof. Bosanquet,
e.g. is " disposed to doubt whether we can interrogate
ourselves " otherwise than rhetorically, and urges that
questions which we cannot answer and know that we
cannot answer cannot be " genuine questions." He con-
cludes that " thus a question cannot be an act of thought
as such, just as a lie is not, and for the same reason, that

it is not an attitude that the intellect can maintain within itself. . . . It is a demand for information ; its essence is to be addressed to a moral agent, not ourselves, in whom it may produce action " (*Logic*, i. p. 36).

Clearly, however, this whole paradox rests on the abstraction of truth from its consequences, on the divorce of 'thought' from its psychical context. The question is taken as unrelated to anything that precedes and follows. If this is done, only two cases remain ; we ask ourselves a question to which we either do, or do not, know the answer. And of course the question is in both cases futile. In actual knowing, however, we only ask ourselves questions where, though we do not yet know the answers, *we want to know them and are willing to take steps to find them out.* A question, therefore, is logically futile only if we decline to *act* on it, and this would be equally true of a question addressed to others, if they, similarly, did not react upon it. Really, therefore, the putting of questions is, as the Greeks well knew, a natural and necessary process as a preliminary to the satisfaction of a cognitive need, and one which may be of the greatest value, if the right questions are clearly formulated.

§ 10. Lastly, not so much because further illustration should be needed, as in order to force a clear issue, let us consider one more case, that which has been most disputed, viz. that of reasoning openly inspired by desire, *i.e.* of a conclusion affirmed because we should like it to be true. Is it always true that we attain truth only by suppressing desire? Take the familiar argument : *The world is bad, therefore there must be a better.* It all rests on the desire for good and the postulate of perfection. Now if postulation is as such invalid, and desire a mere obstacle to truth, it clearly follows that this argument is hopelessly illogical ; which is accordingly what intellectualist logicians have everywhere maintained.[1]   A bad world

---

[1] *Qua* human they have, of course, not infrequently relapsed into the postulatory way of reasoning. Thus it is a favourite inference from the fact that all the parts of the world are imperfect, that the whole must be perfect. But if in this case it is legitimate to argue to the ideal from the defects of the actual, why not in others?

is logically evidence *against*, not *for*, the existence of a better.

Now, against such abstract and *a priori* notions of what is good reasoning, we may lay it down that good reasoning is that which leads us right and enables us to discover what we are willing to acclaim as truth. And so tested the desire-inspired reasoning may clearly often be the better. It may prompt to more active inquiry, to keener observation, to more persevering experiment. The logician who declares *de non apparentibus et non existentibus eadem est ratio*, who declines to look for what he wants but does not see, who does not seek to penetrate beyond the veil of appearances, is, frankly, an ass. He frustrates his avowed purpose, the discovery of truth, by debarring himself from whatever truth lies beneath the surface. His self-approbation, therefore, of the heroic self-sacrifice of his volitional preferences to 'objective truth' which he 'feels himself bound' to commit, is simply silly. What right, indeed, has he even to 'feel bound'? Does not the phrase betray the emotional origin also of *his* attitude to truth? He accomplishes the sacrifice of 'personal preference' to 'objective truth' by dint of an emotional desire to mortify himself (or, more often, others), the satisfaction of which appears to him as a good. How then is he other or better than the voluntarist who makes bold to postulate, and verifies his anticipations?

Moreover, if we supply the missing premiss in the contention of the intellectualist, we find that it must take a form something like this, that it is *wrong* to anticipate nature, to go beyond what you can see, wicked to try whether the apparent 'facts' cannot be moulded or re-moulded into conformity with our desires. He must say 'it is *wrong*.' He cannot say 'it is impossible.' For it is constantly done, and with the happiest effects.

If now we ask, *Why wrong?* we force the intellectualist to reveal the full measure of his prejudice. To defend his assumption he must do one of two things: (1) He may fall back upon his own feeling of the æsthetical or ethical impropriety of the voluntarist's procedure. But if so, his objection ceases to be purely logical. It may be declared to be only his idiosyncrasy, and be met by the retort—"but it does not seem improper to me. I do not, will not, and cannot share your devil-worship of disagreeable fact and unwelcome truth. I do not, cannot, and will not call a universe good which does not satisfy my desires, and I feel strongly that it *ought* to do so. Whether it does, or can be made to do so, I do not know as yet; it is one of the chief things I am staying in the universe to find out. If (*a*) it does, or can, then my desires are to be regarded as a sound, logical indication of the nature of reality and a valid method of penetrating to its core. If (*b*) it does not, I may have, no doubt, to admit unwelcome truths and unpalatable facts. But I shall do so provisionally, and with a clear intention of abolishing them as soon and as far as I am able. If (*c*) it sometimes does, and sometimes not, why then I am entitled, nay bound, to try *both* methods. I have a right both to treat my wishes as clues to reality, and to subordinate them on occasion to facts which are too strong for me. And I observe that (whether you approve or blame) this is what, in fact, men have always done."

If (2) the intellectualist tries to find something more objective than his instinctive feeling of the wrongness of the voluntarist's procedure, what resource has he? Must he not appeal to the consequences of the two methods? Must he not try to show that the consequences of submission are always, or mostly, good—those of postulation always, or mostly, bad? But can he show this? Notoriously he cannot. And in either case has he not used the pragmatic test of logical value?

It is vain, therefore, to seek an escape from the conclusion that actual thinking is pervaded and conditioned through and through by psychological processes, and that Logic gains nothing, and loses all vitality and interest, all touch with reality, by trying to ignore them. To emphasize this is not, of course, to deny that for logical purposes some psychological conditions may sometimes be irrelevant. Thus in using concepts it is generally possible to abstract from the particular nature of the psychological imagery. The reason is that identity of meaning overpowers diversity of imagery ; if this were otherwise, the use of concepts would be impossible. Again an error, say of counting, may be psychologically a very complex fact ; it may, nevertheless, be logically a very simple error. By my counting 2 and 3 as 6, there may hang a lengthy tale ; but for the logician it may be enough to say that the result ought to have been 5. It should be observed, however, even here, that the logical description of this process as an 'error' involves an appeal to psychology ; the error could not be recognized as such but for my capacity to correct it, or at least to admit the validity of processes which enable others to correct it. If I were psychologically incapable of counting 2 + 3 as other than 6, I could not recognize my 'error,' a 'common' arithmetic would disappear, and there would remain no way of deciding which process was counting and which miscounting, but the experience of the respective consequences and the slow test of survival.

§ 11. Whenever, then, the logician abstracts from the concrete facts of reasoning, he should do so with a consciousness of the nature and dangers of his procedure. He should feel that he may have left out what is essential, that he may have failed to notice the actual meaning of the thought he examined, and have substituted for it some wholly different imagination of his own. The proposition which he solemnly writes down an 'error' or a 'fallacy' may not have been a prosaic affirmation at all ; it may have been poetical hyperbole or an hypothesis, a jest or a sarcasm, a trap or a lie. He will, therefore, get a very little way into the analysis of actual thinking if he declines to recognize that in its actual use the same form of words may serve all these purposes, and cannot be treated logically until he has found out what its actual meaning is. A lie is, I presume, a proposition which claims truth like any other. But the claim is for export only ; the liar himself knows it to be 'false,' and has rejected the claim, even though he has persuaded all the

world.   There is no 'lie' unless there is deception, and no
deception unless there are deceivers and deceived.   The
difference of the persons concerned, therefore, is essential.
How then can 'the meaning' of such a proposition be
represented as single and simple?   How can its logical
status even be discussed without going into these facts?
Does it not follow that Formal logicians have no right to
their habit of speaking of 'the meaning' of a proposition
as if it were a logical fixture?   *The actual* meaning is
always a psychical fact, which in the case of an ambiguity
intended, implied, or understood, may be many.   The
'logical' meaning is potential; it is at best the *average*
meaning with which the proposition is most commonly
used.   It is only more or less probable, therefore, as the
interpretation of an actual judgment.   And to build a
system of apodictic doctrine on foundations such as these
what is it but to build a house of cards?

   It would be possible to show in this manner, and with
the utmost fulness and unlimited examples, that vastly
more than the text-books recognize is really relevant to
Logic, that every logical process, conception, method, and
criterion springs naturally and continuously out of psychological soil, and is essentially a *selection from*, and *valuation
of*, a more extensive psychical material.   But enough has
probably been said to suggest that Logic can take nothing
for granted, and itself least of all.   In view of the complete
dependence and reliance of every logical process on the
psychical nature of man in general and of men in particular,
in view of the manifest adjustment of every logical principle to the needs of human life, is it not high time that
*a systematic doubt were cast on the assumption that the
theory of knowledge must abstract from the personality of
the knower*?

   § 12. It should now be clear what is the meaning, the
ground and the aim of our Humanist 'psychologism,' but
we may clinch the argument by supplementing it nega-
tively by a proof that the antagonistic conception of an
'independent' Logic (1) involves unintelligible and self-
contradictory misdescriptions; (2) assumes a standpoint

which it cannot justify, and (3) is so unable to deal with actual knowing, that (4) it ends in scepticism and intellectual collapse. It will be seen, in short, that the intellectualistic treatment of Logic "necessarily conducts to a complete *débâcle* of the intellect."[1]

It has already been implied that it is usual to formulate the conception, and to expound the claims, of Logic in an anti-psychological way radically opposed to ours. One still hears of Logic as the science of 'pure' thought, endowed with a standpoint and nature of its own, which is 'free' and 'independent' of man and human psychology, and anything it may do or say about such merely human processes as 'willing' and 'feeling,' as a science which by 'depersonalizing' itself has risen to communion with the eternal and immutable Ideal, and of course cares not one jot about our personal interests or attitude towards truth.

These epithets, however, are chiefly ornamental, and merely serve to curry favour for the assumptions on which it is attempted to rest the science.

(1) The notion of 'pure thought,' for example, must not be pressed. It is not a fact of actual knowing, but a barefaced fiction, which can at most be defended as a methodological necessity for the purposes of intellectualist logicians. Its fictitious nature has nowadays to be avowed, whenever it is directly challenged. Even Mr. Bradley "agrees" with Prof. Dewey, that "there is no such existing thing as pure thought,"—it is true only just before proceeding to declare that "if there is to be no such thing as *independent* thought, thought that is which in its actual exercise *takes no account of the psychological situation*, I am, myself, in the end, led inevitably to scepticism. The doctrine that *every judgment essentially depends on the entire psychical state* of the individual, and derives from this its falsehood or truth, is, I presume, usually taken to amount to complete scepticism."[2] 'Pure thought,' then, is not to be the

---

[1] Captain H. V. Knox in *Mind*, xiv. p. 210. Cp. *Formal Logic*.
[2] *Mind*, xiii. p. 309 *n*. Italics mine. We learn from this amazing passage that it is complete scepticism to take complete account of the facts in a cognitive procedure, and that if we will not deliberately falsify them, we are doomed to end

same as 'independent.'   But what is 'pure' thought *pure
from*?   Psychological contamination?   If so, will it not
coincide with 'independent' thought?   For that too
"takes no account of the psychological situation."   But
if so, has not an imperious need of Logic been equated
with a non-existent?   The puzzle grows more perplexing
when we recall the pronounced emotionalism which is
somehow combined with Mr. Bradley's intellectualism, and
to which Mr. Sturt has lately drawn attention.[1]   How can
an intellect so emotionally conditioned be either 'pure'
or 'independent'?

The truth, however, seems to be that the sacrifice of
'pure thought' goes greatly against the grain of intellectualism.   Only constant vigilance can prevent it from
wriggling itself back into the claim to be an actual fact,
and whether intellectualism can afford wholly to dispense
with it, especially in its arguments about 'useless' knowledge, seems more than doubtful.

(2) The 'independence' of Logic and its standpoint
is in every way a most difficult notion.   It is hard to
understand, harder to derive, hardest to justify.   Nay, in
the end it will turn out so anarchical as to be fatal to
the theory that entertained it.   For the present, however,
it may suffice to point out the difficulty of ascertaining
the meaning of a word which is constantly employed in
current discussions, and never defined.   Its meaning
appears to vary with the work it has to do.   In its most
rigorous sense it describes the iniquity of pluralism in
claiming 'independence' for its reals, the impossibility of
which provides an *a priori* refutation of this metaphysical
'heresy.'[2]   In this sense it means apparently 'totally
unconnected with.'   A more lenient sense is in vogue

---

as sceptics !   It is surely strange that such falsification should be a necessary preliminary to the search for truth, and one is tempted to reply, that if 'Logic'
demands this falsification, then the sooner the conception of Logic is amended
the better.   But it is evidently Mr. Bradley who is predestined to scepticism ;
every theory of Logic he touches turns to scepticism in his hands, and even
when he flees to metaphysics he fares no better (cp. Essay iv. § 3).   Probably
the peculiarity is, in his case, psychological.

[1] *Idola Theatri*, ch. v. §§ 4-7.

[2] *Appearance and Reality*, ch. x.

when intellectualism has to defend its abstractions against Humanist attacks. For in that case we learn, *e.g.* that every Logic is 'independent' of Psychology, nay, that every well-conducted theoretic truth preserves a virtuous independence. Similarly we are told by 'realists,' that in the act of knowing the object of knowledge is quite 'independent' of the knowing act. And, finally, Mr. Bradley sometimes equates it with 'relative freedom'![1] It is clear that if these ambiguities were done away with, either the argument about the impossibility of pluralism, or that about the independence of pure thought and Logic, would have to disappear from the armoury of our intellectualists.

(3) The 'depersonalization' which is regarded as characteristic of an 'independent' Logic is usually defended by the example of Science, which is said to ignore all human interest as irrelevant. But this assertion is hardly true. The abstraction practised by Science is *not* analogous to that advocated for Logic. It is *not* true that Science as such abstracts from *all* human interest. It does *not* abstract from the scientist's interest in his particular science. And this is still a human interest. For it is what generates the science, and incites men to its study.[2] Psychologically it represents, not an *absence*, but a *concentration* of interest, such as is demanded, more or less, for the attainment of every purpose, and for the satisfaction of every interest. And it can occur *only in a highly developed personality*. The 'depersonalization,' therefore, which is postulated for Logic obtains no support whatever from scientific procedure. And we shall soon see how ill it serves the ends of 'Logic.'

(4) The analysis of psychic process into 'thinking,' 'willing,' and 'feeling,' in order to justify the restriction of 'Logic' to the first and the exclusion of the two latter, appears to be an unwarranted piece of amateur psychologizing. For the analysis in question is valuable

---

[1] *Mind*, xiii. p. 322, and cp. Essay iv. § 9 *s.f.*
[2] This remark, of course, is not inconsistent with the pragmatic doctrine that all science is ultimately useful. For it refers only to the immediate psychological motive.

only as a rough reference for popular purposes, and is really a survival from the old 'faculty' psychology. Scientifically its descriptive, like its explanatory, value is *nil*. No one nowadays seriously supposes that a soul can actually be put together out of 'thought,' 'will,' and 'feeling,' or that this 'analysis' represents its actual genesis.[1] For in actual knowing all three always co-operate. There is no thought-process which is not purposively initiated and directed (*i.e.* more or less 'willed '), or which is not coloured by feelings and emotions. It is false, therefore, to conceive 'thought' in abstraction from 'will' and 'feeling,' if we intend to examine actual knowing. But it is just this intention which intellectualism leaves in doubt. It is hard to see, therefore, why a 'thought,' which has abstracted from purpose, interest, emotion, and satisfaction, should any longer be called thought at all ; at any rate, it is no longer human thought, and can have no relation to human life.

But the unfortunate fact remains that all these phrases have long been taken for granted, with little or no warrant or criticism. They are traditionally part and parcel of an 'independent' Logic *which has begged its 'standpoint.'*

§ 13. Formally this standpoint is bafflingly in-determinate. It is neither consistently descriptive nor consistently normative, but either, or both, as suits the occasion. Sometimes it appeals to what logical procedure actually is, sometimes to what it ideally ought to be ; *i.e.* what *by us* would be called psychological and logical considerations alternate in the most confusing way. In its own phraseology this confusion is cloaked by its conception of 'the logical Ideal,' which can be represented either as what human thought naturally aspires to, or as what controls its wayward vagaries.

Let us consider a few representative examples. Mr. Bradley prefaces his *Principles of Logic* with the confession that he is not sure where Logic begins or ends ; but no attentive reader can fail to see that his 'Logic' begins in

---

[1] Cp. Essay iv. § 10.

Psychology and ends in Scepticism. It is, moreover, just because the standpoints of fact and of validity are so inextricably mingled that nothing can save his 'Logic' from surrender to Scepticism, except a desperate appeal to metaphysics, the aid of which *Appearance and Reality* was subsequently to prove illusory.[1]

Prof. Bosanquet seems to incline more distinctly to the descriptive standpoint. He declines to call Logic normative; but calls its object 'self-normative.'[2] The preface of his *Logic* tells us that "the conception of Logical Science which has been my guide is that of an unprejudiced study of the forms of knowledge in their development, their interconnexion, and their comparative value as embodiments of truth." In his discussion with me he calls it "the science which considers the nature of thought as manifested in a fully self-consistent form."[3]

Still, even here, both sides are observable. A 'study of the forms of knowledge,' and of 'the nature of thought,' sounds like a purely descriptive undertaking. But the notion of 'comparative value' is as distinctly normative;

[1] Cp. Essay iv. § 3. It need not, of course, be denied that nevertheless Mr. Bradley's *Logic* is a great work, which has exercised a well-deserved influence on English thought. But its defects are so glaring that its influence has been very mixed. The sort of thing complained of may be illustrated, *e.g.* by comparing Mr. Bradley's criticism of Mill's conception of induction with his criticism of the syllogism. When he objects to the former that induction is not proof, his standpoint is clearly that of validity. But when he protests that the syllogism is not the universal form of (*de facto*) valid reasoning, and gives 'specimens of inference' which are not syllogistic as they stand and rest on relations evident to us on empirical and psychological grounds, has he not plainly passed over to the standpoint of description of the actual?

[2] *Arist. Soc. Proc.* 1905-6, p. 263. This looks suspiciously like an attempt to run with the hares and to hunt with the hounds. At any rate, it involves the 'depersonalization' we have objected to, and ignores the fact that logical norms are values *for man*, and the offspring of our interests.

[3] *L.c.* p. 237. He gives as an alternative to this, "as manifest in the endeavour to apprehend truth." But it would appear that, even in these definitions, Logic has not succeeded in manifesting herself in a fully consistent form. For even if we make explicit what is presumably intended, viz. that they take 'truth' as = 'the fully self-consistent form' of thought (an essentially formal view which seems to render it a wholly intrinsic affair of thought, and to rule out all testing of our predications on the touchstone of reality), the two definitions cannot be made to coincide. For 'the *endeavour* to apprehend truth' adds a consideration wholly extraneous and alien to the formal self-consistency of thought, and one, moreover, which is plainly psychological.

so is that of a fixed ideal or 'system' which claims to regulate and control the natural development of cognitive procedures, quite irrespective of their use as the means to the ends of human knowing.

§ 14. This whole conception of the logical standpoint is, however, open to the gravest objection. *Qua* descriptive, it either instigates Logic to poach on the preserves of Psychology, and to interfere with its functions, or, if you please, to become itself Psychology. In the latter case it must become bad or ignorant Psychology. In the former case it must either *prohibit* Psychology from describing cognitive processes, or *duplicate* the psychological descriptions. We should get, that is, a twofold description of the same events, the one dubbed 'Logic' and the other 'Psychology.' One or the other of these would surely be superfluous or mistaken. Or if both of them could somehow (*e.g.* by a reference to the different purposes of the two sciences?) be maintained, it would become necessary to consider their relation to each other. This would be just as necessary, and much more difficult, when both sciences are conceived as descriptive, as when one is conceived as normative. For the attempt to adjust their relations would have to start from an open conflict about the ground each was to cover.

Moreover, even as descriptive Psychology, this Logic would be defective. It would either have to ignore the 'willing' and 'feeling' indubitably present in cognition, or to insist on describing them, as far as its purposes required. In the former case it would be certain, in the latter it would be probable, that the description would be incomplete. For the descriptive interest would be restricted by the logical purpose, and in any case, would not extend to the whole psychical context.

But surely, when we describe, we should try to describe completely, without obliterating psychical values and without any *arrière pensée*. The omission of any feature which *de facto* accompanies knowing demands caution and an explicit justification. For how can it be taken for granted that anything is unessential? The context of any reasoning extends indefinitely into the psychological : the actual meaning always depends upon the context, and when we abstract from any of it, we take a risk. Before any train of thought is capable of logical analysis, it must somehow be determined what features in it are important and vital, and what unimportant and unessential. But how can the logician determine this, without the aid either of Psychology or of experience ? There is no prospect then that his descriptions will be adequate, either logically or psychologically.

Even though, therefore, some one should suggest as a compromise that Logic and Psychology should both describe the actual psychic process, but that Logic should have a monopoly of the cognitive features, the compromise would be equally futile and intolerable. For if so, who or what is to decide which is which, and how much of the whole is logically relevant ? What if the parties disagree, and the subjects decline to be separated ?

Finally, in assigning to Logic a descriptive function, a serious concealment has been practised. Its study of cognitive process assuredly was *not* 'unprejudiced.' It has made *de facto*, but secretly and unconsciously, very definite and peculiar assumptions as to the nature of the logical standpoint. A big encroachment has been made on the domain of Psychology, which has been robbed of the most valuable portion of its territory. It has been assumed (as we saw in § 4) that Psychology has no right to treat cognitive values, and must perforce content itself with what is left over after Logic has claimed all it has a mind to for its province. And this despoliation has been committed by sheer importunity, without the least pretence of a rational delimitation of scientific frontiers, and with no attempt at an equitable arbitration of the dispute !

§ 15. The results of this monstrous injustice are not slow to show themselves. First of all, Psychology is reduced to absurdity, to the care of the shreds and dregs of a disrupted soul. And then, by a thoroughly deserved

Nemesis, the unjust abstraction made by Logic ends in her own paralysis!

The first stage of this process, the arbitrary stultification of Psychology, may best be studied in Prof. Bosanquet's Aristotelian Society papers ;[1] the second, the suicide of 'independent' Logic, in Mr. H. H. Joachim's book, *The Nature of Truth*.

"Psychological process," says Prof. Bosanquet, "when it differs from the process which is the object-matter of logic, differs by being inarticulate, circuitous, fragmentary. It is the logical process broken up and disguised," "a Glaucus," whose divine original, however, is "never found typically perfect in actual psychological process."[2] Thus "logical process is the psychological process in its explicit and self-consistent form," freed from the "interruptions" and "irrelevance" of "purely psychical disturbances."

And so the 'self-normative,' 'independent' Logic, "dropping out abstract psychical processes," haughtily "goes forward on the path of concrete fulfilment or individuality"[3]—to what end will presently appear.

Now the division of territories propounded in these words should certainly secure to Logic the most brilliantly prosperous career. It appears to give Logic every advantage. It reduces Psychology to such pulp that its voice can scarce be heard in the Council of the Sciences. One hardly dares to point out in remonstrance that Prof. Bosanquet's "psychological process" with "pure" and "mere" conditions differs radically from the concrete psychical process of Humanist Psychology, and is obviously incapable of performing the functions of the latter. It is conceived as a miserable abstraction, not (as is legitimate in a special science) as regards limitation of standpoint, but as regards the content it is permitted to treat, and is almost deserving of the contempt poured upon it. For what is it but a mere rubbishy residuum, all that is left behind when its values have been ex-

[1] *L.c.* pp. 237-47, 262-5.
[2] *L.c.* pp. 239, 240. [3] *L.c.* p. 265.

tracted from the actual psychic process, and its life has
been extinguished?

Compared with this "misshapen Glaucus" postulated
by logical theory, almost anything may claim to be
concrete. Even Prof. Bosanquet's 'logic-process,' which
has been allowed to select all that seemed to be of value,
and to abstract only from the merest and most worthless
dross. So at least it seems, in the triumphant self-
assertion of an 'independent' Logic. It seems almost
fantastic to suggest a doubt whether after all 'Psychology'
has been despoiled enough, whether after assigning to
the 'logical' the whole purposiveness of psychic process
and leaving the psychological a purposeless chaos, Prof.
Bosanquet has not abstracted from something which was
needed to make thought truly purposive.

§ 16. Meanwhile, what can we reply? Nothing, it is to
be feared, our intellectualist logicians will deign to listen to.

We shall protest in vain that the 'mere' or 'pure'
psychological conditions, which Prof. Bosanquet flung
aside as worthless on the rubbish heap, are pure fictions
which bear no resemblance to the psychical processes of
actual knowing, that we never meant to relate *them* to
Logic, that what we meant was not this fantastic
abstraction, but the most concrete thing imaginable,
viz. the actual psychic process in its all-inclusive activity,
and with nothing at all, however worthless it might seem,
abstracted from. We shall observe in vain that however
'concrete' the logic-process may appear by comparison
with the artificial abstraction of the 'merely psychological,'
it is admitted to be an ideal never realized in actual
thinking, that therefore it *has* abstracted from something,
and that it remains to be seen whether that was really
as unessential as was asserted, or whether an immense
abstraction has unwittingly been made, which in the end
proves ruinous to Logic. We shall ask in vain how
Logic has arrived at a standpoint which gives it such
crushing superiority over Psychology, and entitles it to
take and leave whatsoever it likes, without condescending
to give reasons for its procedure.

We shall ask all these questions vainly, because Logic is 'independent,' nay autocratic. It gives an account of its self-normative procedure to no man or science. "It can only be judged by itself at a further stage," its friends haughtily declare.[1] We must therefore perforce let it go its own way. It cannot be refuted; it can only be developed.

§ 17. Let us therefore follow the developments of 'Logic.' Having successfully maintained her right to 'depersonalize' herself, having got rid of the 'merely psychological' encumbrances of her 'Glaucus,' her 'old man of the sea,' she should be able to soar to the illimitable heights of an infinite 'ideal' of a "timelessly self-fulfilled," "all-inclusive, significant whole," "whose coherence is perfect truth."[2] She proceeds to do so, until only our deep-seated British respect for what we cannot understand hinders us from declaring that in her Hegelian disguise she has become wholly unintelligible, and that clouds of German metaphysics have rendered her invisible in her ascension.

But just as we had despaired of ever seeing her again, to our amazement there ensues a catastrophe which brings her back to earth with more than Icarian suddenness, and in as completely shattered a condition.

There was an error in her calculations which has brought about her fall. Or rather Error was *not* taken into her calculations, when she assumed her standpoint, discarded the merely human as 'merely psychological,' and constructed her ideal. 'The Ideal' does not admit of Error: and yet on earth Error impudently takes the liberty to exist. It is, of course, a mere illusion, but its persistent phantom yields not to the exorcisms of Logic.

The situation must be set forth in the words of one who has seen the vision, and suffered its *dénoûment*: our own would be suspect and inadequate.[3]   "The confused

---

[1] Prof. Bosanquet (*l.c.* p. 265).
[2] H. H. Joachim, *The Nature of Truth*, pp. 169-170 and *passim*.
[3] *Ibid.* pp. 167-8.   For further selections see Essay vi., especially §§ 2, 3.

mass of idiosyncrasies," we are told, which are "my and your thinking, my and your 'self,' the particular temporal processes, and the extreme self-substantiation of the finite 'modes,' which is error in its full discordance : these are incidents *somehow* connected with the known truth, *but they themselves, and the manner of their connexion, are excluded from the theory of knowledge*,"[1] which "*must* rule out as irrelevant *some*·—perhaps *most*, but certainly not *all*—of the temporal and finite conditions under which truth is known." "Truth, beauty, and goodness" (for all the ideals as conceived by intellectualism must break down in the same way when they try to transcend their reference to man) "are timeless, universal, independent structures ; and yet it is also essential to them to be manifested in the thinking of finite subjects, in the actions and volitions of perishing agents."[2] Hence Error is "unthinkable," "a declaration of independence, where that which declares is nothing real, and nothing real is declared."[2]

But why should not 'Logic' free herself from these embarrassments by cutting the last thin thread that attaches her to an earthly existence and a human function which are infested with 'merely psychological' accidents and idiosyncrasies, and vitiated by the errors of human beings of which she ought surely to have divested herself when she proceeded to 'depersonalize' herself? Why do these human trappings cling, like a shirt of Nessus, to the naked Truth? Can it be that 'Logic' could not 'depersonalize' herself completely, nay, that her effort was a sheer delusion?

Mr. Joachim makes answer.[3] Logic "must *render intelligible* the dual nature of human experience. . . . It must show how the complete coherence, which is perfect truth, involves as a necessary 'moment' in its self-maintenance the self-assertion of the finite modal minds : a self-assertion which in its extreme form is Error. It must reconcile this self-assertive independence with the

---

[1] Italics mine, cp. p. 168 *n.* 2.   [2] *L.c.* p. 163.
[3] *L.c.* pp. 170-1.

modal dependence of the self-asserting minds. . . . Otherwise human knowledge remains, for all we can tell, un-related to ideal experience." [1]

In other words, when 'Logic' commenced her nuptial flight towards 'the Ideal,' she quite forgot that after all human forces raised her, that all her beauteous visions were conceived by the eye of human minds, and that she has repaid our devotion by disavowing her creators.

The natural result is sheer, unmitigated, inevitable, and irreparable contradiction, as Mr. Joachim most honourably recognizes. Logic is met by "demands which both *must be* and *cannot be* completely satisfied." [2] To satisfy them completely, complete truth would have to be manifest to itself. Whereas what we can conceive ourselves as attaining is only complete truth *manifest to us*. And as manifested in human truth the opposition of subject and object persists ; our knowledge is always thought *about* an Other: " the opposition of the thought and its Other is apparently vital." It cannot attain to union with its Other ; and so the significant Whole, cleft by a self-diremption, falls into halves.[3] The whole theory, therefore, " falls short of the absolute truth manifest to itself." [4] The " theory of truth, based on the coherence-notion, is not itself true *qua* coherent." [5] It is " not only *de facto* unaccomplished, but is impossible by the very nature of the case." [5]

And so Mr. Joachim, though he tries to soften the effect of his idol-breaking blows for the benefit of his friends by protesting that their common theory is "*as true as a theory can be*," [6] finishes up as a sceptic *malgré lui* amid the ruins of *all* the intellectualistic conceptions of Logic, and of his own 'Hegelian' metaphysic.

§ 18. Of a surety we did well to allow Logic to go on her way, and to be " judged by herself at a further stage," by her " approach to completeness and comprehensive-

[1] *L.c.* p. 172.   [2] *L.c.* p. 171. The italics are Mr. Joachim's.
[3] *L.c.* pp. 171-2 (in substance).
[4] *L.c.* p. 178.   [5] *L.c.* p. 176.   [6] *L.c.* p. 178.

ness."[1]   Her *débâcle* has certainly approached completeness, and is quite comprehensible to us.

For there is nothing either new in her overthrow or
obscure in its causes.

The Hegelian theory of knowledge and reality—for
Mr. Joachim, taught perhaps by the negative outcome
of *Appearance and Reality*, has rightly renounced the
pretence of salving Logic by Metaphysics[2]—has broken
down completely.   It has broken down precisely as it
was predicted that it must break down so soon as it was
thought out consistently and to the end.[3]   It has broken
down precisely as every intellectualistic conception of
Logic has always broken down, at precisely the same
point and for precisely the same reasons.   It has not
failed, assuredly, for any lack of ingenuity or perseverance
in its advocates, who have left no stone unturned to save
a hopeless situation, and could no doubt with ease have
lifted the burden of Sisyphus to the summit of any hill of
hell.   But their labour was more than Sisyphean : they
had, unfortunately, committed 'Logic' to a fundamental
blunder.   It has wilfully, wantonly, and of malice
prepense abstracted from humanity.   Instead of conceiving God as incarnating himself in man, it has sought
God by disavowing and belittling man.   And as a reward
it has itself been terrified to death by an incredible
monster—the creature of its own unhealthy nightmare !

In other words, it has fallen into a χωρισμός, a fatal
separation between the human and the ideal which
renders *both* unmeaning, but was rendered inevitable
and irretrievable by its presuppositions as to the value
of human psychology.   Once our psychic processes are
denied logical value and excluded from the nature of
truth, we are playing with abstractions, even though we
may not realize this until at the end our 'Ideal' is
required to find room for our errors.   Once we exalt the
limited and relative, and merely 'pragmatic,' 'independence' of truth, which remains safely immanent *within the*

---

[1] *Arist. Soc. Proc.* 1906, p. 265.   [2] Cp. Essay iv. § 3.
[3] Cp. *Humanism*, p. 48.

sphere of human valuations and can always be withdrawn
and modified as our needs and purposes require, into an
absolute and infinite 'independence' which entirely transcends our human experience, we have ascribed to truth
the 'dual nature,' which so perplexes Mr. Joachim, and
can by no device be unified. For a dualistic chasm has
been constructed between the human and 'psychological,'
and the ideal and 'logical.' No real relation can be
established between them ; all attempts at connecting
them break down so soon as they are tested. Nor can
any real theoretic progress be made. The utmost
ingenuity only brings 'logicians' to the brink of the
chasm. And that is 'nearer' to the other side only in
an illusory fashion. It remains only to *postulate* a reconciliation of the discrepant halves of a knowledge which
is rent asunder from top to bottom, by a supreme and
mystic act of faith.[1] But as the jejune rationalism of the
theory in question had previously prohibited all acts of
faith, it has manifestly fallen into a pit of its own digging.

Or shall we rather say, of Plato's?[2] For he it was
that first led the way into the pit into which, with a few
despised exceptions, the whole company of philosophers
has followed him, as patiently and submissively as a
flock of sheep follows its bell-wether, and out of which no
one has been able, and not too many have even tried, to
escape.

Throughout the *Theaetetus*, for example, Plato has
made the assumptions that 'knowledge' is of 'universals'
and not concerned or connected with the fleeting and
variable judgments of individual men about their personal
experience, that thought and sense-perception are antithetical and hostile, that the logical concept is something
wholly superior to and independent of the psychical
process (*e.g.* 152 D), and that the Protagorean suggestion,
to start the theory of knowing from the actual knowing
of the individual's perceptions is a proposal for the
abolition of truth. No wonder after this that it becomes for

---

[1] Cp. *The Nature of Truth*, pp. 172, 177.
[2] Compare the last Essay.

him a serious 'contradiction' when A judges to be warm
what B judges to be cold, seeing that 'it' cannot be both.
But 'it' does not exist out of relation to the divergent
judgments : 'it' stands in this case for *the problem of
constructing a 'common' perception* ; if the two 'its' are
to be brought together into an 'objective' scheme of
temperature, A and B must set to work to construct a
thermometer, as to the readings of which they can agree.[1]
Plato, therefore, has merely debarred himself from understanding the *de facto* genesis and development of our
common world of subjective intercourse, and by starting with
abstraction from the *personal* character of both judgments,
he has manufactured a fallacious contradiction.   Can we
wonder after this that the Platonic theory of knowledge
remains plunged in unmitigated dualism, and that in the
end it has to be admitted (209) that 'knowledge' can
never condescend to the particular and personal, and is
unable to discriminate between Theaetetus and Socrates ?
For was it not pledged, *ex vi definitionis*, to leave
out whatever part of reality concerns a '*this*,' '*here*,'
and '*now*'?   But instead of inferring from this impotence, and from the self-abnegation of an 'ideal' of
knowledge which is not even ideally adequate, because it
renounces the duty of knowing the individual perfectly
in its uniqueness,[2] that there must be a radical flaw in a
conception of knowledge which has led to this absurdity,
what does Plato do?   He proclaims the Sensible unknowable and unintelligible as such, attributes to all
'phenomenal' reality an all-pervasive taint of 'Not-being,'
and retains his Ideal Theory though well aware that it
cannot cross the gulf between the truly Real and the
Sensible![3]   How very human are even the greatest of
philosophers !

It would never, therefore, occur to us to be surprised
that not only should the *Theaetetus* in the end leave the
problem of error unsolved and confess to utter inability
to say what knowledge is, but that the whole Platonic

---

[1] Cp. pp. 315-20.   [2] Cp. *Humanism*, p. 126.
[3] Essay ii. § 14-16.

theory of knowledge should remain immersed in obscurity
and contradiction. But one thing is clear, viz. that whoever had learnt the lesson of the *Theaetetus* could have
predicted the failure of all intellectualistic epistemologies
down to *The Nature of Truth.*

§ 19. And the remedy for this sceptical paralysis of
Intellectualism? It is simple—so simple that it will be
hard to get philosophers to look at it. But it cuts very
deep. It demands a complete reversal of inveterate
assumptions, and a re-establishment of Logic on very
different foundations. We have merely to refrain from
the twin abstractions which every intellectualistic logic
makes, and which must, if carried through consistently,
prove fatal to its very existence. These two assumptions,
which have troubled us throughout, may now be called
(1) the *etherealizing*, and (2) the *depersonalizing* of truth,
and together they effect the complete *dehumanizing* of
knowledge.

(1) By the *etherealizing* of truth is meant the abstraction from the actual use and verification of an assertion,
which is made in assuming that its truth is independent
of its *application.* This really destroys its whole significance, although at first it seems to leave its ' truth ' a
matter of self-consistency and intrinsic ' coherence.' But
if we try to take truth in this purely formal way, we
identify truth with claim to truth,[1] and render the testing
of claims extralogical. And it is then discovered that all
reference to reality has been excluded,[2] that ' self-consistency ' means nothing but a juggle with words whose
meanings are presumed to be perfect and stable in their
truth, and that the distinction between truth and error
has become incomprehensible. Error (as contrasted with
self-contradiction, which destroys the meaning wholly)
is nothing inherent in the form of the judgment, but lies
in a failure of its application. It is a failure of *our*

---

[1] Cp. Essay v.

[2] It is characteristic of intellectualist ' logic ' not to have noticed the discrepancy between its two assertions (1) that ' truth ' is wholly a matter of the
intrinsic ' self-consistency ' of its ' ideal,' and independent of all ' consequences ' ;
and (2) that all judgment involves a ' reference to reality ' beyond itself.

thought to attain *its* object. And as our conception of
'truth' is determined by its contrast with error, to
abstract from error is really to abstract from 'truth.'
Hence a Logic which abstracts from error implicitly
despairs also of giving an intelligible account of truth.
It ceases at any rate to be a theory of real knowledge,
and the formal 'truth,' the semblance of meaning, which
it verbally retains, no longer possesses relevance to human
knowing.

(2) But the *depersonalizing* of truth deprives the Logic
of Intellectualism even of this show of meaning. It
makes abstraction from the meaning actually intended,
from the purpose of the meaner. Now as every judgment
is prompted and kept together by a purpose which forms
the uniting bond between its subject and its predicate,
the purpose is logically vital. It is also a concrete fact of
an intensely personal kind, which ramifies indefinitely
into human psychology. Hence it is often logically inconvenient, as complicating the situation beyond the
powers of formal analysis. But to abstract from it,
wholly and systematically, is to disintegrate the judgment.
To do this destroys its intrinsic coherence, as well as its
reference to real truth. It amounts to *a complete annihilation of meaning.*

It is difficult to suppose, therefore, that when intellectualist Logic fully realizes the situation to which
its abstractions lead, it will continue to presume without
trial that the full concreteness of psychic process is
logical irrelevance, and that man is a negligible quantity
in the formation of truth.

A reformed and rehumanized Logic, on the other
hand, will flatly refuse to immolate all human knowledge,
all fact, and all reality to intellectualist prejudices. It will
conceive and value the old abstractions merely as instruments, as methodological simplifications, which may be
freely used, so long as the *limits* of their usefulness are
not overlooked, and their authority is not made absolute.

And here will be the rub. For these abstractions
have been misconceived so long! It is such a time-

honoured custom with philosophers to believe that 'universals' are loftier and more sacred than 'particulars,' that their *formation* is not to be inquired into nor tested, that their value is wholly independent of their application, that they would subsist in unsullied excellence and truth, even though they never were, nor could be, used. It will take, therefore, generations for philosophers to convince themselves that the essential function of universals is to *apply to particulars*, that they are *actually true* only because, and when, they are used, that when they become inapplicable they become unmeaning, that their abstraction, therefore, from time, place, and individuality is only superficial and illusory, and that in short they are instruments for the control and improvement of human experience.

'But will not the attempt to build knowledge on so untried and paradoxical a basis be fraught with unsuspected difficulties, and in its turn conduct us back to scepticism? Is it credible that so many generations of thinkers can have been mistaken in acquiescing in the unproved assertion of the good man, Plato, that Protagoreanism necessitates scepticism?

In view of the outcome of intellectualistic 'Logic,' this menace of scepticism seems a grotesque impertinence, and it might be well to retort that even an untried basis was better than one which had been tried and found to be so self-destructive. But the threat has been used so often that it will hardly be relinquished all at once: so we had better face it. It is a mere bogey—a Chimæra summoned from the House of Hades to scare us back into the Labyrinth of the Minotaur. No proof has ever been vouchsafed of its contention. And seeing that Plato's genius has failed so signally to refute Protagoras, we may await with equanimity the advent of a greater man than Plato to confute the inherent Humanism of man's thought.

IV

TRUTH AND MR. BRADLEY[1]

ARGUMENT

§ 1. Mr. Bradley's attack on Humanism in spite of, § 2, the hesitations in his intellectualism. § 3. His perception of the difficulties in the 'correspondence' view of truth. § 4. Pragmatism as the way to avoid logical scepticism. § 5. Mr. Bradley rejects this way and prefers to stay in 'Jericho.' § 6. The total irrelevance of his criticism. § 7. His reversion to the 'correspondence' view, and its difficulties, which coincide with those of realism. The inability of Absolutism to disavow it. § 8. Mr. Bradley's troubles with the relations of 'truth' and 'fact,' and with the subjective activity in the apprehension of 'fact.' The 'double nature of truth.' § 9. The antithesis of 'practice' and 'theory.' What does the 'independence' of theory mean? § 10. Humanism as overcoming this antithesis and unifying life in voluntarist terms. The advantages of voluntaristic descriptions. § 11. Mr. Bradley's definition of 'practice.' § 12. His failure to distinguish between axioms and postulates. § 13. His intellectualistic conceptions of 'will.' § 14. His summary of his objections. § 15. His attempt to raise the *odium theologicum.* § 16. His relapse into agnosticism. § 17. His concessions. § 18. His preference for a difficult philosophy.

§ 1. MR. F. H. BRADLEY'S characteristic paper on "Truth and Practice" in the July 1904 number of *Mind* (vol. xiii. N.S. No. 51) must be regarded as the most significant, though hardly the most valuable, of the hostile criticisms which the Humanist movement has so far en-

---

[1] The substance of this paper appeared as a reply to Mr. Bradley in *Mind*, vol. xiii. N.S. No. 52 (October 1904). It has, however, been considerably altered, partly by the excision of matters of ephemeral and merely personal interest partly by some expansion of the argument. Mr. Bradley, as might have been expected, did not reply. Other comments on the shifting phases of his struggle to save his absolutism from absorption in scepticism on the one side and pragmatism on the other, will be found in *Mind*, Nos. 63, 67, 73, 76. In the end Mr. Bradley has to confess that his 'philosophy,' *i.e.* his particular amalgamation of a dogmatic absolutism corroded by scepticism and saved from annihilation by an appeal to pragmatism as a 'practical makeshift,' is just his personal preference, which need not appear rational to any one else.

countered. For Mr. Bradley is an acknowledged leader of the sect of absolutists which has long dominated philosophic instruction in this country, and is incomparably the most brilliant and formidable of its champions. Ever since he made his *début* a quarter of a century ago by triumphantly dragging the corpse of Mill round the beleaguered stronghold of British philosophy, he has exercised a reign of terror based on an unsparing use of epigrams and sarcastic footnotes, "more polished than polite," as Prof. Hoernle wittily remarks.[1] He has shown also that however much he may despise personalities in his monistic metaphysics, he yet loves them like a pluralist in his polemics.

§ 2. And yet until this paper appeared, it was quite open to doubt what attitude Mr. Bradley would assume towards the new philosophic movement. It was open to him to disarm revolt by judicious concession, nay to put himself at the head of it, by developing ideas not obscurely implicit in his own writings. It was by no means self-evident that he must utterly condemn even a systematic protest against intellectualism. For though Mr. Bradley no doubt seemed in the end to come down on the intellectualist side of the fence, the reason plainly seemed to be that he had not subjected the notions with which he stopped, those of the 'intellect' and its 'satisfaction,' to stringent scrutiny. And it was evident that his intellectualism had not desiccated his soul, nor did it seem so deeply ingrained, or of so extreme and naïve a type, as that of his more rigidly 'Hegelian' allies. Nay, it seemed at times to have been only by a distinctly wilful fiat that he had arrested himself on the path to pragmatism, as, for example, in *Appearance and Reality*, p. 154. Even the final intellectualism of his description of the false as 'the theoretically untenable' and of the aim of philosophy as 'the satisfaction of the intellect,' might have easily been mitigated into harmony with the Humanist view by shifting the emphasis from the '*intellect*' to the '*satisfaction*,' and by adopting a pragmatic interpretation of the 'intellect's' structure and of its 'theoretic' functioning.

[1] *Mind*, N.S. No. 55, p. 332.

§ 3. Again, from the position Mr. Bradley had reached at the end of his *Principles of Logic*, a pragmatic Logic might well have seemed the promised land. Students of that brilliant and entertaining work will doubtless remember that the situation Mr. Bradley finally found himself in was one of logical scepticism tempered by prophetic allusions to a not yet extant metaphysic. This plight, however, cannot be said to have been mended when his *Appearance and Reality* ended in a far more complete scepticism, tempered only by the postulation of an unknowable Absolute invoked to set all things right 'somehow.'

Yet this whole perplexity arose from a very simple cause. His examination of the function of our thought had irresistibly pointed to the conclusion that knowing, in very many, if not all, cases involves an arbitrary manipulation ('mutilation') of the presented data. Hence if it was assumed that the business of thought was fundamentally to 'copy' reality, it was clear that thought was a failure. It did not 'copy'; it abstracted, it selected, it mutilated, it recombined, it postulated—all in what seemed a thoroughly arbitrary manner.[1] If, therefore, *truth* meant 'correspondence with reality,' it seemed plain that inference as such was invalid, and truth unattainable. Nowhere could Mr. Bradley discover a case where "the truth of the consequence does not rest upon our interference" with the data. In vain he clings to the possibility that "though the function of concluding depends upon my intellect, the content concluded may be wholly unhelped, untouched, and self-developed."[2] This possibility is clearly preposterous, even though it is guaranteed by 'logical postulates' which have constantly to be invoked. "Rightly or wrongly," we are told, "logic assumes that a mere attention, a simple (*sù !*) retaining and holding together before the mind's eye, is not an alteration," and "we are forced to assume that some processes do not modify their consequence,"[3] and that "some operations do

---

[1] *Princ. of Logic*, pp. 500-10.   [2] *L.c.* p. 502.
[3] *L.c.* p. 506.

but change our power of perceiving the subject and leave
the subject itself unaltered . . . even where our wilful
and arbitrary choice selects the process and procures the
result." [1]   But, as we saw, these logical postulates
were then consigned to metaphysics, and finally entered
that cave of the Absolute whence no 'finite' truths ever
issue forth again.

In short the 'correspondence-with-reality' view of
truth is 'riddled with contradictions' in the concluding chapters of Mr. Bradley's *Logic*, and driven to
seek refuge in an arbitrary 'postulate,' to be hereafter
established by metaphysics.   This feat his metaphysic
fails to accomplish : but it solaces the wounds of Logic
by riddling everything else with contradictions too.

§ 4. Yet the remedy was close at hand.   Mr. Bradley
had merely to grasp his nettle firmly, to take his bull
by the horns, to sit down on his praying carpet, in order to
effect a magical transformation of the whole situation, in
the simplest and most satisfying way !   He remarks : "in
A—B, B—C, the identity of B is the bond of the construction.   If I *made* that identity, I should certainly in that
case have manufactured the consequence.   And it may be
contended that it lies in my choice to see or to be blind,
and that hence my recognition does make what it perceives.   Against such a contention I can here attempt no
further answer.   I must simply fall back on the logical
postulate, and leave further discussion to metaphysics." [2]

But now suppose that instead of 'falling back' he had
gone on boldly and stayed in logic ?   Suppose he had
followed the indications of logic and accepted the omens ?
Suppose he had allowed himself to see that we *make
the identity* always and everywhere, that selection and
voluntary manipulation are of the essence of all cognitive
process, and that even our most 'passive' reception of
sensory stimuli is at bottom selective, because it ignores
a multitude of other processes in nature, and volitionally

---

[1] *L.c.* p. 518, where too Mr. Bradley catches a glimpse of the dependence of
'truth' on possibility of application (§ 24).
[2] *L.c.* p. 502.

so, because determined by the organism's choice of life, by the way in which its 'will to live' has moulded it?

If Mr. Bradley had been willing to do this, to say (with me) that logical identity is always made, being a great postulate, by means of which we successfully operate upon our experience,[1] he would have passed easily and naturally on to the pragmatic view of truth and of the nature of logic. If in all thinking identities are 'made,' then this normal procedure cannot possibly be made a reproach to thought. If 'truth' *means* successful operation on 'reality,' then reasoning cannot be invalidated so long as it is successful. If thought has not to 'correspond' or ' copy,' but to be efficacious, then it need not be despised for failing to do what it was not concerned to do. In short the theory of knowledge is out of the wood.[2]

§ 5. What, then, prevented Mr. Bradley from perceiving all this? So far as one can see, nothing but sheer prejudice. He simply will not allow practical success to validate a cognitive process. He will not let us " plead that because logic works, logic cannot be wrong." [3] But at the time when he wrote the *Logic*, Mr. Bradley was still far from " a blind acquiescence in the coarsest prejudices of popular (i.e. *intellectualist*) thought," [4] and it might well seem possible that he would determine to advance instead of retrograding, and hopelessly miring himself in the slough of scepticism.

Unfortunately Mr. Bradley has chosen otherwise. He has preferred to revert to the correspondence view of truth, of which he had formerly so clearly exposed the absurdities.[5] So when the princes of Moab tempted him, he went and cursed the newcomers with a vehemence which must have well-nigh exhausted the resources even of his vocabulary, perhaps because none of his faithful followers dared to open their mouths to utter a word of

---

[1] *Personal Idealism*, pp. 103-4. *Formal Logic*, ch. x. § 10.

[2] Cp. Mr. Sturt's criticism of these notions of Mr. Bradley's in *Idola Theatri*, pp. 291-2.

[3] *L.c.* p. 531.   [4] *L.c.* p. 534.

[5] *Mind*, N.S. No. 51. P. 311, "If my idea is to work, it must correspond to a determinate being it cannot be said to make." P. 312, "The whole of this is fact to which my idea has got first to correspond."

warning. He has chosen to conceive the philosophic controversy of the day as a mere raid by a horde of vagrant
nomads upon the citadel of Absolutism, and mingled
wit with venom in his own inimitable way when he
declares, " I forget before how many blasts of the trumpet
the walls of Jericho fell, but the number, I should judge,
has already been much exceeded. The walls of Jericho,
so far as I can see, have no intention of moving, and the
dwellers in Jericho tend irreverently to regard the sound
as the well-known noise which comes from the setters
forth of new pills or plasters." [1]

One knows of course what is the controversial meaning
of abusing the plaintiff's attorney, but our appreciation of
Mr. Bradley's fun should not deter us, either from regret-
ting his retrogression, or from welcoming his simile.   We
all remember what happened to the walls of Jericho, and
so can value Mr. Bradley's testimony to the ' jerry-built '
character of the defences he has done so much to raise.[2]
Let us therefore accept the omen and proceed to consider
the objections which Mr. Bradley seems to think important.

§ 6. Mr. Bradley boldly begins with an avowal that he
has so far failed to understand the new philosophy.[3]   This
did not seem a very credible or promising premiss for a
critic of Mr. Bradley's calibre to set out from, but long
before I had finished reading I found myself entirely in
agreement with him. What he had failed to understand,
that is, or perhaps, as Prof. James suggested,[4] had not
sought to understand, was the doctrine I had maintained ;

[1] *L.c.* p. 330.
[2] It may be worth noting that this probably indicates the real derivation of
the word. ' Jerry-built ' = ' Jericho-built.' The mythical ' Jerry and Co.' probably
arose by ' tmesis ' from Jeri-cho, and the term thus embodies a jocular ration-
alizing of the recorded miracle.
[3] In his controversial methods this does not preclude a subsequent claim to
understand it much better than its author, who, he informs us, with marvellous,
but too evidently telepathic, insight "has *made no attempt*[1] to realize the true
meaning of his own doctrine" (pp. 322, 333).   Afterwards he reaffirms his
inability to understand (p. 329), which finally (p. 335), with the agnosticism
which seems to be the natural reaction from pretensions to absolute knowledge,
extends itself to all things !
[4] *Mind*, N.S. No. 52, p. 458.

[1] The italics (mine) indicate the point misapprehended.

what he had refuted with much superfluous subtlety was a mass of misconceptions which he had developed into misrepresentations, and finally distorted into absurdities entirely irrelevant to my position. Now if anything I had written had fairly lent itself to such interpretations, I should feel duly contrite, and would gladly remove the occasion for them. It is, however, difficult to see how the text of any of my essays anywhere lends itself to any of Mr. Bradley's interpretations, and in the absence of precise references to it, it seems impossible even to conjecture what occasioned them.

Where, if point-blank questions may be put, has Mr. Bradley ever found it stated that 'no object counts for any more than a *worthless means* [1] [! how can a worthless means be a means at all ?] to one's own *mere* [1] activity,' or that 'truth consists in the *mere* [1] practical working of an idea,' or that 'the words true and false have not a specific meaning,' or that 'truth everywhere subserves practice *directly*,' [1] or that 'the *entire* [1] nature of the situation is first made by the idea,' or that an idea's 'agreement or discord with fact other than my will can be excluded,' or that 'the *entire* [1] truth is made by my end and my ideas' and is 'a *mere* [1] deed,' or 'a means to a *foreign* [1] end' or '*merely* [1] what happens to prevail'? I do not ask, *bien entendu*, for literal quotations in support of these allegations (for I know these do not exist), but even for passages which can legitimately be said to countenance them, and meanwhile must question whether Mr. Bradley has at all entered into the pragmatist conception of the 'making' of 'truth' and 'reality.' Else he would hardly have wholly ignored or dismissed as unessential [2] such cardinal doctrines as the presence of limiting conditions in each experiment and the voluntary acceptance [3] of a basis

---

[1] The italics (mine) indicate the points misapprehended.

[2] Especially *Personal Ideal'sm*, pp. 54-63 and 95, and *Humanism*, pp. 12, 55-60. Indeed one would not suppose that he had read beyond the Preface in the latter work, but for his strange manipulation of the former.

[3] I am gratified to find the importance of this in the recognition of 'fact' so strongly emphasized by Prof. Royce in his valuable paper on "The Eternal and the Practical" (*Phil. Rev.* for March 1904). Strictly, nothing further is needed to establish the pragmatic view of 'fact.'

taken as factual, the distinction of postulate and axiom, the selection and verification of postulates by subsequent experience, and the psychological and social criticism which inevitably purifies the passing wishes of the individual.

Now controversially nothing is more embarrassing than a criticism which is *totally* irrelevant. Absolute irrelevance induces a sort of dazed feeling in its victim, who thinks that his inability to see the application must be due to his own lack of intelligence, especially when it is accompanied by an air of condescension, and a careful avoidance of references. To meet it one must either restate one's own position,[1] or criticize the critic.

In this case I should have been only too glad to show more explicitly what is actually the contention of Humanism regarding the conception of 'truth' and its relation to 'fact,' and how exactly it disposes of Mr. Bradley's difficulties, and achieves what hitherto all idealisms have attempted in vain, viz. the abolishing of the dualisms of 'truth' and 'fact' and 'fact' and 'value.' In view, however, of my critic's reluctance to consider the new doctrines in their connexion, I feel constrained to devote my energies chiefly to showing critically that, whether we are right or wrong, the old doctrine at all events cannot stand.

§ 7. I must observe, therefore, that even Mr. Bradley can state nothing tenable or coherent on either of the points alluded to. As regards the conception of 'truth,' he seems only just to have realized that there is a question as to the 'specific meaning' of the attributions 'true' and 'false' (p. 311).[2] But he excuses himself from telling us what he takes it to be! Surely so long as our critics have no positive conception of what the predication of truth means, their criticisms have no real *locus standi*.

On the relation of 'Truth' and 'Fact' he is somewhat more explicit. But he has not realized how deadly a blow at Absolutism Prof. Dewey has dealt by his admirable proof of the superfluity of an absolute truth-to-be-

---

[1] Cp. for this Essays xviii. and xix.   [2] Cp. p. 144.

copied, existing alongside of the human truth which is *made* by our efforts.[1] Its peculiar deadliness is due to the fact that the absolute idealist can hardly disavow a contention with which he himself is wont to ply the realist, viz. that an existent beyond human knowledge, which does nothing to explain that knowledge, is invalid, alike whether it is called an 'independent' reality or an 'absolute' truth. The fact is that this fundamental difficulty in absolutism and realism is the same. In both cases our knowing has to be related to something which transcends it and claims to be 'independent' of it and unaffected by it, *through the very process of our knowing* ; and the 'correspondence'-notion is merely a verbal cover for this *crux*. It cannot, therefore, be really and wholly discarded. In the last resort human truth must still be conceived as 'corresponding' to absolute truth, whatever obscurities and absurdities this may involve. It is only when we interpret the transcendence pragmatically that we perceive the nullity of the problem, because the 'independent' reality and truth are *not absolutely so*, but alike conceptions *immanently* evolved in human knowing, and do not therefore require to be forced into relation with it.[2] From his own point of view, therefore, Mr. Bradley is in a manner right in reverting to the correspondence-with-reality view of truth, as we saw above (p. 118). But it is indicative of the intellectual disintegration which Prof. Dewey's bombshell has produced in the intellectualist camp that most of his followers have tried to abandon it. Mr. H. W. B. Joseph admits that "the conception of truth as correspondence" is "a difficult notion" and "open to criticism."[3] Prof. A. E. Taylor goes so far as to suppose that his master has dropped it too,[4] while both he and Mr. H. H. Joachim prefer to rely on the notion of

---

[1] Mr. Bradley, who (for purposes of contrast ?) praises Prof. Dewey, also does not seem to have noticed that something faintly like the doctrine of 'doing for doing's sake,' which he vainly tries to fasten on me, appears to be upheld by Prof. Dewey, so that in this important respect his form of Pragmatism would seem to be the most radical in the field.

[2] Cp. Essays vii. § 1 and xx. § 2.   [3] *Mind*, xiv. N.S. No. 53, p. 35.

[4] *Phil. Rev.* xiv. 3, p. 288.

'system,' without perceiving that the difficulty of the 'correspondence' will then occur between the two 'systems,' ideal and human. Hence the latter, after assuming an 'ideal' of a self-supporting systematic coherence, finds himself face to face with the problem of connecting it with actual human knowing. It then turns out that the existence of error is inconsistent with that of his ideal, and so his whole essay on *The Nature of Truth* ends, avowedly, in failure. But surely it should have been obvious from the first that the notion of 'system' is not only purely human but also purely formal. It, therefore, could not be expected to throw any light on the nature of 'truth,' until means had been devised for discriminating systematic 'truth' from systematic 'error.' Thus if Mr. Joachim had condescended to start from human knowing, the problem of error would have formed an initial obstacle and not a final crux. These examples may serve to show that the intellectualist theory of knowledge is as completely nonplussed to-day by the notion of truth as Plato was when he wrote the *Theaetetus* more than 2000 years ago.[1]

§ 8. Mr. Bradley's embarrassments are no less painful.

(1) By retaining perforce this 'correspondence' view he pledges himself to the assumption that Truth is determined by Fact, by which it is 'dictated.' Fact exists whether we will it or not, whether or not we acknowledge it, and to it our "idea has first to correspond" (p. 312). It has naturally to be left obscure what part is played by the intelligence which accepts this 'dictation,' and how the facts manage to 'dictate' to us the ideas with which we work and which we have to acknowledge as true, because they are thus called for. It must not be asked how we ascertain the nature of the eternal text, the supercelestial Koran, which the dictation reveals ; nor yet how we are to authenticate the correctness of the dictates we receive. For it must clearly be ignored, that the 'facts' we recognize are always relative to the 'truths' we predicate ; that of facts-

---

[1] Cp. Essays vi. and ii. § 16.

in-themselves and independent of our knowledge we can know nothing. Neither must we ask whether these imagined facts in their own right are correctly 'represented' by the facts as we take them to be.

(2) But these difficulties are old, and ought to be familiar to all but the naïvest realism, of which Mr. Bradley's language here grows strangely redolent.[1] Let us pass, therefore, to a still more perplexing subject, Mr. Bradley's present handling of what puzzled him before, viz. the subjective activity in the apprehension of 'fact.' For 'truth,' it seems, is after all not mere reproduction of 'fact': the 'right' idea is not merely 'dictated,' it has also to be 'chosen' (p. 311). How then, we ask, can this hapless Truth serve two such different masters? How can it on the one hand adjust itself to human demands and interests, and yet on the other slavishly copy and respectfully reproduce a congenitally 'outer,' and already pre-existing, 'fact'? No 'logical postulate' is invoked to perform this unparalleled feat, but at times this subjective influence which goes to the making of 'Truth' is called merely a *congé d'élire* (p. 312), *i.e.* a formality, presumably, which is not held seriously to impair the dependence of truth upon an already determinate 'fact.' Yet in the same breath a 'selection' is mentioned. If this is not to involve volitional preference and acceptance, what can it mean? Surely it is something more than a mechanical registration of an outside 'fact'? Elsewhere it is admitted that our idea "reacts and then makes the whole situation to be different" (p. 311), that "truth may not be truth at all apart from its existence in myself and in other finite subjects, and *at least very largely* that existence depends on our wills."[2] Nay, our moral ends in their turn 'dictate' even to truth and beauty (pp. 320-1). Indeed In one aspect at least truth is an ideal construction (pp. 324-5).

Now what are we to make of this double nature of

---

[1] As Prof. Hoernle also notices (*Mind*, xiv. p. 442, *s.f.*).
[2] P. 320, italics mine.

Truth? Is it not clear that if there is to be a real selection there must be *real alternatives*, which can be chosen?
And is it not almost as clear that even in a 'forced'
choice such alternatives are really presented? Even the
poor bread-and-butter fly (now extinct) that would live
only on the 'weak tea with plenty of cream in it' which
it could not get, and consequently 'always died,' exemplifies this. We get then this dilemma: if our 'choice,'
'selection,' or '*congé d'élire*' does not affect the rigidity of
'fact,' it is an illusion which ought not even to seem to
exist, and we have certainly no right to talk about it: if,
on the other hand, there really is 'selection' (as is asserted),
will it not stultify the assumption of a rigid fact, introduce
a possibility of *arbitrary* manipulation, and lead to *alternative* constructions of reality? In other words, how
is a belief in a real selection compatible with the denial
of a real freedom of human choice and of a real plasticity
in reality at large?[1]

Mr. Bradley's insistence on the 'determinateness' of
being does not help us in the least. For he does not
specify whether he conceives the determination to be (*a*)
absolute, or (*b*) partial. If (*a*), then how is it to be *altered*
by our 'reaction'? That reaction too, indeed, must be
wholly determinate, and the 'selecting' must be mere
illusion. If (*b*) the determination is only partial, it will
form the starting-point for alternative modes of operating
upon 'fact' and alternative results. That is, 'fact' will
be plastic, and responsive to our will.

In short, a constructive conception of the relation of
Truth to Fact is nowhere to be grasped. Everywhere
Mr. Bradley's meaning seems swiftly to evaporate into
metaphor or to dissipate into ambiguity.

Not that these difficulties are likely to prove a permanent embarrassment. Eventually, no doubt, some
subtlety can be requisitioned from the Christological
controversies of the sixth century wherewith to reconcile
the 'divine' with the 'human' nature in the body of
the one Truth. But at present what Mr. Joachim signi-

[1] Cp. p. 392.

ficantly calls " the dual nature of human experience "[1]
forms the rock on which the logic of Intellectualism
deliberately wrecks itself, and one cannot find that it has
anything even apparently coherent to substitute for the
pragmatist account it rejects so haughtily.

§ 9. Mr. Bradley's second point concerns the relation
of Practice to Theory. The importance of this seems to
me to be secondary, because our differences rest largely
on the connotation of terms whose meaning is somewhat
a matter of convention, and not completely settled.

I should not dream, however, of denying that the end
must be " the fullest and most harmonious development
of our being " (p. 319), and still less than this " coincides
with the largest amount of mere doing "—except in so far
as I repudiate the notion of ' mere doing '! It is gratifying also to find Mr. Bradley so emphatic that " every
possible side of our life is practical," that there is nothing
" to which the moral end is unable to dictate " (p. 320),
" and even truth and beauty, however independent, fall
under its sway." These dicta ought to be decisive dis-
avowals of the old-fashioned intellectualism, and it may be
conjectured that, but for lapses of inadvertence, very little
more will be heard of it.

Difficulties begin when we try to follow Mr. Bradley's
attempt nevertheless to provide for an ' independence ' of
the theoretical. What precisely does he mean by ' independence '? We are told that though all the ends and
aspects of life are practical, yet in a sense they are also
not practical. There exists, it seems, an attitude of ' mere '
theory and ' mere ' apprehension, which has indeed to
demean itself by ' altering things ' and becoming ' practical,' but " so far as it remains independent " is " essentially " *not* practice. Both truth and beauty therefore are
practical incidentally but not in their essence" and at
once dependent and free " (p. 320), ' free ' in their ' nature,'
dependent in their actual functioning. Whether this
claims for theoretic truth something like Kant's noumenal
freedom and phenomenal necessity it is hard to say. But

---

[1] *The Nature of Truth*, pp. 163, 170, etc.

it is clearly an important article of Mr. Bradley's faith:
"we believe in short in relative freedom" and "this is
even dictated by the interest of the spiritual common-
wealth" and identified with "the independent cultivation
of any one main side of our nature" (p. 322).

Now, quite humbly and sincerely, I must here beg for
further elucidation. I cannot in the least conceive how
this semi-detached relation is possible. Evidently there
is here between us a divergent use of terms which must
breed confusion. What (1) means the antithesis of
'*incident*' and '*essence*'? And how are they related to
Aristotle's συμβεβηκός and οὐσία? 'Essence' is a word
which had a definite, though highly technical, meaning in
the philosophies of Plato and Aristotle, but which has
now lost this, and lends itself to much looseness of
thought. It clearly does not imply to Mr. Bradley,
as it does to a pragmatist, a reference to purpose. But
I suppose it means something important. If so, why is
it not divulged? Again (2) does it not evince a serious
laxity of terminology to equate a 'relative freedom' with
'independence'? It would be instructive to watch Mr.
Bradley dealing with the same equation in other contexts,
e.g. in pluralistic attempts to derive the 'unity' of the
world.

§ 10. Whether or not Mr. Bradley sees his way to
answer these questions, it must once more be added that,
be the argument coherent internally or meaningless, it is
at all events irrelevant. It attacks a position which has
never been defended; it fails to repel the real attack.
For it is *not* our intention to turn dualists, to prove that
Theory and Practice are fundamentally different, and
foreign to each other, and then to enslave Theory to
Practice, Intellect to Will. Something of the sort may
possibly be extracted from that great matrix of the most
various doctrines, the philosophy of Kant.[1] But we con-

---

[1] I do not say *justly*, because I am convinced that if Kant had been twenty
years younger when he attained his insight (such as it was) into the nature of
postulation, he must have rewritten his *Critique of Pure Reason* on pragmatist
lines. At all events he lays the foundations of Pragmatism in a remark no pragmatist would seek to better, when he says that "*all interest is ultimately practical,*

tend rather that there can be no independence of theory
(except in popular language) and no opposition to
practice, because theory is an outgrowth of practice and
incapable of truly 'independent' existence. And what
we try to do is to trace this latent reference to practice,
i.e. life, throughout the whole structure, and in all the
functions, of the intellect. There is no question therefore
of degrading, and still less of annihilating, the intellect,
but merely one of its reinterpretation. We deny that
properly speaking such a thing as pure or mere intellection can occur. What is loosely so called is really also
purposive thought pursuing what seems to it a desirable
end. Only in such cases the ends may be illusory, or
may appear valuable for reasons other than those which
determine their value.[1] What, therefore, we have really
attempted is to overcome the antithesis of theory and
practice, and to unify human life by emphasizing the all-
pervading purposiveness of human conduct.

Such attempts at unification are not new, but they
have usually been conducted with an intellectualist bias,
and with the purpose of reducing all 'willing' and 'feeling' to cognition. And this has often been supposed to
be something magnificent and inspiring. But how is it
spiritually more elevating to say *All is Thought* than to
say *all is Feeling* or *Will*? The only advantage which a
voluntarist formulation of the unity of the faculties claims
over its rivals is that 'will' is *de facto* conceived as in a
manner intermediate between 'thought' and 'feeling.'
Hence it is easiest to describe all mental life in voluntarist
terms. If either of the others is taken as fundamental,
'will' easily succumbs to an illusory 'analysis'; it can
be termed the strongest 'desire' or the 'self-realization'
of ideas. But it is not so easy to describe either of
the extremes in terms of the other. Hence 'panlogism'
of the Hegelian type is a height to which intellectualism
rarely rises, and even then only by regarding 'feeling' as

and even that of the speculative reason is merely conditional, and only complete in
its practical use" (*Krit. d. prakt. Vern.*, II. 2, iii. *s.f.*).
[1] Cp. *Humanism*, pp. 58-60.

irrational 'contingency' which is 'nothing for thought,' *i.e.* inexplicable. More commonly intellectualism has to come to terms with 'feeling,' as in Mr. Bradley's own philosophy, which derides the Hegelian's 'unearthly ballet of bloodless categories,' and as Mr. Sturt has shown, in some respects exalts 'feeling' even above intellect.[1]

But the truth is that the whole question seems merely one of the convenience and use of psychological classifications, and that none of these descriptions have explanatory value. All three 'faculties' are at bottom only labels for describing the activities of what may be called indifferently a unitary personality, or a reacting organism.

So when Mr. Bradley wonders (p. 327) what I am " to reply when some one chooses to assert that this same whole is intelligence or feeling," I am not dismayed. I should merely underline the "*chooses*," and beg both parties to observe that this is what they are severally '*choosing to assert*,' and therefore *arbitrary*. *Not more arbitrary*, doubtless, than my own choice, but far more awkward for *their* scheme of classification than for mine. For on mine I should *expect* to find that ultimate questions sooner or later involved *acts of choice* ; as indeed I have repeatedly, though perhaps too unobtrusively, pointed out.[2] Moreover, I have expressly guarded myself against this particular criticism by passages in *Personal Idealism* (p. 86) and *Humanism* (p. 53). These no doubt occur in footnotes, but then Mr. Bradley will hardly accuse me of putting too much into footnotes.

§ 11. Finally, before leaving this part of Mr. Bradley's argument I must say something about his definition of Practice (p. 317) as an *alteration of existence*. This seems altogether too narrow in the sense Mr. Bradley puts upon it. For (1) I cannot possibly assent to his proposal[3] to exclude not only theoretic interests, but all values, ethical and æsthetical, from the sphere of 'practice.' It is an integral part of the Humanist position to contend that

---

[1] *Idola Theatri*, chaps. v. and ix. This homage paid to feeling is, however, really nothing but a reluctant recognition of the difficulties of the situation.
[2] *E.g. Humanism*, pp. 49, 153, 157.   [3] P. 334.

'truths' are values, and that values are all-important and really efficacious, being the real motives which make, unmake, and alter reality, because the whole of our practical activity aims at their attainment. To take the activity in abstraction from the values it aims at, and to conceive the values without reference to the activity which realizes them, seems to me equally preposterous.

Hence (2) the *means* to an alteration of existence must surely be called practical, and among these are of course included almost all of what have hitherto been called the 'purely theoretic' functions. If Mr. Bradley will not concede this, *cadit quaestio*.[1] I, at any rate, should never have asserted the absorption of the theoretical in the practical, if I had thought that the means to an end were to be excluded from the practical. And (3) we do not, even in practice, always seem to aim at alteration of existence. The *preservation* of the desirable seems frequently to be our end.

Again (4) the fruition of the end attained would fall outside Mr. Bradley's definition. Whereas to me it would seem intolerable to exclude from Practice, *e.g.* the Ἐνέργεια Ἀκινησίας, which forms the ideal of life and the goal of effort. I could wish only that it were practicable, as well as practical!

It seems necessary, therefore, to conceive 'practice' more broadly as *the control of experience*, and to define as 'practical' whatever serves, *directly or indirectly*, to control events. So to conceive it will probably render it quite obvious that the aim of the doctrine of the 'subordination' of 'theory' to 'practice' (more properly of the *secondary* character of the former) is merely *voluntarism*, merely to make 'practice' cover practically (*i.e.* with the exception of certain intellectualistic delusions) the whole of life, or in other words to insist on bringing out the *active* character of experience, and the fact that in virtue of its psychological genesis *every thought is an act* just as it is the aim of intellectualism, alike in its sensationalistic and in its rational-

---

[1] He finally (p. 334 *s.f.*) seems to concede this when he says "in a secondary sense anything is practical so far as it is taken as subserving a practical change."

istic forms, to obscure and exclude this character and to declare the conception of activity unmeaning.[1]   Intellectualism, in short, is deeply committed to what Mr. Sturt has well denominated 'the fallacy of *Passivism*' in all its forms.

If, on the other hand, we press Mr. Bradley's remark that "my practice is the alteration by me of existence inward and outward," it would seem that the notion of an 'independent' theoretic life must speedily collapse.   For even the most 'theoretical' of thoughts will induce at least an inward 'alteration' of the thinker.   And this, presumably, will show itself in differences of 'outward' action, and so have 'practical consequences.'

If, again, 'alteration of existence' is not meant unequivocally to imply the activity of a human agent, if it is intended to cover the possibility that it may come about of itself, or as the result of an immanent self-development of a non-human Absolute, it would be interesting to know whether Mr. Bradley would attribute 'practice' also to his Absolute, or whether it would resemble the Aristotelian 'gods' in having none.   In short, the formula is woefully lacking in explicitness.

But even if we accepted Mr. Bradley's definition, we should continue to be perplexed by his needlessly ambiguous use of 'practical.'   We seem to find the 'practical' subdivided into the practical and the non-practical (p. 319): we are told (pp. 322 *s.f.* and 333) that Mr. Bradley is *clear* (!) that in the end there is no distinction between 'theory' and 'practice'; and then again (what I own I had suspected) that there are several senses of 'practical' such that what *in one sense* is practical is not so in another (p. 323).[2]   But is it not the duty of a writer who

---

[1] Cp. Mr. Bradley's teaching on this subject (*Appearance and Reality*,[1] pp. 116-7 and 483-5) and the comments of Prof. James in his admirable chapter on 'the Experience of Activity' in *The Pluralistic Universe*.

[2] In his Note on pp. 332-4 Mr. Bradley recurs to the point in a way which betrays a feeling that his first treatment was not wholly satisfactory.   After again asserting that the distinction of practical and non-practical is ultimately one of degree, he lays it down that nevertheless a 'practical' activity may be so called "when and so far as its product *directly* qualifies the existence which is altered."—This involves a distinct correction of the definition given before.   A little later he admits that "*in a secondary sense* anything is practical so far as it

confessedly uses a term in several senses to explain
distinctly what those senses are?

§ 12. One hardly knows how much notice to take of an
apparently casual remark on page 322 to the effect that if
I understood my own doctrine, I should have to hold that
any end however perverted was rational, and any idea
however mad was truth, so soon as any one insisted on it.
For subsequently (p. 329) Mr. Bradley seems graciously
to decide that he will not attribute so ' insane ' a doctrine
even to me.   Why then did he mention it as if it were
relevant?   Did he not know that he was merely dishing
up an old objection to Protagoras, the effeteness of which
even Plato was candid enough to avow?[1]   Since then
this caricature has often been exposed, most recently in
the explicit account of the development of objective truth
out of subjective valuations given in *Humanism*, pages
58-60.   Its reappearance now that the conceptions of
variation and selection are in universal use is simply
stupefying, and if it is intended as a serious argument, it
shows clearly that Mr. Bradley has yet to grasp the
essential difference between an axiom and a postulate.
In any case Mr. Bradley could do his followers a great
service if, instead of so crudely travestying my argument,
he supplied them with an alternative to it, and showed
them how to deal with the empirical existence of the
infinite variety in ends and ideas.   Or does he not admit
this to constitute a scientific problem, and is it merely in
" appearance " that our views diverge?

§ 13. Mr. Bradley's article is so rich in provocations
of all sorts that I forbear to reply to all of them.   Still
I should have liked to discuss the difficulties he raises
about the conception of Will, which seems to be the

in ᵗ᷅᷄ᵘ ᵃᵃ ᵃᵘᵇᵃᵃᵐᵘᶦᵃᵍ ᵃ ᵖ᷅ᵃ᷅ᵃᵗᶦᵃᵃᶜ ᵃᵇᵃᵃᵍᵃ " This surely would include everything and amply account for the ' perception of a horse ' which Mr. Bradley is
pleased to call a ' revelation.'   For, as the psychologists are daily showing, our
very modes of perception are relative to our practical needs.   The human eye is
not like the eye of an eagle or a cat, because it is *used* differently, and the perception of the horse would never have been attained, unless it had been useful to
such of our ancestors as had acquired eyes.   Presumably the eyes of Micromegas
would be fitted to see a horse as little as Mr. Bradley's are to see a microbe or a
ghost.

[1] *Theaetetus*, 166-7, and cp. Essay ii. § 5-6.

only other point which may be thought to possess some
relevance to the controversy, did we not seem so far
from agreeing on the meaning of the term.   Rather
than plunge into a long disquisition on the proper senses
of 'Will,' and their proper correlation, I will relinquish
the attempt to clear up matters.   I will remark only that
Mr. Bradley's second definition of (a depersonalized) Will
as "a process of passage from idea into existence" is as
intellectualistic and as unacceptable as "the self-realization of an idea," and am curious to know how he gets from
one to the other without exemplifying the pragmatist
doctrine that definitions are relative to purpose.   Moreover, it seems arbitrary and inconvenient to deny the
volitional quality of an achievement simply because the
Will has realized itself, and now accepts and sustains
the situation it has created.   In the theological language
Mr. Bradley affects in this article, this would be equivalent
to the assertion that because God is the Creator, He
cannot also be the Sustainer, of the universe.   I conclude, therefore, by pointing out that all the arguments
which Mr. Bradley bases on *his* conceptions of Will are
to me, once more, corrupted by irrelevance.

I shrink, similarly, from meeting many other interesting points (most of them highly barbed!) with which
Mr. Bradley's paper bristles.   The most relevant of these
would seem to be his curiosity about Bain's theory
of belief (p. 315), but I will not attempt to say how
far I think he has refuted it, because I have always found
it very hard to recognize it in the account given of it in
Mr. Bradley's *Logic* (as usual without specific references).
I have, however, sufficiently justified my conviction that, so
far from refuting Pragmatism by anticipation, Mr. Bradley
appears to have very nearly stumbled into it.

§ 14. On page 331 Mr. Bradley appears to summarize
under four heads that part of his paper which may be
called argumentative.   In the *first* charge that 'the
whole essence' of truth has been subverted, I would read
'analysed' for 'subverted.'   The *second* calls it 'a thoughtless compromise' to treat the result of past volitions as

being my will and choice. But why a 'compromise'?
With whom or what? What have I compromised but
Mr. Bradley's preconceptions, by declining to ignore the
volitional acceptance in the recognition of 'fact' or to
plunge into the flagrant contradictions of his own
account? And why 'thoughtless'? Because it does not
lend itself to Mr. Bradley's travesties? The *third* charge
is partly irrelevant, in so far as it rests on definitions of
'will' which I reject, partly answered by the account I
have given of the factual basis in our cognitive procedure.

As for Mr. Bradley's *fourth* difficulty, I should never
have guessed from his very perfunctory and obscure
exposition of it that he attached any importance to
it. And even after I had perceived that it was to be
made into a capital charge, it failed to impress me.
So it seems sufficient to point out that if knowledge be
conceived as secondary without being *divorced* from
action, and if due reflection is thus rendered a useful
habit, there is no paradox in holding that it may also
profitably reflect on its own genesis. So far from condemning philosophic reflection, I could even wish that
its use, especially when conducted on the right humanist
lines, were more extensive.

§ 15. These replies would perhaps suffice, were it not
that Mr. Bradley's paper contains much more than arguments. He makes also what looks like an attempt to
arouse theological prejudice against us.

It is very surprising to observe the general air of
religiosity in which Mr. Bradley has enveloped himself.
I looked in vain for my beloved *bête noire*, the Absolute,
and wondered why it had been sent to dwell with Hegel
in eternal night. In its place one found not only the old
ambiguous use of 'God' in all its philosophic deceptive-
ness,[1] but even allusions to the Jehovah of Mr. Bradley's
youth, and wondered why the Baal of 'Jericho' received
no honourable mention. Now, as I had always respected
Mr. Bradley's philosophy for never seeking to curry
favour with theology by playing on ambiguous phrases,

---

[1] Cp. Essay xii. § 6.

I was naturally puzzled by this change of face. Was it to be regarded as a reversion, like the return to the 'correspondence' view of truth, or respected as an indication of a change of heart, of a pathetic recrudescence of what Mr. Bradley had learnt (or, as he says, 'imbibed') in his youth about Jehovah (p. 332)? Or were we witnessing a strategic movement of the absolutist host, necessitated by the unexpected force of the enemy, and a recoil of its 'left' upon its 'right' wing? Or lastly, was it to be interpreted, less charitably, as an attempt to enlist religious prejudices against the new philosophy by unfair appeals to a few travestied formulas of a musty theology?

The last seemed the boldest and riskiest strategy, and I should have thought Mr. Bradley too prudent to attempt it. The controversial maxim *verketzern gilt nicht* has not yet taken such firm root in Oxford that it should be superfluous for us to safeguard ourselves by repudiating an interpretation and an impression which his language may countenance. I must protest therefore against the insinuation that because our views do not conform with the dogmatic definition of religion it has pleased Mr. Bradley to impose, we may fitly be branded as irreligious and as blasphemers against the deity whom Mr. Bradley so strangely denominates "the lord of suffering and of sin and of death" (p. 315). Now I am well aware that the definition of religion is a difficult matter, and that many of its empirical manifestations accord ill with any of its definitions. But since the publication of James's *Varieties of Religious Experience*, I should have thought that there were two things that even the hardiest apriorist would have shrunk from. The first is dogmatizing concerning what religion *must* mean, without troubling to inquire what *psychologically* the various forms of religious sentiment *have* meant and do mean. Now if Mr. Bradley had condescended for a moment to contemplate the objective facts of concrete religion, he could not but have been struck with the fact that Humanism has the closest affinities with such important religious phenomena as

Newman's 'grammar of assent' and the widespread theology of Ritschl. And from James also he might have learnt that amid all the varieties of religious feeling the one most constant conception of the divine has been, not some desiccated formula about the Unity of the Universe, but a demand for *something* to respond to the outcry of the human heart.

I should have thought, therefore, secondly, that whatever might be said about the logical subversiveness of the new views, their value for religion was secured against attack. For has not James's doctrine of the Will to believe made manifest the pragmatic value of faith, and put the religious postulates on the same footing with those of science?[1] Nay, has not the common charge against us been that our doctrines pander to all the crudest superstitions of the vulgar? Mr. Bradley, I suppose, acquits us on this charge; but his own is far less plausible.

When one remembers further how Mr. Bradley has himself described religion as mere 'appearance' riddled with contradictions and denied that "a God which is all in all is the God of religion,"[2] it seems—well —slightly humorous to find him now setting up standards of 'orthodox' theology and solemnly anathematizing those who have doubted the omnipotence of *their* 'God' and the religious value of *his* (p. 331, cp. p. 316). One is inclined merely to retort in the words of Valentine— "*Lass unsern Herr Gott aus dem Spass.*"

His attacks (p. 331) on the two clerical contributors to *Personal Idealism*, Dr. Rashdall and particularly Dr. Bussell, are peculiarly invidious as being *ad captandum* appeals to "the more orthodox theologians" and prejudicial to their professional status. But it seems somewhat doubtful whether he will find any one naïvely 'orthodox' enough to reduce Christianity to a sort of Crypto-Buddhism at the behest of the author of *Appearance and Reality*.

Mr. Bradley must have been well aware that his

---

[1] Essay xvi. §§ 2, 9.
[2] *Appearance and Reality*, p. 448 (1st ed.). Cp. Essay xii. § 6.

language was wholly 'popular.' He must have known, as well as Dr. Rashdall or I, that the 'omnipotence' he claims for his Absolute is *not* the 'omnipotence' of the theologians, and that his Absolute is not obviously identical with the superhuman power, adequate to all human needs, which the religious sentiments legitimately postulate. He must know too that in *no* religion is the Divine, the principle of Help and Justice, ever actually regarded as omnipotent in practice.[1] Again, seeing that he has plainly shown us that his Absolute possesses the religious attributes only as it possesses all else, and that for all human purposes it is impotent and worthless, was it not most injudicious to attack us on religious grounds? And has he not justly provoked the retort that *we* feel his whole Absolutism to be a worthless technicality, if its true character *is* revealed, and a fulsome fraud upon all man's most sacred feelings, if it is *not*?

§ 16. Curiously enough, however, Mr. Bradley's paper does not close with the enigmatic piety which has provoked these strictures. It is followed by a fit of agnosticism which might have come straight out of Herbert Spencer's *Autobiography*.[2] The promise of philosophy " even in the end is no clear theory nor any complete understanding or vision "; " its certain reward is a continual evidence and a heightened apprehension of the ineffable mystery of life." Only Spencer and Mr. Bradley tend in opposite directions: the former, more truly, feels that this final incomprehensibility is a " paralysing thought," and inclines towards the authoritative dogma of some religion that will claim to know; the latter seems to regard it as edifying, and abandons the religious formulas to disburden himself of his contradictions in the bottomless pit of the Absolute. To the one, religion holds out *more* hopes of knowledge than philosophy, to the other, *less*. But as a satisfaction to the philosophic craving, to the will-to-know, neither policy, alas, seems to promise much. The philosopher's reasoning is rewarded merely with the sorry privilege accorded by Polyphemus to Odysseus.

[1] Cp. Essay xii. § 6.   [2] Cp. that work, ii. pp. 469-471.

For what profit is it, if break down it must, that it
should perish somewhat later?   What a satire too it is
upon a philosophic quest that started with the most confident anticipations of the rationality of the universe to
have to end in such fiasco!   Can Mr. Bradley wonder, if
this is really all his philosophy can come to, that philosophy is disregarded and despised, or that other philosophers prefer to bend their footsteps in more promising
directions?   And it seems still stranger that it should be
deemed appropriate to scathe all fresh attempts at ex-
ploration with unmeasured contumely *a priori*.   Surely a
somewhat humbler and less 'hybristic' note would better
become the actual situation!

§ 17. One notes indeed with satisfaction that in places
Mr. Bradley seems to evince some dim consciousness of
the real predicament.   At all events he is growing more
liberal in throwing open for discussion questions which
we have always been assured on his side had been
definitively closed.   We may welcome, therefore, and note
for future use, Mr. Bradley's admission of "well-known
difficulties" in the infinity of God (p. 331), his description
of pluralism as "a very promising adventure," and the
"pleasure" it would give him to learn that its difficulties can be surmounted (p. 327).   The tone of these
admissions, it is true, still smacks of the judge who was
'open to conviction, but by Jove would like to see the
man who could convince him.'   And he hastens to add
that there are 'obvious difficulties' (not stated) on the
other side.   Nor does he make it clear why, if real anti-
nomies exist on these points, he should have so decisively
adopted the one alternative, instead of suspending judgment
and looking out for a real solution.

But on the whole I read these admissions as a hopeful
sign that the dwellers in 'Jericho' are not so content with
their gloomy ghettoes as they had seemed, nor so sure that
it is in very deed the heavenly Jerusalem.   Ere long they
may come out to parley of their own accord and offer us
terms, nay themselves dismantle antiquated defences that
are useless against modern ordnance!   And when the

stronghold of the Absolute is once declared an open town,
no longer cramped within walls, nor serving as a strait
prison for the human soul, it can be refurbished and
extended for those to dwell in whose tastes its habitations
please. We too shall then have no further motive to molest
an Absolutism which has ceased to oppress us and to be
a menace to the liberty of thought. We may still decline
to go to 'Jericho,' and prefer the open country, abiding
in our tents with the household gods who suffice for our
needs and need our co-operation because of their "pathetic
weakness." [1]   But why should we contend against the
genial Absolutes of Prof. Taylor, which is finally reduced
to an emotional postulate,[2] or of Prof. Royce,[3] which
becomes the ultimate satisfaction of our social instincts
and forms a sort of *salon* where all are at home and
can meet their friends, so long as we escape the grim
all-compelling monster of Mr. Bradley's nightmare?
When we are no longer treated as Ishmaelites, there will
be peace in the land, a peace attained, not by what must
surely by this time seem the impossible method of snub-
bing and snuffing out the new philosophy, but by a
mutual toleration based on respect for the various idiosyncrasies of men.[4]   Nor will there then any longer be
occasion to reproach Philosophy that its favourite *idolon
fori* is simply Billingsgate.

§ 18. Life will be easier in those days, and with it philosophy. For philosophers will have ceased to confound
obscurity with profundity, difficulty with truth, and to
expect that because some truths are hard, therefore all
hard sayings are true. Nor will they any longer feel
aggrieved, like Mr. Bradley (p. 335 *s.f.*), at the prospect
of everything that would render philosophy easier and
more attractive. For they will realize that the intrinsic

---

[1] In Dr. Bussell's striking phrase (*Personal Idealism*, p. 341).
[2] *Elements of Metaphysics*, p. 317 ; cp. p. 253. Prof. Taylor's disclaimer in
Mind, N.S. No. 57, p. 86, upholds the claim to universal cogency and represents the argument for a postulated Absolute as only *ad hominem*. But my
objection to a postulated Absolute is not to the postulation, but merely to the
fact that this postulate frustrates itself.
[3] *On the Eternal and the Practical.*
[4] Cp. Essay xii. §§ 8, 10.

difficulties of thinking as an exercise of faculty will always suffice to preserve the ' dignity ' of philosophy, and that it is needless to enhance them by adding unintelligibilities and aimless word-play.

Philosophy will always be hard, I agree. In some respects and for three reasons : because thinking is the hardest of exercises, because it presupposes much special knowledge to grasp the *use* of general conceptions which are devoid of meaning in abstraction from the experience they serve to organize, and because to rethink *old* conceptions into *new* ones is irksome and frequently demands a flash of insight before we can really ' see ' it all. But one might well despair of the human reason if what had once been clearly thought could not always be lucidly expressed. Obscurity of expression is nothing admirable ; it is always a bar to the comprehension of any subject, and it is fatal in a subject where the intrinsic difficulties are so great and the psychological variations of the minds which apprehend them so extreme ; it is, moreover, an easy refuge for confusion of thought. And it is surely one of the quaintest of academic superstitions to think that obscurity and confusion of thought have as such, ' pedagogical value.' In view of these facts what reason can there be for making Philosophy anything like so obscure, hard, repulsive, and unprofitable as the intellectualist systems which have obfuscated us so long ?

V

THE AMBIGUITY OF TRUTH [1]

ARGUMENT

The great antithesis between Pragmatism and Intellectualism as to the nature of Truth. I. The predication of truth a specifically human habit. The existence of *false* claims to truth. How then are *false* claims to be dis-criminated from *true*? Intellectualism fails to answer this, and succumbs to the *ambiguity of truth* ('claim' and 'validity'). Illustrations from Plato and others. II. Universality and importance of the ambiguity. The refusal of Intellectualism to consider it. III. The pragmatic answer. Relevance and value relative to purpose. Hence 'truth' a valuation. The convergence of values. IV. The evaluation of claims proceeds pragmatically. 'Truth' implies relevance and usually reference to proximate ends. V. The pragmatic definition of 'Truth': its value for refuting naturalism and simplifying the classification of the sciences. VI. A challenge to Intellectualism to refute Pragmatism by evaluating any truth non-pragmatically

THE purpose of this essay is to bring to a clear issue, and so possibly to the prospect of a settlement, the conflict of opinion now raging in the philosophic world as to the nature of the conception of 'truth.' This issue is an essential part of the greater conflict between the old in-tellectualist and the new 'pragmatist' school of thought, which extends over the whole field of philosophy. For, in consequence of the difference between the aims and methods of the two schools, there is probably no intel-lectualist treatment of any problem which does not need, and will not bear, restatement in voluntarist terms. But the clash of these two great antithetical attitudes towards life is certainly more dramatic at some points than at others. The influence of belief upon thought, its value

[1] A revised form of a paper which appeared in *Mind* for April 1906 (N.S. No. 58).

and function in knowledge, the relation of 'theory' to 'practice,' the possibility of abstracting from emotional interest, and of ignoring in 'logic' the psychological conditions of all judgment, the connexion between knowing and being, 'truth' and 'fact,' 'origin' and 'validity,' the question of how and how far the real which is said to be 'discovered' is really 'made,' the 'plasticity' and determinable indetermination of reality, the contribution of voluntary acceptance to the constitution of 'fact,' the nature of purpose and of 'mechanism,' the value of teleology, the all-controlling presence of value-judgments and the interrelations of their various forms, the proper meaning of 'reason,' 'faith,' 'thought,' 'will,' 'freedom,' 'necessity,' all these are critical points at which burning questions have arisen or may arise, and at all of them the new philosophy seems able to provide a distinctive and consistent treatment.   Thus there is throughout the field every promise of interesting discoveries and of a successful campaign for a thoroughgoing voluntarism that unsparingly impugns the intellectualist tradition.

But the aim of the present essay must be restricted. It will be confined to one small corner of the battlefield, viz. to the single question of the making of 'truth' and the meaning of a term which is more often mouthed in a passion of unreasoning loyalty than subjected to calm and logical analysis. I propose to show, (1) that such analysis is necessary and possible ; (2) that it results in a problem which the current intellectualist logic can neither dismiss nor solve ; (3) that to discard the abstractions of this formal logic at once renders this problem simple and soluble ; (4) that to solve it is to establish the pragmatist criterion of truth ; (5) that the resulting definition of truth unifies experience and rationalizes a well-established classification of the sciences ; and (6) I shall conclude with a twofold challenge to intellectualist logicians, failure to meet which will, I think, bring out with all desirable clearness that their system at present is as devoid of intellectual completeness as it is of practical fecundity.

This design, it will be seen, deliberately rules out the

references to questions of belief, desire, and will, and their ineradicable influence upon cognition, with which Voluntarism has made so much effective play, and this although I am keenly conscious both that their presence as psychical facts in all knowing is hardly open to denial,[1] and that their recognition is essential to the full appreciation of our case.   But I am desirous of meeting our adversaries on their own ground, that of abstract logic, and of giving them every advantage of position.   And so, even at the risk of reducing the real interest of my subject, I will discuss it on the ground of as ' pure,' *i.e.* as *formal*, a logic as is compatible with the continuance of actual thinking.

I

Let us begin then with the problem of analysing the conception of ' truth,' and, to clear up our ideas, let us first observe the extension of the term.   We may safely lay it down that the use of truth is ἴδιον ἀνθρώπῳ, a habit peculiar to man.   Animals, that is, do not attain to or use the conception.   They do not effect discriminations within their experience by means of the predicates ' true ' and ' false.'   Again, even the philosophers who have been most prodigal of dogmas concerning the nature of an ' infinite ' intelligence (whatever that may mean !), have evinced much hesitation about attributing to it the discursive procedures of our own, and have usually hinted that it would transcend the predication of truth and falsehood.   As being then a specific peculiarity of the human mind, the conception of ' truth ' seems closely analogous to that of ' good ' and of ' beautiful,' which seem as naturally to possess antithetical predicates in the ' bad ' and the ' ugly,' as the ' true ' does in the ' false.'   And it may be anticipated that when our psychology has quite outgrown the materialistic prejudices of its adolescence, it will probably regard all these habits of judging ex-

---

[1] In point of fact such denial has never been attempted : inquiries as to how logic can validly consider a ' pure ' thought, abstracted from the psychological conditions of actual thinking, have merely been ignored.   My *Formal Logic* may now, however, be said to have established that such ' logic ' is meaningless.

periences as just as distinctive and ultimate features of
mental process as are the ultimate facts of our perception.
In a sense, therefore, the predications of 'good' and 'bad,'
'true' and 'false,' etc., may take rank with the experiences
of 'sweet,' 'red,' 'loud,' 'hard,' etc., as ultimate facts which
need be analysed no further.[1]

We may next infer that by *a truth* we mean a proposition to which this attribute 'true' has somehow been
attached, and which, consequently, is envisaged *sub specie
veri.* *The Truth*, therefore, is the totality of things to
which this mode of treatment is applied or applicable,
whether or not this extends over the whole of our experience.

If now all propositions which involve this predication
of truth really deserved it, if all that professes and seems
to be 'true' were really true, no difficulty would arise.
Things would be 'true' or 'false' as simply and un-
ambiguously as they are 'sweet' or 'sour,' 'red' or 'blue,'
and nothing could disturb our judgments or convict them
of illusion.   But in the sphere of knowledge such, notoriously, is not the case.   Our anticipations are often falsified, our claims prove frequently untenable.   Our truths
may turn out to be false, our goods to be bad : falsehood
and error are as rampant as evil in the world of our
experience.

This fact compels us (1) to an enlargement, and (2) to
a distinction, in the realm of truth.   For the logician
'truth' becomes a problem, enlarged so as to include
'falsity' as well, and so, strictly, our problem is the contemplation of experience *sub specie veri et falsi.*   Secondly,
if not all that claims truth is true, must we not distinguish
this initial claim from whatever procedure subsequently
justifies or validates it ?   *Truth, therefore, will become
ambiguous.*   It will mean primarily a claim which may or
may not turn out to be valid.   It will mean, secondarily,
such a claim *after* it has been tested and ratified, by

---

[1] The purport of this very elementary remark, which is still very remote from
the real problem of truth, is to confute the notion, which seems dimly to
underlie some intellectualist criticisms, that the specific character of the truth-
predication is ignored in pragmatist quarters.

processes which it behoves us to examine. In the first sense, as a claim, it will always have to be regarded with suspicion. For we shall not know whether it is really and fully true, and we shall tend to reserve this honourable predicate for what has victoriously sustained its claim. And once we realize that *a claim to truth is involved in every assertion as such,* our vigilance will be sharpened. A claim to truth, being inherent in assertion as such, will come to seem a formal and trivial thing, worth noting once for all, but possessing little real interest for knowledge. A formal logic, therefore, which restricts itself to the registration of such formal claims, we shall regard as solemn trifling ; but it will seem a matter of vital importance and of agonized inquiry what it is that validates such claims and makes them really true. And with regard to any ' truth ' that has been asserted, our first demand will be to know what is *de facto* its condition, whether what it sets forth has been fully validated, or whether it is still a mere, and possibly a random, claim. For this evidently will make all the difference to its meaning and logical value. That ' $2 + 2 = 4$ ' and that ' truth is indefinable ' stand, *e.g.* logically on a very different footing : the one is part of a tried and tested system of arithmetical truth, the other the desperate refuge of a bankrupt or indolent theory.

Under such conditions far-reaching confusions could be avoided only by the unobtrusive operation of a beneficent providence. But that such miraculous intervention should guard logicians against the consequences of their negligence was hardly to be hoped for. Accordingly we find a whole cloud of witnesses to this confusion, from Plato, the great originator of the intellectualistic interpretation of life, down to the latest ' critics ' of Pragmatism with all their pathetic inability to do more than reiterate the confusions of the *Theaetetus*. For example, this is how Plato conducts his refutation of Protagoras in a critical stage of his polemic :—[1]

" *Socrates.* And how about Protagoras himself ? If

---

[1] *Theaetetus,* 170 E–171 B, Jowett's translation. Italics mine.

neither he nor the multitude thought, as indeed they do
not think, that man is the measure of all things, must it
not follow that the truth (*validity*) of which Protagoras
wrote would be true (*claim*) to no one? But if you
suppose that he himself thought this, and that the multitude does not agree with him, you must begin by allowing
that in whatever proportion the many are more than one,
his truth (*validity*) is more untrue (*claim*) than true?" (not
necessarily, for all truths start their career in a minority
of one, as an individual's claims, and obtain recognition
only after a long struggle).

" *Theodorus.* That would follow if the truth (*validity*)
is supposed to vary with individual opinion.

" *Socrates.* And the best of the joke is that he acknow-
ledges the truth (*as claim*, Protagoras ; *as validity*, Plato)
of their opinion who believe his own opinion to be false ;
for he admits that the opinions of all men are true " (*as
claims* ; cp. also p. 309).

For a more compact expression of the same ambiguity
we may have recourse to Mr. Bradley. " About the *truth*
of this Law " (of Contradiction) " so far as it applies, there
is in my opinion no question. The question will be rather
as to how far the Law applies and how far *therefore* it is
true." [1] The first proposition is either a truism or false.
It is a truism if ' truth ' is taken in the sense of ' claim ' ;
for it then only states that a claim is good if the question of its application is waived. In any other sense of
' truth ' it is false (or rather self-contradictory), since it
admits that there *is* a question about the application of
the ' Law,' and it is not until the application is attempted
that validity can be tested. In the second proposition it
is implied that ' truth ' depends, not on the mere claim,
but on the possibility of application.

Or, again, let us note how Prof A. E. Taylor betters
his master's instruction in an interesting article on ' Truth
and Practice ' in the *Phil. Rev.* for May 1905. He first lays
it down that " true propositions are those which have an
unconditional *claim* on our recognition " (of their *validity*,

<hr>
[1] *Mind*, v. N.S., 20, p. 470.   Italics mine.

or merely of their *claim*?), and then pronounces that
"truth is just the system of propositions which have an
unconditional *claim* to be recognized as *valid*."[1]   And lest
he should not have made the paradox of this confusion
evident enough, he repeats (p. 273) that "the truth of a
statement means not the actual fact of its recognition"
(*i.e.* of its *de facto* validity), "but its *rightful claim* on our
recognition" (p. 274).[2]   In short, as he does not distinguish between 'claim' and 'right,' he cannot see that the
question of truth is as to when and how a 'claim' is to
be recognized as 'rightful.'   And though he wisely refrains
from even attempting to tell us how the clamorousness of
a claim is going to establish its validity, it is clear that
his failure to observe the distinction demolishes his
definition of truth.

Mr. Joachim's *Nature of Truth* does not exemplify
this confusion so clearly merely because it does not get
to the point at which it is revealed.   His theory of
truth breaks down before this point is reached.   He
conceives the nature of truth to concern only the question
of what 'the ideal' should be, even though it should be
unattainable by man, as indeed it turns out to be.
Thus the problem of how *we* validate claims to truth
is treated as irrelevant.[3]   Hence it is only casually
that phrases like 'entitled to claim' occur (p. 109),
or that the substantiating of a claim to truth is said to
consist in its recognition and adoption " by all intelligent
people " (p. 27).   Still on p. 118 it seems to be implied
that a " thought which claims truth as affirming universal
meaning" need not undergo any further verification.   It
is evident, in short, that not much can be expected from
theories which have overlooked so vital a distinction.
Their unawareness of it will vitiate all their discussions
of the nature of 'truth,' by which they will mean now the
one sense, now the other, and now both, in inextricable
fallacy.

---

[1] Pp. 271, 288.   Italics mine.
[2] Cp. also pp. 276 and 278.
[3] As it is by Mr. Bradley, who, as Prof. Hoernle remarks, "deals with the
question how *we* correct our errors in a footnote ! " (*Mind* xiv. 321).

II

Our provisional analysis, therefore, has resulted in our detecting an important ambiguity in the conception of truth which, unless it can be cleared up, must hopelessly vitiate all discussion. In view of this distressing situation it becomes our bounden duty to inquire *how an accepted truth may be distinguished from a mere claim, and how a claim to truth may be validated.* For any logic which aims at dealing with actual thinking the urgency of this inquiry can hardly be exaggerated. But even the most 'purely' intellectual and futilely formal theory of knowledge can hardly refuse to undertake it. For the ambiguity which raises the problem is absolutely all-pervading. As we saw, a formal claim to truth is co-extensive with the sphere of logical judgment. No judgment proclaims its own fallibility; its formal claim is always to be true. We are always liable, therefore, to misinterpret every judgment. We may take as a validated truth what in point of fact is really an unsupported claim. But inasmuch as such a claim may always be erroneous, we are constantly in danger of accepting as validly true what, if tested, would be utterly untenable. Every assertion is ambiguous, and as it shows no outward indication of what it really means, we can hardly be said to know the meaning of any assertion whatsoever. On any view of logic, the disastrous and demoralizing consequences of such a situation may be imagined. It is imperative therefore to distinguish sharply between the formal inclusion of a statement in the sphere of *truth-or-falsity*, and its incorporation into a system of tested truth. For unless we do so, we simply court deception.

This possibility of deception, moreover, becomes the more serious when we realize how impotent our formal logic is to conceive this indispensable distinction and to guard us against so fatal a confusion. Instead of proving a help to the logician it here becomes a snare, by reason of the fundamental abstraction of its standpoint. For if, following Mr. Alfred Sidgwick's brilliant lead, we regard as Formal Logic every treatment of our cognitive processes which abstracts from the concrete application of our logical functions to actual cases of knowing, it is easy to see that no such logic can help us, because the meaning of an assertion can never be determined apart from the actual application.[1] From the mere verbal form, that is, we cannot tell whether we are dealing with a valid judgment or a sheer claim. To settle this, we must go behind the statement : we must go into the rights of the case. Meaning depends upon purpose, and purpose is a question of psychical fact, of the context and use of the form of words in actual knowing. But all this is just what the abstract standpoint of Formal Logic forbids us to examine. It conceives the meaning of a proposition to be somehow inherent in it as a form of words, apart from its use. So when it finds that the same words may be used to convey a variety of meanings in various contexts, it supposes itself to have the same form, not of words, but of judgment, and solemnly declares it to be as such ambiguous, even though in each actual case of use the meaning intended may be perfectly clear to the meanest understanding ! It seems more than doubtful, therefore, whether a genuine admission of the validity of our distinction could be extracted from any formal logician. For even if he could be induced to admit it in words, he would yet insist on treating it too as purely formal, and rule out on principle attempts to determine how *de facto* the distinction was established and employed.

Although, therefore, our distinction appears to be as clear as it is important, it does not seem at all certain that it would be admitted by the logicians who are so enamoured of truth in the abstract that they have ceased to recognize it in the concrete. More probably they would protest that logic was being conducted back to the old puzzle of a general criterion of truth and error, and would adduce the failures of their predecessors as a valid excuse for their present apathy. Or at most they

[1] Cp. Essays i. § 2, and iii. § 10.

might concede that a distinction between a truth and a claim to truth must indeed be made, but allege that it could not take any but a negative form. The sole criterion of truth, that is, which can be given, is that truth is not self-contradictory or incoherent.

This statement, in the first place, means a refusal to go into the actual question how truth is made : it is an attempt to avoid the test of application, and to conceive truth as inherent in the logical terms in the abstract. But this is really to render 'truth' wholly *verbal*. For the inherent meanings are merely the established meanings of the words employed. It is, secondly, merely dogmatic assertion : it can hardly inspire confidence so long as it precedes and precludes examination of the positive solutions of the problem, and assumes the conceptions of ' self-contradiction ' or ' incoherence ' as the simplest things in the world. In point of fact neither of them has been adequately analysed by intellectualist logicians, nor is either of them naturally so translucent as to shed a flood of light on any subject. As, however, we cannot now enter upon their obscurities, and examine what (if anything) either ' coherence ' or ' consistency ' really means, it must suffice to remark that Capt. H. V. Knox's masterly article in the April (1905) number of *Mind*[1] contains ample justification for what I have said about the principle of contradiction. If on the other hand the ' negative criterion' be stated in the form of incoherence, I would inquire merely how intellectualist logic proposes to distinguish the logical coherence, to which it appeals, from the psychological coherence, which it despises. Until this difficult (or impossible ?) feat has been achieved, we may safely move on.[2]

III

Let us proceed therefore to discard old prejudices and to consider how in point of fact we sift claims and discriminate between ' claims ' and ' truths,' how the raw

[1] N.S. No. 54 ; cp. *Formal Logic*, ch. x.   [2] *Cf.* also *Humanism*, pp. 52-53.

material of a science is elaborated into its final structure,
how, in short, truth is made. Now this question is not
intrinsically a hopeless one. It is not even particularly
difficult in theory. For it concerns essentially facts
which may be observed, and with care and attention it
should be possible to determine whether the procedures
of the various sciences have anything in common, and if
so what. By such an inductive appeal to the facts,
therefore, we greatly simplify our problem, and may
possibly discover its solution. Any obstacle which we
may encounter will come merely from the difficulty of
intelligently observing the special procedures of so
many sciences and of seizing their salient points and
general import ; we shall not be foredoomed to failure
by any intrinsic absurdity of our enterprise.

Now it would be possible to arrive at our solution
by a critical examination of every known science in
detail, but it is evident that this procedure would be
very long and laborious. It seems better, therefore,
merely to state the condensed results of such investigations.
They will in this shape stand out more clearly and better
exhibit the trend of an argument which runs as follows :—

It being taken as established that the sphere of logic
is that of the antithetical valuations 'true' and 'false,'
we observe, in the first place, that in every science the
effective truth or falsity of an answer depends on its
relevance to the question raised in that science. It does
not matter that a physicist's language should reek of
'crude realism' or an engineer's calculations lack 'exactness,' if both are right enough for their immediate purpose.
Whereas, when an irrelevant answer is given, it is justly
treated as non-existent for that science ; no question
is raised whether it is 'true' or 'false.' We observe,
secondly, that every science has a definitely circumscribed
subject-matter, a definite method of treating it, and a
definitely articulated body of interpretations. Every
science, in other words, forms a system of truths about
some subject. But inasmuch as every science is concerned with some aspect of our total experience, and no

science deals with that whole under every aspect, it is
clear that sciences arise by the limitation of subjects, the
selection of standpoints, and the specialization of methods.
All these operations, however, are artificial, and in a
sense arbitrary, and none of them can be conceived to
come about except by the action of a purposing intelligence. It follows that the nature of the *purpose* which
is pursued in a science will yield the deepest insight into
its nature ; for what we want to know in the science will
determine the questions we put, and their bearing on the
questions put will determine the standing of the answers
we attain. If we can take the answers as relevant to
our questions and conducive to our ends, they will yield
' truth ' ; if we cannot, ' falsity.' [1]

Seeing thus that everywhere truth and falsity
depend on the purpose which constitutes the science and
are bestowed accordingly, we begin to perceive, what
we ought never to have forgotten, that the predicates
' true ' and ' false ' are not unrelated to ' good ' and
' bad.' For good and bad also (in their wider and
primary sense) have reference to purpose. ' Good ' is what
conduces to, ' bad ' what thwarts, a purpose. And so it
would seem that ' true ' and ' false ' were valuations, forms
of the ' good '-or-' bad ' which indicates a reference to an
end. Or, as Aristotle said long ago, "in the case of
the intelligence which is theoretical, and neither practical
nor productive, its ' good ' and ' bad ' is ' truth ' and
' falsehood.' " [2]

Truth, then, being a valuation, has reference to a
purpose. What precisely that reference is will depend
on the purpose, which may extend over the whole range
of human interest. But it is only in its primary aspect,
as valued by individuals, that the predication of ' truth '
will refer thus widely to any purpose any one may
entertain in a cognitive operation. For it stands to
reason that the power of constituting ' objective ' truth

[1] But cp. note on p. 154.
[2] *Eth. Nic.* vi. 2, 3. Cp. *De Anim.* iii. 7, 431 b 10, where it is stated
that " the true and false are in the same class with the good and bad,"
i.e. are valuations.

is not granted so easily. Society exercises almost as severe a control over the intellectual as over the moral eccentricities and nonconformities of its members ; indeed it often so organizes itself as to render the recognition of *new* truth nearly impossible. Whatever, therefore, individuals may recognize and value as ' true,' the ' truths ' which *de facto* prevail and are recognized as objective will only be a *selection* from those we are subjectively tempted to propound. There is, therefore, no real danger lest this analysis should destroy the ' objectivity ' of truth and enthrone subjective licence in its place.

A further convergence in our truth-valuations is produced by the natural tendency to subordinate all ends or purposes to the ultimate end or final purpose, ' the Good.' For in theory, at least, the ' goods,' and therefore the ' truths,' of all the sciences are unified and validated by their relation to the Supreme Good. In practice no doubt this ideal is far from being realized, and there arise at various points conflicts between the various sorts of values or goods, which doubtless will continue until a perfect harmony of all our purposes, scientific, moral, æsthetic, and emotional has been achieved. Such conflicts may, of course, be made occasions for theatrically opposing ' truth ' to (moral) ' goodness,' ' virtue ' to ' happiness,' ' science ' to ' art,' etc., and afford much scope for dithyrambic declamation. But a sober and clear-headed thought will not be intolerant nor disposed to treat such oppositions as final and absolute : even where under the circumstances their reality must provisionally be admitted, it will essay rather to evaluate each claim with reference to the highest conception of ultimate good which for the time being seems attainable. It will be very chary, therefore, of sacrificing either side beyond recall ; it will neither allow the claims of truth to oppress those of moral virtue nor those of moral virtue to suppress art. But it will still more decidedly hold aloof from the quixotic attempt to conceive the sphere of each valuation as independent and as wholly severed from the rest.

IV

We have seen so far that truth is a form of value, and
the logical judgment a valuation ; but we have not yet
raised the question as to what prompts us in bestowing
or withholding this value, what are our guiding principles
in thus evaluating our experience. The answer to this
question takes us straight into the heart of Pragmatism.
Nay, the answer to this question *is* Pragmatism, and gives
the sense in which Pragmatism professes to have a criterion
of truth. For the pragmatist contends that he has an
answer which is simple, and open to inspection and easily
tested. He simply bids us go to the facts and observe
the actual operations of our knowing. If we will but do
this, we shall 'discover' that in all actual knowing the
question whether an assertion is 'true' or 'false' is
decided uniformly and very simply. It is decided, that is,
by its consequences, by its bearing on the interest which
prompted to the assertion, by its relation to the purpose
which put the question. To add to this that the consequences must be *good* is superfluous. For if and so far
as an assertion satisfies or forwards the purpose of the
inquiry to which it owes its being, it is so far 'true'; if
and so far as it thwarts or baffles it, it is unworkable,
unserviceable, 'false.' And 'true' and 'false,' we have
seen, are the intellectual forms of 'good' and 'bad.' Or
in other words, a 'truth' is what is useful in building up
a science ; a 'falsehood' what is useless or noxious for
this same purpose.[1] A 'science,' similarly, is 'good' if it
can be used to harmonize our life; if it cannot, it is a
pseudo-science or a game. To determine therefore whether
any answer to any question is 'true' or 'false,' we have
merely to note its effect upon the inquiry in which we
are interested, and in relation to which it has arisen. And
if these effects are favourable, the answer is 'true' and
'good' for our purpose, and 'useful' as a means to the

[1] After allowance has been made for methodological assumptions, which may
turn out to be 'fictions.' 'Lies' exist as such only after they have been
detected ; but then they have usually ceased to be useful.

end we pursue.[1] Here, then, we have exposed to view the whole rationale of Pragmatism, the source of the famous paradoxes that 'truth' depends on its consequences, that the 'true' must be 'good' and 'useful' and 'practical.' I confess that to me they have never seemed more than truisms so simple that I used to fear lest too elaborate an insistence on them should be taken as an insult to the intelligence of my readers. But experience has shown that I was too sanguine, and now I even feel impelled to guard still further against two possible misapprehensions into which an unthinking philosopher might fall.

I will point out, in the first place, that when we said that truth was estimated by its consequences for some purpose, we were speaking subject to the social character of truth, and quite generally. What consequences are relevant to what purposes depends, of course, on the subject-matter of each science, and may sometimes be in doubt, when the question may be interpreted in several contexts. But as a rule the character of the question sufficiently defines the answer which can be treated as relevantly true. It is not necessary, therefore, seriously to contemplate absurdities such as, *e.g.*, the intrusion of ethical or æsthetical motives into the estimation of mathematical truths, or to refute claims that the isosceles triangle is more virtuous than the scalene, or an integer nobler than a vulgar fraction, or that heavenly bodies must move not in ellipses but in circles, because the circle is the most perfect figure. Pragmatism is far less likely to countenance such confusions than the intellectualist theories from which I drew my last illustration. In some cases, doubtless, as in many problems of history and religion, there will be found deep-seated and enduring differences of opinion as to what consequences and what

---

[1] Strictly both the 'true' and the 'false' answers are, as Mr. Sidgwick says, subdivisions of the 'relevant,' and the irrelevant is really unmeaning. But the unmeaning often seems to be relevant until it is detected ; it is as baffling to our purpose as the 'false'; while the 'false' answer grows more and more 'irrelevant' as we realize its 'falsity'; it does not mean what we meant to get, viz. something we can work with. Hence it is so far unmeaning, and in a sense all that *fails* us may be treated as '*false.*'

tests may be adduced as relevant ; but these differences already exist, and are in no wise created by being recognized and explained. Pragmatism, however, by enlarging our notions of what constitutes relevant evidence, and insisting on *some* testing, is far more likely to conduce to their amicable settlement than the intellectualisms which condemn all faith as inherently irrational and irrelevant to knowledge. And, ideally and in principle, such disagreements as to the ends which are relevant to the estimation of any evidence are always capable of being composed by an appeal to the supreme purpose which unifies and harmonizes all our ends : in practice, no doubt, we are hardly aware of this, nor agreed as to what it is ; but the blame, surely, attaches to the distracted state of our thoughts and not to the pragmatic analysis of truth. For it would surely be preposterous to expect a mere theory of knowledge to adjudicate upon and settle offhand, by sheer dint of logic, all the disputed questions in all the sciences.

My second caution refers to the fact that I have made the predication of truth dependent on relevance to a proximate rather than an ultimate scientific purpose. This represents, I believe, our actual procedure. The ordinary ' truths ' we predicate have but little concern with ultimate ends and realities. They are true (at least *pro tem.*) if they serve their immediate purpose. If any one hereafter chooses to question them he is at liberty to do so, and if he can make out his case, to reject them for their inadequacy for his ulterior purposes. But even when the venue and the context of the question have thus been changed, and so its meaning, the truth of the original answer is not thereby abolished. It may have been degraded and reduced to a methodological status, but this is merely to affirm that what is true and serviceable for one purpose is not necessarily so for another. And in any case it is time perhaps to cease complaining that a truth capable of being improved on, *i.e.* capable of *growing*, is so far not absolutely true, and therefore somewhat false and worthy of contempt. For such complaints spring from an *arbitrary* interpretation of a situation that might more sensibly be envisaged as meaning that none of the falsehoods, out of which our knowledge struggles in its growth, is ever wholly false. But in actual knowing we are not concerned with such arbitrary phrases, but with the bearing of an answer on a question actually propounded. And whatever really answers is really 'true,' even though it may at once be turned into a stepping-stone to higher truth.[1]

[1] Cp. Essay viii. § 5. If therefore we realize that we are concerned with human 'truth' alone, and that truth is ambiguous, there is no paradox in affirmatively answering Prof. A. E. Taylor's question (*Phil. Rev.* xiv. 268) as to whether "the truth of a newly discovered theorem is created" (it should be "made," *i.e.* out of earlier 'truth') "by the fact of its discovery." He asks "did the doctrine of the earth's motion become true when enunciated by the Pythagoreans, false again when men forgot the Pythagorean astronomy, and true a second time on the publication of the book of Copernicus?" The ambiguity in this question may be revealed by asking : 'Do you mean "true" to refer to the valuation of the *new* "truth" by us, or to the *re-valuation* of the old?' For the 'discovery' involves *both*, and both are products of human activity. If then we grant (what is, I suppose, the case) that the Pythagorean, Ptolemaic and Copernican systems represent stages in the progress of a successful calculation of celestial motions, it is clear that each of them was valued as 'true' while it seemed adequate, and revalued as 'false' when it was improved on. And 'true' in Prof. Taylor's question does not, for science, mean 'absolutely true.' The relativity of motion renders the demand for absolute answers scientifically unmeaning. As well might one ask, 'What exactly *is the* distance of the earth from the sun?' Moving bodies, measured by human instruments, have *no* fixed distance, no absolute place. The successive scientific truths about them are only *better* recalculations. Hence a very slight improvement will occasion a change in their valuation. Prof. Taylor has failed to observe that he has conceived the scientific problem too loosely in grouping together the Pythagorean and the Copernican theory as alike cases of the earth's motion. No doubt they may both be so denominated, but the scientific value of the two theories was very different, and the Ptolemaic system is intermediate in value as well as in time. He might as well have taken a more modern instance and argued that the emission theory of light was true 'all along' because the discovery of radio-activity has forced its undulatory rival to admit that light is sometimes produced by the impact of 'corpuscles.'

The reason then why it seems paradoxical to make the very existence of truth depend on its 'discovery' by us, is that in *some* cases there ensues upon the discovery a transvaluation of our former values, which are now re-valued as 'false,' while the new 'truth' is *antedated* as having been true all along. This, however, is conditioned by the special character of the case, and would have been impossible but for the human attempt to verify the claim. When what is 'discovered' is gold in a rock, it is supposed to have been there 'all along' ; when it is a burglar in a house, our common-sense rejects such antedating. So the whole distinction remains *within* the human evaluation of truth, and affords no occasion for attributing to 'truth' any real independence of human cognition : the attempt to do so really misrepresents our procedure ; it is a mere error of abstraction to think that because a 'truth' may be judged 'independent' *after* human manipulation, it is so *per se*, irrespectively of the procedure to which it owes its 'independent' existence. And to infer further that therefore logic should wholly abstract from the human side in knowing, is exactly like arguing that because children grow 'independent' of their parents, they must be conceived as essentially independent, and must have been so 'all along.'

V

We now find ourselves in a position to lay down some Humanist definitions. Truth we may define as logical value, and a claim to truth as a claim to possess such value. The validation of such claims proceeds, we hold, by the pragmatic test, *i.e.* by experience of their effect upon the bodies of established truth which they affect. It is evident that in this sense truth will admit of degrees, extending from the humble truth which satisfies *some* purpose, even though it only be the lowly purpose of some subordinate end, to that ineffable ideal which would satisfy *every* purpose and unify all endeavours. But the main emphasis will clearly fall on the former : for to perfect truth we do not yet attain, and after all even the humblest truth may hold its ground without suffering rejection. No truth, moreover, can do more than do its duty and fulfil its function.

These definitions should have sufficiently borne out the claim made at the beginning (p. 142), that the pragmatic view of truth unifies experience and rationalizes the classification of the normative sciences ; but it may not be amiss to add a few words on both these topics. That, in the first place, the conception of the logical judgment as a form of valuation connects it with our other valuations, and represents it as an integral part of the ἔφεσις τοῦ ἀγαθοῦ, of the purposive reaction upon the universe which bestows dignity and grandeur upon the struggle of human life is, I take it, evident. The theoretic importance of this conception is capital. It is easily and absolutely fatal to every form of Naturalism. For if every 'fact' upon which any naturalistic system relies is at bottom a valuation, arrived at by selection from a larger whole, by rejection of what seemed irrelevant, and by purposive manipulation of what seemed important, there is a manifest absurdity in eliminating the human reference from results which have implied it at every step. The Humanist doctrine, therefore, affords a protection

against Naturalism which ought to be the more appreciated
by those interested in taking a 'spiritual' view of life now
that it has become pretty clear that the protection
afforded by idealistic absolutism is quite illusory. For
the 'spiritual nature of the Absolute' does nothing to
succour the human aspirations strangled in the coils of
materialism : 'absolute spirit' need merely be conceived
naturalistically to become as impotent to aid the theologian
and the moralist as it has long been seen to be to help
the scientist.[1]

The unification of logic with the other normative
sciences is even more valuable practically than theoretically. For it vindicates man's right to present his claims
upon the universe in their integrity, as a demand not for
Truth alone, but for Goodness, Beauty, and Happiness as
well, commingled with each other in a fusion one and
indiscerptible ; and what perhaps is for the moment more
important still, it justifies our efforts to bring about such
a union as we desire. Whether this ideal can be
attained cannot, of course, be certainly predicted ; but
a philosophy which gives us the right to aspire, and
inspires us with the daring to attempt, is surely a
great improvement on monisms which, like Spinoza's,
essay to crush us with blank and illogical denials of
the relevance of human valuations to the truth of
things.

In technical philosophy, however, it is good form to
profess more interest in the formal relations of the
sciences than in the cosmic claims and destinies of man,
and so we may hasten to point out the signal aid which
Humanism affords to a symmetrical classification of the
sciences. If truth also is a valuation, we can understand
why logic should attempt normative judgments, like ethics
and æsthetics : if all the natural sciences make use of
logical judgments and lay claim to logical values, we can
understand also how and why the normative sciences
should have dominion over them. And lastly, we find
that the antithetical valuations and the distinction

[1] Essay xii. § 5.

between claims and their selection into norms run through all the normative sciences in a perfectly analogous way. Just as not everything is true which claims truth, so not everything is good or right or beautiful which claims to be so, while ultimately all these claims are judged by their relation to the perfect harmony which forms our final aspiration.

VI

This essay was pledged at the outset to conclude with a twofold challenge, and now that it has set forth some of the advantages proffered by the pragmatic view of truth, we must revert to this challenge, in a spirit not of contentiousness so much as of anxious inquiry. For it is to be feared that a really resolute adherent of the intellectualist tradition would be unmoved and unconvinced by anything we, or any one, could say. He would simply close his eyes and seal his ears, and recite his creed. And perhaps no man yet was ever convinced of philosophic truth against his will. But there are beginning to be signs (and even wonders) that our intellectualism is growing less resolute. So perhaps even those who are not yet willing to face the new solutions can be brought to see the gaps in the old. If therefore we bring these to their notice very humbly, but very persistently, we may enable them to see that the old intellectualism has left its victims unprovided with answers to two momentous questions. Let us ask, therefore, how, upon its assumptions, they propose (1) to evaluate a claim to truth, and (2) to discriminate between such a claim and an established truth? These two questions constitute the first part of my challenge. They are, clearly, good questions, and such that from any theory of knowledge with pretensions to completeness an answer may fairly be demanded. And if such an answer exists, it is so vital to the whole case of intellectualism, that we may fairly require it to be produced. If it is not produced, we will be patient, and hope that some day we may be vouchsafed a revelation of

esoteric truth ; but human nature is weak, and the longer
the delay the stronger will grow the suspicion that there
is nothing to produce.

The second part of our challenge refers to the intellectualist's rejection of our solution. If we are so very
wrong in our very plain and positive assertion that the
truth (validity) of a truth (claim) is tested and established
by the value of its consequences, there ought surely to be
no difficulty about producing abundant cases in which the
truth (validity) of a doubtful assertion is established in
some *other* way. I would ask, therefore, for the favour
of *one clear case of this kind*.[1] And I make only one
stipulation. It should be a case in which there really
was a question, so that the *true* answer might have, before
examination, turned out *false*. For without this proviso
we should get no illustration of actual knowing, such as
was contemplated by the pragmatist, whose theory professes to discriminate cases in which there is a real
chance of acquiring truth and a real risk of falling into
falsity. If on the other hand specimens merely of
indubitable or verbal truths were adduced, and it were
asserted that these were true not because they were
useful, but simply because they were true, we should end
merely in a wrangle about the historical pedigree of the
truth. We should contend that it was at one time doubtful,
and accepted as true because of its tested utility : our
opponent would dispute our derivation and assert that it
had always been true. We should agree that it was *now*
indisputable, we should disagree about the origin of this
feature ; and the past history would usually be too little
known to establish either view. And so we should get
no nearer to a settlement.

By observing on the other hand *truth in the making*,
inferences may be drawn to the nature of truth *already
made*. And whether truth is by nature pragmatic, or
whether this is a foul aspersion on her character, it is

---

[1] Prof. Taylor attempted to answer an earlier form of this challenge in *Mind*,
N.S. No. 57. My reply in N.S. No. 59, entitled ' Pragmatism and Pseudo-
Pragmatism,' showed that he had misunderstood even the elementary ' principle
of Peirce.'

surely most desirable that this point should be settled. Hitherto the chief obstacle to such a decision has been the fact that while in public (and still more in private) there has been much misconception, misrepresentation and abuse of our views, there have been no serious attempts to contest directly, unequivocally, and outright, *any* of our cardinal assertions.[1] And what perhaps is still more singular, our critics have been completely reticent as to what alternative solutions to the issues raised they felt themselves in a position to propound. They have not put forward either any account of truth which can be said ultimately to have a meaning, or one that renders it possible to discriminate between the 'true' and the 'false.' The whole situation is so strange, and so discreditable to the *prestige* of philosophy, that it is earnestly to be hoped that of the many renowned logicians who so vehemently differ from us some should at length see (and show us!) their way to refute these 'heresies,' as clearly and articulately as their θυμοειδές [2] permits their φιλόσοφον,[2] and as boldly as their φιλόσοφον permits their θυμοειδές, to express itself.

[1] Prof. Taylor has now supplied this desideratum, by denying that psychology has any relevance to logic (*Phil. Rev.* xiv. pp. 267, 287). Yet immediately after (p. 287) he feels constrained to argue that the efficient cause of his accepting any belief as true is a specific form of emotion ! Surely the fact that no truth can be accepted without this feeling constitutes a pretty substantial connexion between psychology and logic. Cp. Essay ii'.

[2] The 'spirited' and 'philosophic' parts of the soul, according to Plato.

VI

THE NATURE OF TRUTH[1]

ARGUMENT

I. The making of ideals is vain if they are divorced from human life. II. Mr. Joachim's abstraction from the human side of truth. III. The consequent failure of his 'ideal.' IV. Truth and error in the Hegelian 'Dialectic.' The 'concrete' universal really abstract. Scientific 'laws' truly concrete and not timeless, as alleged. The chasm between the human and the ideal in intellectualist epistemology. V. Contrast with the Humanist solution. The 'correspondence' and the 'independence' view of truth. Both are inevitable for intellectualism, as is the scepticism in which they end.

I

OF all the animals that creep and breathe upon the earth man is the most iconoclastic—because he is also the most iconoplastic. He is ever engaged in forming ideals for his delectation and worship, and continually discovering his worship to be idolatry and shattering his own creations.

The reason for this absurdly wasteful procedure is always the same. The ideal has been constructed, the idol has been set up, too uncritically. Too little care has been devoted to the foundations of the ideal to build upon them an enduring structure. The requirements which an ideal must satisfy have been ignored. Yet these requirements are simple. They may be formulated as follows :—

1. The ideal must be attainable by a thought which starts from our actual human standpoint.

[1] This essay appeared, as a review of Mr. H. H. Joachim's book with the same title, in the *Journal of Philosophy*, iii. 20 (27th Sept. 1906). It has been somewhat expanded.

2. When constructed it must be relevant to actual human life.

3. The ideal must be realizable by the development of man's actual life.

4. Yet it must have 'independent' authority over actual human life. Or, more briefly, the ideal must (*a*) *be an ideal for man*, and yet (*b*) *have authority over man*.

Unless the first condition is complied with, it is evident that the ideal will be the arbitrary creation of a fancy which uses the actual only as a jumping-off place into cloudlands and dreamlands. And any ideal, which is arrived at thus *per saltum*, is bound to reveal its illusory nature so soon as an attempt is made to *get back* from the ideal to the actual, *i.e.* to *apply* the ideal to human life. We then find that we *cannot* get back from the standpoint of the ideal; with its glamour in our eyes the actual seems hideous and distorted, alien and unintelligible. Whereat, enraged, we may feel tempted to pronounce, not the ideal, but the actual, radically false and vicious, and to build out our 'ideal' into a veritable paradise of fools.

Unless the second condition is complied with, our ideal becomes non-functional, and therefore really meaningless. A real ideal for man must be applicable to the world of man's experience. An ideal which is not so applicable is no ideal for man, even though it might entrance angels and redeem Absolutes. And clearly an ideal which has been reached by a jump is pretty certain to prove thus inapplicable. As it was not reached by a gradual approach from the actual, it cannot return to the actual world and enlighten its gropings. It owed its being to invalid fancy; it owes its application to an irrational fiat.

Unless the third condition is complied with the ideal loses its compelling power. The impossible is no source of obligation, no centre of attraction : nor is it rational to aim at its attainment. The notion that an ideal would not be an ideal if it were realizable, is a false inference from the fact that ideals are progressive, and expand as actuality approaches the level of what once seemed the ideal. It overlooks the fact that throughout this whole process the ideal has to be conceived as essentially realizable. If this belief in its possibility failed us, our devotion would at once be stultified.

It is, however, to the fourth condition that the other three have usually been sacrificed. Ideals have been unnaturally projected into a non-human sphere, they have been rendered inefficacious and impossible by being dissociated from human life, in order to guarantee their independence and to enhance their authority. That this procedure is self-defeating has already been explained. It may be shown also to rest on radically false conceptions of the authority and 'independence' of ideals. Their 'authority' must not be conceived as imposed on man; it must be freely constituted and recognized by him. Nor can their 'independence' be conceived as absolute; it cannot mean absence of relation to human life. It can at most be relative, a tentative simplification of the actual facts, an exclusion of this or that unimportant circumstance, of this or that discrepant desire, of this or that discordant claim. But to set up an ideal *wholly* independent of terrestrial conditions, human psychology, and individual claims, to argue that because experience shows that *some* such features may be set aside, all may in a body be excluded *a priori*, seems merely to exemplify the fallacy of 'composition.' It should never be forgotten that in any actually working ideal the 'independence' is functional, and strictly limited to the sense and extent which its efficacy requires.

II

These reflections have not been wholly inspired by Mr. Joachim's interesting and instructive essay, but they find in it abundant illustration. It is always an affecting spectacle to behold the good man conscientiously practising the idol-breaking art upon the idols of his soul, but the total failure of Mr. Joachim's investigation of the nature of truth, which he himself confesses in such handsome terms (pp. 171-180), might have been predicted by any one who had examined the functioning of human ideals.

Mr. Joachim has courted failure by the fundamental assumptions which pervade his ideal of Truth.

(1) He has assumed that the 'Critical' question is out of date. Nowhere does he betray any consciousness of the need for asking, 'How can I know all this that I have assumed? How are the facts assumed compatible with my knowing them?' He has not in consequence raised the question how his ideal was arrived at.

(2) He has thereby been enabled to assume an impossible standpoint, without realizing until it was too late that nothing could be said from it that was in the least degree relevant to the facts of human life. Assuming that 'the nature of truth' concerned "the character of an ideally complete experience," and not the actual procedures of human minds, he inevitably lays it down that "there can be one *and only one* such experience: or only one significant whole the significance of which is self-contained in the sense required. For it is absolute self-fulfilment, *absolutely* self-contained significance, that is postulated ; and nothing short of absolute individuality— nothing short of *the* completely whole experience—can satisfy this postulate. And human knowledge, not merely *my* knowledge or *yours*, but the best and fullest knowledge in the world at any stage of its development—is clearly not a significant whole in this ideally complete sense. Hence the truth is—*from the point of view of the human intelligence*—an Ideal, and an Ideal which can never *as such*, or in its completeness, be actual as human experience."[1]

(3) Having assumed such an ideal, he is compelled to abstract, as far as possible, from everything human, real, and concrete. But ultimately this abstraction proves

---

[1] Pp. 78-9. The ideal described is clearly not an ideal for man. And, naturally, Mr. Joachim finds the resources of human language inadequate to describe it. So on p. 83 *n.* he declares that though he calls it 'experience,' the word is 'unsatisfactory,' and only used because 'God' would be 'misleading,' and 'the Absolute' and 'the Idea' have become bywords.

impracticable, and when at last his conception of truth is brought into contact with the fact of human error, its breakdown is as irretrievable as it was inevitable : for it is the collapse into its interior emptiness of the bubble of a false ideal under pressure from the real it had scouted.

That Mr. Joachim has really made all these assumptions can be made plain in his own words. He thus describes on p. 178 his assumption of the standpoint " That the truth itself is one and whole and complete, and that all thinking and all experience moves within its recognition and subject to its manifest authority ; this I have never doubted." Perhaps if he had been more willing, not necessarily to doubt, but, let us say, to examine, this assumption, he would not have been forced to doubt so much in the end. For it was decidedly uncritical thus to rule out the question of whence came the features in the ideal he postulated. It was also by definition that he had ruled out the conception of truth as a *human* ideal. Hence it was quite superfluous to state in the preface that he was not going to discuss the Humanist conception of truth. He could not : from his point of view the Humanist position was invisible, and was bound to seem " a denial of truth altogether."

From Mr. Joachim's standpoint human knowing could not possibly appear as anything but an inexplicable falling away from the serenity, purity, and perfection of 'the Ideal,' as a chaos of 'unreal abstractions' which it is his duty 'to do his best to discredit' (p. 59). Or, as he says more fully (pp. 167-8), " The differences of *this* and *that* knowing mind—*a fortiori*, the confused mass of idiosyncrasies which together distinguish *this* 'person' or 'self' from *that*—are recognized only to be set aside and, if necessary, discounted. They are accidental imperfections, superficial irregularities, in the medium through which truth is reflected ; limitations in the vessels through which knowledge is poured. They are, so to say, bubbles on the stream of knowledge ; and the passing show of arbitrary variation, which they create on the surface, leaves the depths untroubled—a current uniform and timeless. My and your thinking, my and your self, the particular temporal processes, and the extreme self-substantiation of the finite 'modes' which is error in its full discordance : these are incidents somehow [1] connected with the known truth, but they themselves and the manner of their connexion are excluded from the theory of knowledge." [2]

The theory of knowledge, then, " studies the known truth *qua* timeless and universal " (p. 168), and the judgments of science cannot be "concerned with the concrete thinking of the individual mind *qua* 'this' or 'that,' *qua* differentiated by the idiosyncrasies developed through its particular psychological history" (p. 93), "in all the accidental and confused psychical setting " (p. 115).

Or lastly and most frankly (p. 118), " I do not inquire how the logician can pass from the 'psychological individual' to the 'logical subject,' from *this* actual thinking (with all its psychical machinery and particular setting) to the thought which claims truth as affirming universal meaning. The logician, I am convinced, never really starts with *this individual thinker* in the sense supposed ; and, if he did, the passage from this psychological fiction to the subject of knowledge would be impossible."

It is clear that Mr. Joachim at any rate has never started with 'this individual thinker,' but equally so

---

[1] The magic word, to which the logic, like the metaphysic, of intellectualism always in the end appeals, when its false abstractions fail ! A critic's brutal candour is tempted to substitute Humpty Dumpty's favourite word 'Nohow !' in all such passages.

[2] Mr. Joachim has protested against my use of this passage in *Mind*, N.S. No. 63, p. 412, and declared that it expresses a view he is attacking. It is true that as a whole he does not seem entirely satisfied with it, but I cannot see that any injustice was done him by quoting part of it as illustrating a general difficulty which is common to him and it. His (very friendly) 'attack' on it appears to concern only a part I did *not* quote, viz. the verbal question whether what has got into a mess is to be called 'metaphysics' or 'theory of knowledge,' and if the latter, whether 'metaphysics' may be invoked to come to the rescue. He rightly objects that the difficulty cannot be evaded thus. But on the main question I was illustrating from him, as to how terrestrial error is compatible with the celestial 'ideal,' he merely remarks (p. 169) that "we must be able to show *both* the extreme opposition *and* the overcoming of it, as essential moments in that self-fulfilment." Aye, but what is this but an unfulfilled postulate on his own showing ?

that he never gets to him. He has, like Plato, assumed his 'logical' standpoint, and never doubts, even when it proves unworkable, that the discrepancy of psychical fact is mere irrelevance and confusion. "We have been demanding all along," he says (p. 82), "an entire reversal of this attitude" (of starting from the actual). "In our view it is the Ideal which is solid and substantial and fully actual. The finite experiences are rooted in the Ideal. They share its actuality[1] and draw from it whatever being and conceivability they possess. It is a perverse attitude to condemn the Ideal because the conditions under which finite experiences exhibit their fragmentary activity do not as such restrict its being, or to deny that it is conceivable, because the conceivability of such incomplete expressions is too confused and turbid to apply to it."

III

What, then, is this standpoint of the Ideal? Page 76 tells us that "Truth in its essential nature is that systematic coherence which is the character of a significant whole. A 'significant whole' is an organized individual experience, self-fulfilling and self-fulfilled. Its organization *is* the process of its self-fulfilment, and the concrete manifestation of its individuality."

Brave words, if only the standpoint of 'the Ideal' could be maintained, if only the 'individual thinker' could be wholly dismissed from the inquiry! Unluckily he cannot.

The tree of knowledge cannot be guarded against human profanation, even in the logician's paradise, once it is 'somehow' revealed to man. Nay, the logician is ultimately driven out by the diabolical machinations of "the dual nature of human experience," which has "its universality and independence and yet also its individuality and its dependence on personal and private conditions" (p. 29). "Truth, beauty, goodness are timeless, universal,

---

[1] This is how Mr. Joachim glides over the 'participation' difficulty. Plato at least perceived its seriousness.

independent structures ; and yet also it is essential to them to be manifested in the thinking of finite subjects, in the actions and volitions of perishing agents " (p. 163). They "appear in the actual world and exist in finite experience . . . and their life (at least on one side of itself) is judgment, emotion, volition—the processes and activities of finite individuals. Truth, if it is to be *for me*, must enter into my intellectual endeavour," however 'independent' it is "of the process by which *I* come to know it " (p. 21).

No wonder 'human experience' is 'paradoxical' (p. 23), and that in the end its 'dual nature' is too much for 'the Ideal'! It has no room for Error ; and yet Error inexplicably exists. Thus Error becomes the "declaration of independence" of the finite, something utterly 'unthinkable' "where that which declares is nothing real and nothing real is declared " (p. 163).

So 'the Ideal of coherence' "suffers shipwreck at the very entrance of the harbour " (p. 171). " It must render intelligible 'the dual nature of human experience'" (p. 170) ; it fails to meet 'demands' which "both *must be* and *cannot be* completely satisfied " (p. 171). The whole "voyage ends in disaster, and a disaster which is inevitable " (p. 171).

It would be ungenerous in those who declined to commit themselves to the ill-found craft which Mr. Joachim has gallantly navigated to foredoomed failure to crow over this catastrophe ;[1] but it is permissible to point out *why* it was inevitable from the start.

The whole ideal, despite its protestations of 'concreteness' and aspirations towards a 'self-fulfilling individuality,' rested all along on an unjustified abstraction from the most essential features of the only knowledge and truth we are able or concerned to attain and examine. As Prof. Stout says,[2] "The only knowing with which we are primarily acquainted is knowing on the part of individuals,

---

[1] But in view of it Mr. Bradley's boasting about the security of 'Jericho' seems particularly misplaced ! Cp. Essay iv. § 5.

[2] *Arist. Soc. Proc.* 1905-6, p. 350.

of empirical, historical selves." All actual truth is human, all actual knowing is pervaded through and through by the purposes, interests, emotions, and volitions of a human personality. Mr. Joachim had no right to treat these facts as distorting disturbances : they are the roots of the tree of knowledge. He had no right to treat knowledge as if it were impersonal : the 'personal equation' is never really eliminated even in science,[1] and in philosophy the attempt to abstract from its all-pervasive influence stands self-condemned. He had no right to assume that to take our knowledge in its full concreteness would be fatal to its 'objectivity'; he should have studied how men proceed from individual judgments to social agreements about truth, and ultimately construct ideals which are intended to guide our aspirations, but are at once bereft of their significance when they lose touch with human knowing.

Mr. Joachim has had, of course, to pay the penalty of these uncritical assumptions. He has failed to describe anything at all resembling the actual processes of human knowing. He has failed equally to portray the operations of science. He has failed even to render his abstract ideal self-supporting : it crumbles under its own weight ; for all its claim to absoluteness it possesses no authority ; for all its aspirations to 'coherence' it does not cohere, even in itself.

These defects, moreover, are closely intertwined. Because he has assumed the absolute standpoint and abstracted from the personal context of every judgment, he can never seize the actual meaning of any judgment. He cannot see that it lies in the use of the judgment, in its relation to a cognitive end, in its adjustment to a particular case, in its satisfaction of a need. By ignoring (what is obvious from the opposite point of view) that meaning depends on purpose and demands application, he has restricted himself to potential meaning, and moves in a world of impotent phantoms. It is only in such a phantasmagoria of depersonalized, hypostasized abstrac-

---

[1] Compare my discussion of another paper by Mr. Joachim in *Mind*, No. 71, pp. 404-5.

tions that truth can appear timeless and unalterable, that judgments can *bear meaning* in isolation (p. 90), and *are* possessed of a 'truth' which *they* 'affirm' and 'demand' (pp. 108-9), that thoughts move and live and expand out of space and time (p. 176).

But these are all illusions incidental to an impracticable standpoint, and the whole Witches' Sabbath of the Hegelian Dialectic is really started by the wanton and impossible dehumanizing of knowledge.

IV

The Hegelian Dialectic is essentially an attempt to determine the concatenation of meanings *per se* and in abstraction from their application and actual function, and in a sense the culmination of all such attempts. But it fails because it too has not realized that *per se* 'categories' do not mean anything, and that the meaning of a càtegory lies in the purpose with which it is employed. Hegel had perceived—and it is greatly to his credit that he should have done so—that taken *per se* the 'higher' abstractions were also the emptier : thus in the 'philosophic' (*i.e.* abstract) contemplation of thought there seemed to occur a progressive loss of meaning, a gradual evisceration of content, until the highest 'category' of all, 'Being,' appeared to be *de facto* indistinguishable from 'nothing.' Seeing that this was wrong, Hegel set himself to find a remedy for this disease of thought, and prescribed his 'Dialectic' as the way by which thought might return to the concreteness of 'spirit.' He perceived, that is, that the concrete is really higher than the abstract, and so demanded that a universal which was to be really valuable should be conceived as 'concrete' The 'concrete universal' is thus a demand for a something to rectify the error of abstraction. But unfortunately it does not go far enough. For Hegel did not see (1) that his problem was unreal ; and (2) that his solution of it was illusory.

(1) The disease of thought which Hegel undertook to

cure does not really exist : it is a figment of the philosophers, the product of a defective analysis of actual human
knowing.   If we refrain from abstracting from the actual
functioning of thought, there is no need to evolve a
concrete universal, by the convolutions of the Dialectic.
For in their actual use all universals are concrete.   For
they are applied to a concrete situation.   And this is as
true of ' Being ' as of ' Spirit.'   Whenever we actually
have occasion to predicate ' being,' *i.e.* to include anything
in that *summum genus*, we *mean to relate it to the concrete
whole of reality*, not to include it in an empty category.
And if the purpose of the train of thought which led to
the predication had not been abstracted from, this would
have been evident throughout.   All abstractions are made
for a purpose, and are meant to be applied, and recover
full concreteness in their power over the particular cases
of their application.   Their ' abstractness,' therefore, constitutes no problem for a humanist theory of knowledge,
and the ' error of abstraction ' is cured simply by a
perception of the use of abstraction.

(2) Even if Hegel's difficulty had not been one of
those which one gets out of by never getting into, his
' concrete universal ' is no way out of it.   In its unapplied
condition, it is *never* fully concrete.   The ' Dialectic ' no
more gets back to the concrete individual, from which
the (purposive) process of abstraction started, than the
Platonic Idea.   It stops short with the ' category ' of
' Spirit,' and *assumes* that it applies to reality and cannot
be misapplied.   But its *application* to concrete ' spirits ' is
the real problem, seeing that an inapplicable ' category ' is
plainly unmeaning.   Of this problem the Dialectic is no
solution ; indeed, it does not even suspect its existence.
Hence the ' concrete universal's ' claim to be concrete,
is a mere ' bluff.'   It is and remains a rank abstraction, because it has not comprehended the function of
abstractions.   It has abstracted from the personal aspects
of the knowing process, without perceiving that in so
doing it has abolished its own *raison d'être*.   Nor is it
what it pretends to be in other respects.   It is not even a

true universal, because it has no power over particulars ;
and for all its theoretical assurances, in practice it repels
them as confusing and irrational. Whereas *the 'universals'
which are really functional and are used in actual knowing
are always particulars, i.e.* they are *applied* to a '*this*' in a
'*here*' and '*now*.'

Hence the Hegelian 'universal' never occurs either in
ordinary or in scientific knowing. The 'universals'
('laws') of the sciences live only in their application to
particular cases ; they try to formulate the habits of
things, and are intended to be rules which guide us in our
treatment of them. It is, therefore, the less important
half of the truth to assert (p. 110) that "scientific thought
moves in universals" and that "in the science of botany
a judgment of perception like 'this tree is green' finds,
as such, no place."   For in reality the universals are
applied universals, and the science of botany would be
valueless if it did not deal with the behaviour of particular
trees, nor would it value the more abstract judgments if
they did not show their *pragmatic power* by applying
to a greater number of 'particulars.' Our scientific procedure, in short, gives no sanction whatever to the
notion that universals which cannot be applied have
any value, and the alleged 'eternity' of scientific truth
is merely an illusion engendered by the abstraction from
purpose.[1]

The Hegelian 'universal,' however, not merely misrepresents the scientific 'law,' it no less distorts our vision
of the 'particular.'   An abstraction itself, it constructs
the bogey of 'the individual mind,' presumably in order
that something more monstrous than itself may deter us
from acknowledging plain facts. But its 'individual
mind' is a figment, formed by expunging all values from
the concrete mind.[2] In actual minds the values are all
present, *as psychical facts*, with the ideals and the idiosyn-

[1] As Prof. Hoernle neatly says, "Science only formulates its conceptions and
laws apart from their temporal setting in any given case, that it may be the
better able to understand and control the succession of phenomena in time"
(*Mind*, xiv. 329). Cp. *Humanism*, pp. 103-5 ; *Formal Logic*, ch. xxi.
[2] Cp. Essay iii. § 14.

crasies, all capable of contributing harmoniously to the conservation of the individual life.[1]

There is no occasion or temptation, therefore, to oppose ' particular' to ' universal,' and to reject any of the mind's actual contents as ' accidental,' ' irrelevant,' or ' confused.' For one, that is, who really starts from the ' finite experiences.' But it is only an amiable delusion of Mr. Joachim's to imagine that he has tried to do so (p. 115). His assumption of ' the Ideal' has really incapacitated him from describing human experience as it is. He has in reality dissevered it into a part which is (to his thinking) superhuman, and another which is despicable, if not bestial. But the two will not cohere, nor even come into contact, and between them his theory of knowledge founders.

In other words, Mr. Joachim has contrived to reopen an old wound that was never really healed. In every absolutist theory of knowledge, when it is really thought out to the end, there is and must be a dualistic chasm gaping between the ' human' and the ' absolute' aspects of truth. Across this chasm there is no bridge; but the mystic often fancies that he can be wafted across it on the wings of desire. Mr. Joachim is too sceptical and too honest to play such tricks, but the old mistakes have conducted him to the old *impasse*. Once more the ideal has been severed from its roots in the real ; once more it has been incited to transcend our experience ; once more it has refused to return to earth and to redeem it. It is vain to protest (p. 62) that a "universal is not another entity existing alongside of its particulars." He himself has made it such, by refusing to conceive it as human and as humanly inhabiting them.

If he will not conceive the universal as a human instrument, as existing in and for its use, if he will insist that it must be ' independent,' it *must* be so exalted as to lose all real significance for us. Thus the old Aristotelian protest against the Platonic Idea has still to be reiterated against the Hegelian universal. If it holds aloof from

[1] Cp. Essay iii. § 3.

human knowing, it manifestly fails, because it becomes a vain duplication, which has no meaning or interest for us : if it essays to dea! with human knowing, it becomes an inhuman monster which tries to absorb the human and, still more manifestly, fails, and then revenges itself by abusing and depreciating us. In neither case can the human and the ideal be harmoniously combined, or their ' duality ' overcome. But this duality was produced by the initial assumption of a non-human standpoint ; if the inquiry had commenced by investigating how ' truths ' are verified and errors detected, no ' duality ' need ever have arisen to bar the way.[1]

V

To discuss Mr. Joachim's standpoint really implies the highest praise that could be bestowed on Mr. Joachim's essay. For it means that having assumed it, he has worked out its implications with consistency and rigour to the bitter end. Indeed, it seems that of all the writers of the ' Anglo-Hegelian ' school he has most firmly grasped their central problem, most honestly faced their difficulties, most clearly shown what their doctrines really mean and to what they really lead. That his conclusions should be welcome to all (or even to any) of the members of the school is not, perhaps, to be expected ; but it is no slight service to philosophy to have set the issue in so clear a light. Other philosophers, who stand remote enough to enjoy the light of Mr. Joachim's criticism without being scorched by its fire, will appreciate that service at its true value. Humanists, in particular, will derive much instruction from the uncompromising expression Mr. Joachim has given to an attitude diametrically opposed to theirs. They will note with satisfaction how close is the parallel, and how complete the antithesis, between him and them on all essential points, and regard this as testimony to the inner consistency

[1] Cp. for all this the argument in Essays ii. §§ 16-18, and iii. §§ 17-18.

of rival views whose divergence springs from different answers to the same question.   They will rejoice that Mr. Joachim has unequivocally expressed a multitude of notions they had long suspected their opponents of harbouring, and desired to see stated in cold print.   Nor will they regret the negative outcome of Mr. Joachim's labours.   On the contrary, the more extensively it is recognized as the final breakdown of intellectualistic attempts to explain 'how knowledge is possible' without regard to the actual functioning of knowledge in human life, the better they will be pleased.

In view of the fundamental value of Mr. Joachim's work it seems ungracious to allude to secondary blemishes. But it is a pity that instead of starting from the simplest form of the 'correspondence-with-reality' view of truth, he has altogether omitted to consider it.   For it is in its *sensationalistic* form, as referring thoughts to the test of perceptions, that this view is most plausible and least inadequate.   Indeed, apart from ulterior interpretations, it is plainly descriptive of processes which actually occur in our knowing, and is not so much false as incomplete. It ordinarily means no more than that when our judgments anticipate perceptions, the perceptions do not belie them.

Again, one feels that the most consistent attempt to work out the notion of the 'independence' of reality on intellectualistic lines, viz. that made by Messrs. Bertrand Russell and G. E. Moore, is rejected rather than refuted on pp. 51-55.   At any rate the objections urged against the theory seem to press equally upon that to which, in spite of its collapse, Mr. Joachim remains attached : the fundamental assumption is the same for both, viz. that experiencing *ought not* to make a difference to the 'facts' ; so is their fundamental difficulty, that of getting this 'independent' truth into relation with human minds after it has been postulated.   Now such a relation *has* to be conceived as a 'correspondence' somehow ;[1] and so it would seem that in criticizing the correspondence

[1] Cp. Essay iv. § 7.

notion Mr. Joachim has once more refuted his own assumptions.[1]

This, indeed, would seem to be the conclusion of the whole matter: when we find the logic of Mr. Joachim and Mr. Russell failing just where that of Plato had failed in the *Theaetetus*, viz. over the existence of error, and failing just for the same reason, viz. on account of its wanton abstraction from the human knowing which falls into error, failing just where that of Mr. Bradley had failed, failing just where its failure was predicted;[2] when we find logicians unable to account for the empirical fact of knowledge, and plunging deeper and deeper into the quicksands of scepticism the more they try to explain it, when inference becomes a 'paradox' and a mystery exceeding those of theology, when our reasoning has to be treated as either 'irrational' or extra-logical, and when we contrast the fact to which Prof. A. W. Moore has justly drawn attention,[3] that all the time our actual knowledge is growing and progressively ameliorating the lot of man, is it not high time that we should stop and bethink ourselves of a possible alternative to a course which is both fatal and ridiculous? Has not the time come when Kant's 'Copernican change of standpoint' might at last be put into practice seriously, and when Truth, instead of being offered up to idols and sacrificed to 'ideals,' might at length be depicted in her human beauty and simplicity?

[1] Of course the problem has, in both cases, been wrongly formulated. Instead of asking, 'How can our judgments reveal independent facts?' we ought to have inquired when and why and in virtue of what *intrinsic* peculiarities, *some* of our judgments have this transcendent 'reference to an independent fact' ascribed to them. It would then appear that the reason is pragmatic: those judgments refer to 'independent facts' which have reached (relative) stability and pragmatic trustworthiness.

[2] Cp. *Humanism* p. 18 and *Essays* §§ 0 5

[3] *The Functional versus the Representational Theory of Knowledge in Locke's Essay*, ch. i.

VII

THE MAKING OF TRUTH

ARGUMENT

§ 1. The problem of relating 'truth' to 'fact.' Difficulties of conceiving 'fact' as 'independent' of our knowing : (*a*) The paradoxes of realism ; (*b*) the additional contradictions of rationalism. The old assumptions to be given up. (1) *Truth is human* ; (2) *fact is not 'independent,'* but (3) *dependent and relative to our knowing.* § 2. The problem of validating claims to truth, and avoiding error. § 3. Actual knowing our starting-point : its seven features dominated by the *pragmatic test of truth.* § 4. The fact of previous knowledge. § 5. The acceptance of a basis of fact. The ambiguity of fact : 'real' fact evolved from 'primary,' by a process of *selection.* Individual variations as to acceptance of fact. Fact never merely objective. § 6. The problem of 'objectivity.' It does not = unpleasantness. Pragmatic recognition of 'unpleasant fact' and its motives. § 7. The place of interest and purpose in our knowing. 'Goods' and 'ends.' § 8. The validation of a claim by its consequences. § 9. (*a*) Complete success ; (*b*) partial and conditional success leading to methodological or practical 'truth' ; (*c*) failure, to be variously explained. § 10. The growth of knowledge a growth of efficiency as well as of 'system,' but 'system' tested by its efficiency. § 11. The making of truth in its application to the future and the past. Antedating and re-valuing of truth. Can all truth be conceived as 'made'? Difficulties. No 'creation out of nothing.' The problems of 'previous knowledge' and 'acceptance of fact.' § 12. The 'previous knowledge' to be treated pragmatically. Uselessness of fundamental truths which cannot be known. § 13. The 'making of truth' *ipso facto* a 'making of reality' : (*a*) beliefs, ideas, and desires, as real forces shaping the world ; (*b*) the efficacy of ideals ; (*c*) the dependence of 'discovery' upon endeavour. § 14. The further analysis of the factual basis is really metaphysics, and pragmatic method need not be carried so far. Conflict between the pragmatic value (1) of the real world of common-sense, and (2) of the making of truth. But (2) is of superior authority because (1) is a pragmatic construction. Also the real making of reality may be analogous to our own.

§ 1. THE problem of 'the making of truth' issues from the epistemological situation of the day at two points. It arises out of two burning questions—(1) how 'truth' is related to 'fact'; and (2) how 'truth' is discriminated from 'error,' or how 'claims' to truth are 'validated.'

On both these questions we have already abundantly seen that the intellectualistic theories of knowledge have argued themselves into a complete *impasse*. They have put the questions in such a way that no answer is possible. Their 'doctrines' in the end amount merely to confessions of failure. They cannot understand how error is possible, or how, if it nevertheless exists, it can be discriminated from truth ; and the only answer they can give to the question how truth is made, is to declare that it is never really *made*, but must pre-exist ready-made as an eternal ideal (whether in a non-human mind, or a supercelestial space, or in independent being, is a matter of taste), to which our human truths have to approximate. But when it turns out *on their own showing* that the attainment of this ideal by us is eternally impossible, what option have we but to treat this answer as no answer at all?

Again, they involve themselves in insuperable difficulties as to the relation of truth to fact. They start from an uncriticized assumption that truth must be the apprehension of 'independent' fact ; but they cannot understand how 'fact' can be 'independent' of our knowing. For how, if it is in any way dependent on us, can it remain 'fact,' or 'truth' remain true? Can we *make* 'truth' and 'fact'? Away with the monstrous, impious thought! And yet it is too plain that *our human knowing* seems to do these very things. And that in what must seem to them the most dubious ways. For it employs a multitude of arbitrary processes, commended only by the psychological hold they have over our mortal nature, and, when these are abstracted from, it simply ceases to work. But how, Intellectualism must ask, can such processes be more than subjective, how dare we attribute them to an eternal mind, to an independent reality? It would be flat absurdity. But if they are merely subjective, must they not hopelessly vitiate the facts, distort the image of reality, and utterly unfit *our* 'truth' to be the passionless mirror of reality which it is assumed it has to be?

Nor does it matter from what side this puzzle is approached. If it is approached from the 'realist' side, we come upon the sheer, unmitigated, incredible paradoxes that the 'independent fact' is (1) to be known by and in a process which *ex hypothesi* it 'transcends'; (2) to be apprehended by a subjective activity which is confessed to be largely, if not wholly, arbitrary; that (3) this is to make *no difference whatsoever* to the fact; and (4) that *we are to know this also*, to know, that is, that the 'correspondence' between the 'fact,' as it is in itself and outside our knowledge, and the fact as it appears in our knowledge, is somehow perfect and complete!

If we come upon it from the absolutist side, we find an 'eternal ideal of truth' supervening upon, or perhaps taking the place of, the 'independent fact.' In the former case we have, evidently, achieved nothing but a complication of the problem. For it will now be a question how 'eternal truth' is related to 'independent fact,' and also how both of them are to be related to 'truth' and 'fact' for us. But even in the latter case there is no gain, because this ideal also is still supposed to be 'independent' of us and our doings. The difficulties, therefore, remain precisely the same. Nay, they are added to by the demand that we are to know that the 'correspondence' between the human and the ideal *must be imperfect as well as perfect*! For the ideal has been so constructed that our knowledge *cannot* fully realize it, while yet it *must* fully realize it, in order that we may assure ourselves of its 'truth,' by observing its 'correspondence' with the ideal! Absolute truth, therefore, as conceived by absolutism, is not merely *useless* as a criterion of *our* truth, because we do not possess it, and cannot compare it with our truth, nor estimate where and to what extent our truth falls short of its 'divine' archetype; it is not merely the adding of one more to the multitude of (human) truth-conceptions which have to be accommodated to one another, and out of which there has to be compounded the 'objective' truth and the 'common' world of practical life. It is positively *noxious*, actively disruptive of the whole notion of truth, and pregnant with self-destructive consequences.

Surely this situation, the development of which has been traced in Essays ii., iii., iv., §§ 3-5 and 7-8, and vi., should be painful and irrational enough to stagger even the most rationalistic faith in the sufficiency of intellectualistic assumptions, and to impel it at least to investigate the alternative conception of the problem which Pragmatism has had the boldness to propound!

To us, of course, it will be as clear as daylight that *the old assumptions are wrong*, proved to be wrong by the absurdity of their consequences, and must be given up. We shall infer frankly—(1) that whether or not we have constructed a wholly unexceptionable theory of knowledge, it is folly any longer to close one's eyes to the importance and all-pervasiveness of subjective activities in the making of truth. It must frankly be admitted that *truth is human truth*, and incapable of coming into being without human effort and agency; that human action is psychologically conditioned; that, therefore, the concrete fulness of human interests, desires, emotions, satisfactions, purposes, hopes, and fears is relevant to the theory of knowledge and must *not* be abstracted from.

(2) We shall perceive that the futile notion of a really 'independent' truth and fact, which cannot be known or related to us or to each other, even by the most gratuitous of miracles, must be abandoned. If we insist on preserving the word, it must at any rate be used no longer as a label for the problem of relating the human to a non-human which cannot possibly be related to it. It must, at least, be interpreted pragmatically, as a term which discriminates certain behaviours, which distinguishes certain valuations, *within* the cognitive process which evolves *both* 'truth' and 'fact' for man.[1]

(3) Instead of wasting our ingenuity, therefore, in

---

[1] Cp. Essay xix. § 10.

trying to unite conceptions which we have ourselves
made contradictory, let us try the alternative adventure of
a thoroughly and consistently dependent truth, dependent,
that is, on human life and ministering to its needs, made
by us and referring to our experience, and evolving
everything called 'real' and 'absolute' and 'transcendent'
immanently in the course of its cognitive functioning.
It will have at least this great initial advantage over
theories which assume an antithesis between the human
and the 'ideal' or the 'real,' that its terms will not have
to be laboriously brought into relation with each other
and with human life.

§ 2. The second question, as to how claims to have
judged 'truly' are to be made good, and how 'truth' is
to be distinguished from 'error,' raises the problem of the
'making of Truth' in a still more direct fashion. Indeed
it may in this form be said to be the pragmatic problem
par excellence, and we have already taken some steps
towards its solution. We have seen the nature of the
distinction between 'claim' and 'validity' and its importance (Essay v.). We may also take it for granted
that as there is nothing in the claim itself to tell us
whether it is valid or not (Essay iii. § 18), the validation
of claims must depend on their consequences (Essay i.).
We have also vindicated the right of our actual human
knowledge to be considered by Logic in its full concreteness (Essay iii.). We have noted, lastly, that the
collapse of the rationalistic theory of truth was to be
traced to its inveterate refusal to do this (Essays v., ii., vi.,
and iii.), and more particularly to recognize the problem
of error, and to help human reasoners to discriminate
between it and truth.

But all this is not enough to give us a positive grasp
of the making of truth. To do this we must analyse a
simple case of actual knowing in greater detail. But this
is difficult, not so much because of any intrinsic difficulty
of being aware of what we are doing, as because the contemplation of actual human knowledge has fallen into
such disuse, and the simplest facts have been translated

into the language of such weird fictions, that it is hard
to bespeak sufficient attention for what actually occurs.
Philosophers have strained their ingenuity to prove that
it is impossible, or at least indefensible, to test the simplest
truth in the most obvious manner, without dragging in
'the *a priori* Deduction of the Categories,' or the
'Dialectic of the Notion.' And all the while they are
oblivious of the very real presuppositions of our knowing,
and systematically exclude from their view the fact that
all our 'truths' occur as personal affirmations in the life
of persons practically interested to attain truth and to
avoid error. Thus, when I take some one coming
towards me from a distance to be my brother, and
subsequently perceive that he is not, this correction of a
false claim seems an act of cognition well within the
powers of any man : it seems gratuitous to regard it as a
privilege reserved for the initiates of 'the higher Logic,'
the seers of 'the Self-development of the Absolute
Idea,' while totally ignoring such facts as that I was (*a*)
anxiously expecting my brother, but also (*b*) unfortunately
afflicted with short-sightedness.

§ 3. Let us begin, then, quite simply and innocently,
with our immediate experience, with the actual knowing,
just as we find it, of our own adult minds. This proposal may seem hopelessly 'uncritical,' until we realize—
(1) that our actual minds are always the *de facto* starting-
points, from which, and with the aid of which, we *work
back* to whatever 'starting-points' we are pleased to call
'original' and 'elementary'; (2) that we always read
our actual minds into these other starting-points; (3)
that no subtlety of analysis can ever penetrate to any
principles really certain and undisputable *to start with* ;
(4) that such principles are as unnecessary as they are
impossible, but that we only need principles which will
work and grow more certain *in their use*, and that so
even initially defective principles, which are improved,
will turn out truer than the truest we could have started
with ; (5) that in all science our actual procedure is
'inductive,' experimental, postulatory, tentative, and that

the demonstrative form, into which the conclusions may afterwards be put, is merely a trophy set up to mark the victory. If we are met with reluctance to accept our contentions, let us not delay in order to argue them out, but proceed with the pragmatic confidence that, if they are provisionally assumed, the usefulness of the resulting view of knowledge will speedily establish them.

By tentatively assuming, then, this ‘common sense’ starting-point, we are enabled to observe that even one of the simplest acts of knowing is quite a complicated affair, because in it we are (1) using a mind which has had some prior experience and possesses some knowledge, and so (2) has acquired (what it greatly needs) some basis in reality, which it is *willing to accept as ‘fact*,’ because (3) it needs a ‘platform’ from which *to operate further on a situation* which confronts it, in order (4) to realize some *purpose* or to satisfy some *interest*, which defines for it an ‘end’ and constitutes for it a ‘good.’ (5) It consequently *experiments* with the situation by some voluntary interference, which may begin with a tentative predication, and proceed by reasoned inferences, but always, when completed, comes to a *decision* (judgment’) and issues in an *act*. (6) It is guided by the results (‘consequences’) of this experiment, which go to verify or to disprove its provisional basis, the initial ‘facts,’ predications, conceptions, hypotheses, and assumptions. Hence (7) if the results are satisfactory, the reasoning employed is deemed to have been *pro tanto good*, the results *right*, the operations performed *valid*, while the conceptions used and the predications made are judged *true*. Thus successful predication extends the system of knowledge and enlarges the borders of ‘fact.’ Reality is like an ancient oracle, and does not respond until it is questioned. To attain our responses we make free to use all the devices which our whole nature suggests. But when they are attained, the predications we judge to be ‘true’ afford us fresh revelations of reality. Thus Truth and Reality grow for us *together*, in a single process, which is *never* one of bringing the mind into relation with a fundamentally alien reality, but always one of improving and extending an already existing system which *we know*.

Now this whole process is clearly dominated by the *pragmatic test of truth*. The claims to truth involved are validated by their consequences when used. Thus Pragmatism as a logical method is merely the *conscious* application of a *natural* procedure of our minds in actual knowing. It merely proposes (1) to realize clearly the nature of these facts, and of the risks and gains which they involve, and (2) to simplify and reform logical theory thereby.

§ 4. We may next consider some of these points in greater detail. First as to the use of an already formed mind (§ 3 (1)). That empirically knowledge arises out of pre-existing knowledge, that we never operate with a raw and virgin mind, has been an epistemological common-place ever since it was authoritatively enunciated by Aristotle, though the paradox it involves with regard to the first beginning of knowledge has never quite been solved. For the present, however, we need only add that the development of a mind is a thoroughly *personal* affair. Potential knowledge becomes actual, because of the purposive activity of a knower who brings it to bear on his interests, and uses it to realize his ends. Knowledge does not grow by a mechanical necessity, nor by the self-development of abstract ideas in a psychological vacuum.

§ 5. Next, as to the acceptance of a basis of fact (§ 3 (2)). It is extraordinary that even the most blindly hostile critic should have supposed Pragmatism to have denied this. It has merely pointed out that the *acceptance* must not be ignored, and that it is fatal to the chimera of a 'fact' for us existing quite 'independently' of our 'will.'

It is, however, important to note the *ambiguity of* '*fact*.' (1) In the wider sense everything is 'fact,' *qua* experienced, including imaginings, illusions, errors, hallucinations. 'Fact' in this sense is anterior to the distinction of 'appearance' and 'reality,' and covers *both*. To distinguish it we may call it 'primary reality.'[1] For though it is always perceived by us in ways defined, or 'vitiated,' by our past interests and acts (individual and racial), and we are rarely conscious of all we read into our data, there is undeniably a 'given' in experience, or rather a givenness about it.   We never experience it as purely given, and the nearer it comes to this the less we value it, but in a sense this 'primary reality' is important. For it is the starting-point, and final touchstone, of all our theories *about* reality, which have for their aim its transformation.   It may, certainly, in a sense, be called 'independent' of us, if that comforts any one.   For it is certainly not 'made' by us, but 'found.'   But, as it stands, we find it most unsatisfactory and set to work to remake it and unmake it.   It is not what we mean by 'real fact' or 'true reality.'   For, as immediately experienced, it is a meaningless chaos, merely the raw material of a cosmos, the stuff out of which real fact is made. Thus the need of operating on it is the real justification of our cognitive procedures.

These make it into (2) 'fact' in the stricter and more familiar sense (with which alone scientific discussion is concerned), by processes of analysis, *selection* and *valuation*, which *segregate* the 'real' from the 'apparent' and the 'unreal.'   It is only *after* such processes have worked upon 'primary reality' that the distinction of 'appearance' and 'reality' appears, on which intellectualism seeks to base its metaphysic.   But it has failed to observe that the ground it builds on is already hopelessly vitiated for the purpose of erecting a temple to its idol, the 'satisfaction of pure intellect.'   For in this selection of 'real reality' our interests, desires, and emotions inevitably play a leading part, and may even exercise an overpowering influence fatal to our ulterior ends.

Individual minds differ as greatly in their acceptance of 'facts' as in other respects.   Some can never be got to face *unpleasant* 'facts,' or will accept them only at the

---

[1] Cp. *Humanism*, pp. 192-3, and Essays viii. § 11, ix. § 4.

point of the sword. Most prefer to contemplate the more agreeable alternative. A few are driven by their fears unduly to accept the worse alternative. The devices for ideally rectifying the harshnesses of actual experience are endless. We console ourselves by postulating ideal realities, or extensions of reality, capable of transfiguring the repugnant character of actual life. We so conceive it, or interpret it, as to transform it into a 'good.' Or sometimes plain and generally recognized 'facts' are disposed of by a sheer assertion of their 'unreality,' as is, *e.g.*, the existence of pain by 'Christian Science,' and of evil by absolutist metaphysics. It is clear that psychologically all these attitudes towards 'fact' more or less work, and so have a certain value.

It is clear also that the recognition of 'fact' is by no means a simple affair. 'Facts' which can be excluded from our lives, which do not interest us, which mean nothing to us, which we cannot use, which are ineffective, which have little bearing on practical life, tend to drop into unreality. Our neglect, moreover, really tends to make them unreal, just as, conversely, our preference for the ideals we postulate makes them real, at least as factors in human life.

The common notion, therefore, that 'fact' is something independent of our recognition, needs radical revision, in the only sense of 'fact' which is worth disputing. It must be admitted that without a process of selection by us, there are no real facts for us, and that this selecting is immensely arbitrary. It would, perhaps, be infinitely so, but for the limitations of human imagination and tenacity of purpose in operating on apparent fact.

§ 6. Through this atmosphere of emotional interest, how shall we penetrate to any 'objective' fact at all? Where shall we find the 'hard facts' our forefathers believed in, which are so whether we will them or not, which extort recognition even from our sturdiest reluctance, whose unpleasantness *breaks* our will and does not *bend* to it?

Certainly it may not be quite easy to discern the old

objective facts in their new dress, but that is a poor reason for denying them the subjective atmosphere in which they have to live.

(1) We may begin, however, by remarking on the curious equating of 'objective' with 'unpleasant' facts and truths. Its instinctive pessimism seems to imply a mind which is so suspicious of fact that it can be driven to recognize the reality of anything only by pains and penalties, which is so narrowly contented with its existing limitations as to be disposed to regard all novelties as unwelcome intrusions, which has, in short, to be *forced* into the presence of truth, and will not go forth to seek it and embrace it. Such, certainly, is not the frame of mind and temper of the pragmatist, who prefers to conceive 'the objective' as that which he aims at and from, and contends that though 'facts' may at times coerce, it is yet more essential to them to be 'accepted,' to be 'made,' and to be capable of being '*remade*.'

(2) At all events, he thinks that the coerciveness of 'fact' has been enormously exaggerated by failure to observe that it is never sheer coercion, but always mitigated by his choice and acceptance, by which it ceases to be *de facto* thrust upon him, and becomes *de jure* 'willed.' Even a forced move, he feels, is better than no power to move at all; and the game of life is not wholly made up of forced moves.

(3) He finds no difficulty, therefore, in the conception of *unpleasant* 'fact.' It indicates the better of two disagreeable alternatives. And he can give good reasons for accepting unpleasant fact, without on that account conceiving 'fact' as such to be unpleasant and coercive. He may (a) accept it as the *less unpleasant* alternative, and to avoid worse consequences, much as man may wear spectacles rather than go blind. He may (b) prefer to sacrifice a cherished prejudice rather than to deny, *e.g.*, the evidence of his senses, or to renounce the use of his 'reason.' He may (c) accept it *provisionally*, without regarding it as absolute, merely for the purposes of the

act or experiment he is contemplating. For to recognize the *pragmatic reality* of an unpleasant fact means nothing metaphysical, and entails no serious consequences. It only implies willingness to accept it for the time being, and is quite compatible with a disbelief in its ultimate reality, and with its subsequent reduction to unreality or illusion. Hence (*d*) such a pragmatic acceptance of unpleasant fact does not impair our liberty of action ; it is no obstacle to subsequent experimentation, which may 'discover' the illusoriness of the presumed 'fact.' But even where it does not lead to this, it may (*e*) be a preliminary to making the unpleasant fact *unreal*, and putting something better in its place ; thus proving, in another way, that it never was the absolute hard fact it was supposed to be, but dependent on our inaction for its continued existence.

Thus (4) it turns out that the existence of unpleasant fact, so far from being an objection to the pragmatic view of fact, is an indispensable ingredient in it. For it supplies the motive for that transformation of the existing order, for that unmaking of the real which has been made amiss, which, with the making fact of the ideal and the preservation of the precious, constitutes the essence of our cognitive endeavour. To attain our 'objective,' the 'absolutely objective fact,' which would be absolutely satisfactory,[1] we need a 'platform' whence to act and aim. 'Objective fact' is just such a platform. Only there is no need to conceive it as anchored to the eternal bottom of the flux of time : it *floats*, and so can move with the times, and be adjusted to the occasion.

§ 7. As to § 3 (4), we have already seen that interest and purpose can be eliminated from cognitive process only at the cost of stopping it (Essay iii § 7.) A being devoid of interests would not *attend* to anything that happened, would not *select* or *value* one thing rather than another, nor would any one thing make more of an impression on its apathy than any other. Its mind and its world would remain in the chaos of primary reality

---

[1] Cp. Essay viii. § 12 ; and *Humanism*, pp. 198-203.

(§ 5), and resemble that of the 'Absolute'[1] (if it can be said to have a mind).

The human mind, of course, is wholly different. It is full of interests, all of which are directly or indirectly referable to the functions and purposes of life. Its organization is biological and teleological, and in both cases selective. If we except a few abnormal and morbid processes such as idiocy, insanity, and dream, mental life may be called wholly purposive; that is, its functioning is not intelligible without reference to actual or possible purposes, even when it is not aiming at a definite, clearly-envisaged end. Definite purposes are, it is true, of gradual growth. They arise by selection, they crystallize out from a magma of general interestedness and vaguely purposive actions, as we realize our true vocation in life, much as 'real' reality was selected out of 'primary.' Thus we become more and more clearly conscious of our 'ends,' and more and more definite in referring our 'goods' to them. But this reference is rarely or never carried through completely, because our nature is never fully harmonized. And so our 'desires' may continue to hanker after 'goods' which our 'reason' cannot sanction as conducive to our ends, or our intelligence may fail to find the 'good' means to our ends, and be deceived by current valuations of goods which are really evils. Thus the 'useful' and the 'good' tend to fall apart, and 'goods' to seem incompatible. But properly and ideally, there are no goods which are not related to the highest Good, no values which are not goods, no truths which are not values, and therefore, none which are not useful in the widest sense.

§ 8. As to § 3 (5), Experience is experiment, *i.e. active.* We do not learn, we do not live, unless we try. Passivity, mere acceptance, mere observation (could they be conceived) would lead us nowhere, least of all to knowledge.

(1) Every judgment refers sooner or later to a concrete situation which it analyses. In an ordinary judgment of sense-perception, as, *e.g.*, 'This is a chair,' the

[1] Cp. Essay ix. § 5.

subject, the 'this,' denotes the product of a selection of the relevant *part* of a given whole.   The selection is arbitrary, in that it ignores all the rest of the situation 'given' along with the 'this.'   If taken in abstraction, as intellectualism loves to do, it seems *wholly arbitrary*, unintelligible, and indefensible.   In the concrete, however, the judgment *when made* is always purposive, and its selection is justified, or refuted, by the subsequent stages of the ideal experiment.   The 'objective control' of the subjective freedom to predicate is not effected by some uncomprehended pre-existing fact : it comes *in the consequences of acting out the predication.*   So our analyses are arbitrary only if and in so far as we are not willing to *take* their consequences upon us.   Similarly the predicate, which includes the 'this' in a conceptual system already established, is arbitrary in its selection.   Why did we say 'chair,' and not 'sofa' or 'stool'?   To answer this we must go on to *test* the predication.

For (2) every judgment is essentially an experiment, which, to be tested, must be acted on.   If it is really true that 'this' is a chair, it can be sat in.   If it is a hallucination, it cannot.   If it is broken, it is not a chair in the sense my interest demanded.   For I made the judgment under the prompting of a desire to sit.

If now I stop at this point, without acting on the suggestion contained in the judgment, the claim to truth involved in the assertion is never tested, and so cannot be validated.   Whether or not 'this' was a chair, cannot be known.   If I consent to complete the experiment, the consequences will determine whether my predication was 'true' or 'false.'   The 'this' may not have been a chair at all, but a false appearance.   Or the antique article of ornamental furniture which broke under my weight may have been something too precious to be sat in.   In either case, the 'consequences' not only decide the validity of my judgment, but also alter my conception of reality. In the one case I shall judge henceforth that reality is such as to present me with illusory chairs ; in the other, that it contains also chairs *not* to be sat in.   This then is what is meant by the pragmatic testing of a claim to truth.[1]

§ 9. As to the reaction of the consequences of an experimental predication upon its 'truth' (§ 3 (6)), the simplest case is that (1) of a successful validation. If, in the example of the last section, I can sit in the 'chair,' my confidence in my eyesight is confirmed and I shall trouble little whether it ought not rather to have been called a 'sofa' or a 'stool.' Of course, however, if my interest was not that of a mere sitter, but of a collector or dealer in ancient furniture, my first judgment may have been woefully inadequate, and may need to be revised. 'Success,' therefore, in validating a 'truth,' is a relative term, *relative to the purpose* with which the truth was claimed. The 'same' predication may be 'true' for me and 'false' for you, if our purposes are different. As for a truth in the abstract, and relative to no purpose, it is plainly unmeaning. Until some one asserts it, it cannot become even a claim, and be tested, and cannot, therefore, be validated. Hence the truth of 'the proposition' 'S is P,' when we affirm it on the strength of an actually successful predication, is only potential. In applying it to other cases we always take a risk. The next time 'this' may not be a 'chair,' even though it may look the 'same' as the first time. Hence even a fully successful predication cannot be converted into an 'eternal truth' without more ado. The empirical nature of reality is such that we can never argue from one case to a *similar* one, which *we take to be* 'the same,' with absolute assurance *a priori*; hence no 'truth' can ever be so certain that it need not be verified, and may not mislead us, when applied. But this only means that no truth should be taken as unimprovable.

(2) Experiments, however, are rarely quite successful. We may (*a*) have had to purchase the success we attain by the use of artificial abstractions and simplifications, or even downright fictions, and the uncertainty which this

---

[1] Cp. Dewey's *Logical Studies* for the experimental nature of predication especially ch. vii.

imports into the ' truth ' of our conclusions will have to
be acknowledged.   We shall, therefore, conceive ourselves
to have attained, not complete truths without a stain
upon their character, which there is no reason to doubt,
but only ' approximations to truth ' and ' working hypotheses,' which are, at most, ' good enough for practical
purposes.'   And the principles we used we shall dub
methodological ' truths ' or ' fictions,' according to our bias.
And, clearly, the cognitive endeavour will not in this case
rest.   We shall not have found a ' truth ' which fully
satisfies even our immediate purpose, but shall continue
the search for a more complete, precise, and satisfactory
result.   In the former case, the cognitive interest of the
situation could be renewed only by a change or growth
of purpose leading to further judgments.

(3) The experiment may fail, and lead to unsatisfactory results.   The interpretation then may become
extremely complex.   Either (*a*) we may put the blame
on our subjective manipulation, on our use of our cognitive
instruments.   We may have observed wrongly.   We may
have reasoned badly.   We may have selected the wrong
conceptions.   We may have had nothing but false conceptions to select from, because our previous knowledge
was as a whole inadequate.   Or we may be led to doubt
(*b*) the basis of fact which we assumed, or (*c*) the
practicability of the enterprise we were engaged in.   In
either of the first two cases we shall feel entitled to try
again, with variations in our methods and assumptions ;
but repeated failure may finally force even the most
stubborn to desist from their purpose, or to reduce it to
a mere postulate of rationality which it is as yet impossible to apply to actual experience.   And, needless to say,
there will be much difference of opinion as to where, in
case of failure, the exact flaw lies, and how it may best
be remedied.   Herein, however, lies one reason (among
many) why the discovery of truth is such a personal
affair.   The discoverer is he who, by greater perseverance
or more ingenious manipulation, makes something out of
a situation which others had despaired of.

§ 10. We see, then, *how truth is made*, by human operations on the data of human experience. Knowledge grows in extent and in trustworthiness by successful functioning, by the assimilation and incorporation of fresh material by the previously existing bodies of knowledge. These 'systems' are continually verifying themselves, proving themselves true by their ' consequences,' by their power to assimilate, predict and control fresh ' fact.' But the fresh fact is not only assimilated ; it also transforms. The old truth looks different in the new light, and really changes. It grows more powerful and efficient. Formally, no doubt, it may be described as growing more ' coherent ' and more highly ' organized,' but this does not touch the kernel of the situation. For the ' coherence ' and the ' organization ' both exist in our eyes, and relatively to our purposes : it is *we* who judge what they shall mean. And what we judge them by is their conduciveness to our ends, their effectiveness in harmonizing our experience. Thus, here again, the intellectualist analysis of knowledge fails to reach the really motive forces.

§ 11. It is important, further, to point out that *looking forward* the making of truth is clearly a continuous, progressive, and cumulative process. For the satisfaction of one cognitive purpose leads on to the formulation of another ; a new truth, when established, naturally becomes the presupposition of further explorations. And to this process there would seem to be no actual end in sight, because in practice we are always conscious of much that we should like to know, if only we possessed the leisure and the power. We can, however, conceive an ideal completion of the making of truth, in the achievement of a situation which would provoke no questions and so would inspire no one with a purpose to remake it, and on this ideal the name absolute truth may be bestowed.

Looking backwards, the situation, as might have been expected, is less plain. In the first place there are puzzles, which arise from the natural practice of *re-valuing* superseded ' truths ' as ' errors,' and of *antedating* the new truths as having been ' true all along.' So it may

be asked: 'What were these truths *before* they were
discovered?' This query is essentially analogous to the
child's question: 'Mother, what becomes of yesterday?'
and by any one who has understood the phraseology of
time in the one case and of the making of truth in the
other, the difficulty will be seen to be merely verbal. If
'true' means (as we have contended) 'valued by us,' of
course the new truth becomes true only when 'discovered';
if it means 'valuable *if* discovered,' it was of course hypothetically 'true'; if, lastly, the question inquires whether
a past situation would not have been *altered for the better*,
if it had included a recognition of this truth, the answer
is: 'Yes, probably; only unfortunately, it was not so
altered.' In none of these cases, however, are we dealing
with a situation which can be even intelligibly stated
apart from the human making of truth.[1] Again, it is by
no means easy to say how far our present processes of
making truth are validly to be applied to the past, how
far *all* truth can be conceived as having been made by
the processes which we now see in operation.

(1) That we must try to conceive it thus is, indeed,
obvious. For why should we gratuitously assume that
the procedure by which 'truth' is now being made differs
radically from that whereby truth initially came into
being? Are we not bound to conceive, if possible, the
whole process as continuous, truth made, truth making,
and truth yet to be made, as successive stages in one and
the same endeavour? And to a large extent it is clear
that this can be done, that the established truths, from
which our experiments now start, are of a like nature
with the truths we make, and were themselves made in
historical times.

(2) Before, however, we can generalize this procedure, we
have to remember that on our own showing, we disclaimed
the notion of making truth out of nothing. We did not
have recourse to the very dubious notion of theology
called 'creation out of nothing,' which no human operations ever exemplify. We avowed that our truths were

---

[1] Cp. p. 157 *note*, and Essay viii. § 5.

made out of previous truths, and built upon pre-existing knowledge ; also that our procedure involved an initial recognition of ' fact.'

(3) Here, then, would seem to be two serious, if not fatal, limitations upon the claim of the pragmatic ' making of truth' to have solved the mystery of knowledge. They will need, therefore, further examination, though we may at once hasten to state that they cannot affect the validity of what the pragmatic analysis professed to do. It professed to show the reality and importance of the human contribution to the making of truth ; and this it has amply done. If it can carry us further, and enable us to humanize our world completely, so much the better. But this is more than it bargained to do, and it remains to be seen how far it will carry us into a comprehension also of the apparently non-human conditions under which our manipulations must work.

§ 12. Now as regards the previous knowledge assumed in the making of truth, it may be shown that there is no need to treat it in any but a pragmatic way. For (1) it seems quite arbitrary to deny that the truths which we happen to assume in making new truths are the same in kind as the very similar truths we make by their aid. In many cases, indeed, we can show that these very truths were made by earlier operations. There is, therefore, so far, nothing to hinder us from regarding the volitional factors which actual knowing now exhibits, viz. desire, interest, and purpose, as essential to the process of knowing, and similarly the process by which new truth is now made, viz. postulation, experiment, action, as essential to the process of verification.

Moreover (2), even if we denied this, and tried to find truths that had never been made, it would avail us nothing. We never can get back to truths so fundamental that they cannot possibly be conceived as having been made. There are no *a priori* truths which are indisputable, as is shown by the mere fact that there is not, and never has been, any agreement as to what they are. All the ' *a priori* truths,' moreover, which are commonly alleged, can be conceived as postulates suggested by a previous situation.[1]

(3) Methodologically, therefore, it leads us nowhere to assume that within the truth which is made there exists an uncreate residuum or core of elementary truth, which has not been made. For we can never get at it, or know it. Hence, even if it existed, the theory of our knowing could take no note of it. All truth, therefore, must, methodologically, be treated as if it had been 'made.' For on this assumption alone can it reveal its full significance. In so far, therefore, as Pragmatism does not profess to be more than a method, it has no occasion to modify or correct an account of truth which is adequate to its purpose, for the sake of an objection which is methodologically null.

(4) It seems a little hard on Pragmatism to expect from it a solution of a difficulty which confronts alike all theories of knowledge. In all of them the beginning of knowledge is wrapped in mystery. It is a mystery, however, which even now presses less severely on Pragmatism than on its competitors. For the reason that it is not a retrospective theory. Its significance does not lie in its explanation of the past so much as in its *present* attitude towards the *future*. The past is dead and done with, practically speaking; its deeds have hardened into 'facts,' which are accepted, with or without enthusiasm; what it really concerns us to know is *how to act with a view to the future*. And so like life, and as befits a theory of human life, Pragmatism faces towards the future. It can adopt, therefore, the motto *solvitur ambulando*, and be content if it can conceive a situation in which the problem would *de facto* have disappeared. The other theories could not so calmly welcome a 'psychological' solution as 'logically' satisfactory. But then they still dream of 'theoretic' solutions, which are to be wholly 'independent' of practice.

§ 13. The full consideration of the problem involved in the initial 'acceptance of fact' by our knowing will

[1] Cp. 'Axioms as Postulates' in *Personal Idealism*.

have to be reserved for the essay on 'Making of Reality,' which will have to examine the metaphysical conclusions to which the Pragmatic Method points. At present it must suffice to show (1) that the 'making of truth' is necessarily and *ipso facto* also a 'making of reality'; and (2) what precisely is the difficulty about accepting the making of truth as a *complete* making also of reality.

(1) (*a*) It is clear, in the first place, that if our beliefs, ideas, desires, wishes, etc., are really essential and integral features in actual knowing, and if knowing really transforms our experience, they must be treated as *real forces*, which cannot be ignored by philosophy.[1] They really alter reality, to an extent which is quite familiar to 'the practical man,' but which, unfortunately, 'philosophers' do not yet seem to have quite adequately grasped, or to have 'reflected on' to any purpose. Without, however, going into endless detail about what ought to be quite obvious, let us merely affirm that the 'realities' of civilized life are the embodiments of the ideas and desires of civilized man, alike in their material and in their social aspects, and that our present inability wholly to subdue the material, in which we realize our ideas, is a singularly poor reason for denying the difference between the present condition of man's world and that of his miocene ancestors.

(*b*) Human ideals and purposes are real forces, even though they are not yet incorporated in institutions, and made palpable in the rearrangements of bodies. For they affect our actions, and our actions affect our world.

(*c*) Our knowledge of reality, at least, depends largely on the character of our interests, wishes, and acts. If it is true that the cognitive process must be started by subjective interest which determines the direction of its search, it is clear that unless we seek we shall not find, nor 'discover' realities we have not looked for. They will consequently be missing in our picture of the world, and will remain non-existent for us. To become real

---

[1] Cp. Prof. Dewey's essay on 'Beliefs and Existences' in *The Influence of Darwin on Philosophy*, which makes this point very forcibly.

for us they (or cognate realities—for we do not always discover just what we went forth to find, as witness Saul and Columbus) must have become *real objects of interest* hypothetically ; and as this making of 'objects of interest' is quite within our power, in a very real sense their 'discovery' is a 'making of reality.'[1]   Thus, in general, the world as it now appears to us may be regarded as the reflexion of our interests in life : it is what we and our ancestors have, wisely or foolishly, sought and known to make of our life, under the limitations of our knowledge and our powers.   And that, of course, is little enough as compared with our ideals, though a very great deal as compared with our starting-point.   It is enough, at any rate, to justify the phrase 'the making of reality' as a consequence of the making of truth.   And it is evident also that just in so far as the one is a consequence of the other, our remarks about the presupposition of an already made 'truth' will apply also to the presupposition of an already made 'reality.'

§ 14. The difficulty about conceiving this 'making of reality,' which accompanies the 'making of truth,' as more than 'subjective,' and as affording us a real insight into the nature of the cosmic process, lies in the fact that it is complicated with the difficulty we have already recognized in trying to conceive the making of truth as a completely subjective process, which should yet be self-sufficient and fully explanatory of the nature of knowledge (§ 11).   It is because the making of truth seemed to presuppose a certain 'acceptance of fact,' which was indeed volitional *qua* the 'acceptance' and even optional, but left us with a surd *qua* the 'fact,' that it seems impossible to claim complete objectivity for the making of reality, and that our knowing seems to many merely to select among pre-existing facts those which we are interested to 'discover.'

It is inevitable, moreover, that the pre-existing facts,

---

[1] For the reason why we distinguish between these two cases at all, see Essay xix. § 5.

which the making, both of truth and of reality, seems to presuppose as its condition, though, properly speaking, it only implies the pre-existence of 'primary reality' (§ 5), should be identified with the 'real world' of common-sense, in which we find ourselves, and which we do not seem to have made in any human sense.   In other words, our theory of knowledge is confronted at this point with something which claims ontological validity, and is requested to turn itself into a metaphysic in order to deal with it.

This, of course, it may well refuse to do.   It can insist on remaining what it originally was, and has so far professed to be, viz. a method of understanding the nature of our knowledge.   And we shall not be entitled to censure it, however much we may regret its diffidence, and desire it to show its power also in coping with our final difficulties.

We ought, however, to be grateful, if it enables us to perceive from what the difficulty really arises.   It arises from a conflict between pragmatic considerations, *both* of which are worthy of respect.   For (1) the belief in the world theory of ordinary realism, in a 'real world' into which we are born, and which has existed 'independently' of us for æons before that event, and so cannot possibly have been made by us or any man, has very high pragmatic warrant.   It is a theory which holds together and explains our experience, and can be acted on with very great success.   It is adequate for almost all our purposes.   It works so well that it cannot be denied a very high degree of truth.[1]

(2) On the other hand, it is equally plain that we cannot deny the reality of our cognitive procedure and of the human contribution it imports into the making of reality.   It, too, is a tried and tested truth.   The two, therefore, must somehow be reconciled, even though in so doing we may have to reveal ultimate deficiencies in the common-sense view of the world.

The first question to be raised is which of the two

[1] Cp. Essay xx. § 6.

pragmatically valuable truths should be taken as more ultimate.

The decision, evidently, must be in favour of the second.   For the 'reality of the external world' is not an original datum of experience, and it is a *confusion* to identify it with the 'primary reality' we recognized in § 5. It cannot claim the dubious 'independence' of the latter, just because it is something better and more valuable which has been 'made' out of it.   For it is a pragmatic construction *within* primary reality, the product, in fact, of one of those processes of selection by which the chaos is ordered.   The real external world is the pragmatically efficient part of our total experience, to which the inefficient parts such as dreams, fancies, illusions, after-images, etc., can, for most purposes, be referred.   But though this construction suffices for most practical purposes, it fails to answer the question—how may 'reality' be distinguished from a consistent dream?   And seeing that experience presents us with transitions from an apparently real (dream) world into one of superior reality, how can we know that this process may not be repeated, to the destruction of what now seems our 'real world'?[1]

We must distinguish, therefore, between two questions which have been confused—(1) 'Can the making of truth be conceived as a making also of " primary reality "?' and (2) 'Can it be conceived also as a making of the real " external world " of ordinary life?'—and be prepared to find that while the first formulates an impossible problem,[2] an answer to the second may prove feasible.   In any case, however, it cannot be affirmed that our belief in the metaphysical reality of our external world, which it is in some sense, or in no sense, possible to 'make,' is of higher authority than our belief in the reality of our making of truth.   The latter may pervade also forms of experience other than that which gets its pragmatic backbone from the former.   Indeed, one cannot imagine desiring, purposing, and acting as ceasing to form part of our cognitive procedure, so long as 'finite' minds persist at all.   All we

---

[1] Cp. Essay xx. §§ 19-22.   [2] Essay xix. § 7.

can say, therefore, is that so long as, and in so far as, our experience is such as to be most conveniently organized by the conception of a pre-existing real world (in a relative sense), 'independent' of us, it will also be convenient to conceive it as having been to a large extent 'made' before *we* took a part in the process.[1]

Nevertheless, it is quite possible (1) that this 'pragmatic' recognition of the external world may not be final, because it does not serve our ultimate purposes ; and (2) that the human process of making reality may be a valuable clue also to the making of the pragmatically real world, because even though it was not made by us, it was yet developed by processes closely analogous to our own procedure, which this latter enables us to understand.   If so, we shall be able to combine the *real* 'making of reality' and the human 'making of reality' under the same conception.   But both of these suggestions must be left to later essays to work out.[2]   Before we embark upon such adventurous constructions, we must finally dispose of the metaphysical and religious pretensions of the Absolutism whose theory of knowledge has ended in such egregious failure.

[1] Cp. *Riddles of the Sphinx*, chap. ix. § 32.
[2] Essays xix. and xx.

VIII

ABSOLUTE TRUTH AND ABSOLUTE REALITY

ARGUMENT

I. *The Conception of Absolute Truth.* § 1. The sceptical tendency of the historical study of Thought is due to reflection on the falsifying of human truths. § 2. The Ideal of an absolute truth as a standard to give stability to human truths. § 3. But, being conceived as separate, it turns out to be futile. (1) It guarantees nothing, and (2) it is different in kind. § 4. It is also pernicious, as leading either to scepticism or to stagnation. § 5. The real growth of Truth is by a constant revaluation of truths which are 'verified' as well as falsified. § 6. The real meaning of 'absolute' truth.

II. *The Conception of Absolute Reality.* § 7. The character of scientific reality which absolute reality is supposed to guarantee. § 8. It is, however, futile, because (1) its notion is no help to finding it *de facto*, and (2) it must be kept away from our reality. § 9. Is it also pernicious, as disintegrating human reality and discouraging efforts to improve it. § 10. The real growth of reality never involves the notion of absolute reality. § 11. 'Primary' would be accepted as ultimate reality by 'purely' cognitive beings. § 12. 'Real' reality selected by human interests. The real meaning of 'absolute' reality.

I.—THE CONCEPTION OF ABSOLUTE TRUTH

§ 1. *The Sceptical Tendency of the Historical Study of Thought*

THE reflective student of the history of human knowledge is apt to receive an overwhelming impression of the instability of opinion, of the mutability of beliefs, of the vicissitudes of science, in short of the impermanence of what is, or passes for, 'truth.' Despite the boastful confidence of Platonically-minded system-builders that they have 'erected monuments more perennial than bronze' and coerced 'eternal' truth to abide immutably within the flimsy shelters which their speculations have erected, the universal flux of reality sways the world of ideas even more rapidly and visibly than the world of things. What truths have lasted like the Alps, or even like the Pyramids? All human truth, as it actually is and historically has been, seems fallible and transitory. It is of its nature to be liable to err, and of ours to blind ourselves to this liability. The road to truth (if such a thing there is) grows indiscernible amid the many bypaths of error into which it branches off on either side,[1] and whichever of these mazes men adopt, they plunge into it as gaily, follow it as faithfully, and trust it as implicitly, as if it were the one most certain highroad. But only for a season. For sooner or later they weary of a course that leads to nothing, and stop themselves with a shock of distressed surprise at the discovery that what they had so long taken to be 'true' was really 'false.' And yet so strong is the dogmatic confidence with which nature has endowed them, that they start again almost at once, all but a very few of the wisest, upon the futile quest of a truth which in the end always eludes their human grasp.

Thus human truth cannot substantiate its claim to absoluteness : the truths of past ages are at present recognized as errors ; those of the present are on the way to be so recognized. They can inspire us with no more confidence, they ought to inspire us with far less, than that with which exploded and superseded errors inspired our forefathers, who in their day were equally con-temptuous of the errors of an earlier age. We have no right to hold that this universal process will be arrested at this single point, and that our successors will find reason to spare our present truths and shrink from discarding them when they have had their day.

Nor can the feeling of conviction which has gathered

---

[1] Cp. Poincaré, *La Valeur de la Science*, p. 142 : toute vérité particulière peut évidemment être étendue d'une infinité de manières. Entre ces mille chemins qui s'ouvrent devant nous, il faut faire un choix, au moins provisoire.

round our present 'truths' guarantee them permanent validity. All 'truths' claim to be 'true' without a hint of doubt, and come upon the scene with similar assurance and similar assurances. And all alike evoke the feeling of loyalty which truth - seeking men are anxious to bestow upon whatever comes to them in the guise of truth. But all too often our trust is woefully misplaced. The truths we trusted are transformed into hideous errors in our hands, and after many bitter disappointments we are driven to grow wary, and even sceptical.

Thus our faith in the absoluteness of our truth grows ever fainter, shrinks ever more into an unreasonable instinct, until, in our most lucid intervals, we may even come to doubt whether our 'truth' is ever more than the human fashion of the ruling fancy.

§ 2. *The Conception of Absolute Truth*

In this distress, for man by nature is the most credulous of creatures, the thought of an absolute truth, serenely transcending all this turmoil, so distinct in nature as to be independent of the misfortunes and exempt from the vicissitudes of human truth, presents itself as a welcome refuge from the assaults of scepticism. If such a thing can be conceived, it will form a model for human truth to imitate, a standard for evaluating our imperfect truths, and an impregnable citadel into which no change can penetrate. The wish is so urgent, the thought is so natural, that we are not disposed to be critical, and it is no wonder that it has become nearly universal. And yet when we force ourselves really to scrutinize the habitation which our hopes have built, we may have reason to fear that it is founded on illusion, and results in disaster to the very hopes to which it promised satisfaction.

The notion of an absolute truth suggested itself as an expedient for escaping from the continuous revaluation and transvaluation of truths, which forms the history of human knowledge. The efficacy of the expedient consists essentially in constituting a distinction between actual or human, and absolute or ideal truth, and in so separating them that the latter can be fished up out of the flux of reality and set up aloft on an immutable pedestal for the adoration of the faithful.   But in this very separation lurk the dangers which render vain our idolatry and our sacrifices, and in the end conduct the whole conception to failure and futility.

For the conception of an absolute truth was not won without cost.   We had to value it above our human truth, and so to derogate from the latter's authority, and yet to keep the two related ; and so these sacrifices will be vain if we fail to show (1) that the conception of absolute truth solves our original problem and really guarantees our truths ; and (2) that the new problem it provokes as to the relation of the actual changing human truth to its superhuman stable standard is capable of satisfactory solution.

§ 3. *The Futility of Absolute Truth*

Now as to (1) we soon see reason to doubt whether the conception of an immutable truth really gives our actual truths the guarantee we sought.   Rather it seems to leave the problem where we found it.   For manifestly we cannot argue that because absolute truth exists and is immutable, therefore our truths do not need correction.   On the contrary, we shall have to admit as a general principle that, just because human, they cannot be absolute.   Still less can we assume that any particular truth that is recognized at a particular time is absolute and destined to be permanent.   Even though therefore the logician's heaven were packed tight with a mass of absolute and eternal verities, rigid and immutable, they could not miraculously descend to transform our truths and to cure the impermanence of our conceptions.   Neither could the latter aspire to their superhuman prerogatives.   Or even if they could so descend, we could never discover this, and, like other deities, they would have lost heaven without redeeming earth.

Absolute truth, therefore, to benefit human truths, must be conceived as capable of being identified with them. So long as it is not so conceived, it does nothing to redeem them from suspicion. And conversely, so long as human knowledge is not absolute, so long as it cannot even seriously claim to be so, absolute truth is irrelevant to human knowledge, and it is gratuitous to assume its existence.

(2) To save the conception, therefore, we must examine the relation of human to absolute truth, in order to see whether they may not be so connected that some divine virtue from the latter may magically be instilled into the former. Let us try to conceive, that is, human truth as a reflexion of absolute, imperfect indeed but valid, being mysteriously transubstantiated by the immanence of the absolute and sharing in its substance.

The first point which, on this assumption, must excite surprise is that the appearance of our truth, in spite of the sanctification it is said to have undergone, remains strangely unregenerate. Its salient features are in complete contrast with those of the original it claims to reproduce. It is fluid, not rigid ; temporal and temporary, not eternal and everlasting ; arbitrary, not necessary ; chosen, not inevitable ; born of passion and sprung (like Aphrodite) from a foaming sea of desires, not 'dispassionate' nor 'purely' intellectual ; incomplete, not perfect ; fallible, not inerrant ; absorbed in the attaining of what is *not* yet achieved ; purposive and struggling towards ends, and not basking in their fulfilment. Surely if the two are really one, and the distortion which dissevers them lies only in the human eye that sees amiss, our trust in the competence of our cognitive apparatus will be worse shaken than before.

And secondly, these features of human truth seem definitely bound up with the conditions that make it truth at all. Human truth is discursive, because it cannot embrace the whole of reality ; it is fallible, because it never knows the whole, and so may ever need correction by wider knowledge. It is, in a word, essentially partial.

Absolute truth, on the other hand, extends to and depends on a knowledge of the whole. Its absoluteness rests on its all-embracingness. If there is not completely adequate knowledge of a completed system of reality there can be no absolute truth.

But can such knowledge be ascribed to human minds? Can we conceive ourselves as contemplating the whole from the standpoint of the whole? If not, our truth, *just because it is partial,* and rests on partial data, and is generated by the partialities of selective attention, and is directed upon partial ends, which it achieves by playing off parts of the universe against the others, can never aspire to the absoluteness which pertains only to the whole.

Thus the chasm of a difference in kind begins to yawn between truth human and truth absolute. And this perhaps we ought to have expected. For did we not succeed in postulating an absolute truth by exempting it from all the defects that seemed to mar our truth? We have been only too successful ; the separation we enforced has been too effectual ; absolute truth is safe from contamination, but it can do nothing to redeem our truth : the two are different in kind, and have no intercourse or interaction.

Must we not conclude, therefore, that our assumption of absolute truth is futile and has availed us nothing? Even if it existed, it could not help us, because we could not attain it. Even if we could attain it, we could not know that we had done so. Even, therefore, if it could remove doubt, it would not do so to our blinded eyes.

§ 4. *The Perniciousness of the Conception of Absolute Truth*

But there is more to be said against the notion of absolute truth. Its futility, perhaps, will seem no serious drawback. It does but little harm, and induces at the worst a loss of time which leisurely philosophy can well afford to part with. What is that compared with the delight of rolling in our mouths such dainty words as 'absolute' and 'truth'?

To which it may be replied that those who conceive philosophy, not as a game for indolent spectators of the battle of life, but as the culmination of our efforts to grasp and control the struggle, will not easily condone a futile waste of time.

But they will condemn the conception of an absolute truth also on more weighty grounds. They will proceed to urge against it—(1) that it leads to a shipwreck of the theory of knowledge; that (2) it interposes itself between us and the truth we need; and (3) by obfuscating the real nature of the problem, it prevents us from recognizing the true solution.

(1) The pernicious influence of the notion of absolute truth on our theory of knowledge will differ according as the difference between it and human truth is (*a*) perceived, or (*b*) not.

If (*a*) it is perceived (in the manner shown above), we shall of course be tempted to suppose that absolute truth is something grander and more precious than ours. It will, therefore, cast a slur upon all human knowledge, which will be despised as a ludicrous and vain attempt to achieve the impossible, viz. to reflect the absolute. To the pain and loss of discovering that our 'truths' are null— the malady which afflicted us before—there is now added contempt for the human presumption which tries to inflate man into a measure of the universe.

The more clear-sighted of absolutists therefore will to all practical intents be sceptics, and even though they will contend that it is only for the greater glory of the Absolute that they have shattered human truth, they will find it hard even theoretically, to draw the very fine line which marks them off from the downright sceptic. The most eminent of absolutists, Mr. F. H. Bradley, has signally illustrated this inevitable consequence.[1]

---

[1] To him may now be added Mr. Joachim, whose 'ideal' of knowledge breaks down just in the way anticipated, although this was written before his book appeared. Cp. Essay vi.

(*b*) If the difference is not perceived, if by drugs and prayers the eye of the soul is sufficiently dimmed to take our truth for absolute, the consequences will be very nearly as disastrous. It will not indeed be *all* truth that will run the risk of rejection, but all *new* truth. For if a recognized 'truth' is regarded as 'absolute,' it is naturally stereotyped. (1) Alteration will become impossible, the effort to improve it will be discouraged and will cease ; in short, the path of progress will be blocked. And even formally, a theory of knowledge which cannot account for its growth has no great claim upon our veneration. (2) The belief that our truth is absolute is pernicious, not only as checking its development, but also as incapacitating us from understanding its real nature, and (3) the true nature of the problem presented by the growth of knowledge, and its true solution. For it renders us impatient of following the real clues to the development of truth, and so prevents us from perceiving that, properly understood, this affords no ground for the sceptical inferences to escape from which we vainly appealed to the notion of absolute truth.

§ 5. *The Real Nature of the Growth of Truth*

If we adopt the Humanist view that 'truth' is essentially a valuation, a laudatory label wherewith we decorate the most useful conceptions which we have formed up to date in order to control our experience, there is not the slightest reason why the steady flow of the stream of 'truths' that pass away should inspire us with dismay. Every 'truth' has its day, but what matters it, if sufficient for the day is the truth thereof? That a 'truth' should turn out 'false' is a calamity only if we are unable to supplant it by a 'truer.' But if instead of practising dialectics in the study, we condescend to observe the actual growth of knowledge, we find that we change 'truths' only for the better. We are enabled to declare an old 'truth' 'false' because we are able to find a new one which more than fills its place. We do not discard a valuable and serviceable conception, until we have something more valuable and convenient, *i.e.* truer, to serve us in its stead. Even where it is necessary to condemn the old truth as 'false'— a harsh necessity commonly imposed on us only by the pertinacity with which unprogressive thinkers cling to it—its 'falsity' does not mean revolution so much as development. The 'false' is absolute as little as the 'true.' It is commonly a term attached to an earlier phase of the process which has evolved the 'truth.' Hence to regard the discarded ex-truth as merely 'error' is to fail to do justice to its record, to fail to express the continuity of the process whereby knowledge grows.

Thus the abstract intellectualist view of truth creates a dialectical difficulty which does not really exist. Our 'truth' is not merely being 'falsified,' but also being 'verified' in one and the same process; it is corrected only to be improved. So the Humanist can recognize necessary errors as well as necessary truths, errors, that is, which are fruitful of the truths which supersede them.

Herein lies the explanation also of the otherwise paradoxical fact that those who have most experience of the fallibility of human truth are least disposed to be sceptical about it. For being actively engaged in 'making' or 'discovering' truth, they are too busy with anticipating achievement to reflect upon the failures that strew the path of every science. It is not to the invalidation of the old truths, but to the establishment of the new, that they are attending. Thus the whole procedure carries with it a feeling of fulfilment, which is encouraging and not depressing. They see the new truth continuously growing out of the old, as a more satisfactory mode of handling the old problems. The growth of truth cannot therefore suggest to them a growth of doubt, as it naturally does to the indolent spectator.

Nor is it really a paradox to maintain that our 'errors' were 'truths' in their day. For they were the most adequate ways we then had of dealing with our experience. They were not, therefore, valueless. Nor were they gratuitous errors. More commonly they were natural, or even indispensable, stages in the attainment of better ' truths.'

And so the prospect of further improvements in the formulas whereby we know the world, which will supersede our present truths, does not appal us. They will be welcome when and as they come. They will not put us to intellectual confusion, unless we narrow-mindedly exclude them : on the contrary they will mean a more adequate fulfilment of what we now desire.

Viewing truth in this way, we shall regard it neither disdainfully nor unprogressively. We shall regard no truth as so rigidly 'absolute' as to be incapable of improvement. But we shall not despise it for displaying so tractable a flexibility. We shall honour it the more for thus adjusting itself to the demands of life. It will fulfil its function, even if it perishes in our service, provided that it. has left behind descendants more capable of carrying on its salutary work.

§ 6. *Absolute Truth as an Ideal*

Shall we conclude, then, that the conception of an absolute truth is a mere will-o'-the-wisp ?

No ; rightly conceived, it has the value of a valid ideal for human knowledge. The ideal of a truth wholly adequate, adequate that is to every human purpose, may well be called truth absolute. Nor did the absolutist err in describing its formal character. It would be, as he says, stable, immutable, and eternal. His fatal mistake is to conceive it as *already actual*. For by thus attributing actual existence to it in a non-human sphere, he spoils it as an ideal for man ; he dissevers it from the progress of human knowledge, and disables it as an encouragement to human effort.

Moreover, so to conceive it is at one blow to reduce our actual knowledge to superfluity and illusion. If *the* truth is already timelessly achieved, what meaning can our struggles to attain it ultimately claim? They cannot make a truth already made, they cannot add to a perfection already possessed, they cannot enrich a significance already complete. They must inexorably be condemned as unmeaning surplusage. Thus the real function of the ideal has been destroyed by untimely haste to proclaim its reality.

II.—THE CONCEPTION OF ABSOLUTE REALITY

§ 7. It is an integral part of the Humanist theory of knowledge that the System of Truth and the world of Reality are constructed by one and the same purposive manipulation out of the materials provided by crude or immediate experience, and that consequently the processes of *knowing reality* and of *establishing truth* must not be separated even in statement. The discussion, therefore, of the conception of Absolute Reality will naturally run parallel to that of Absolute Truth ; but as the pragmatic handling of this theme is still sufficiently novel to be frequently misunderstood, it will be advantageous to reiterate the general argument in its special application to a distinct question.

And to begin with, we must consider the characteristics of Reality which our science recognizes and *de facto* deals with. Scientific reality, *i.e.* as it enters into and is treated in the sciences, normally exhibits the following features. (1) It is not rigid, but plastic and capable of development ; (2) it is not absolute nor unconditionally real, but relative to our experience and dependent on the state of our knowledge ; (3) our conception of it changes, and so (4) often reduces to unreality what had long been accepted as real ; (5) initial reality (like initial truth) is claimed by everything in experience ; (6) we need therefore a principle which acts selectively to discriminate between initial reality, or primary experience, and 'real' reality which has survived the fire of criticism and been promoted to superior rank ; (7) even more markedly than in the case of truth, the constant substitution of more for less adequate conceptions of reality does *not* engender scepticism.   At every step we are confident that here at last we have reached the goal ; but even though the next step may show that we were too sanguine, we are never undeceived and never doubt our powers to attain reality.

Nevertheless the idea of an Absolute Reality has cropped up here also as a device for avoiding the restlessness of a dynamic reality, and as a short cut to intellectual repose.   Here also it is supposed to support and guarantee, to round off and confirm, the realities we actually deal with.

§ 8. *The Futility of Absolute Reality*

Here also the notion is delusive.   For (1) the Absolute Reality gives us no aid in dealing with the realities we actually recognize ;   (2) it cannot be related to them ; (3) it therefore disparages the value of our realities, and (4) obstructs a more adequate knowledge of reality ;   (5) as before, the mistake consists in the attempt to project into reality a misconceived ideal, with the result that the ideal loses its value, and the nature of the real is obscured.

(1) It is an entire mistake to suppose that the general conviction that there is absolute reality is a reason for declaring absolute any apparent reality.   It is not even a help in discriminating between conflicting realities which claim to be truly real.   For how are we to decide that anything in particular is (or is not) as real as it seems ? The belief in an absolute reality will but justify us in looking for it; the risk in identifying it when found will remain precisely what it was.   And will it not always be presumptuous to assume that we have attained it ? And if we had assumed it, how could we prove it ?   All the old difficulties which arise from the growth of our knowledge of reality, from the discarding of old superstitions, from the ' discovery ' of new facts, would beset us as before.   Beyond the satisfaction of believing that absolute reality existed somewhere in the world, our practical gain would be *nil.*

(2) It would be very difficult, moreover, to establish any effective connexion between the absolute reality we had postulated, and our own. Our reality seems in all respects to fall short of the ideal of a reality, stable, immutable, perfect, unconditional, self-sufficing, and worthy to be dignified with the title of 'absolute.' The reals we know all seem corruptible and transitory ; they are incessantly changing ; they are penetrated through and through with imperfections ; it is their nature to depend on others and to be as little able to satisfy them as themselves. To realize our ideal, therefore, they would have fundamentally to change their nature.

These defects the notion of absolute reality does nothing to alleviate. It cannot even affect them, for it can never get into touch with them. Absolute reality must in self-defence eschew all relation with ours. For such relation would involve a dependence on the imperfect which would disturb its own perfection. Relation among realities implies interaction, and interaction with the un-stable and changing must import a reflected instability into the nature of the absolute reality and destroy its equipoise. The only way therefore for the perfect to preserve its perfection is to keep aloof : but if it does that, how, pray, shall it be known by us ?

§ 9. *The Perniciousness of the Notion of Absolute Reality*

(3) The mere notion, moreover, of an absolute reality has a disintegrating effect on the realities of human knowledge. The more glowing the colours, the greater the enthusiasm, with which absolute reality is depicted, the more precarious grows the status of human reality. It sinks into the position of an illusion, adjusted no doubt to the imperfection of 'finite' being, but for this very reason ineradicable and irremediable. For from the standpoint of absolute reality there is no difficulty to sur-mount. *Sub specie absoluti* there is no imperfection at all. We have no case against absolute reality, because our woes are illusory. So are we. It need not and cannot

help us, because neither they nor we exist for it.   If we start from the other side, we come upon the same *impasse* : if, in defiance of all that is rational, finite beings nevertheless seem to themselves to exist and to battle with imperfect realities, this shows that such illusion is not repugnant to the perfection of absolute reality.   But if such illusion does not impair this perfection now, there is no reason why it ever should in times to come (if it is not nonsense to speak of future times in connexion with the Absolute) : for all the Absolute knows or cares, 'finite' beings may continue to seem to exist and continue to seem imperfect to themselves and to each other for evermore. We have not therefore altered the dimensions or the urgency of our troubles : we have merely denied the cosmic significance of human life.

Or, looked at from the standpoint of human reality, all that the thought of an absolute reality effects is subtly and all-pervasively to discredit whatever reality we have felt it right to recognize.   It merely warns us that there is something more real, but unattainable, beyond.

The conclusion therefore is inevitable, that the notion of an absolute reality is doubly pernicious : (a) as reducing our reality to unreality in comparison with a higher reality, and (b) as making the ideal of reality seem unattainable.   These results follow if the disparity between absolute reality and reality for us is perceived.

(4) If there is no perception of the difference, if, that is, the two notions are confused, all sorts of realities will be taken for absolute merely because they happen to exist.   They will accordingly be regarded with the respect due to absolute reality, and the disastrous consequence will ensue that it will be impious to experiment with the purpose of (1) rendering them unreal, (2) improving them, and (3) discovering further realities to supersede or supplement them.

The effects of this superstition will indeed here be more deleterious than in the parallel case of 'absolute' truth.   For the old 'truths' which could not be got rid of because they were taken to be absolute, were, after all, not wholly bad. If they had not been valuable, they would never have been called truths ; they worked and served our purposes fairly well, and *faute de mieux* we could get on with them.   The realities we have to accept, on the other hand, are often intrinsically abominable and worthy of destruction, and to perpetuate their reality is wantonly to inflict unnecessary suffering.   The belief, therefore, that they are ultimate and sanctioned by a fixed order of things, prevents the attainment of what is good, as well as preserving what is evil.

To symbolize numerically the extent of this mischief, we might represent the known and accepted realities as, say, one million.   But these, as we have learnt from past experience, do not exhaust the possibilities of the universe.   There may (1) exist in addition, say, ten million other realities which may be ' discovered,' *i.e.* found to be ' real,' if certain experiments are performed which are, or will be, in our power.   Moreover (2) of the million known realities one-half, say 500,000, may deserve to be rendered unreal, and may be removable from the world they contaminate.   (3) There may be as many more potential realities, unreal at present, but capable of being brought into existence by our efforts.

Now all these three desirable operations are barred by the notion that our existing realities are absolute. The rigidly monistic way of conceiving the universe is singularly unimaginative and lacking in variety.   It cuts down the possibilities to the actualities of existence.   It shuts us off from infinite possibilities of things beautiful, good, and true, by the wanton dogmatism of its assumption that the absolute is already real, and that the attempt to remake it is as vain as it is blasphemous.

Consider, on the other hand, the advantages of discarding this notion.   We can then permit ourselves to recognize that reality is still in the making.   Nothing is *absolutely* settled.   Human operations are real experiments with a reality that really responds, and may respond differently to different manipulations.   Reality no doubt has its habits, good and bad, useful and inconvenient (as we have), and is not easily induced to change them. But at bottom they are habits, and leave it plastic. Consequently at every point at which we have alternative ways of manipulating either ourselves or other reals there exists a choice between two really, and for ever, divergent universes. Thus our actual experience contains literally infinite possibilities of alternative universes, which struggle for existence in the minds of every agent who is capable, in however limited a degree, of choosing between alternatives.[1] Every impulse we repress or yield to, every act we do or leave undone, every inquiry we pursue or neglect, realizes a new universe which was not real, and need never have become so. Thus it is our duty and our privilege to co-operate in the shaping of the world ; among infinite possibilities to select and realize the best. That is not much perhaps, though it is as much as God could do in the intellectualistic scheme of Leibniz ; but it is enough to encourage us and to confirm our faith. For herein surely lies the most bracing of responsibilities, the chief attraction of pluralism, and the most grievous wrong which monism has inflicted upon our aspirations and our self-respect.

§ 10. *How Reality really grows*

(5) After proving that the assumption of absolute realities is futile, *i.e.* unnecessary and self-defeating, and pernicious, it might seem superfluous to show that they are also ' untrue,' *i.e.* that they caricature the development of reality as it actually takes place in our knowledge.

But it is so difficult to get even ' philosophically-trained ' minds to look at the simple facts of actual knowing that no means of illumination should be neglected.

It is a simple fact that the *conception of absolute reality does not enter into our actual knowing of reality.* The conceptions of ' primary,' ' ulterior ' and ultimate, of ' lower ' and ' higher ' realities do. Yet our epistemo-

---

[1] Cp. Essay xviii. §§ 9-12.

logy has hitherto allowed itself to be so dazzled by the supernatural effulgence of the former as to blind itself to the really important function of the latter. And so the attainment of epistemological knowledge has been sacrificed to the pursuit of metaphysical will-o'-the-wisps.

§ 11. *The Conception of Primary Reality*

We start uncritically with the acceptance of whatever seems to be. 'Whatever is, is real,' is what we begin with. If we were purely cognitive beings, we should also stop with this. For it is utterly false to imagine *purely intellectual* 'contradictions of appearance' as initiating the process of real knowing, and the dialectical diversions of the young men of Athens some 2000 years ago have been treated far too seriously by staid philosophers who did not appreciate Platonic humour. The problem as to how Socrates, being greater than a flea and less than a whale, can be both greater and less, has very little to do with the difficulties of real knowing. But there are no contradictions in appearance so long as we are merely *contemplating* it : so long as we do not care what appears, no course of events can be any more 'contradictory' than the shifting scenes of a kaleidoscope. Whatever appears 'is,' even though it lasts only for a second.[1] Its reality, such as it is, is not impaired by its impermanence, nor by the fact that something else comes up and takes its place in the twinkling of an eye.

There is no contradiction in change—until we have ourselves imported it by developing a desire to control the changes by means of identities we trace in them. For until then we do not seek for identities in the changeful ; change, taken merely as such, is merely what Kant called 'alternation.' As it presents nothing 'identical' either in the object or in the subject, the

---

[1] Mr. Bradley here bears us out by saying (*Appearance and Reality*, p. 132) "what appears, for that sole reason, indubitably *is*; and there is no possibility of conjuring its being away from it." Capt. H. V. Knox has, however, shown that the coherence of this doctrine with the rest of Mr. Bradley's metaphysic is very dubious (*Mind*, xiv. 217).

problem as to how anything can 'change,' and yet remain 'the same,' does not arise. Events flit across the stage of Reality in the theatre of Being, to adapt Hume's famous simile; but a merely intellectual spectator would see no reason for rejecting anything, for selecting some things as more real and important than others, no occasion to criticize and to wonder how things got there. Even though he were privileged to become a 'spectator of all time and all existence,' he would not be able to 'spectate' to any purpose, nor be really an intelligent spectator. Having no interest to guide his contemplations he would not analyse the flow of events, because he would not attend to anything in particular. He would not even be interested to distinguish 'subject' from 'object.' This distinction too is teleological, and rooted in feeling.

In short, at the level of primary reality, conceived as 'purely' cognitive, everything would be, and remain, in an unmeaning, undiscriminated flow.

§ 12. 'Real' Reality versus Appearance

But the mind is not of such a nature as to put up with this imaginary situation. It is interested, and purposive, and desirous of operating on, and controlling, its primary reality. So it proceeds to discriminate, to distinguish between 'appearance' and 'reality,' between 'primary' and 'real' reality, to accept what appears with mental reservations and provisionally, to operate upon it, and to alter it. As interests grow various and purposes are differentiated, 'real reality' grows more complex. It is differentiated into a series of realities which are referred to a series of systems co-ordinated and subordinated to each other. But as yet only imperfectly. The ultimate reality which we envisage as the goal of our interpretations of primary reality, recedes into a more and more distant ideal. It forms the further pole of our cognitive attitude towards the primary reality, the control of which is the motive for the whole procedure, and ever

forms our final criterion. Fof it is upon this touchstone
of direct experience that we test the value of the assumed
realities which claim authority to interpret it.

Thus by a painful and laborious process we supplement the inadequacies of our actual experience by
assumed realities whose reality is assured to us by their
value, by the salutary transformations which they help us
to effect in our life. The process is as unending as the
pursuit of happiness. We are never wholly satisfied ; we
are never therefore wholly willing to accept reality as it
appears. So we conjure into existence the worlds of the
' higher ' realities, from mathematics to metaphysics, from
the idealized abstractions of the humblest science to the
heaven of the loftiest religion. Their function, one and all,
is to control and to transform the reality we have. But
to do this they have to remain related to it, to sympathize
with its career, to share in its vicissitudes. So long
as they succeed in this, they have their reward : they
are not called in doubt, however much, and however
often, they are required to transform themselves. For at
every transformation we can feel ourselves to be advancing
from a less to a more adequate plane of operations, and
can say, ' This then, which we mistook until now, was real
all along.'

So soon, however, as this dependence on and interaction with immediate experience is renounced, *i.e.* so
soon as the higher reality is taken to be something apart
and absolute, its whole function is destroyed. It can no
longer serve even as an ideal ; for an ideal can only be
functional if it is conceived as attainable, though not
attained.[1] If therefore absolute reality is either unattainable, or already attained, or, worst of all, *both* (*i.e.*
attained, but unattainable by us), it ceases to he a valid
ideal.

Yet it was a beautiful ideal until it was misconceived. It could inspire our efforts to reach a perfect
harmony, and justify our aspirations. For the humanist
also may cherish an ideal of absolute Reality. Nay,

[1] Cp. Essay vi. § 1.

he can even determine its formal character. Nothing is easier. That reality (and that alone) will be pragmatically absolute, which every one will accept as real and no one will seek to alter. For a universe completely satisfied would not seek to change itself, and indeed could not so much as entertain the thought of change.

The real difficulty lies not in framing ideals, but in achieving them, and this is a difficulty, not of philosophy, but of life. And the noblest service philosophy can render us is to pass a self-denying ordinance, and to draw our attention away from idle and inactive speculation about reality in the abstract, to the real ways in which ideals are realized and the world of reality is rendered fit to live in.

IX

EMPIRICISM AND THE ABSOLUTE[1]

ARGUMENT

§ 1. The conflict between Evolutionism and a static metaphysic. The back-sliding of Spencer. § 2. The protest of Humanism. Its acceptance of common-sense, and criticism of metaphysical, assumptions. The new issues. Prof. Taylor's attempts at compromise. § 3. Can purpose be ascribed to the Absolute ? The external contemplation of purpose false. Hume's trick. § 4. Prof. Taylor on selective attention and Berkeley's passivism. § 5. His own Berkeleian basis. The impossibility of selection in the Absolute, which cannot be teleological. § 6. Other mitigations of intellectualism. § 7. Impossibility of combining Absolutism and Humanism, exemplified (a) in the doctrine of appearance and reality ; § 8 (b) of the dual criteria of reality ; § 9 (c) the relations of axioms and postulates ; § 10 (d) intellectualism ; and § 11 the Absolute. Its derivation, which, § 12, depends wholly on the validity of the 'ontological' argument. § 13. The Absolute is really a postulate, § 14, intended to satisfy the craving for unity, and to yield an *a priori* guarantee for the future. The fear of the future as the root of rationalism. § 15. The inadequacy of the postulated Absolute.

§ 1. PHILOSOPHY just now is in a very interesting condition. For Evolutionism, the great scientific movement of the nineteenth century, is at length investing the

---

[1] This discussion of Prof. A. E. Taylor's *Elements of Metaphysics* appeared in *Mind* for July 1905 (N.S. 55), and in its original form treated his views as possibly intended to be crypto-pragmatic. His reply, however, in N.S. 57, exonerated him from the charge of talking Pragmatism (except in the way in which M. Jourdain talked prose) ; his doctrines can now only be treated as 'pseudo-pragmatic,' and as in some respects seriously inconsistent. My reasons for this estimate were set out in full in N.S. 59, pp. 375-390 ; but the discussion, though instructive also for its bearing on the question of 'useless knowledge,' of which Prof. Taylor attempted to produce some examples (cp. pp. 384-8), grew too minute, controversial to be included here. I have, however, profited by it to make some modifications, additions, and omissions, and have tried to note the gist of Prof. Taylor's replies in footnotes. That Prof. Taylor has since abandoned Absolutism and returned to Theism appears from his contribution to a symposium on Pluralism in the Aristotelian Society's *Proceedings* (1909). Hence my criticisms no longer apply to him personally, but only to the views of which he has been an unusually lucid expounder.

last well-nigh inaccessible stronghold of 'pure' metaphysics,[1] and systematically grappling with the ultimate
abstractions which human thought has recognized and
respected for ages, but has never succeeded in rendering
really useful and intelligible. In saying this I am of
course well aware that the application of Evolutionism to
metaphysics is supposed to have been accomplished by
the Synthetic Philosophy of Herbert Spencer. This
popular belief, however, is easily shown to be a misapprehension. If we take as the essence of Evolutionism
the doctrine that the world is in process, and as its chief
corollaries its vindication of the reality of change and of
the belief that real (and not merely apparent) novelties
occur, it is easily seen (1) that the old metaphysic must
ultimately reject these doctrines, and (2) that Spencer's
final surrender to its prejudices involves a failure to work
out a truly evolutionist philosophy.

As to the first point, it has always been assumed
that ultimately Reality must be a closed system, a fixed
quantity, immutable substance, or absolute whole. What
has not always been perceived to be an inevitable consequence is that Reality must, in the last resort, be
stationary, that if so, there can be neither increase nor
decrease in Being, and that the changes, processes, and
novelties we suppose ourselves to experience and observe
do not really mean alterations in the substance of the
All. They must, in other words, be human illusions (or,
more politely, "appearances"), which do not penetrate to,
or affect, the eternally complete and immutable Reality.
If, resenting this paradox of metaphysics, we plead that
these "appearances" are inextricably intertwined with the
whole reality of human life, we are baffled by the retort
that this only shows that we too are 'appearance.'

Such metaphysic plainly is not to be silenced by mere
common-sense: it must be fought with its own weapons.
And so it is probably more profitable to point out that in
strict consistency these metaphysicians should demand,
not merely that change, etc., should be illusions, but also

[1] Felicitously entitled 'Jericho' by Mr. Bradley (*Mind*, xiii. p. 330).

that such illusions should be impossible. As Prof. Stout
has pointed out, you can call all 'reality' illusion, but in
so doing you imply the reality of the illusion. If then
change is truly irrational and unthinkable, it should not
be able to maintain even an illusory existence in a
rational universe ; and the very existence of such an
illusion is itself as irrational and unthinkable as the reality
which was condemned as illusory. Abstract metaphysic,
therefore, is unable to explain, and unwilling to accept,
phenomenal change, process, and novelty : if it desires to
be consistent, it must simply *deny* them, and revert as
nearly as possible to its earliest form, viz. Eleaticism. To
evoke a philosophic meaning from the everyday facts of
change and novelty and from the scientific testimonies to
vast cosmic processes, we need a different method, which
will deign to consider whether we should not do as well,
or better, by frankly accepting the apparent facts of
ordinary life and science, and regarding rather our preference for the constant and immutable as an artificial
device which is susceptible of derivation and limited in
application. In other words, we need Humanism.

(2) Now Spencer, in his attempt at an evaluation of
the idea of Evolution, unfortunately committed himself to
a use of physical principles which belong inalienably to
the static series of conceptions, and are designed to satisfy
our craving for constancy. The indestructibility of matter
and the conservation of energy ('persistence of force')
are constitutionally incapable of yielding a justification
for the belief in a real process, a real progress, and a real
alteration in the meaning of the world. In consequence,
the phenomena of life and consciousness, in which the
reality of such evolution is most manifest (for psychically
every experience is more or less 'new'), have to be reduced
by Spencer to physical terms. And thus the whole
evolutionary process becomes nugatory in the end.
Spencer has to admit that the differentiation-process
which forms the cosmic *diastole* has for its counterpart a
systole which restores all things to homogeneity, and that
throughout both processes the axiom of the Persistence of

Force remains uninfringed. In terms of ultimate reality, therefore, both processes mean *the same*, and at the end of the infinite toil and struggle of the cosmic agony, the universe is where it was, neither richer nor poorer, neither better nor worse. Evolution therefore has turned out a merely subjective illusion, engendered by our incapacity to follow the giant swing of the cosmic pendulum.

§ 2. But can we hesitate to declare this result to be, humanly speaking, most unsatisfactory, and indeed profoundly irrational? And is it not worth while at least to entertain proposals for the radical revision of the metaphysical prepossessions that have brought us to such a pass? Why, after all, should we insist on starting from the conception of an absolute Whole presumed to be unalterable? Why should we not set out rather from the facts of *our* 'finite' struggling life, and pluck up courage to scrutinize the construction of the scientific, or rather metaphysical, bogies that stand in the way of a thorough-going Evolutionism? So at least the Humanist must argue. He takes for granted all those features of our experience which are undeniable on the common-sense level of life. He takes as the sole essential problem of philosophy the harmonizing of a life, which is as yet inharmonious, but which he is willing to believe may be transmuted into harmony. And instead of contenting himself with a verbal 'proof' that all evil is 'appearance' which is 'transcended' *sub specie aeternitatis*, and then submitting tamely to the cosmic nightmare *in saecula saeculorum*, he accepts all the apparent features of life, its transitoriness, cruelty, ignorance, uncertainty, struggle; the reality of its chances and changes, of its gains and losses, of its pains and pleasures, of its values, ethical, logical, and æsthetical, of its goods and evils, truths and errors, as alike *data* for thought to grapple with and to transform, and holds that only by achieving this does our thought vindicate its use, and our truth become truly true. Not that the Humanist imagines that all these features will in the end turn out to be equally significant; he contends only that they cannot be proved delusions *a priori*, that the sole way of proving them unreal is by abolishing them, and that until they have been so abolished they must be reckoned with as facts.

In the rationalistic intellectualism,[1] on the other hand, in which the method of abstract metaphysics culminates, all these initial facts of common life are contemptuously ignored. Nothing less than the absolute totality of existence is worthy of its notice or worth assuming. This totality it supposes itself to demonstrate by some version of the ontological proof, and aims at developing, by *a priori* reasoning, into a coherent and consistent, self-determined and unalterable system.

To the Humanist, on the other hand, this whole procedure seems a tissue of fallacious and futile assumptions. Why should he assume that experience necessarily forms a whole before he has got it all together? that it forms a system before he has traced it out? that the system is *one*, before he has found that his actual world can intelligibly be treated as such? that the system is perfect (in any but a verbal, intellectualist sense) before he has tried it? And if he assumes these things because he would like them to be true, what does he make the totality of Reality but a conceptual postulate, perhaps of rationality, perhaps of a subtler irrationality, which can be tested only by its working, and can in no case be argued from *a priori*? What in general are the *a priori* truths but *claims*, what are axioms but postulates? As for the complete determination of the universe, is not both the fact and its value open to doubt? As for its unity, is not its value emotional and illusory rather than scientific, so long as we can neither avoid assuming a plurality of factors in all scientific calculation, nor identify our actual world with the one immutable universe, so long as it seems to us subject to

[1] It is better to avoid the term 'idealism,' as being too equivocal to be useful. There are too many 'idealisms' in the market, many of them more essentially opposed to each other than to views classified as 'realism.' Plato, *e.g.*, has an indefeasible claim to the title of 'idealist,' but Mr. G. E. Moore, in reviving the Platonic hypostasization of abstract qualities in an extreme form, prefers to call himself a 'realist.' Berkeley again is firmly established in the histories of philosophy as the typical idealist, but his sensationalism constitutes a most irritating challenge to the rationalists' claim to monopolize the name. In addition, there are 'subjective' and 'personal' and 'empirical' 'idealists' galore.

irruptions from without its known limits and to the erup-
tion of novelties within them?[1]   As for its immutability,
is it not a direct defiance of our primary experience and
a wanton stultification of the evolutionist method?   And
finally, is not the fundamental intellectualism of the old
metaphysic a gross parody of our actual thought, which
proceeds from a purposive intelligent activity, and was
not, and is not, and never can be, separated from the
practical needs of life?

Humanism therefore challenges all the assumptions on
which rationalistic intellectualism has reposed ever since
the days of Plato.   Against such a challenge the old
catchwords of its warfare with the sensationalistic intellectualism of the British empiricists are no longer adequate.
They are as plainly outranged by the novelty as its prejudices are outraged by the audacity of the voluntarist
attack.   A complete change of front, and a thorough re-
arrangement of its forces, have become imperative.   And
by the younger men among its exponents this is beginning to be perceived.   Prof. A. E. Taylor has not yet
perhaps fully realized the magnitude and difficulty of the
readjustment which is needed in his camp, and he has
certainly not succeeded in repelling the attack ; but he has
perceived that the creed of the ' Anglo-Hegelian '[2] Intellectualism rests on a dangerously narrow basis.   The lucid
and agreeable form of his *Elements of Metaphysics*, his
manifest anxiety to assimilate at least as much of the new
material as may be needed to leave the old positions
tenable, and the importance of making clear just where
the difficulties of mediating between Absolutism and
Humanism lie, amply warrant a detailed examination of
this side of his work.

As the result of such examination, it will be found that
though Prof. Taylor has not been able to bridge the gulf
between the old philosophy and the new—indeed, he has
hardly been invested with full authority by his party—he
has effected some instructive modifications, and discovered
some interesting jumping-off places.

[1] Cp. Essay xii. § 9.   [2] As he calls it (*Mind*, xv. p. 90).

§ 3. (1) Perhaps the most striking of Prof. Taylor's innovations is his constant use of the language of purpose and teleology.[1] For, in words at least, this seems to concede the main principle for which Humanism has contended, viz. the purposiveness of human thought and experience.

Unfortunately, however, for the fruitful application of this principle, Prof. Taylor hardly seems to conceive purpose in the natural way. He habitually regards it rather from the external standpoint of the contemplative *spectator* than from that of the purposing *agent*, and it will always be found that a philosophy which refuses to enter into the feelings of the agent must in the end pronounce the whole conception of agency an unmeaning mystery. Now this *ab extra* way of conceiving agency from the standpoint of a bystander was Hume's fundamental trick, the root of all his naturalism, and the basis of his success as a critic of causation. It seems curious, therefore, that rationalists should never try to emancipate themselves from it, but should accept it meekly and without question, the more so as their ' answers to Hume ' are always upset by it. For it would be possible to show that once this assumption is made, there is (1) no real answer to Hume, (2) no escape from naturalism, and (3) no room left for the conception of agency ; and it may be suggested that the radical unsoundness of the transcendentalists' position at this point is the real reason for the obscurity and unsatisfactoriness of their own treatment of causation ever since the days of Kant. So long as Hume's specious arguments against our immediate experience of agency are accepted, agents and activities cannot be recognized anywhere in the universe, and we are driven to the desperate contradiction of ascribing an ' activity ' to the whole which is denied to all its parts and ought not to exist, even as a word ; it is *a fortiori* impossible, therefore, to see how we

---

[1] Cp. especially pp. 55, 58, 66, 106, 162, 204. Prof. Taylor retorted that his debt was to Professors Ward and Royce (*Mind*, N.S. xv. 88). I replied (1) that neither of these fitted into a Bradleian metaphysic ; (2) that it was necessary to have an explanation with Humanist teleology ; and (3) that he had been challenged to explain how an Absolute could have a purpose (*Mind*, xv. p. 377).

could be active enough to lay down 'rules' for the apprehending of events.[1]

Prof. Taylor, therefore, seems to fall into an insidious
but far-reaching error when he says (p. 55) "all that I
mean is that the processes of conscious life are as a matter
of fact only *intelligible* with reference to the results in
which they culminate . . . or again that they all involve
the kind of continuity of interest which belong (*sic*) to
attention."[2]   Similarly in defining spirit (p. 99), "where
you have a connected system of factors which can only
be understood" (why not *understand themselves*?) "by
reference to an explicit or implicit end which constitutes
their unity, you have spirit."[3]   On this it seems obvious
to remark that unless 'you' *were* an actively purposing
spirit, you could never regard any connexion of things as
teleological.   And the human spirit is, of course, teleological, because it attends and operates selectively.   But
these very facts suggest the deepest doubt as to the
transfer of these features to the Whole.   Can an Absolute
attend or act selectively, can it be 'teleological' or
'spiritual' in any humanly intelligible sense ?

§ 4. To answer this question, let us examine Prof.
Taylor's treatment of selective attention.   It is most
instructive.   The conception does not occur in his master,
Mr. F. H. Bradley, who is too much under the spell of
Hume to admit the notion of activity.   He has taken it
from Prof. Stout, and is eager to use it as a good stick
for beating the elder (and saner) brother, whom 'absolute'
idealists are always so anxious to disparage and so unable
to dispense with, viz. Berkeleian idealism.   Accordingly
he points out (p. 66)—what is true of intellectualism as
such, but less patently applicable to Berkeleianism than
to most rationalistic forms of intellectualism—viz. that
Berkeley conceived the mind as passive, and did not allow
for its interests and purposes.   "Berkeley," he says,
"omits selective attention from his psychological estimate
of the contents of the human mind.   He forgets that it

---

[1] Cp. James in *The Pluralistic Universe*, p. 370-94.
[2] Italics mine.   [3] P. 3 ; cp. also pp. 5 and 44.   Italics mine.

is the interests for which I take note of facts that in the
main determine which facts I shall take note of, an over-
sight which is the more remarkable, since he expressly
lays stress on 'activity' as the distinguishing property of
'spirits.' When we make good the omission by emphasizing the teleological aspects of experience, we see at
once that the radical disparity between the relation of the
supreme and the subordinate mind to the world of facts
disappears. I do not receive my presented facts passively
in an order determined for me from without by the
supreme mind; in virtue of my power of selective attention, on a limited scale, and very imperfectly, I recreate
the order of their succession for myself. . . .

The very expression 'selective attention' itself carries
with it a reminder that the facts which respond to my
interests are but a selection out of a larger whole. And
my practical experience of the way in which my own
most clearly defined and conscious purposes depend for
their fulfilment upon connexion with the interests and
purposes of a wider social whole possessed of an organic
unity, should help me to understand how the totality of
interests and purposes determining the selective attention
of different percipients can form, as we have held that it
must, the harmonious and systematic unity of the absolute
experience. . . . It is hardly too much to say that the
teleological character which experience possesses in virtue
of its unity with feeling is the key to the idealistic interpretation of the universe."

§ 5. Philosophy would become delightfully easy if the
fundamental deficiencies of intellectualism could be cured
in the facile fashion of this passage; but Prof. Taylor's
whole procedure is, alas, illusory. It should be observed,
in the first place, that in spite of his continual protests
against Berkeley, he himself has to proceed from a subjective basis. He has to argue, that is, from the behaviour
of his mind to that of the Absolute. His mind attends
selectively, he finds, and thereby constitutes reality; *ergo*
the Absolute is conceived to act similarly.

It must be conjectured that when Prof. Taylor argued

thus, he had lapsed into happy oblivion of the nature of the absolute mind and the meaning of which it is the expression.   Otherwise he could not but have been impressed by the difference between its functioning and that of a human mind.

A human mind initially commences its career in a jumble resembling a chaotic rag-bag.   It finds itself containing things valuable, worthless, and pernicious, dreams, illusions, fancies, delusions, incongruities, inconsistencies, etc., all jostling the materials for what are subsequently construed as realities.   If, therefore, any approach to a harmonious life is to be constructed out of such stuff, a large amount of selection is necessary.   The pernicious contents must be kept under and as far as possible eliminated ; the worthless and useless must be neglected ; and so chaos must be turned into something like a cosmos. This we do by selectively attending to what turns out to be valuable, and by ignoring those elements in our experience which we cannot use.

Similarly in our actions we never operate with or upon the universe as a whole.   We choose our ends and select our means ; we dissect our 'effects' and 'causes' from the unaccentuated flow of events ; it is essential to our science to select limited and partial subjects of inquiry. In short, 'action' seems to connote selection, and selection must seem arbitrary and indefensible if human purposes have been abstracted from.

Now compare the 'absolute mind' of philosophic theory.   It was conceived as all-inclusive ; its business and function is to contain everything.   It must therefore *ex officio* and *ex vi termini* include all the rubbish every human mind is encumbered with and has such trouble to get rid of.   For though *we* can condemn it as 'appearance,' the Absolute cannot.   For ultimately even 'appearance' is a sort of 'reality,' and must be included in its proper place.   And this place is the Absolute, which has room for all things, for which all things are valuable, nay essential, seeing that if they were not, they would not exist !   Or if it be maintained that the Absolute can purify itself by recognizing nothing but 'reality' in the fullest sense, will it not inevitably follow that the human mind and *all* its belongings are cast out upon the rubbish-heap of appearances which are unworthy of the Absolute's notice? And in that case of what value is the Absolute as a conception to explain *our* experience?

If, then, the Absolute has to include everything to fulfil its function, if it exists for us in order to include what we reject, how can it selectively attend to *part* of its contents? Must not all that is be valuable to All-that-is? What private, limited, and partial interests can it have to compel it to 'select' facts out of a larger whole? It is itself the 'larger whole,' and its sole interest must be to represent *that*. It cannot abnegate this function, and 'select' like 'finite' man, without becoming partial and ceasing to be itself.

Manifestly, therefore, no argument holds from selective attention in us to selective attention in the Absolute. For one can hardly press Prof. Taylor's language as seriously advocating a naïve fallacy of composition to the effect that because all (distributively) are interested in some things, therefore all (collectively) are interested in a totality in which *all special emphasis* has disappeared.

And his further procedure in arguing from selective attention in the individual to the recognition of a social, and ultimately of an absolute, environment is equally fallacious. He has failed to observe that the mere practice of selective attention does *not* carry him off the subjective ground he started on. We have seen that a selective ordering of experiences is a vital necessity. It would be so equally to a solipsist who had refrained from postulating an 'external world' populated by 'other' minds. He too would have to order his experiences and to discriminate their values. Only he would reach analogous results by different methods. It is only when our various postulates have been made and found to work, that our experience can be systematized in ways which recognize them by name, and that so we speak of our 'social' environment.

And even then the taking account of wider environments must, it would seem, stop short of the whole. The Absolute, strictly and properly conceived, can never be the explanation of anything in particular. It can therefore enter any valid purpose as little as it can itself have a purpose, or aim at completing what is already the whole. Neither, therefore, has it teleological value itself, nor is its own nature teleological. What warrant, then, has any absolutist philosophy to treat human purposiveness as more significant than anything else included in the whole, or to attribute cosmic value to human teleology?

We must conclude, therefore, that Prof. Taylor's recognition of the purposiveness of human thought and action is either illusory or so inconsistent with his fundamental views that it could not but lead him away from the absolutism he professes, if he would work it out. And the objections to this particular eclecticism have turned out to be sufficiently general to render it one of the most urgent *desiderata* of absolutist metaphysics to show how the typically human conception of purpose can be attributed to the Absolute and conceived as a specific function of the Absolute. But the omens augur ill for such an undertaking.

§ 6. (2) His psychological studies seem to have somewhat emancipated Prof. Taylor from the fatal fiction of a disinterested intellect. He even dares to represent metaphysics as the product of an "*instinctive demand* of our intellect for coherency and consistency of thought."[1] In science this interest is definitely practical, and its original object "is practical success in interference with the course of events" (p. 226). Historically, therefore, science is an offshoot of the arts (p. 385), and to this day "the ultimate object of all physical science is the successful formulation of such practical rules for action" (p. 284).[2]

Hence (3) Science, Prof. Taylor agrees, makes use of

---

[1] P. 3 ; cp. also pp. 5 and 44. Italics mine.

[2] Cp., however, pp. 121-2, where to aim at "practical success in action rather than at logical consistency in thinking" is called a *pre-scientific* attitude, and the aim of Science is reduced to that of 'metaphysics,' viz. consistent systematization.

Postulates, which serve its practical purposes without being ultimately true. Thus the principle of causality " must be pronounced to be neither an axiom nor an empirical truth, but a postulate, in the strict sense of the word, *i.e.* an assumption which cannot be logically justified, but is made because of its practical value, and depends for confirmation on the success with which it can be applied. In the sense that it is a postulate which experience may confirm but cannot prove, it may properly be said to be *a priori*, but it is manifestly not *a priori* in the more familiar Kantian sense of the word " (p. 167).[1]

Similarly (pp. 175-6) the analysis of events into independent series, and their mathematical calculability, are postulates. It is too " a practical methodological postulate that the reign of law in physical nature is absolute " (p. 223), and a possible failure of experience to confirm it is disregarded because of our *interest* to discover such uniformities. . " We treat all sequences as capable, by proper methods, of reduction to uniformity, for the same reason that we treat all offenders as possibly reclaimable. We desire that they should be so, and we therefore behave as if we knew that they were so " (p. 200). " Space and Time are phenomenal, the result of a process of construction forced on us by our practical needs " (p. 230).[2]

---

[1] Cp. also pp. 227-9. It is difficult to estimate how far this doctrine is modified in Prof. Taylor's interesting "Side Lights on Pragmatism" (in the *M'Gill University Magazine*, iii. 2). For though Prof. Taylor again instances (p. 61) among the " beliefs which are useful but cannot be proved independently to be true," "our scientific beliefs in causation or in the existence of laws of nature," and tells us that " for the purpose of formulating practical rules for the manipulation of bodies it is advantageous to be assured that . . . whatever happens . . . *will* happen again without variation," he is by no means clear about the logical position of this postulate. Immediately after he goes on to say that because such assumptions are merely considered true because they are convenient, " we have no right to say that they are true except within the limits in which they *have been* verified by actual experience." This would again invalidate them as methods of prediction, and exactly parallels Mill's famous stultification of the causal principle when he admitted that it might not hold in distant parts of the stellar regions. Prof. Taylor exhibits this contradiction in a more compact form, but with as profound an unconsciousness of its logical import.

[2] I cannot see why after this Prof. Taylor should insist on treating the Conservation of Mass and of Energy as only empirical generalizations (p. 177). In his reply he treats the recognition of postulates as something which might have occurred to any one, but denies that they are found in arithmetic (*Mind*, xv. p. 89). I commented on the awkwardness of the anomaly, etc. (*l.c.* p. 378).

It will be clear from the above that Prof. Taylor has no mean grasp of the epistemological convenience of postulates, and though their relations to the axioms are far from clear, and he does not apparently perceive their importance as an epistemological clue, it seems indisputable that he has surrendered some of the most characteristic features of the Kantian and post-Kantian apriorism.[1]

(4) Occasionally Prof. Taylor catches still deeper glimpses of the function of thought in the service of humanity. Rightly denying the possibility of an *a priori* theory of knowledge, he remarks (p. 17) that " the *instrument* can only be studied in its work, and we have to judge of its possibilities by the nature of its products." [2]

After two such *aperçus* a relapse into intellectualism would hardly seem logically possible, the more so as Prof. Taylor also recognizes the teleological character of the construction of identity, and regards it as a methodological assumption that " there are situations in the physical order which may be treated, with sufficient accuracy for our practical purposes, as recurring identically " [3] (p. 284). It is difficult not to take this as subordinating the conception of 'identity' to practical purposes. In the physical order, at all events, 'identity' would seem to be not 'found' but 'made' or 'taken' with a purpose which conditions its existence, and when we remember the terrible embarrassments in which the fact of this 'arbitrary making' of identities involves intellectualistic logic,[4] it will seem strange that after departing so far from the spirit of Mr. Bradley's scepticism, he should have stopped short of recognizing *all* logical identifying to be a pragmatically justified experiment.[5]

---

[1] Kant personally he is only too eager to throw overboard, accusing his epistemological position of confusion (pp. 40, 134, 242).

[2] Cp. p. 32 ; italics mine.   Prof. Taylor denies that this was intended to bear a pragmatic meaning, but proceeds to explain what he meant in a way which seems to me to bring out still more clearly the pragmatism logically implicit in his dictum.

[3] Cp. also pp. 335 and 98.

[4] Cp. Essays, iii. § 8, iv. § 4.

[5] In spite of saying that "all identity appears in the end to be teleological" (*Elem. of Met.* p. 335), he denies, however, that he meant to conceive logical identity as a postulate. Cp. *Pers. Ideal.* pp. 94-104 ; and *Mind,* xv. p. 380.

And so finally (5) Prof. Taylor is sometimes beguiled into what looks suspiciously like the most radical empiricism. He says (p. 23) that "the real is experience, and nothing but experience, and experience consists of psychical matter-of-fact. Proof of this proposition can *only*[1] be given in the same way as of *any other*[1] ultimate truth, *by making trial of it.*[2] Again (p. 38) "the true character of any scientific method can *of course only*[1] be discovered by *the actual use* of it."[3]

Prof. Taylor hereupon explains (*Mind*, xv. 91) that the remark only means that "you cannot analyse the methods of a science properly until you have them embodied before you in examples," and has no bearing on the issue between rationalists and empiricists. After this one is more at a loss than ever to understand how the definition of truth can be laid down *a priori* and the nature of logic be determined without reference to their actual functioning when applied to experience. Are we to suppose that a methodological rule which applies to all the sciences is not to be applied to knowledge in general?

§ 7. It should be sufficiently apparent from the above samples that Prof. Taylor's book exhibits an interesting development of Absolutism, which, until he disclaimed the intention, and protested his innocence, might well be conceived as an attempt to transfer to it some of the most distinctive features of Humanism, in order to enrich the barren doctrine that the Absolute is absolute. In view of his disclaimer, however, it must be assumed that the approximations are more apparent than real, and that his 'pragmaticoid' utterances are in reality pseudo-pragmatic, even where they seem incompatible with his system, and where pragmatism would seem to be their logical implication. It remains, therefore, only to show that Absolutism and Humanism cannot be combined, and that Prof. Taylor's work, so far from affording a basis for such a combination, really remains open to all

[1] Italics mine.
[2] Cp. p. 319 *s.f.* and p. 351 *n.*
[3] Italics mine. Prof. Taylor now wishes it to be understood that "the trial referred to was purely logical and *a priori.*"

the insuperable objections which have often been urged against the Absolute from a human point of view. Fortunately Prof. Taylor's lucidity greatly facilitates the proof of this fundamental incompatibility : he has not cared to remember that there are views which flourish best, like fungi, in obscurity, and which it is fatal to expose to the light, and so has probably done Absolutism doubtful service by making too clear its constitutional inability to meet the demands either of the human intellect or of the human heart.

In proof of which let us select for consideration (*A*) Prof. Taylor's account of the relations of 'appearance' and 'reality,' (*B*) his *criteria* of ultimate reality, (*C*) his conception of axioms and postulates, (*D*) his intellectualism, and (*E*) his derivation of the Absolute, with the doctrine of 'degrees of reality' and the 'ontological proof.'

(*A*) The antithesis of 'appearance' and 'reality' is the bed-rock of Prof. Taylor's as of Mr. Bradley's philosophy. But its assumption seems inadequately justified by the simple remark that we must rid experience of its contradictions (p. 2). Getting rid of contradictions is no doubt *one* aspect of our efforts to harmonize our experience, but it is by no means the easiest or most logical starting-point. For (1) before we can use the test of contradiction we have to make sure that we know what 'self-contradiction' is to mean. (2) We have to make sure that it does not mean that what we have to get rid of is, not the 'self-contradictory' 'appearance,' but the conceptions by which we have tried to know it. And (3) as regards the self-contradiction itself, before we can get rid of a contradiction we have to make sure that we *have* a *real* contradiction to get rid of. Before making contradiction our criterion, therefore, we must find a criterion to discriminate between real and apparent contradictions. Thus the antithesis, which it was to transcend, breaks out again *within* the 'absolute criterion' itself.[1]

[1] The levity with which these difficulties have been ignored is admirably brought out in *Mind*, N.S. xiv. 54, by Capt. Knox's masterly paper on "Mr. Bradley's Absolute Criterion," and it is to be hoped that henceforth appeals to it will be more cautious.

Nor again is success in removing contradictions quite the alpha and omega of philosophy as intellectualists are fond of assuming. If it were, philosophy would be in a bad way. A severe construction of the principle would work sad havoc with most philosophic systems, and Prof. Taylor also would have been more judicious not to plume himself upon a consistency too great for mortal logic. For to a harsher stickler for literal consistency than myself, many of Prof. Taylor's statements would seem to need a good deal of reconciling.

What does appear to me to be somewhat deplorable is the way in which he misconceives the logical implications of this doctrine. He fails to make it clear that (1) Nothing whatsoever can be condemned as 'appearance,' unless the superior reality which corrects it, is *already known*; and (2) that even then, whenever the superior reality is not a matter of immediate experience, its validity has to be established by the control it gives us over the 'appearance.'[1] It is fallacious, therefore, to claim ultimate reality for anything that is not (1) known or knowable, and (2) *useful* in operating on our apparent realities. Now as the Absolute has never yet been shown to be capable of satisfying either of these tests, this would conduct us to the distressing dilemma that we must either renounce the Absolute or the favourite antithesis between appearance and reality.

§ 8. (*B*) Incidentally it has already been mentioned that Prof. Taylor liberally allows himself *two* criteria of metaphysical reality. This seems to exceed the legitimate luxury of speculation, and may perhaps seem as gross a self-indulgence to the strict metaphysician as bigamy does to the moralist. There is, however, no doubt of the fact[2] The first of Prof. Taylor's criteria is empirical, and its formulations have been quoted in § 6. Its ultimateness cannot be doubted, either as stated or intrinsically. For any principle can be con-

---

[1] For both these points see my essay on "Preserving Appearances," *Humanism*, pp. 191, 195.

[2] Prof. Taylor's reply on this point has seemed to me so unconvincing that I have not altered this passage. Cp. *Mind*, xv. p. 91, with p. 381.

ceived as a postulate, the value of which is established
by trial.   It must be supposed therefore that Prof. Taylor,
when he states it, really means what he says, and is not
merely lax in his language.   But Prof. Taylor retains
also an intellectualistic criterion which announces itself as
ultimate, and is put forward independently and indeed
with more formal pomp.   It is Mr. Bradley's familiar
maxim that Reality is not self-contradictory.   This it
is argued (p. 22) must be a metaphysical as well as
a logical principle.   For to think truly about things is to
think in accord with their real nature.   But to think
them as contradictory is not to think them *truly*.

In its essence this would seem to be a form of the
'ontological' argument whereby a claim of our thought is
turned into a revelation about reality.   But in addition
there is surely involved a twofold fallacy, viz. (1) an
equivocation in the word 'truth,' which is used both of
the internal self-consistency of thought *and* of its 'correspondence with reality,' and (2) the unworkable view of
truth as the correspondence of thought with reality.[1]

And so it must surely be suggested that the principle
of Non-contradiction is a postulate, if ever there was one.
At one time (p. 19) Prof. Taylor seems to perceive this,
and speaks of the *audacity*[2] of making "a general statement about the whole universe of being" as resulting
from our "*refusing*[2] to accept both sides of a contradiction as true."   But on the next page his faith in the
infallibility of postulation has become so robust that he
proceeds to treat it as *knowledge* about reality, and as
justifying a "confident" assertion that "it is positively
certain that Reality or the universe is a self-consistent
systematic whole!"   A mere pragmatist would gasp at
the audacity of such expeditious modes of overleaping all
distinctions between wish and fact, assertion and proof,
postulate and axiom; but when Prof. Taylor is in the
mood no obstacles can check him.

§ 9. (C) It seems doubtful whether he has quite

---

[1] For the first point see *Humanism*, p. 98 ; for the second, pp. 45-6.
[2] Italics mine.

arrived at the perfect clearness which is so desirable with regard to the relations of axioms and postulates. His procedure, however, is instructive. Without formal discussion he assumes (1) that there are axioms which belong to the fundamental structure of our intellect (pp. 19, 378); (2) that postulates are methodological assumptions, defensible on the ground of their practical usefulness, but only so far as they actually succeed (pp. 227, 167, 169), and sometimes to be spoken of contemptuously as " mere practical postulates " (p. 239); (3) that questions of 'origin' (*i.e.* past history) have no bearing on the 'validity' of our conceptions. Origins, indeed, he concedes whole-heartedly to the pragmatists (p. 385): historically the true is the useful, science an offshoot of the arts (and why not all axioms promoted postulates?). But this does not matter, once the intellectual ideal has been developed. It can judge, and condemn, the very process which constituted the tribunal. Hence (4) it is more likely than not that postulates do not yield us final truth, as is indeed the case with the postulates of which Prof. Taylor makes most explicit mention. Hence (5) it appears that not only do logical defects not impair the usefulness of a conception (p. 168), but (p. 182) "any form of the causal postulate of which we can make effective use necessitates the recognition of that very Plurality of Causes, which we have seen to be logically excluded by the conception of cause with which science works" (or rather *doesn't*!), and "any form of the principle in which it is true is useless, and any form in which it is useful is untrue." This sweeping affirmation of the validity of useless truth and methodological fiction may be commended to the timid souls who shrink from the more moderate inferences from the facts of postulation, which are drawn by the pragmatists, viz. that *the true is useful* and that *the useless is untrue*.[1] To others it will seem queer that a doctrine of the thorough rationality of the universe should reach the result that the highest truths (*e.g.* the metaphysics of the Absolute) should be

---

[1] Cp. *Humanism*, p. 38; *Formal Logic*, ch. xx. § 2.

useless, while the useful, viz. the postulates, are mostly untrue! It should be noted (6) as a final perplexity that on the same page (29) the psychical nature of Reality is called *both* an initial postulate *and* a fundamental metaphysical principle. Are we to infer from this that the fundamental principles are seen to be postulates, or that Prof. Taylor's language has relaxed under the strain of accommodating his theory to the actual procedure of our minds?

These, then, are Prof. Taylor's dicta on the subject of axioms and postulates, and certainly they seem variegated beyond necessity. A living and rapidly growing philosophy will no doubt always find it hard to sustain the appearance of a rigid verbal consistency, and I do not in the least hold with the cynics that demanding consistency from a metaphysician is as absurd as demanding demonstration from a logician—because in neither case will you get it! A certain amount of inconsistency, therefore, is human and pardonable. But I somewhat doubt whether Prof. Taylor has not occasionally exceeded these limits. I am more interested to observe (1) that it seems a great exaggeration of the pragmatist doctrine of methodological assumptions to infer that because they are useful they are probably untrue. For *usefulness is no presumption of untruth*, but rather the reverse. It is not *qua* useful that our assumptions are judged untrue, but *qua* useless. To assume a principle, therefore, for methodological reasons, *i.e.* as conducive to some proximate purpose, in nowise *prejudices* its claim to ulterior truth. It is 'true' so far as it goes, and whether it goes all the way is still an open question. The more useful, therefore, it turns out to be, the truer we judge it: whatever limitations it develops render it useless for our ulterior purposes, and become *pro tanto* motives for judging it untrue, and for trying to recast it into a more widely applicable form. It is therefore for pragmatism the reverse of true that logical defects do not matter: only it contends that in abstraction from its use a conception has no actual meaning, and that it is the limitations which its use reveals which persuade us of its logical defectiveness, rather than *vice versa*.

(2) Prof. Taylor hardly seems to dispose of the strong appeal which Pragmatism makes to the history of our axioms by merely trotting out the musty old antithesis of origin and validity. For in the first place to say that 'origin' does not decide 'validity' gives no positive information on the very vital questions as to what it does decide, and what is the connexion of the two; and, secondly, overlooks the fact that the appeal is not really to *origin* so much as to *past history*.[1]

Concerning the origin indeed of anything whatsoever not more than *two* fundamentally distinct views can be entertained. We may either (1) welcome its novelty and originality, and ascribe its appearance to a providential interposition (θεῖα μοῖρα), hailing it as a gift of the gods, *or* we may reluctantly recognize it as an 'accidental variation.' Metaphysically these explanations are equivalents. Or (2) we may sacrifice the recognition of novelty to the vindication of systematic connexion, and labour to show that, much as the apparent novelty has perturbed us, nothing has occurred that was not fully contained in, and determined by, its antecedents, so that the identical content of Reality has suffered no alteration from the occurrence. It is easy to predict that Intellectualism is sure to prefer the second of these views, and to regard the first as the very acme of irrationality.

But when it argues thus, it only shows, perhaps, how far it is from understanding wherein irrationality consists for its opponents. For to a pragmatist there is nothing essentially irrational in the first account, because he has *not* assumed that the value of a thing depends on, and is eternally determined by, its origin. If the value of everything depends on its *efficiency* in use, it is clear that the rationality of the universe will consist not in its *a priori* inclusion in a metaphysical Absolute, but just in the actual way in which things manage to fit and work together. Things, therefore, neither acquire nor lose any

[1] Cp. *Personal Idealism*, pp. 123-5.

real rationality by their mode of origin. Axioms may arise
as postulates, thoughts as wishes, values as 'accidents'—
their real validation in every case comes from subsequent
experience. Not that our *Humanism* can be indifferent
to the pragmatic equivalents 'chance *or* purposing intelligence.' Only it seems that this further question also
can only be decided *ex post facto*, when the novelties that
burst into the dull routine of a mechanically calculable
world have run their course, and we can judge them by
their fruits whether indeed they *were* of God.

Thus Pragmatism can rebut the charge of irrationality,
and indeed retort it, by pointing out that desirable as it
is for all our scientific purposes to regard the world as
wholly calculable, our anxiety may yet involve us
ultimately in absurdity, if it leads us totally to deny
the occurrence of real novelty. What should, therefore,
be pointed out to Prof. Taylor is that Pragmatism, in
appealing to the past history of conceptions for light upon
their value, is *not* laying stress on their *origin*. It is
assuming merely that the nature of a thing is revealed
empirically in its behaviour, and that therefore to understand it, we should do well to make the most extensive
study of that behaviour. If, moreover, it should be in
process, it will be from a study of its history that we shall
see the drift of that process, and if that process should
admit of, or demand, teleological interpretation, we shall
thus be enabled to forecast its end, and to anticipate its
future, sufficiently for our purposes, even though the
whole nature of a thing could only be fully expressed in
its whole history. The attempt, on the other hand, to
determine the 'validity' of a thing apart from its history
and prospects would seem sheer folly. For it tries to
contemplate in abstraction a mere cross-section of Reality
and claims final validity for what may only be a misleading present phase of its total evolution.

Of course, however, the comparative merits of these
two procedures might be completely altered if it were
possible to pronounce upon the nature of a thing *a priori*.
For in that case there would be no need to wait upon

experience, and science and history would have no bearing upon ultimate Reality. This, no doubt, would be convenient, and forms perhaps the hidden motive for the anxiety of metaphysicians to attain some sort of *a priori* at any cost.

(3) Just as Prof. Taylor failed to see the full logical force of the pragmatist treatment of axioms, so too, I fear, he has not quite apprehended the place which the new views assign to intellection. For he appears to think that pragmatist appeals to practical results can be sufficiently met by saying that the intellect is not wholly practical (pp. 121-2). It aspires beyond practical success in action to logical consistency in thinking, and so the ideals of truth and moral goodness fall asunder, and metaphysics 'plays its game' according to its own rules, and demands that ultimate truth shall satisfy the intellect, and that alone (pp. 384-6).

Unfortunately, however, these propositions do not meet the pragmatist contentions, and, in so far as relevant, are disputable. Not only does Prof. Taylor appear to confuse the proposition that every (valid) thought aims at a practical end with the assertion that it aims at moral goodness (p. 385), but he has not realized that the position he has to refute is that *the intellect itself is practical throughout.* If this be true, the truths of metaphysics (if there are any) will be just as practical as the rules of conduct and the methods of science, and it is vain to pit 'logic' against 'practice.' For the reference to the use which verifies them can no more be eliminated from the logical than from the ethical valuations.[1]

§ 10. (*D*) As a natural result of his failure to perceive the full scope of Pragmatism, Prof. Taylor can never really overcome the intellectualism of his school. He does not indeed carry it to the extreme of denying the rationality of the existence of anything but thought, and follows Mr. Bradley in recognizing the existence of 'Feeling,' though he too leaves its relation to intellect in obscurity. But the aim of philosophy is still for him to

---

[1] Cp. *Humanism,* pp. 55, 160-3.

EMPIRICISM AND THE ABSOLUTE 247

understand, and *not* to *transform* and improve experience,
and that there is an inherent connexion between the two,
that we 'understand' in order to transform, and that it
is the 'transforming' which assures us of the 'understanding,' has not yet dawned upon him. He too, that is, has
not yet asked himself by what tests other than the pragmatic we can or do pronounce upon the claim of a
proposition to validity. The intellectualist prejudice
which he has consequently been able to retain oozes out
spontaneously in all sorts of places. Thus (1) the
purposive operations of our intelligent manipulation of
experience are constantly striking him as '*arbitrary*'
(*e.g.* pp. 35, 145, 175, 178, 256). He regards (2) an
'indefinite regress' as a mark of unreality or 'appearance,'
without discriminating between the cases where it means
the defeat of a purpose, and those in which it means a
successful accomplishment of the same, and indicates
that an intellectual operation (*e.g.* 'counting' or assigning
what for our purpose is the 'cause' of an event) can be
performed as often as we *please* and *need.* Again (3), to
be *free,* he says, is to *know* one's own mind (p. 381).
And lastly, and most flagrantly, (4) Evil is merely the
intellectual incompleteness incident to the restricted purview
of 'finite' beings (pp. 113-5, 121-2, 340, 387, 389, 393,
396).

§ 11. (*E*) And so we come to the infinite being to
which all else is 'appearance.' The Absolute appears
early in Prof. Taylor's philosophy and stays to the bitter
end. It is regarded as so axiomatic a principle that its
derivation is somewhat perfunctory (pp. 53-61). We
may, however, represent the steps of this derivation and
the assumptions they involve as follows :—

1. The universe is ultimately a system [= an application *a priori* of a human conception to reality, depending
on the validity of the 'ontological proof '].

2. If it is a system at all, it must be a rigid system,
and "must finally have a structure" (why only *one* ?) " of
such a kind that any purpose which ignores it will be
defeated." [But must not the sort of system which the

universe is be determined by experience rather than *a priori*? And why should a system be absolutely rigid? Might it not be plastic, with no *predetermined* structure, but with potentialities of varying response to varying efforts? Determinism (which, by the way, Prof. Taylor professes to reject in Book iv. chap. iv.) is not so absolute a postulate that a determinable indetermination in Reality should be inconceivable. And why, lastly, should the purposes which ignore the Absolute be defeated by it? Why should there not be purposes which, though they ignore the Absolute, are ignored by it? Where, indeed, is there an indisputably valid purpose which needs to take the Absolute into account?]

3. Hence to deny the Absolute would be to reduce the world to a mere chaos. [I have never found this to be so. And do we as a matter of fact *ever* import order into our experience by arguing down from the Absolute? Do we not rather start from apparent chaos, and work our way out by the most empirical experiments?]

4. The whole of Reality is the one and only perfect and complete individual (p. 113). [' *Complete*,' however, we must be careful to understand in a merely intellectual way as = 'all-embracing,' 'not omitting anything,' rather than as 'feeling no want.' And yet I doubt whether Prof. Taylor's readers will always succeed in distinguishing these two senses when they peruse his eulogies on the perfection and harmony of the Absolute.]

5. The Absolute is infinite experience, not like ours limited, and still less collective.[1] Though neither a self nor a person,[2] it is a conscious life which embraces the totality of existence all at once and in a perfect, harmonious, systematic unity,[3] as the contents of its experience. [But how, if it is *not* limited, can 'purpose' be ascribed to it? The time has surely come when the apparently self-contradictory notion of an infinite purpose should be either explained or dropped. How again can one life embrace another, *i.e.* not merely *know* it, but

---

[1] Pp. 343, 396.   [2] Pp. 343, 346.   [3] P. 60.

experience it with its unique limitations? And this in an indefinite number of conflicting and mutually contradictory cases! Surely the difficulties of the *Kenosis* in Christian theology, of the combination of divine omniscience with human ignorance, are child's play in comparison with these vagaries of what calls itself a rational metaphysic!]

6. The Absolute is out of Time and Space and cannot evolve. Hence all things in our experience are for it contradictory appearance. But this does not mean 'illusion.' For (p. 109) there are degrees of Reality or individuality, and those things which are more complete and more systematic are more real. Or, put otherwise, things are more real the more they approximate to the ideal of perfect self-consistency and the less the modification which our knowledge would require to transform them into complete harmony with themselves (pp. 37, 105, 108).

On this I remark that by the time Prof. Taylor has proved Space and Time 'appearances' which cannot be attributed to the Absolute, he appears to have quite forgotten the vital distinction between perceptual and conceptual Space and Time which he began (p. 243) by calling of 'fundamental importance.'

This, however, is a slight matter compared with the 'saving doctrine' of the Degrees of Reality, in stating which Prof. Taylor does not seem to have materially improved its Bradleian form. (1) It still seems to be a pure assumption that what *appears to us* to be the order of ascertained reality, must coincide with the absolute order of merit. (2) Nor is it in the least self-evident that what seems to need less modification is actually nearer to ultimate Reality and more likely to attain it. The little more may be unattainable, and something worlds away may be on the right line of development. If, *e.g.*, Prof. Taylor had cast his prophetic eye on the Jurassic age would he not have prognosticated the descent of the fowls of the air from soaring Pterodactyls of the period rather than from clod-hopping Dinosaurs? And yet it is certain that the former never evolved into

the true avian form, while the latter very probably did!
(3) How, we may ask, are we to know *how much*
'modification' or 'transformation' a thing may need
to become ultimate reality? Is this also to be known
a priori, or judged by casual appearances? How can
we tell what the difficulties really are until we have
overcome them? For our finite apprehension, therefore,
the doctrine of degrees is quite unworkable, and indeed
unmeaning. And (4) the criterion in any case is quite
delusive. For *ex hypothesi* it fails us : nothing ever *de
facto* reaches ultimate reality, or can be conceived as so
doing. We are carefully warned that a 'finite' appearance could do so only by ceasing to be finite. But
impossibility has no degrees, and hence to say 'you shall
become perfectly harmonious and fully real when you
become the Absolute' is like saying 'you shall catch the
Snark on the Greek Kalends.'

7. Despite, however, the manifestly illusory character
of our hopes of becoming real by becoming the Universe,
we are still bidden to believe (p. 16) that the Absolute
realizes our aspirations and satisfies our emotions.
Even though (p. 411) "the all-embracing harmonious
experience of the Absolute is the *unattainable*[1] [!] goal
towards which finite intelligence and finite volition are
alike striving," we must have faith (p. 394) that "all
finite aspiration must *somehow*[1] be realized in the
structure of the Absolute whole, though not necessarily
in the way in which we . . . actually wish it to be
realized"! For (p. 386) "it is simply inconceivable in
a rational universe that our abiding aspirations should
meet with blank defeat." It is not to this final
apocalypse that Prof. Taylor applies the incisive words
"an uncritical appeal to unknown possibilities": but
the phrase seems singularly apt

§ 12. Now that we have seen what the claims of the
Absolute are, we can proceed to examine its logical
foundations. No great acuteness is needed to perceive
that the whole tissue of affirmations concerning the

---

[1] Italics mine.

Absolute depends logically on the question whether the
conception of a whole can be applied to Reality *a priori*,
and whether consequently it can validly be taken as
certain that Reality forms a harmonious system.

In other words, the 'ontological proof,' *i.e.* the transmutation of a conceptual ideal into absolute fact, is a
vital necessity for Prof. Taylor's metaphysic. He himself is well aware of this, and furnishes us (pp. 402-3)
with a revised version of it, drawn from the armoury of
Bradleian logic.

Every idea, he tells us, has a reference to reality,
outside its own existence, which it means or stands for.
" In its most general form, therefore, the ontological
argument is simply a statement that reality and meaning
for a subject mutually imply each other." But (as we
saw) thoughts represent the reality they mean with very
different degrees of adequacy, and so, of reality. Only
the thought of a perfectly harmonious system can be an
adequate representation of the reality which it means.
As therefore we have in the Absolute a way of thinking
about Reality " which is absolutely and entirely internally
coherent, *and from its own nature must remain so, however
the detailed content of our ideas should grow in complexity*,[1]
we may confidently say that such a scheme of thought
faithfully represents the Reality for which it stands."

In this form, then, the 'ontological proof' satisfies Prof.
Taylor ; but it hardly brings out what is really its
cardinal feature, viz. the *a priori* character of its claim.
Unless reality can be predicated *a priori* of its ideal, the
'proof' is worthless for the purposes of absolutist metaphysics. For the conception of the Absolute must be
valid of any and every course of experience in a wholly
non-empirical and *a priori* way, to enable us to pronounce our knowledge and our opinion of it to be
incapable of modification by the course of events. It
follows that the Absolute must be *rigid*, and its conception one which differs radically in its nature and
meaning from any other idea. For other ideas *acquire*

---

[1] Italics mine.

their meaning in the process of experience, which moulds and modifies them, and is continually *testing the validity* of their 'reference to reality.' Their 'objective reference' is at first no more than a formal *claim*, which experience must confirm and develop and show to be really applicable. Whereas in the Absolute's case, the mere making of a claim, by reason, I suppose, of its peculiarly sweeping and impudent character, is held to be sufficient warrant of its *a priori* truth.

In other words, Prof. Taylor's argument is a *petitio principii*; it amounts only to a covert re-statement of the contested claim. The dispute was whether a subjective demand of ours could authenticate the existence of something which satisfies that demand.[1] The 'proof' consists in reiterating that the meaning of the conception involves this same claim to reality. But what we still want to know is whether this claim can be sustained, whether reality will actually conform itself to our conceptions, whether the meaning we attribute to them is actually true. And to assure us of this we are given nothing but the Absolute's own assurance! This may be rationalism, but it does not look rational.

§ 13. Yet the facts are, of course, plain enough. The Absolute is a postulate of the extremest and most audacious kind. And so far from its being true that our concept's claim to reality is in this instance independent of experience, it is dependent upon every experience and distinguished from other such claims only by the greater difficulty of subjecting it to any adequate verification. The question of whether, say, my idea of 'dog' 'corresponds with the reality,' is easily settled by observing whether what I take to be a 'dog' behaves in the manner I expect a 'dog' to behave. But to establish that all Reality behaves in a manner conformable with my notion of a perfectly harmonious system, and that my notion may consequently be safely predicated of

---

[1] It is amusing that this should turn out to be the essence of the 'onto-logical proof,' when one remembers how wroth rationalists get when they imagine that pragmatists are attempting this very feat!

Reality, is a desperate undertaking. Well might rationalists imagine that if it was not done *a priori*, it could not
be done at all! For the claim is so large that its
empirical proof might well seem impracticable : because
the Absolute is all-embracing, the claim has to be
substantiated in the case of all things in existence.

Of course it can still be postulated, and indeed this
may be expedient. For it is doubtless methodologically
just as judicious to give the universe, as the dog, a good
name, if you do not wish to quarrel with it. But to prove
my postulate, to make sure that the universe really
deserves my praises, and that my eulogy is not a fabric
of adulation on a basis of desire, I should have to be in a
position to explain away every trace and appearance of
disharmony! It is only our interested bias, therefore, that
leads us to argue [1] that the apparent evil must be really
good. If we were quite impartial, *i.e.* void of interest in
the matter, it would be intellectually just as easy, and as
tenable, to infer from our mixed universe that the apparent
good was really evil.

That the Absolute is really a postulate is all but conceded by Prof. Taylor in one passage,[2] where he argues
that as it is the satisfaction of a human aspiration, and
as his peace of mind depends on speculation about it, it
must be regarded as pragmatically 'useful,' and therefore
valid.

To which I reply that the path from usefulness to
validity leads through verification. Not that Pragmatism
has the slightest objection to the principle of an Absolute
conceived as a postulate. And if it makes Prof. Taylor
happy to believe that there is such a thing, and he won't
be happy till he gets it, by all means let him try it, and
see whether it will give him his heart's desire. In matters
of postulation all are called, and all may hope to be

[1] As Prof. Taylor does on p. 396.
[2] P. 317 *n.* The passage may be read as an *argumentum ad hominem*, but
fails as such, because (1) we have always conceded the fullest liberty to postulate,
and (2) Prof. Taylor has ignored, as our critics have usually done, the necessity
of verifying postulates. Besides, the Absolute is palpably a postulate, so mistaken
and ineffective that it never develops into the 'necessity of thought' it is assumed
to be.

chosen. But this reduces the claim originally made to quite modest dimensions. The Absolute was put forward as an actually existing reality which no sane intelligence could deny. What, therefore, we have rejected was a pretended axiom of universal cogency; what it may yet be possible to retain is a queer sort of emotional postulate.

§ 14. Yet I wonder whether the Absolute, after undergoing so capital a diminution of its logical status, will continue to find favour with our metaphysicians. It was cherished for two reasons. In the first place, as a response to a supposed necessity of thought, that of conceiving the universe as one, *i.e.* as a systematic order. This has turned out to be a mere craving, and a doubt has arisen as to whether this postulate fully understands its own nature. Is it really all that we need demand of our experience that it should be an ordered whole? Do we not demand also that its order should be worthy of our *approbation*? To any one not pledged to intellectualism at all costs, the thesis must seem indefensible. For the demand for *intellectual* order is but part of a greater *moral* claim, without which it is not really intelligible. For what has happened? We claim to have been enabled by the 'Absolute' to think the universe as a whole: but only by *leaving out*, as irrelevant and unreal 'appearance,' all of its initial features. The result is the self-contradiction that the world is said to become a whole only by extruding its parts. Surely a grotesque derision of our postulate! To satisfy its real meaning, therefore, we must retrace our steps, and argue either that the world is not a whole at all, if that conception involves the reduction of all empirical reality to illusion, or that if it is, the conception has been grossly misconceived, and must be amended in such wise as to admit of a real interaction of the world's constituents, of a real purpose, and a real history, and a real achievement of a good end. Either, therefore, it is no use to postulate an Absolute, because as conceived it cannot explain the facts of experience, or we must postulate an Absolute which is plastic, and not rigid, and not subversive of the 'appearances' in which we live.

But this latter alternative is ruled out by the other main incentive to Absolutism. The Absolute was cherished, in the second place, as a means to what all Rationalism craves, viz. an indefeasible guarantee against the contingency of experience. This needs, perhaps, a word of explanation. When we have seen that as there is no such thing as 'pure reason' we can no longer define the rationalist as one who is guided by it, it becomes necessary to redetermine his essential type of mind in pragmatic terms. And when we make a psychological study of his character and his works, we shall find that his master passion is not so much a love of reason as a *fear of experience*. I should define him, therefore, as essentially a person who *will not trust experience*, who wants at all costs to be insured against the risks, surprises, and novelties of life, and to feel that, in principle, nothing can occur which has not been provided for in the closed circle of existence. What he has failed to perceive is merely that such a guarantee can be obtained only at the cost of rendering all change and process unmeaning and illusory. For he can only obtain it by dissociating the stable, immutable, ideal Reality from the flux of human reality ; but once these are dissevered, what power can the former retain over the latter? The Absolute is set above change and process ; certainly : but change and process as illusions continue to dominate the illusory world wherein we are involved inextricably, nor can any demand for their cessation be urged upon an Absolute which already possesses eternally the absolute reality to which we everlastingly aspire in vain.

Regarding them, then, from this point of view we see that all the infinite convolutions and contortions of *a priori* philosophies mean just this, that the contingency of the future, the dependence on experience of what most we value, must 'somehow' be eliminated. It was thus as a method of satisfying a natural (and not wholly ignoble) instinct that rationalists had recourse to the Absolute. But its power to satisfy this emotional demand *depended on its strict apriority to all experience*. It is not enough that the universe should really be a harmonious system and that we should *gradually* come to 'discover' this. It is not enough that the potential harmony should be a valid postulate which we may help to realize. What was demanded was an initial and absolute assurance beyond all possibility of peradventure. And if the ontological argument is disallowed, the Absolute no longer yields this. Why then should it continue to be postulated?

§ 15. But may not the Absolute still retain its place as a postulated satisfaction for other desires? I hardly think so. Man craves no doubt for an object of worship, and when in sore distress will worship almost anything. But how can the Absolute afford him this satisfaction, if finite minds can hardly worship it without "a certain element of intellectual contradiction" (p. 399)? Again, we desire a moral ideal: but though Prof. Taylor desperately invokes the doctrine of degrees to show that goodness possesses more reality than badness, and that therefore the Absolute is not morally indifferent, he is driven to confess that it is "not one of the combatants; it is at once both the combatants and the field of combat." [1] Again, those of us in whom intellectual abstractions have not dried up the fount of human sympathy and feeling desire *at least* an explanation of the existence of Evil (pending the achievement of its entire obliteration): but what is the response to this demand which Absolutism proffers? It regards Evil merely as the necessary incompleteness of the parts of a whole!

It is difficult to discuss this proposition in a temperate manner. For all I know there may be people intellectualist enough to contemplate without a twinge the dismembered corpses on a reeking battlefield and to say: 'That only shows how incapable the parts are of becoming the whole.' But that this defect is regarded as the source of all evil is certainly not true, *psychologically*, of ordinary human feeling. Man is not miserable because he is not the universe, but because he seems to be flung without rhyme or reason into a discordant scheme of things, and

[1] P. 399 *n.*

exposed to cruelty, injustice, and disappointment, disease, decay, and death. I should imagine too that a desire to be the Absolute was a sufficiently rare idiosyncrasy. Certainly I myself have no trace of it; the prospect would appal me, not only because of its responsibilities, but also on account of its dulness.[1]   Prof. Taylor, of course, may be differently constituted. If so, psychologic science should certainly record this curious fact about him ; but I sincerely hope that there may be an error in his auto-diagnosis, and that his grievances are really of a more human calibre. And *logically* also the proposition that *because the Whole is perfect, all its parts must be imperfect* seems far from obvious : to me it would seem far more plausible that *if the Whole were perfect, all its parts must be perfect too*, and that if any part so much as *seems* imperfect, the Whole *cannot* be perfect. And why, to raise a prior question, should it be assumed, *apart from our interests and desires*, that a whole is necessarily perfect? Why should not the intrinsic scheme of things be evil at the core, *i.e.* utterly discordant or imperfect in any nameable degree ? Has any philosopher the right to allow his intellectualist proclivities to burke the whole question of pessimism in this flagrant way?

It would seem, then, that regarded as a postulate, the Absolute is a *bad* one, *because it does not work*, nor secure us what we wanted : regarded as an axiom it stands— and falls—with the ontological fallacy. Is it not therefore as a mere private fad, rooted in the idiosyncrasy of a few philosophic minds, that it can continue to figure, and that we must continue to respect it? But will not those who desire real answers to the real questions of life more and more audibly protest against the imprisonment of all human thought in the dismal void of the conception of a Whole which can neither be altered nor improved, and demand the liberty to think the world as one in which progress and goodness can be real?

[1] For the Absolute, were it conscious, would have to be a solipsist. Cp. Essay x.

X

IS 'ABSOLUTE IDEALISM' SOLIPSISTIC?[1]

ARGUMENT

§ 1. The affinity of solipsism to idealism as such. § 2. An amended definition of solipsism; § 3, applies to the Absolute; and, § 4, escapes the stock objections. § 5. The difficulties of absolute solipsism; § 6, destroy absolute idealism; and, § 7, are avoided only by its self-elimination.

§ 1. THE possibility of solipsism and its consequences is one of many important philosophic questions which after long and undue neglect seem now at length to be attracting attention. The question of solipsism in its various aspects really has a most vital bearing on the ultimate problems of metaphysics. It is easy to see that every idealistic way of interpreting experience cannot honestly avoid an explicit and exhaustive discussion of its relations to solipsism. For every approach to idealism is so closely beset on either side by the precipices of solipsism that every step has to be careful, and a false step must at once be fatal. The course of realistic philosophies, no doubt, is in this respect less dangerous: but they, too, are interested in the problem. They have a direct interest in precipitating all idealisms into solipsism. They tend, however, to treat it too lightly as a *reductio ad absurdum*, without sufficiently explaining why. Its absurdity appears to be regarded as practical rather than as theoretical, but even so the instinctive feeling that solipsism 'won't do' should be elaborated into a conclusive

[1] This appeared in the *Journal of Philosophy, Psychology, and Scientific Methods* for Feb. 15, 1906 (vol. iii. No. 4).

proof that it must of necessity lead to impracticable consequences.   And this might not prove to be quite so easy
as it is customary to assume.   Lastly, as a final proof of
the prevalent vagueness of philosophic thought on this
subject, it may be mentioned that it has even been
debated whether radical empiricism is not solipsistic.[1]

It would seem, therefore, decidedly opportune to
inquire further into the philosophic affinities of solipsism,
and more particularly into its unexplored relations to
absolute idealism.   For that form of idealism has hitherto
escaped suspicion by reason of the loudness of its protestations against solipsism.   But such excessive protests
are themselves suspicious, and it should not be surprising
to find that whether or not solipsism is a bad thing and
an untenable, whether or not other idealisms can escape
from it, absolute idealism, at all events, contains implications which reduce it to a choice between solipsism and
suicide.

§ 2. To show this, our first step will have to be the
amending of the current definition of solipsism.   For by
reason, doubtless, of the scarcity or non-existence of
solipsists interested in their own proper definition, its
statement is usually defective.   When solipsism is defined
as the doctrine that *as all experience is my experience, I
alone exist*, it is taken for granted (1) that there can be
only one solipsist, and (2) that he must be ' I ' and not
' you.'

Both of these assumptions, however, are erroneous.
Indeed, the full atrocity of solipsism only reveals itself
when it is perceived that solipsists may exist in the
plural, and attempt to conceive *me* as parts of *them*.
The definition, therefore, of solipsism must not content
itself with providing for the existence of a single solipsist,
i.e. with stating how ' I ' could define ' my ' solipsism (if I
were a solipsist).   It should provide me also with a basis
for argument against ' your ' solipsism and that of others.
For that is the really intolerable annoyance of solipsism.
If I felt reckless or strong enough to shoulder the respon-

[1] See the *Journal of Philosophy*, vol. ii. No. 5 and No. 9.

sibility, I might not object to a solipsism that made *me* the all by emphasizing the inevitable relation of experience to an experient ; the trouble comes when *other* experients claim a monopoly of this relation in the face of conflicting claims, and propose to reduce *me* to incidents in *their* cosmic nightmare.

Solipsism, therefore, should be conceived with greater generality. It should cover the doctrine that the whole of reality has a single owner and is relative to a single experient, and that beyond such an experient nothing further need be assumed, without implying that I am the only 'I' that owns the universe. *Any 'I' will do.* Any I that thinks it is all that is, is a solipsist. And solipsism will be true if *any one* of the many 'I's' that are, or may be, solipsists is right, and really is all that is. Provided, of course, he knows it.

§ 3. How, now, can this amended definition be applied to the case of absolute idealism ? We must note first that my (our) experience is not to be regarded as wholly irrelevant to that philosophy. Indeed, in all its forms it seems to rest essentially on an argument from the ideality of my (our) experience to the ideality of all experience. For the former is taken as proof that all reality is relative to a knower, who, however, is not necessarily the individual knower, but may (or must) be an all-embracing subject, sustaining us and all the world besides. Indeed absolute idealists have so convinced themselves of the moral and spiritual superiority of their absolute knower that they habitually speak in terms of contemptuous disparagement of their 'private self' as 'a miserable abstraction.'[1] And from the standpoint of *their* private self such language is no doubt justified ; it inflicts on it salutary humiliations and represses any tendency it might otherwise have to expand itself solipsistically into the all.

But how does it look from the standpoint of the absolute self? For that, too, has been conceived as a self, and therefore as capable of raising solipsistic

---

[1] *E.g.* Mr. Bradley, *Appearance and Reality*, p. 259.

claims. Can the absolute self be deterred from excesses of self-elation by the reflection that it is not, after all, the totality of existence? Assuredly not; for *ex hypothesi* that is precisely what it is. It includes all things and is all things in all things. If it cannot be said to 'create' all things, it is only on the technical ground that since a subject implies an object, and the world must be coeternal with its 'creator,' 'creation' is an impossible idea. Nevertheless, the dependence of all things on the absolute self must be absolute. *And if it is conscious, it must know this.* For else the ultimate truth about reality would be hidden from the absolute knower, though apparently revealed to the (comparative) ignorance of quite a number of philosophers.

But is not this equivalent to saying (1) that *the Absolute must be a solipsist,* and (2) that *solipsism is the absolute truth*?

§ 4. The inference is plain, and confirmed also by the admirable fitness of the Absolute to play the solipsist in other ways. For the arguments against solipsism have derived what success they have achieved from the habit of conceiving it as the freak of an individual self; they recoil helplessly from an absolute solipsism. Even Mr. Bradley would probably admit, *e.g.* that the Absolute, being out of time, would not be perplexed by the necessity of transcending its present experience in order to complete itself.

Indeed, it may here be remarked that Mr. Bradley's refutation of solipsism in *Appearance and Reality,* ch. xxi., seems to fail for (at least) three reasons. (1) Solipsism no doubt does not rest upon 'direct' experience merely, *i.e.* it is not a congenital, but an acquired, theory. Still 'indirect' experience must sooner or later return to and enter into direct present experience, under penalty of ceasing to be 'experience' at all. And so the solipsistic hypothesis, though doubtless it is not what any one starts with, may suggest itself as the explanation of experience and be confirmed, even as the solipsistic interpretation of part of it, viz. our dream-experience, is now confirmed, namely by the discovery that there is after all nothing

in direct experience which forbids its adoption. Mr.
Bradley, therefore, fails to pin solipsism down to the
alternative 'based either on direct or on indirect experience.'
It can rest on *both*. (2) He objects to the enriching of
the 'this' of direct experience by the results of indirect
experience, on the ground that they are *imported, i.e.* were
not *originally* in it (p. 251). Yet immediately after, on
p. 254, he disavows the relevance of the argument from
origins! (3) His argument never really gets to, and
consequently never really gets at, the solipsistic standpoint, and he always presupposes the more usual assumptions as to "a palpable community of the private self
with the universe." But the solipsist has not, and cannot have, a private self to distinguish (except in appearance) from the universe, just because he is a solipsist and
includes all things. His position, therefore, leaves no
foothold for Mr. Bradley's argument.

§ 5. But though the inference from absolute idealism
to solipsism thus seems unavoidable, it would be affec-
tation to pretend that it involves no difficulties. We need
not count among these the fact that it will probably be
exceedingly unpalatable to many absolute idealists, and
may even compel them to temper their denunciations
of subjective idealism. For, after all, they are men (by
their own confession) accustomed to follow truth where-
soever she flits, and to sacrifice their personal feelings.
But there does seem to arise a deplorable difficulty about
bringing into accord the Absolute's point of view with
our own.

For the Absolute, solipsism is true and forms a standpoint safe, convenient, and irrefragable. But for us there
arises an antinomy. We have on the one hand to admit
that solipsism is absolute truth, seeing that the standpoint of the Absolute is absolute truth, and that our imperfect human truth is relative to this standard. Now
it is highly desirable, from the standpoint of absolute
idealism, that human truth should be identified with
absolute wherever this is possible. For to admit any
divergence between the two is very dangerous. If such

divergence should culminate in the assertion that human truth can never attain to absoluteness, it would at once destroy the value of absolute truth as a human ideal.[1] An absolute truth which no human mind can enunciate and hold to be true acts only as a sceptical disparagement of human knowledge, which, moreover, would be gratuitous and untenable.   The absolute idealist, therefore, must seek to maintain that every absolute truth which human minds can entertain is also human truth.   And here, fortunately, this is feasible.   Solipsism is a view which human minds can entertain.   If, therefore, solipsism is true *sub specie Absoluti*, and we can know it to be so, we ought to think it so.   We ought, that is, to think it true that ' I am all that is.'   The Absolute has proved it.   And not only for itself, but equally for any other ' I.'   For regarded as a function to which all experience is related, no ' I ' differs from any other.   Any ' I,' therefore, may claim to profit by the truth of solipsism.   Indeed this is only reasonable ; for if there is only to be one self, why not let it be the only self of which one is directly sure, viz. oneself?   It will be awkward, no doubt, at first, to have to conceive a plurality of solipsists, each claiming to be the sole and sufficient reason for the existence of everything—but I suppose we might get used to that.

§ 6. It seems, however, a more serious implication that each of them, if his claim were admitted, would render superfluous the assumption of an Absolute Knower beyond himself.   Instead of being absorbed in the Absolute, as heretofore, each individual solipsist would swallow up the Absolute.   This consequence may seem bizarre, but in metaphysics at least we must not refuse to follow valid arguments to the queerest conclusions.

The same conclusion follows also in another way. The Absolute *ex hypothesi* is and owns each 'private self.' And the Absolute is a solipsist.   This feature, therefore, of the truth must be reflected in each private self.   They must all be solipsists.   But this is merely the truth of solipsism looked at from the standpoint of the private

[1] Cp. Essay viii. § 4.

self. It must claim to be all because the Absolute is all, and it is the Absolute as alone the Absolute can be known. The absorption of the Absolute and the individual thus is mutual, because it is merely the same truth of their community of substance differently viewed.

On the other hand, it seems most unfortunate that in practice we all negate the truth of solipsism, and Absolute or no, must continue so to do. Even if the impracticability of solipsism had been exaggerated, and philosophy had been too hasty in assuming this, the working assumptions of ordinary life would be rendered ridiculous, and our feelings would be hurt, if solipsism were true. It may be contended, however, that the practical absurdity and inconvenience of a theory is no argument against it, at least in the eyes of a thoroughgoing intellectualism. And a thoroughgoing intellectualism would be a very formidable philosophy, if any one had had the courage to affirm it.

But even waiving this, does it not remain an intellectual difficulty that we have ourselves destroyed the path that led from idealism to the Absolute? The Absolute was reached (rightly or wrongly) as a way of avoiding the solipsistic interpretation of experience, which it was feared idealism might otherwise entail. It now turns out that the Absolute itself is the reason for insisting on the truth of solipsism. And yet if solipsism is true, there is no reason at all for transcending the individual experience of each solipsist! It would seem, therefore, that we cannot admit the truth of solipsism without ruining our Absolute, nor admit our Absolute without admitting the truth of solipsism. We are eternally condemned, therefore, *either* to labour under an illusion, viz. that that is false which is really true, and which we really know to be true though we cannot treat it as true without leaving our only standpoint, the human, *or* to reject the very source and standard of truth itself.

§ 7. In conclusion, I can only very briefly indicate what seems to me to be a way by which absolute idealism can escape these difficulties, even though it may perhaps lead it into further troubles. Of course, from the standpoint of absolute idealism the truth of solipsism is only valid if the Absolute is assumed to be conscious. We can, therefore, avoid the fatal admission by assuming that it is not. The Absolute, that is, is unconscious mind, as von Hartmann long ago contended. But what is unconscious mind? The inherent weakness of the 'proof' of absolute idealism lies in its proceeding from the finite human mind, which we know, to an 'infinite' non-human mind very imperfectly analogous to it, and (apparently) incapable of being known by us. This transition becomes more and more hazardous the further we depart from the analogy with human minds. It may fairly be disputed, therefore, whether there is any sense in calling an unconscious mind a mind at all. But if the unconscious Absolute ceases to be conceived as mind, what becomes of the idealistic side of absolutism? Among the absolutists many, no doubt, would be quite willing (under pressure) to move towards the conclusions thus outlined ; but would not this involve a final breach with their theological allies, to whom the chief attraction of absolute idealism has always been that it appeared to provide for a 'spiritual' view of existence? But it might possibly be contended, on the other hand, that neither philosophy nor theology would suffer irreparable loss by the self-elimination of absolute idealism. And this contention is at least deserving of attention.

XI

ABSOLUTISM AND THE DISSOCIATION OF PERSONALITY [1]

ARGUMENT

I. The discrepancy between absolutist theory and the apparent facts of life arising from (1) the *imperviousness* and (2) the *discords* of the individual minds supposed to be included in the Absolute. II. But if experience is appealed to, a plurality of minds can be conceived as subliminally united, and communicating 'telepathically.' III. The possibilities of a 'dissociated personality' as exemplified in the 'Beauchamp' family. IV. These may be transferred to the Absolute. Its dissociation = the 'creation of the world.' The solution of the 'one and many' problem. V. Would a dissociated Absolute be defunct or mad?

§ 1. AMONG the major difficulties which Absolutism encounters in its attempts to conceive the whole world as immanent in a universal mind, must be reckoned what may be called the *imperviousness* of minds, which seem capable of communicating with each other only by elaborate codes of signalling and the employment of material machinery, and the very unsatisfactory character of the relations between the subordinate minds which are supposed to be included in the same Universal Consciousness. There appear, indeed, to exist very great contrasts between the internal contents of the alleged Universal Mind and the contents of a typically sane human mind. In a sane human mind the contents of its consciousness exist harmoniously together; they are not independent of, nor hostile to, each other; they succeed or even supplant each other without a pang, in a rational and

[1] This essay appeared in the *Journal of Philosophy, Psychology, and Scientific Methods* for Aug. 30, 1906 (iii. 18).

agreeable way; even where there is what is meta-
phorically called a mental 'struggle,' the process is not
painful to the contents, but if to any one, to the mind as
a whole which feels the struggle and the distress.   If, on
the other hand, we conceive ourselves as thoughts of a
Universal Mind, what a chaos we must think that mind
to be!   How strangely dissevered into units which seem
independent and shut up in themselves!   How strange
that each of its thoughts should fight for its own hand
with so little regard for the rest, and fight so furiously!
How strange, in short, upon this hypothesis that the
world should appear as it does to us!   Well may
absolutists be driven to confess "we do not know why
or how the Absolute divides itself into centres, or the
way in which, so divided, it still remains one." [1]

On the face of the apparent facts, therefore, it cannot
be denied that the assertions of absolute idealism are not
plausible.   In contrast with its monism the world on the
face of it looks like the outcome of a rough-and-tumble
tussle between a plurality of constituents, like a coming
together and battleground of a heterogeneous multitude
of beings.   It seems, in a word, essentially pluralistic in
character.   And if, nevertheless, we insist on forcing on it
a monistic interpretation, does it not seem as though that
monism could only be carried through on the lowest
plane, on which existences really seem to be continuous,
viz. as extended bodies in space?   In other words, must
not our monism be materialistic rather than idealistic?
The ideal union of existences in an all-embracing mind
seems a sheer craving which no amount of dialectical
ingenuity can assimilate to the facts, and no metaphysic can *a priori* bridge the gulf between them and
this postulate.

There are, however, so many to whom the idealistic
monism of Absolutism forms a faith which satisfies their
spiritual needs, that it should be doing them a real service
to aid them in thinking out their fundamental conception
with the utmost clearness and precision, and it should not

---

[1] F. H. Bradley, *Appearance and Reality* [1], p. 527.

be taken as an impertinence to point out how much more
there is to be said in its favour than its advocates appear
as yet to have discovered. For if only 'absolute idealists'
will consent to appeal to experience and empirical evidence,
modern psychology provides analogies which remove some
of the difficulties which most embarrass them.

§ 2. The imperviousness and mutual exclusiveness of
individual minds may be conceived and explained by an
extended use of the conception of the threshold of consciousness. It is, of course, well known that this is variable, that, *e.g.*, the raising of the *limen* which accompanies
intense mental concentration, thrusts into subconscious-
ness a multitude of processes which normally are conscious.
On the other hand, much that normally goes on in the
organism without consciousness, or full consciousness,
may become conscious by an abnormal lowering of the
threshold. There is nothing absurd, therefore, in the
idea that we might become conscious again of every
function of the body, say, of the circulation of the blood,
of the growth of every hair, of the life of every cell.
Indeed, the only reason why we are not now so conscious
would seem to be that no useful end would be served
thereby, and that it is teleologically necessary to restrict
consciousness to those processes which cannot yet be
handed over with impunity and advantage to a material
mechanism.

Now it is clearly quite easy to push this conception
one step further, and to conceive individual minds as
arising from the raising of the threshold in a larger mind,
in which, though apparently disconnected, they would
really all be continuously connected below the *limen*, so
that on lowering it their continuity would again display
itself, and mental processes could pass directly from one
mind to another. Particular minds, therefore, would be
separate and cut off from each other only in their visible
or supraliminal parts, much as a row of islands may
really be the tops of a submerged mountain chain and
would become continuous if the water-level were suddenly
lowered. Or to use a more dynamic analogue, they

might be likened to the pseudopodia which an amœba
puts forth and withdraws in the course of its vital
function. Empirically this subliminal unity of mind might
be expected to show itself in the direct transmission of
ideas from one mind to another, of ideas, moreover, that
would spring up casually, mysteriously, and vaguely, in a
mind in which they do not seem to originate. Now this
is on the whole the character of the alleged phenomena
of 'telepathy,' and if absolutists really want to convince
men of the plausibility of their ideas, they could adopt no
more effective policy than that of establishing the reality
of telepathy on an irrefragable basis.

§ 3. Abnormal psychology, moreover, yields further
enlightenments. No one can read Dr. Morton Prince's
fascinating book on the *Dissociation of a Personality*[1]
without being dazzled by the light thrown on the nature
of personality by the tribulations of the 'Beauchamp'
family. Here were B. I., 'the Saint'; B. III., 'Sally';
and B. IV. 'the Idiot' (not to mention the minor
characters) all apparently complete beings with expressions, beliefs, tastes, preferences, etc., of their own, so
diverse and distinctive that no one, who had once discriminated them, could doubt which of them was at any
time manifesting through the organism they shared in
common. And yet they were all included in a larger
self, which was sometimes aware of them and through
which knowledge occasionally passed from one to the
other. 'The Saint' and 'the Idiot' were shown to be
nothing but products of the dissociation of 'the original
Miss Beauchamp,' who, when she was recalled into existence by the astute manipulations of Dr. Prince and put
together again, remembered the careers of both, and
recognized them as morbid states of herself. In the
relations between 'Sally' and 'the real Miss Beauchamp'
the common ground lay apparently still deeper, and the
restoration of the latter did not mean the reabsorption of
the former, but only her suppression; still it may fairly
be assumed that their common relation to the same

[1] Longmans, 1906.

body must indicate the existence of a plane on which (if it could be reached) 'Sally' and 'the real Miss Beauchamp' would be unified, and would coalesce into a single being. It was thereby shown that a large amount of superficial diversity and dissociation might co-exist with a substantial unity beneath the surface. The several 'Miss Beauchamps' were to all appearance independent personages, variously cognitive of each other, hating, loving, despising, pitying, fearing, fighting each other, capable of combining together or opposing each other, and so enjoying their troubled life that most of them were determined to maintain their existence, and resented the restoration of 'the real Miss Beauchamp' as their own extinction. The amusing history of their contentions reads very much like that of a very disorderly girls' school ; but we can hardly flatter ourselves that the case is too abnormal to have any application to ourselves, because our normal life too plainly exhibits the beginnings of similar dissociations of personality in us, *e.g.* in dreams, which the 'Sallies' within us clearly weave out of the contents of our minds whenever we are sufficiently disturbed to be susceptible to their wayward pranks.

The great philosophic lesson of the case is, however, this, that the unity of a common substance only constitutes a very partial and imperfect community of interests, and is no sort of guarantee of harmony in the operations and aspirations of the personalities that possess it.

§ 4. If now we apply this lesson to the universe, it is clear that we have only to multiply indefinitely the phenomena presented by this remarkable case to get an exact representation of the cosmic situation as conceived by Absolutism. On this theory all existences would be secondary personalities of the one Absolute, differing infinitely in their contents, character, and capacity, and capable of co-existence and concurrent manifestation to a much greater extent than were the members of the 'Beauchamp' family, in which this power was possessed only by 'Sally.' We should accordingly all be the

'Idiots,' 'Saints,' and 'Sallies' of the Universal Beauchamp Family which had been engendered by the 'dissociation' of the Absolute. This might not be altogether pleasing to all of us (especially to those who, like the writer, would seem to have been predestined to be among the 'Sallies' of the Absolute); but the idea itself would be quite conceivable and free from theoretical objection.

Indeed, it would throw much light upon many theoretic problems. If discordance of contents is no bar to unity of substance, the extraordinary jumble of conflicting existences which the world appears to exhibit would become intelligible, and would cease to be a cogent argument in favour of pluralism. The disappearance, again, of personalities at death might merely portend that they were temporarily driven off the scene like 'B. I.' or 'B. IV.,' when the other, or 'Sally,' controlled the organism ; 'dead,' that is, in the sense of unaware of what was going on and unable to manifest, but yet capable of reappearing and resuming the thread of their interrupted life after 'losing time.' And so support might here be found for the doctrines of palingenesia and of a cyclic recurrence of events in an unchanging Absolute.

Again, it would become possible to explain the nature and to define the date of 'Creation' better than hitherto. The 'Creation of the World' would mean essentially the great event of the 'dissociation' of the original 'One' into a 'Many,' and would be comparable with the catastrophe which broke up 'the original Miss Beauchamp' in 1893. In the Absolute's case the date itself could not, of course, be fixed with such precision, but the date of the disruption of the One into a Many and consequent creation (or, perhaps, rather 'emanation') of the world might be defined as the date at which its present 'dissociation' set in. This change itself it would hardly be possible, and would certainly not be necessary, to regard as an intelligible event. For we should be absolved from the duty of trying to explain it by the fact that *ex hypothesi* it was the dissociation of the rational repose of the One.

As regards that One again some very pretty problems

would arise, *e.g.* as to whether it continued to exist
subliminally, able though not willing to recover its unity
and to reabsorb the world, or whether its existence was
really suspended, pending the restoration of its unity and
the reabsorption of the Many, or whether its ' dissociation '
into a plurality of related beings was to be regarded as a
final and irretrievable act entailing the permanence of the
plural world thus generated.   The last alternative no
doubt would be that most directly indicated by the
analogy of the ' Beauchamp ' case.   For Miss Beauchamp
could hardly have recovered her unity without the skilful
intervention (from the outside) of Dr. Morton Prince.
But in the world's case nothing analogous would seem to
be conceivable.   As by definition the Absolute is the
totality of things, it can never be exposed to outside
stimulation, and therefore could not, if once ' dissociated,'
reunite itself, under curative suggestions from without.

The same conclusion results from a comparison of this
conception of the relation of the One and the Many with
the very interesting anticipation of it which may be found
in Mainländer's *Philosophie der Erlösung.*   Mainländer
very acutely pointed out that in order to explain the
unity of the universe it was quite superfluous to assume a
still existing One.   It was quite enough to ascribe to the
Many a common origin, a common descent from the One.
Being a pessimist, he further suggested, therefore, that the
One had committed suicide, *i.e.* dissolved itself into a
Many, who sharing in its original impulse were also
slowly dying out, so that the aimless misery of existence
would in the end be terminated by a universal death.
By substituting, however, the notion of a ' dissociation ' of
the One for that of its ' suicide,' it is possible not only to
adduce a definite psychological analogy, but also to render
the process more intelligible and to safeguard the continuance of the world.   Altogether, therefore, the vexed
problem of the One and the Many, the puzzle of how to
conceive the reality of either without implicitly negating
that of the other, seems to be brought several steps nearer
to an intelligible solution by these empirical analogies.

§ 5. Not that, of course, these conceptions would entail no drawbacks. It is a little startling, *e.g.*, at first to have to think of the Absolute as morbidly dissociated, or even as downright mad. But a really resolute monist would not allow himself to be staggered by such inferences. For, in the first place, the objection to a mad Absolute is only an ethical prejudice. And he would have read Mr. Bradley to little purpose,[1] if he had not learnt that ethical prejudices go for very little in the realm of high metaphysics, and that the moral point of view must not be made absolute, because to make it so would be the death of the metaphysic of the Absolute. The fact, therefore, that to our human thinking a dissociated Absolute would be mad, would only prove the limitations of our finite intelligence and should not derogate from its infinite perfection. Moreover, secondly, if the Absolute is to include the whole of a world which contains madness, it is clear that, anyhow, it must, in a sense, be mad. The appearance, that is, which is judged by us to be madness, must be essential to the Absolute's perfection. All that the analogy suggested does is to ascribe a somewhat higher 'degree of reality' to the madness in the Absolute, and to render it a little more conceivable just *how* it is essential.

Less stalwart monists may, no doubt, be a little dismayed by these implications of their creed, and even disposed to develop scruples as to whether, when pursued into details, its superiority over pluralism is quite so pronounced as they had imagined; but in metaphysics at least we must never scruple to be consistent, nor timorously hesitate to follow an argument whithersoever it leads. It must, therefore, be insisted on that absolutism is in these respects a perfectly thinkable, if not exactly an alluring, theory. And we may well display our intellectual sympathy with it by helping to work out its real meaning more clearly than its advocates have hitherto succeeded in doing, or the public in understanding.

[1] See *Appearance and Reality*, ch. xxv.

XII

ABSOLUTISM AND RELIGION

ARGUMENT

§ 1. The philosophic breakdown of Absolutism. But may it not really be a religion, and to be judged as such? § 2. The pragmatic value of religion, and academic need of a religious philosophy. § 3. The history of English Absolutism : its importation from Germany as an antidote to scientific naturalism. § 4. Its success and alliance with theology. Its treatment of its own 'difficulties.' § 5. Its revolt against theology. The victory of 'the Left.' § 6. The discrepancy between Absolutism and ordinary religion, exemplified in (1) its conception of 'God,' and (2) its treatment of 'Evil.' § 7. The psychological motives for taking Absolutism as a religion. § 8. Its claim to have universal cogency compels us, § 9, to deny its rationality to our minds. (1) The 'craving for unity' criticized. (2) The guarantee of cosmic order unsatisfactory. (3) An *a priori* guarantee illusory. (4) The meaninglessness of monism. An 'Infinite whole' a contradiction. The inapplicability of absolutist conceptions. § 10. The inability of Absolutism to compromise its claim to universality, leads it to institute a *Liberum Veto* and to commit suicide.

§ 1. WE have constantly had occasion to criticize the peculiar form of rationalistic intellectualism which styles itself Absolute Idealism and may conveniently be called Absolutism, and to observe how it has involved itself in the most serious difficulties. It has been shown, for example (in Essay ix.), that the proof of the Absolute as a metaphysical principle, and its value when assumed, were open to the gravest objections. It has been shown (in Essays ii.-vii.) that the absolutist theory of knowledge has completely broken down, and must always end in scepticism. It has been shown (in Essay x.) that if the idealistic side of the theory is insisted on, it must develop into solipsism. It has been shown (in Essay xi.) that if a serious attempt is made to derive the Many from the One, to deduce individual existences from the Absolute, the result inevitably is that the Absolute is either 'dissociated,' or mad, or defunct, because it has committed suicide in a temporary fit of mental aberration.

In short, if a tithe of what we have now and formerly [1] had to urge against the Absolute be well founded, Absolutism must be one of the most gratuitously absurd philosophies which has ever been entertained. And if so, how comes it that men professedly and confessedly pledged to the pursuit of pure unadulterated truth can be found by the dozen to adhere to so indefensible a superstition ?

To answer this question will be the aim of this essay.

It is not enough to reply, in general terms, what at once occurs to the student of human psychology, viz. that intellectual difficulties are hardly ever fatal to an attractive theory, that logical defects rarely kill beliefs to which men, for psychological reasons, remain attached. This is doubtless true, but does not enable us to understand the nature of the attraction and attachment in this case. Nor can it be reconciled with the manifest acumen of many absolutist thinkers to suppose that they have simply failed to notice, or to understand, the objections brought against their theory. If, therefore, they have failed to meet them with a logical refutation, the reason must lie in the region of psychology.

This reflection may suggest to us that we have, perhaps, unwittingly misunderstood Absolutism, and done it a grave injustice.

For we have treated it as a *rational* theory, resting its claim on rational grounds, and willing to abide by the results of logical criticism. But this may have been a huge mistake. What if this assumption was wrong? What if its real appeal was not logical, but psychological, not to the 'reason' but to the feelings, and more particularly to the religious feelings? Does not Mr. Bradley himself hint that philosophy (his own, of course)

[1] Cp. *Humanism*, pp. 2-4, 14, 59, 191, 371-2 ; and *Riddles of the Sphinx*, ch. x.

may be " a satisfaction of what may be called the mystical side of our nature " ? [1]

If so, a fully-developed case of Absolutism would never yield to merely philosophic treatment. It might be driven to confess the existence of logical difficulties, but these would not dismay it. It would go on believing in what to its critics seemed the absurd and impossible, with a pathetic and heroic faith that all would ' some day ' [2] be explained ' somehow.' [3]

§ 2. This possibility, at any rate, deserves to be examined. For religions are as such deserving of respectful and sympathetic consideration from a Humanist philosophy. They are pragmatically very potent influences on human life, and the religious instinct is one of the deepest in human nature. It is also one of the queerest in the wide range of its manifestations. There are no materials so unpromising that a religion cannot be fashioned out of them. There are no conclusions so bizarre that they cannot be accepted with religious fervour. There are no desires so absurd that their satisfaction may not be envisaged as an act of worship, lifting a man out of his humdrum self.

There is, therefore, no antecedent absurdity in the idea that Absolutism is at bottom a religious creed, a development of, or a substitute for, or perhaps even a perversion of, some more normal form of religious feeling, such as might well be fomented in an academic atmosphere.

Once this theory is mooted, confirmations pour in on every side. The central notion of Absolutism, the Absolute itself, is even now popularly taken to be identical with the ' God ' of theism. It seems, at any rate, grand and mysterious and all-embracing enough to evoke, and in a way to satisfy, many of the religious feelings, as being expressive of the all-pervasive mystery of existence.

There is, moreover, in every university, and especially

<hr/>

[1] *Appearance and Reality*, p. 6.
[2] Cp. Dr. McTaggart's *Hegelian Dialectic*, ch. v.
[3] Cp. Mr. Bradley's *Appearance and Reality, passim*.

in Oxford, a standing demand for a religious, or quasi-religious, philosophy. For, rightly or wrongly, established religions always cater in the first place for the unreflective. They pass current, and are taught, in forms which cannot bear reflection, as youthful minds grow to maturity. Consequently, when reflection awakens, they have to be transformed. This is what gives his opportunity to the religious philosopher. And also to the irreligious philosopher, who 'mimics' him. They both offer to the inquiring minds of the young a general framework into which to fit their workaday beliefs—a framework which in some respects is stronger and ampler, though in others more meagre and less lovely, than the childlike faith which reflection is threatening to dissolve, unless it is remodelled. Hence the curious fascination, at a certain stage of mental development, of some bold 'system' of metaphysics, which is accepted ·with little or no scrutiny of its wild promises, while in middle age the soul soon comes to crave for more solid and less gaseous nutriment. It is proper, then, and natural, that an absolutist metaphysic should take root in a university, and flourish parasitically on the fermentation of religious instincts and beliefs.

§ 3. The history of English Absolutism distinctly bears out these anticipations. It was originally a deliberate importation from Germany, with a purpose. And this purpose was a religious one—that of counteracting the anti-religious developments of Science. The indigenous philosophy, the old British empiricism, was useless for this purpose. For though a form of intellectualism, its sensationalism was in no wise hostile to Science. On the contrary, it showed every desire to ally itself with, and to promote, the great scientific movement of the nineteenth century, which penetrated into and almost overwhelmed Oxford between 1850 and 1870.

But this movement excited natural, and not unwarranted, alarm in that great centre of theology. For Science, flushed with its hard-won liberty, ignorant of philosophy, and as yet unconscious of its proper limitations,

was decidedly aggressive and over-confident. It seemed
naturalistic, nay, materialistic, by the law of its being.
The logic of Mill, the philosophy of Evolution, the faith
in democracy, in freedom, in progress (on material lines),
threatened to carry all before them.

What then was to be done ?   Nothing directly ; for on
its own ground Science seemed invulnerable, and had
a knack of crushing the subtlest dialectics by the knock-
down force of sheer scientific fact.   But might it not be
possible to change the venue, to shift the battle-ground
to a region *ubi instabilis terra innabilis unda*, where the
land afforded no firm footing, where the frozen sea could
not be navigated, where the very air was thick with mists,
so that phantoms might well pass for realities—the
realm, in short, of metaphysics ?   Germany in those days
was still the promised land of the metaphysical mystery-
monger, where everything was doubted, and everything
believed, just because it had been doubted, and the
difference between doubt and belief seemed to be merely
a question of the point of view : it had not yet become
great by the scientific exploitation of 'blood and iron '
(including organic chemistry and metallurgy).

Emissaries accordingly went forth, and imported
German philosophy, as the handmaid, or at least the
governess, of a distressed theology.   Men began to speak
with foreign tongues, and to read strange writings of Kant's
and Hegel's, whose very uncouthness was awe-inspiring
and terrific.   Not that, however, it should be supposed
that the Germanizers were all consciously playing into
the hands of clericalism, as Mark Pattison insinuated.
T. H. Green, for example, was, by all accounts, sincerely
anxious to plunge into unfathomed depths of thought,
and genuinely opposed to the naturalistic spirit of the
age ; and if there was anything transparent about his
mind, it was assuredly its sincerity.   His philosophy—so
it was commonly supposed by Balliol undergraduates in
the eighties—was encouraged by the Master (Jowett) on
the ground that, inasmuch as metaphysics was a sort of
intellectual distemper incidental to youth, it was well

that it should assume a form not too openly divergent from the established religion.[1]

Others, again, welcomed the new ideas on pedagogical grounds, being haunted by the academic dread lest Mill's *Logic* should render philosophy too easy, or at least contrast too markedly with the crabbed hints of the *Posterior Analytics.* So German Absolutism entered the service of British theology, soon after its demise in its native country.

§ 4. The results at first seemed excellent, theologically speaking. The pressure of 'modern science' was at once relieved. It soon began to be bruited abroad that there had been concocted in Germany a wonderful 'metaphysical criticism of science,' hard to extract and to understand, but marvellously efficacious. It was plain, at any rate, that the most rabid scientists could make no reply to it—because they had insuperable difficulties in comprehending the terms in which it was couched. Even had they learnt the lingo, the coarser fibre of their minds would have precluded their appreciating the subtleties of salvation by Hegelian metaphysics. So it was rarely necessary to do more than recite the august table of the *a priori* categories in order to make the most audacious scientist feel that he had got out of his depth ; while at the merest mention of the Hegelian Dialectic all the 'advanced thinkers' of the time would flee affrighted.

The only drawback of this method was that so few could understand it, and that, in spite of the philosophers, the besotted masses continued to read Darwin and Spencer, Huxley and Haeckel. But even here there were compensations. What can never be popularized, can never be vulgarized. What cannot be understood, cannot be despised or refuted. And it is grateful and comforting to feel oneself the possessor of esoteric knowledge, even when it does not go much beyond ability to talk the language and to manipulate the catchwords.

---

[1] In reality, however, he seems latterly to have deplored Green's influence as tending to draw men away from the practical pursuits of life.

As regards the *direct* support German philosophy afforded to Christian theology, on the other hand, it would be a mistake to lay too much stress on it. Kant's three-fold postulation of God, Freedom, and Immortality could not add much substance to an attenuated faith. And besides the agnostic element in Kant, which had seemed well enough so long as Mansel used it to defend orthodoxy, was recognized as distinctly dangerous, when Spencer, soon afterwards, proceeded to elaborate it into his doctrine of the Unknowable. Hegel's 'philosophy of religion,' indeed, promised more. It professed to identify God the Father with the 'thesis,' God the Son with the 'antithesis,' and God the Holy Ghost with the 'synthesis' of a universal 'Dialectic,' and thus to provide an *a priori* rational deduction of the Trinity. But it could hardly escape the acuteness of the least discerning theologians that, though such combinations might seem 'suggestive' as 'aids to faith,' they were not quite demonstrative or satisfactory. The more discerning realized, of course, the fundamental differences between Hegelian philosophy and Christian theology. They recognized that the Hegelian Absolute was not, and could not be, a personal God, that its real aim was the self-development, not of the Trinity, but of an immanent 'Absolute Idea,' and that the world, and not the Holy Ghost, was entitled to the dignity of the Higher Synthesis. They felt also the awkwardness of supporting a religion which rested its appeal on a unique series of historical events by a philosophy which denied the ultimate significance of events in Time.

So, on the whole, Absolutism did not prove an obedient handmaid to theology, but rather a useful ally : their association was not service so much as symbiosis, and even this was eventually to develop into hostile parasitism.

The gains of theology were chiefly *indirect*. Philosophy instituted a higher, and not yet discredited, court for the trial of intellectual issues, to which appeal could be made from the decisions of Science. And it checked, and gradually arrested, the flowing tide of Science, if not among scientific workers, yet among the literary classes.

It supported theology, moreover, by a singularly useful parallel. Here was another impressive study of the abstrusest kind, with claims upon life as great and as little obvious as those of theology, and yet not open to the suspicion of being a pseudo-science devised for the hoodwinking of men. For was not philosophy a purely intellectual discipline, a self-examination of Pure Reason ? If it was abstract, and obscure, unprofitable, hard to understand, and full of inherent 'difficulties,' why condemn theology as irrational and fraudulent for exhibiting, though to a less degree, the like characteristics ?

Thus could theologians use the defects of philosophy to palliate those of theology, and to assuage the doubts of pupils, willing and anxious to clutch at whatever would enable them to retain their old beliefs, by representing them as inevitable, but not fatal, imperfections incidental to the make-up of a ' finite ' mind.

These services, moreover, were largely mutual. It was the religious interest, and the need of studying theology, which brought young men to college, and so provided the philosophers with hearers and disciples.

Theology reciprocated also by infusing equanimity into philosophy with regard to its own intrinsic 'difficulties.' For, alas, nothing human is perfect, not even our theories of perfect knowledge ! The new philosophy soon developed most formidable difficulties, which would have appalled the unaided reason. It was taught to 'recognize' these 'difficulties' (when they could no longer be concealed), and to plead the frankness of this recognition as an atonement for the failure to remove them, to analyse their grounds, or to reconsider the assumptions which had led to them. Or, if more was demanded, it was shown that they were old, that similar objections had been brought ages ago (and remained similarly unanswered) ; and, finally, the philosophic exposition of the nature of Pure Reason would end in an exhortation to a reverent agnosticism, based on a recognition of the necessary limitations of the human mind! Only very rarely did bewildered pupils note the discrepancy between the mystical conclusion and the initial promise of a completely rational procedure: after a protracted course of abstract thinking the exhausted human mind is only too apt to acquiesce in a confession of failure, which seems to equalize the master's and the pupil's intellect. Lest we should seem, however, to be talking in the air, let us adduce a notorious example of such a 'philosophic' treatment of a 'difficulty.'

It has now for more than a quarter of a century been recognized by absolutist philosophy that there exists at its core a serious gap between the human and the super-human 'ideal' which it deifies, and that it possesses no logical bridge by which to pass from the one to the other. Thus T. H. Green professes to discover that knowledge is only possible if the human consciousness is conceived as the 'reproduction' in time of an Eternal Universal Consciousness out of time. But as to the nature of the connexion and interaction between them, as to how the Eternal Consciousness renders human minds its 'vehicles,' he can, of course, say nothing. Nay, he is finally driven to confess that these two 'aspects' of consciousness, *qua* human and *qua* eternal, "cannot be comprehended in a single conception."[1] In other words, 'consciousness' is merely a *word* used to cover the fundamental discrepancy between two incompatible conceptions, and an excuse for shirking the most fundamental of philosophic problems.

This being so, it is interesting to see what his friends and followers have made of a situation which ought surely to be intolerable to a rational theory. Has its rationalistic pride been in any way abated? Not a whit. Has its doctrine ceased to be taught? Not at all. Has it been amended? In no wise. Have attempts been

---

[1] *Prolegomena to Ethics*, § 68. Capt. H. V. Knox has drawn attention to the vital importance of this extraordinary passage (*Mind*, N.S. No. 33, vol. ix. p. 64), and Mr. Sturt has also commented on it in *Idola Theatri*, p. 238.

made to bridge the chasm? No; but its existence has
repeatedly been 'recognized.' Mr. Bradley 'recognizes'
it as the problem how the Absolute 'transmutes'
'appearances' (= the world of our experience) into
'reality' (= his utopian ideal); but his answer is merely
that the trick is achieved by a gigantic 'somehow.' Mr.
Joachim 'recognizes' it as 'the dual nature of human
experience,'[1] but will not throw over it even a mantle of
words. Prof. J. S. Mackenzie 'recognizes' it by remarking "that a truly conceptual object cannot, properly
speaking, be contained in a divine mind, any more than in
a human mind, unless the divine mind is *something wholly
different from anything* that we understand by a mind."[2]
Has the difficulty led to any analysis of its grounds, or
revision of its assumptions? Not to my knowledge. It
has been 'recognized,' and is now recognized as 'old'[3]
and familiar and venerable; and what more would you
have? Surely not an answer? Surely not a Rationalism
which shall be rational? It is, and remains, a 'difficulty,'
and that is the end of it!

§ 5. But though in point of intellectual achievement
our 'Anglo-Hegelian' philosophy must be pronounced to
be stationary, its mundane history has continued, and its
relations to theology have undergone a startling change.
As it has become more firmly rooted, and as, owing to
the reform of the universities, the tutorial staff of the
colleges has ceased to be wholly clerical, the alliance
between Absolutism and theology has gradually broken
down. Their co-operation has completely disappeared.
It now sounds like an untimely reminiscence of a bygone
era when Mr. Bradley vainly seeks to excite theological
odium against his philosophic foes.[4]

In part, no doubt, the need for the alliance has grown
less. Science is far less aggressive towards theology than
of yore. It has itself probed into unsuspected depths of
being, which make blatant materialism seem a shallow

---

[1] Cp. Essay vi. § 3.
[2] *Mind*, xv. N.S. 59, p. 326 *n*. Italics mine.
[3] As we have seen, it is essentially as old as Plato.
[4] Cp. Essay iv. § 15.

thing, and have destroyed the illusion that it knows all about 'matter.' It has become humble, and begun to wonder whether, after all, its whole knowledge is more than 'a system of differential equations which work'; in other words, it has ceased to be dogmatic, and is discovering that its procedure is, in truth, *pragmatic*.

Absolutism, on the other hand, has grown secure and strong and insolent. It has developed a powerful 'left wing,' which, as formerly in Germany, has triumphed within the school, and quarrelled with theology. Mr. F. H. Bradley, Dr. McTaggart, Prof. B. Bosanquet, Prof. A. E. Taylor, Mr. H. H. Joachim, Prof. J. S. Mackenzie are among its best-known representatives. The 'right wing' seems to have almost wholly gone from Oxford, though it still appears to flourish in Glasgow. As for the 'centre,' it is silent or ambiguous.[1]

But about the views of the Left there can be no doubt. It is openly and exultingly anti-theological. It disclaims edification. It has long ago made its peace with Naturalism, and boasts that it can accept all the conclusions of the latter, and reproduce them in its own language. It has now swallowed Determinism whole and without a qualm.[2] As a whole, it has a low opinion of ethics, and it has even lapsed into something remarkably resembling hedonism.[3] In short, its theological value has become a formidable *minus* quantity, which is mitigated only by the technicality of its onslaughts, which in their usual form can be appreciated only by the few. Still, even this consolation fails in dealing with Dr. McTaggart's most recent and entertaining work, *Some Dogmas of Religion*, which puts the case against Christianity quite popularly, with a lucidity which cannot be surpassed, and a cogency which can be gainsaid only by extensive reliance on the pragmatic considerations which Dr. McTaggart has conspicuously

[1] Prof. J. A. Stewart's invitation to the school to refute Mr. Bradley before continuing the use of edifying phrases has met with no response whatever (see *Mind*, N.S. xi. p. 376).
[2] T. H. Green was a 'soft' determinist.
[3] Cp. F. H. Bradley's *Appearance and Reality*, ch. xxv. ; A. E. Taylor's *Problem of Conduct* ; and J. M. E. McTaggart's *Hegelian Cosmology*.

neglected. He has, indeed, relented in some few respects, and no longer defines 'God' as an *impossible* being, as he did in his *Hegelian Cosmology*, and now admits that a finite God is thinkable ; but he still prefers to call himself an atheist, and there is no saying how much mischief his popular style might not do among the masses were not his book published at half-a-guinea *net*.

All this is very sad in many ways ; but one could pardon these attacks on theology if only they advanced the cause of truth. For we, of course, in no wise hold a brief for theology, which we have reason to regard as in the main an intellectualistic corruption of an essentially pragmatic religion. Unfortunately, however, the prosperity of Absolutism does not mean an end to our intellectual troubles. We have already seen that, when consistently thought out, it ends in scepticism. And it has not merely quarrelled with theology, but is undermining a far greater thing, namely, religion, in its ordinary acceptance, as we must now try to understand.

§ 6. Absolutism may be itself a religion, but it diverges very widely from what is ordinarily known as such, and relies on motives which are not the ordinary religious feelings. This may be shown as regards the two most crucial cases—the problem of 'God' and the problem of Evil.

(1) As regards the conception of 'God' the absolutist and the religious man differ essentially. The term 'God' is used by philosophers, perhaps unavoidably, with a great latitude of meanings, and so disputants too often finish with the confession "your 'God' is my 'devil'!" But still, if we apply the pragmatic test, it must be possible to discover some points in which the consequences of a belief in a 'God' differ from those of a belief in *no* 'God.' 'God,' that is, if we really and honestly mean something by the term, must stand for something which has a real influence on human life. And in the ordinary religious consciousness 'God' does in point of fact stand for something vital and valuable in this pragmatic way. In its most generalized form 'God' probably stands for two connected principles. It means

(*a*) a human *moral* principle of Help and Justice ; and (*b*) an aid to the *intellectual* comprehension of the universe, sometimes supposed to amount to a complete solution of the world-problem. In the ordinary religious conscious-ness, however, these two (rightly) run together, and coalesce into the postulate of a Supreme Being, because no *intel-lectual* explanation of the world would seem satisfactory, if it did not also provide a *moral* explanation, and a response to human appeals.

But in Absolutism these two sides of ' God ' fall hope-lessly asunder. In vain does T. H. Green, after conceiving ' God ' as a purely intellectual principle, declare that ' God ' for religious purposes must *also* be such as to render morality possible.[1] For Absolutism conceives pure in-tellectual satisfaction as self-sufficing, and puts it out of relation to our moral nature, nay, to all *human* interests. But if so, the moral side of ' God ' must wholly disappear. If the Absolute is God, ' God ' cannot be personal, or interested in persons as such. Its relation to persons must be a *purely logical* relation of inclusiveness. The Absolute includes everything, of course, and *ex officio*. But the Whole cannot be *partial*, in either sense of the term. It must sustain *all* its ' parts ' impartially, because it approves of them all alike—inasmuch as it maintains them in existence.

The ordinary religious consciousness, on the other hand, definitely postulates a partial God, a God to succour and to sympathize with us poor ' finite ' fragments of a ruthless Whole. As Mr. Bradley scornfully but quite truly puts it,[2] " the Deity, which they want, is of course finite, a person much like themselves, with thoughts and feelings mutable in the process of time.[3] They desire a person in the sense of a self, among and over against other selves, moved by personal relations and feelings towards these others — feelings and relations which are altered by the conduct of

[1] *Works*, ii. p. 74 *n.*
[2] *Appearance and Reality*[1], p. 532. Italics mine.
[3] Cp. Plato's description of an ' Idea ' which should be really human in the *Sophist*, 249 ; and p. 67.

the others. *And, for their purpose, what is not this, is really nothing.* Of course for us to ask seriously if the Absolute can be personal in such a way would be quite absurd." The absolutist 'God,' therefore, is no *moral* principle. Neither has it *scientific* value, even when taken as an intellectual principle. For it is not the explanation of anything in particular, just because it is the explanation of everything in general; and what is the meaning of a general explanation which explains nothing in particular, is apparently a question it has not yet occurred to our absolutists to ask.

It is quite clear, however, that the Absolute is not God in the ordinary sense, and many of our leading absolutists are now quite explicit in avowing this, and even in insisting on it. As we have already seen what Dr. McTaggart thinks (§ 5), let us once more consult Mr. Bradley's oracle. "We may say that God is not God, till he has become all in all, and that a God which is all in all, is not the God of religion." "We may say that the God, which could exist, would most assuredly be no God." "Short of the Absolute, God cannot rest, and having reached this goal, he is lost and religion with him." Nor has any theologizing absolutist ever dared to question these responses.[1]

(2) The problem of Evil is probably the most funda-mental, and certainly the most pressing, of religious problems; it is also that most manifestly baffling to ordinary religious feeling. It is, however, divisible into a practical and a theoretic problem. The former of these is simply the problem of how *de facto* to get rid of evils. This is a difficult, but not a desperate or irrational, endeavour. The theoretic problem, on the other hand, has been mainly manufactured by theology. It arises from the impossibility of reconciling the postulated goodness with the assumed omnipotence of God. This problem troubles the religious consciousness only in so far as it assents to these two demands. Now this in a manner it may certainly be said to do. The postulate of God's

---

[1] *Appearance and Reality*[1], pp. 448, 449, 447.

goodness is, as we have seen, essential. But the assent to the notion of divine omnipotence is never more than verbal. In practice no real religion can ever work with a single, unrestricted principle. Without a duality, or plurality, of principles the multiplicity of the cosmic drama cannot be evolved. Hence the religious consciousness, and all but the most 'philosophic' forms of theology, do in point of fact conceive evil as due to a power which is not God, and somehow independent: it is variously denominated 'matter,' 'free-will,' or 'the devil.' The more 'philosophic' theologians try to conceive a 'self-limitation' either of the divine power or of the divine intellect; in the latter case following Leibniz's suggestion that in creating the world God chose the best universe he could think of. But on the whole the theoretic explanation of Evil is acknowledged to form a serious 'difficulty.'

What now has Absolutism to say on the subject? It cannot, of course, construe God's omnipotence with the amiable laxity of popular religion; it must insist on the strictest interpretation. Its 'God' must be really all in all; the Whole cannot be controlled or limited by anything, either within it or without it. It must be perfect: its seeming imperfection must be an illusion of imperfect finite beings — though, to be sure, that illusion again would seem to be necessary and essential to the perfection of the Whole.

It is clear that such a theory—which at bottom coincides with that of Eleaticism—must make short work of the religious attempts to understand the existence of Evil. Human 'free-will' it has long schooled itself to regard as "a mere lingering chimera";[1] the resistance of 'matter' it gaily consigns to 'the devil,' who in his turn is absorbed with 'God' in the 'Higher Synthesis' of the Absolute. Evil, therefore, is not ultimately and metaphysically real. It is 'mere appearance,' 'transcended,' 'transmuted,' etc., in the Absolute along with all the rest.

[1] *Appearance and Reality*[1], p. 435 *n*.

All this is very pretty and consistent and 'philosophical.' But it is hardly a solution of the problem,
either practically or theoretically. Not practically because it throws no light on the question why anything
in particular should be as it is ; nor yet theoretically,
because it is avowedly a mystery *how* the Absolute
contrives to transcend its 'appearances.'

Thus the net outcome is that the religious consciousness, so far from obtaining from 'philosophy' any
alleviation of its burdens, not to speak of a solution of
the problem of Evil, is driven forth with contumely and
rebuked for having the impudence to ask such silly
questions! Assuredly Mr. Bradley does well to remark
that (absolutist) " metaphysics has no special connexion
with genuine religion." [1]

§ 7. How, then, can Absolutism possibly be a religion ?
It must appeal to psychological motives of a different
sort, rare enough to account for its total divergence from
the ordinary religious feelings, and compelling enough
to account for the fanaticism with which it is held and
the persistence with which the same old round of
negations has been reiterated through the ages. Of
such psychological motives we shall indicate the more
important and reputable.

(1) It is decidedly flattering to one's spiritual pride
to feel oneself a 'part' or 'manifestation' or 'vehicle' or
'reproduction' of 'the Absolute Mind,' and to some this
feeling affords so much strength and comfort and such
exquisite delight that they refrain from inquiring what
these phrases mean, and whether the relation they
indicate would seem equally satisfactory if regarded
conversely from the standpoint of the Absolute Mind.
It is, moreover, chiefly the strength of this feeling which
explains the blindness of absolutists towards the logical
defects of their theory. It keeps them away from
'Plato's Chasm,' the insuperable gap between the human
and the ideal ;[2] for whenever they imagine that they

[1] *Appearance and Reality*[1], p. 454.
[2] Cp. Essays ii. and vi.

have 'advanced towards a complete solution' by approaching its brink, they find that the glow of feeling is chilled.

(2) There is a strange delight in wide generalization merely as such, which when pursued without reference to the ends which it subserves, and without regard to its actual functioning, often results in a sort of logical vertigo. This probably has much to do with the peculiar 'craving for unity' which is held to be the distinctive affliction of philosophers. At any rate, the thought of an all-embracing One or Whole seems to be regarded as valuable and elevating, quite apart from any definite function it performs in knowing, or service it does, or light it throws on any actual problem.

(3) The thought of an Absolute Unity is cherished as a guarantee of cosmic stability. In face of the restless vicissitudes of phenomena it seems to secure us against falling out of the universe. It assures us *a priori*—and that is its supreme value—that the cosmic order cannot fall to pieces, and leave us dazed and confounded among the *débris* of a universe shattered, as it was compounded, by the mere chance comings and goings of its fortuitous constituents. We want to have an absolute assurance of the inherent coherence of the world; we want to have an absolute assurance *a priori* concerning the future; and the thought of the Absolute seems designed to give it. It is probably this last notion that, consciously or unconsciously, weighs most in the psychology of the absolutist creed.

§ 8. Such, if we are not mistaken, are the essential foundations of the absolutist's faith—the things which he 'believes upon instinct' and for which he proceeds to 'find bad reasons,' to quote Mr. Bradley's epigram about (his own?) metaphysics.[1] And we, of course, to whom human instincts are interesting and precious and sacred, should naturally incline to respect them, whether or not we shared them, whether or not the reasonings prompted by them struck us as logically cogent. We should

[1] *Appearance and Reality*, p. xiv.

respect Absolutism, like any other religion, if we were allowed to.

Unfortunately, however, Absolutism is absolutism, and will not let us.   It will not tolerate freedom of thought, and divergence of opinion, and difference of taste.   It is not content to rest on wide-spread feelings which appeal to many minds : it insists on its *universal cogency*.   All intelligence as such must give its assent to its scheme ; and if we will not or cannot, we must either be coerced or denied intelligence.   Differences of opinions and tastes and ideals are not rationally comprehensible : hence it is essentially intolerant, and where it can, it persecutes.

We are compelled, therefore, to fight it in self-defence, and to maintain that its contentions are *not* logically cogent.   For unless we can repulse its tyrannical pretensions, we lose all we cared for, viz. our liberty to think our experience in the manner most congenial to our personal requirements.

§ 9. But in order that we may not imitate its bad example, let us not contend that because Absolutism fails of being a rational system cogent for all minds, it collapses into incoherent self-contradictory nonsense ; but let us merely, quite mildly, explain why and where it falls short of perfect rationality *to our individual thinking*.   For then, even if we succeed in making good our case, we shall not have attacked the absolutist's *amour propre*, which is the ' *amor intellectualis Dei* ' ; he can still escape defeat by the unassailed conviction that *to his mind* his case remains unanswerable.   And so we shall both be satisfied ; if only he will recognize a plurality of types of mind, and consequent thereon, a possibility of more than one ' rational ' and ' logically cogent ' system of philosophy.

Armed, then, with the consoling assurance that our ' logical ' criticism is at bottom *psychological*, and cannot therefore, in defending our own disputed rationality, hurt the religious feelings of the absolutist, let us proceed to declare roundly that the grounds of Absolutism are (*to our minds*) logically quite inadequate.

(1) In pragmatic minds the emotional 'craving for unity' described in § 7 (2) is not an all-absorbing passion. It is rationally controlled by calm reflection on its functional value. Merely to be able to say that the universe is (in some sense) one, affords them no particular delight. Before they grow enthusiastic over the unity of the universe, they want to know a good deal more about it ; they want to know more precisely what are the consequences of this unity, what good accrues to anything merely in virtue of its inclusion in a universe, how a world which is one is superior as such to a congeries of things which have merely come to act together. All these matters can doubtless be explained, only Absolutism has not yet condescended to do so ; it will be time to welcome it when it has. Moreover, when these questions have been answered, it will be asked further as to why it feels justified in ascribing its ideal of unity to our experience, and how it proposes to distinguish between the two cases of a real and a pseudo-unity. How, in short, can it be ascertained whether a world, of which unity can be predicated in some respects, possesses also, and will evermore continue to manifest, all the qualities which have been included in our ideal of unity ?

(2) We shall further be desirous of inquiring what is the value of the apparent guarantee of cosmic order by the 'systematic unity,' the 'self-fulfilling' coherence of the Absolute? What precisely are (a) its benefits, and (b) the grounds of the guarantee?

(a) From a human point of view the benefits of the postulate of cosmic order, though great, are not nearly enough fully to rationalize existence. And they have to be paid for. On the one hand, there can be no indeterminism in the rigid real. Absolutism is absolute determinism. And there can be no intervention of a higher power in the established order of nature. That is, there can be neither 'free' choice nor 'miracle.' Both are the acme of irrationality from the absolutist's point of view, and would put him to intellectual confusion. On the other hand, this sacred 'order' of the Absolute does not exclude the most stupendous vicissitudes, the most appalling catastrophes, in the phenomenal world.

Let us, therefore, take a concrete case, viz. (1) the total volatilization of the earth and all that creeps upon it, in consequence of the sun's collision with another star ; and (2) an opportune miracle which enables those who will avail themselves of it to escape, say to Mr. H. G. Wells's 'Utopian double' of our ill-starred planet. Now it is clear that *intellectually* (1) would not be a catastrophe at all. The established laws of the 'perfect' universe provide such 'catastrophes' in regular course. They happen one or two a year. And *we* do not mind. We think them rather pretty, if the 'new stars' flare up brilliantly enough, and are gratified to find that the 'reign of law' obtains also in 'distant parts of the stellar regions'; (2), on the other hand, would be intellectually a real disaster. An irruption of miracle, however beneficent, destroys the (conception of a) system of nature. A consistent absolutist, therefore, would not hesitate to choose. (He has no freedom of choice anyhow !) He would decline to be saved by a miracle. He would refuse to be put to intellectual confusion. He would prefer to die a martyr's death in honour of an unbroken order of nature.

A Humanist would not be so squeamish. He would reflect that the conception of an 'order of nature' was originally a human device for controlling human experience, and that if at any time a substitute therefor turned up, he was free to use it. He would have no ingrained objection even to a miraculous disorder, provided that it issued in a sequence of events superior to that which 'inexorable laws' afforded. And he would marvel that the absolutist should never, apparently, have thought of the possibility that his whole martyrdom might be stultified by his *ignorance* of what the cosmic order included or excluded ; so that if he had known more, he might have seen that the 'miracle' he had scouted was really part of a higher and more humanly 'rational' order, while the collision he had so loyally accepted was nothing of the kind, but in truth an 'accident.' And in either case is it not clear that each man's choice would be determined, not by the pure rationality of the alternatives and an irresistible logic of the situation, but by the preferences of his individual idiosyncrasy?

(3) (*b*) We have already often hinted that our ignorance and the difficulties of identifying our actual knowledge with the ideal truth, are continually undermining the value of rationalistic assumptions and defeating the aims it sets out to attain. So in this case. When the *a priori* guarantee of the coherence and predictability of the universe by means of the Absolute comes to be examined, it turns out to be of the flimsiest kind.

It rests on three assumptions—(1) that the order of nature which we have postulated, and which has, for the last few hundreds or thousands of years, shown itself (more or less) conformable to our demand, is really adequate to our 'ideal' and will fully realize it. This assumption manifestly rests in part on non-intellectual considerations, in part on the dubious procedure of the ontological proof,[1] in part on the assumed correctness of the 'ideal.' (2) It is assumed that we know (*a*) the Whole, (*b*) the world, and (*c*) our own minds, well enough to know that we shall continue to make the same demands and to find that reality will continue to conform to them. Now it seems to be distinctly hazardous to affirm that even the human mind must continue to make even its most axiomatic demands to all eternity : that even the known world contains many more surprises for us, seems quite probable ; while it seems fantastic to claim that we know the total possibilities of existence well enough to feel sure that nothing radically new can ever be evolved. Yet any irruption of novelty from any of these three sources would be enough to invalidate our present Absolutism, and to put it to intellectual confusion. It is false, therefore, to assume (3) that what would now seem to be 'irrational,' and to put us to 'intellectual confusion,' may not really be part of a larger design, and

[1] Cp. Essay ix. § 12.

possessed of a higher rationality. Hence the rationalist's protest against irrationalism must always fail, if the latter chooses to claim a higher (and other) rationality.

Now all these assumptions may be more or less probable, but it cannot surely be asserted that their acceptance is obligatory, and that their rejection entails intellectual suicide. Hence there remains, in Absolutism, as in all other philosophies, an empirical element of risk and uncertainty, which 'the Absolute' only conceals, but does nothing to eradicate.

(4) Lastly, and perhaps most fundamentally and cogently, what sense is there in calling the universe a universe at all? How, that is, can the notion be *applied* at all? To call our world 'the universe' is to imply that it is somehow to be conceived as a whole. But we could never actually treat it as such. For we could never know it well enough. It might be of such a kind as not to be a completed whole, and never to become one, either because it was not rigid, but unpredictably contained within itself inexhaustible possibilities of new developments, or because it was really a mere fragment, subject to incalculable influxes and influences from without, which, if reality were truly infinite, might never cease. But either of these possibilities would suffice entirely to invalidate reasonings based on the assumed identity of *our* world with *the* universe.[1]

It is somewhat remarkable that this difficulty should not, apparently, have been perceived by absolutists, and it is significant of the emotional character of their whole faith, that they should habitually delight in the collocation of 'infinite' with 'whole,' without suspecting the gross contradiction this implies. The 'infinite' is that which cannot be got together into a whole, and the whole is that which must be complete. But the truth is that, as used by Absolutism, neither term is used with much precision. Both are mainly labels for emotions.

It would be possible, but not very instructive, to go through the whole series of absolutist catchwords, to

[1] Cp. p. 333.

expose their vagueness and ambiguity, and to show that in the end they are all meaningless, because *they are all inapplicable to our actual experience.* Inapplicable, that is, *without risk.* But if they are once admitted to involve risks, they are in the first place *empirical,* and in the second *lacking in complete intellectual cogency.* Whoever wills may decline to take the risks, and by so doing renounce the absolutist interpretation of experience. And his procedure may be *for him* quite as rational as that of the absolutist. But is not this to have shown that Absolutism can *rationally* be rejected?

§ 10. This conclusion is all we need, and if only it can be similarly accepted by the absolutist, will constitute a true eirenicon. This is the last possibility we have to examine.

Our arguments were satisfactory to us because they seemed rational to us. We only undertook to show that we could make out a rational case *for ourselves.* Of course, however, in calling them rational we implied a claim that all similar minds would assent to them. We did not dogmatize about *all* minds, because, for all we can know *a priori,* there may be minds differently constituted from our own. Only, if there are, they are not 'similar' minds (for our present purposes). The differences in functioning and constitution between these minds and ours are worthy of examination, and may (or may not) be capable of explanation. But it is at any rate useless to *argue* with them. That is all.

But the case looks materially different from the absolutist's standpoint. He was, *ex hypothesi,* unable to combat our case with arguments which seemed rational to us. But, at the same time, he does not accept the arguments which seem rational to us. They seem to him as little 'cogent' as his do to us. To resolve this deadlock, he is offered the suggestion that in some respects there exist intrinsic differences in the logical texture of human minds, and that consequently we may, and must, agree to differ. Thus if he accepts this, he too is secured against attack, and peace must ensue.

But can the absolutist content *himself* with this solution? If he does, will he not debar himself from his original claim that his theory is absolutely cogent and valid for intelligence as such? For was it not part of his theory that such complete cogency existed, and was possessed by his arguments? He cannot therefore compromise his claim. He must insist on proving his case *literally to every one of his adversaries*, and similarly on disproving theirs to *their* own complete (logical) satisfaction, and not merely to his! It is evident that this imposes on him a stupendous burden of proof. To fail to admit the logical cogency of a single step in his argument is to shake the whole structure to its foundations. To renounce it, is to refute it. A single dissentient, therefore, will be, not merely a theoretical impeachment and a practical nuisance, but actually an unanswerable argument against the truth of the theory, of which it will be at all costs necessary to persuade him! Is it a wonder that absolutists are irritated by the mildest of protests against the least of their beliefs? Their whole view of the universe is imperilled : they are put to intellectual confusion, if the objector is not 'somehow' silenced or removed.

But have they any one to thank for their dilemma but themselves? Why did they devise a theory which, by its very hostility to individual liberty, by its very insistence on absolute conformity, is finally forced to sanction the *Liberum Veto* in philosophy, and thereby to ensure its own destruction? It was not prudent. Nor is it a wise theory which offers such facilities for its own refutation. The situation might move to compassion the most relentless enemy. But we are helpless. The equitable compromise we offered has been rejected. Absolutism has foisted upon us the *Liberum Veto*, and forced us to exercise it. It has thrust the sword into our hands upon which it proceeds to fall. And we, after all, shall not be inconsolably afflicted. It saves much argument when one's opponent commits the happy dispatch.

THE PAPYRI OF PHILONOUS

THE manuscripts from which the two following papers have
been translated were found ' in a battered leaden casket
among the ruins of the temple of Dionysus at Mende on
the Thracian coast,' and conclude with a statement that
they were records of conversations held with Antimorus,
the wisest of priests, in the month before he died, written
down by Philonous, the son of Antinous, and by him
dedicated to the god, before he set out to war with the
Olynthians.

To us their value is threefold.   If they are authentic,
and their portrait of Protagoras is quite as likely to be
authentic as Plato's of Socrates, they may, in the first
place, supply an intelligible and much-needed context to
the bare dicta about the gods and Man the Measure, to
which the thought of that great thinker has practically
been reduced for us, and show that the true significance
of Protagorean theology was not agnosticism any more
than the true significance of Protagorean epistemology
was scepticism.   And though they cannot undo the
irreparably fatal work of Athenian bigotry in collecting
and publicly burning Protagoras's book on *Truth*, they
may at least lead us to hesitate before condemning
him on the evidence of two short sentences.

They may serve, in the second place, as a wholesome
corrective of Plato's brilliant but partisan picture of Greek

philosophic activity at the close of the fifth century B.C.
And especially they may vindicate the memory of Protagoras.

The greatness of Protagoras was indeed sufficiently
evident to the discerning eye even before this discovery.
For Plato's own account of him to some extent supplied
its own corrective. In the *Protagoras* he seems as clearly
to excel Socrates in nobility of moral sentiment as he
falls short of him in dialectical quibbling. In this
dialogue it is Protagoras who is the moralist, and
Socrates who is the ' sophist.' In the *Theaetetus* Plato,
while still expressing his respect for the moral character
of Protagoras, makes a desperate attempt to convict his
Humanist theory of knowledge of scepticism and sensationalism. But he clearly shows that he has not understood the doctrine he criticizes,[1] and, but for the magic of
his writing, no one would be beguiled into supposing that
the charming digressions and the irrelevant by-play
about timid boys and Thracian handmaids which follow
(168-179) on the candid and powerful defence of Protagoras in 166-8, contain any answer to the essential
points, to wit, the contention that the dialectical paradoxes, which the recognition of truth-making by individual men may seem to involve, vanish so soon as
it is observed that such ' truths' are claims, that claims
to truth vary in value, and that the ' wise ' man is he whose
claims are valuable, and so are accepted as valid. Plato
manifestly evades this issue of the validation of claims ;
he reverts instead to the old abstraction which treats it
as irrelevant to truth *who* makes a claim (171), and is
content to show that a chaos of opinions must result.
The fallacy is the same as that of the Shah of Persia,
mentioned by James,[2] who refused to go to the Derby on
the ground that he already knew that one horse could run
faster than another. Similarly, if different individuals put
forward different valuations, and we refuse to evaluate these
claims, ' the ' opinion on any subject must remain a chaos,
and every ' truth ' will be judged to be both ' true ' and

---

[1] See also Essays ii. § 5, iii. § 17, and v. § 1.   [2] *Princ. of Psych.* ii. 675.

'false.' But not by the same people, and not so as to render the right to put forward individual claims (which is all that the Protagorean maxim amounts to) intrinsically contradictory. It is mere *ignoratio elenchi*, therefore, to treat Plato's argument as a refutation of Protagoras or as an answer to his proposal to evaluate the conflicting claims. After this Plato passes off into a magnificently eloquent description of the philosophic character, which ever since has served as an apologia for the futilities of countless pedants. And finally (179 B), having taken his readers off the scent by these digressions, he triumphantly proves that one man is wiser than another, and that therefore not every one is 'the measure'; as if 'wiser' were identical with 'truer,' instead of being an equivocation between it and 'better,' and as if he had not himself attributed to Protagoras a distinction between the claim to truth, which any one can make, and its validation, which is achieved only by the 'wise.' In short, he merely reiterates the objection which his own 'Protagoras' had refuted.[1]

In the third place, we may gather from these MSS. how men of high spirituality and great acuteness of mind, but nurtured in a religious creed absurd and outworn beyond anything we can easily imagine, might confront the uncertainties of human fate. And it is curiously instructive to note how very modern, in spite of the immense progress which both science and religion have made, the Protagorean attitude towards theology still sounds to us.

The reason probably is that human nature has changed but little. Man himself is still the greatest obstacle in the way of man's knowledge of what it most concerns man to know. His indolence and his fears still prompt him to declare impious and forbidden, or impos-

---

[1] It is not, however, by any means so certain that Protagoras regarded all views as equally 'true,' as that he regarded some as 'better' than others. Plato's way of extracting this admission (*Theaet.* 152 C) rather suggests that it may be only a bit of intellectualist misunderstanding, and it is quite possible that Protagoras already distinguished between a 'claim' and a 'truth,' and only attributed to individual judgments the value of 'claims.'

sible, the knowledge which would transform his cosmic outlook. He still prefers to conceive religion conservatively rather than progressively. He still keeps the treasures of divine revelation hidden away in his sanctuaries, for fear lest the attempt to make use of them should lead to their loss, and not to their augmentation. There is a most instructive contrast between the hypocrisy of science and of religion ; that of the former, while professing abject obedience to nature, has stealthily mastered it ;[1] that of the latter, while claiming to commune with the supernatural, has secretly shrunk away from it ; and so the faith which in the one case expands into knowledge, in the other shrivels into make-believe.[2]

---

[1] *Natura* non nisi *parendo vincitur*, Bacon could humorously write, with a pen on paper and in a study, man had made by moulding reality to his purposes. But to keep on repeating this as a reply to Humanism is not humorous, but stupid.

[2] Cp. Essay xvi. §§ 9, 10.

XIV

PROTAGORAS THE HUMANIST

ANTIMORUS { of Mende, a small Greek city in Chalcidice, devoted
PHILONOUS { to the production and consumption of wine.

PROTAGORAS, of Abdera.
MOROSOPHUS, an Eleatic philosopher.
SOPHOMORUS, his son.

Time—About 370 B.C.   *Place*—Before the temple of Dionysus at Mende.

ARGUMENT

Philonous consults Antimorus about his project of studying philosophy
under Plato, and is warned by him that Plato's accounts of Athenian
philosophy cannot be trusted.   For example, he had wholly misrepresented Protagoras.   In proof whereof Antimorus reads out his
notes concerning a discussion by Protagoras and two Eleatics of the
dictum that Man is the Measure of all things.   Philonous professes himself to be converted, but his enthusiasm is restrained by Antimorus.

Antimorus.   Desire of what, Philonous, has driven
you now first to visit me?
Philonous.   I hope you will pardon my boldness,
Antimorus, in venturing to visit uninvited one who I
hardly thought would have known me.
A.   It is always an honour for an old man to be visited
by the young and fair; and, fortunately, I was able to
recognize you at once.   You are like your mother, and
singularly like your grandmother.
P.   Was not my grandmother very beautiful?
A.   So beautiful that when I was your age, Philonous,
I should have preferred Eudora to any other gift of the
gods.   But her father esteemed Philoenus the better
match.   You are welcome, therefore—not only on your
own account.

P. How strange!

A. And you are the more welcome, and by far more wonderful, Philonous, in that you have come to me instead of looking on at the show. For I fancy that you and I alone of the Mendeans will this day be absent from the theatre. Surely it is not a slight matter that has brought you?

P. It is one so great that I came with trepidation, and even now hardly know how to put it.

A. Tell me. Are you in love?

P. Yes, but very strangely.

A. How? With a Lamia?

P. I am in love with Wisdom, and deem that you of all men here can best tell me how to obtain her.

A. Unhappy boy, Wisdom is worse than any Lamia, excelling them all in the perplexing shapes she takes, and in the enchantments whereby she lures her victims to destruction!

P. But is it not true, Antimorus, that in your youth you, too, were zealous to pursue Wisdom, and shrinking from no danger, journeyed far, even to Athens, and listened to the converse of the great sages of antiquity?

A. To Athens, aye, and farther. You will not easily find another, either in Hellas or among the barbarians, who has asked the Sphinx her riddles and questioned also the priests of the Egyptians, and Judeans, and Hyperboreans, the Magians, and the Gymnosophists.

P. How wonderful! How much wisdom you must have learnt!

A. A bitter wisdom, to be ignorant of which you might well prefer to much money!

P. Will you not tell me what it was? For money seems to me as nothing in comparison with wisdom.

A. First, that priests are priests throughout the world, however different the gods they serve. Next, that the god whom sophists serve is everywhere the same. Next, that wisdom is as hard to find in a barbarian land and in unintelligible speech as in the familiar commonplaces of our tongue and country. Next, that folly is everywhere at

home, and densest in the densest crowd. Next, that to
war with folly is the luxury of gods, and that for mortals
it is enough to make a living. For as the poet says—

> With folly even gods contend in vain.

P.   A bitter wisdom, truly ! And not acceptable to
one who is aiming at being sent at the public expense to
study the wisdom of Athens.

A.   Ah, you wish to do as the scholars from Rhodes !
But be not discouraged, and learn rather how many times
the greater includes the less. When you have learnt the
folly of Athens you will be glad to return to Mende.

P.   And is this the reason why *you* have returned to
us, and are content to live here in seclusion, instead of
becoming, as was hoped, the most famous of the teachers
of Hellas ?

A.   That, and sheer weariness. But if I had not
returned ill and with great difficulty, from vainly searching
the icy Caucasus for the most glorious victim of divine
malignity, Prometheus, I should hardly have taken to piety
and drink by accepting this priesthood of Dionysus, nor
would you now every year admire the skill with which I
exhort the Mendeans at the great festival to get merry in
honour of the god. Not that they need the exhortation ;
but my speeches are considered most stimulating and
pleasing to gods and men ! However, there are compensations, and the old wine in the temple cellars is really
excellent.

P.   So I have heard.

A.   You shall celebrate with me your election to a
studentship at Athens !

P.   I thank you. But just now I would rather hear
about the sages you have met Were none of them truly
great and wise ?

A.   One there was upon whose like the sun will not
shine again for ten thousand years.

P.   And that, I suppose, was Socrates ?

A.   What ! The boon companion of all the dissolute
young swells in Athens ! I knew him well, as well as I

wanted to.   At times, and for a little while, he was not
unamusing.   It was as stupid as it was cruel to make
him drink the hemlock.   But he had angered the
Athenians beyond endurance, and when fools get angry
they are as likely to commit a crime as a blunder.   No
one, however, who knew him, and wished to speak the
truth, would speak of him as I have spoken of the wisest
of men from the foolishest of cities, Protagoras from
Abdera !

P.   It is true, then, that you were his companion ?

A.   Only for a little while, alas !   For in the fifth year
of my intercourse with him the Athenians condemned
him for impiety—because he had both spoken and written
'the Truth ! '

P.   Yes, I have heard.   He preached atheism, did he
not, and said "concerning the gods I have never been
able to discover whether they exist or not : life is too
short and the subject too obscure " ?

A.   That is how they slandered him !   For of all the
men that ever lived Protagoras was the most anxious to
know about the gods.   Whereas the many have no wish
to *know* ; it is enough for them to believe what they
have heard.   And of the gods they will believe anything,
whether it be holy or unholy, provided that it makes a
pleasing tale.   What alone they will not endure is that
any one should *think* about divine things, or *do* what he
believes the gods desire rather than what *they* desire.   Now
Protagoras wanted to know and tried to find out.   But
he was not allowed.   For in every city they told him
other tales about the gods, and when he compared their
several versions they said that he was impious !   And so,
taking one sentence out of many, they condemned him
unjustly, in word indeed because of his impiety, but in
fact because he had refused to give Hypocrites the
Sycophant a talent wherewith to celebrate the shameful
mysteries of Cotillon.[1]

P.   And did the Athenians give him poison too ?

[1] So the MS., but we should no doubt read Cotytto (an unsavoury Thracian
goddess popular in Athens).

A. No, that they keep for their own citizens. Nor did my master stay to be condemned. But they drove him out, and forced him to flee for refuge to Sicily. The ship was unseaworthy, and he never arrived.

P. The Athenians seem to attract wise men only to destroy them! I marvel that men call their city the Lamp of Hellas!

A. Not unreasonably. Does not the lamp attract moths and destroy them?

P. It would seem then, Antimorus, that you think very differently concerning Protagoras from Plato, who has mentioned him in several dialogues, and indeed you also once.[1] Did you know Plato? and have you read him? They say that no one now at Athens will listen to any philosophy but his.

A. If that be true, I would counsel him to change his philosophy frequently! For the Athenians are ever eager for something that *sounds* new. They are always demanding new truth, lest they should be asked to put some old truth into practice. As for Aristocles the son of Ariston, whom you call by his nickname, he was but a lad when we left Athens, promising indeed and full of poetry, but not as yet taking part in philosophical discussion.

P. But do you not think his writings wonderful?

A. He is a poet still. But if he had not become imbued with the belief that virtue is knowledge, and that knowledge is concerned about the eternal and super-human, he might have done more than most to render virtue beautiful and knowledge profitable in the eyes of men.

P. And what do you think of his portrait of Protagoras? You know that he has named a dialogue after him?

A. Very little. You must not believe a word he says.

P. Is his account untrue then?

A. Pure and malicious fiction.

---

[1] *Protagoras*, 315 A, where our MSS. read 'Αντιμοῖρος instead of 'Αντιμῶρος.

P. What! the whole story of the encounter of Socrates and Protagoras?

A. Certainly. You can easily see for yourself that there is not a word of truth in it.

P. You astonish me!

A. You will be still more astonished to learn that the Callias, at whose house the conversation is said to have taken place, did not succeed to the fortune of the Daduchs until his father Hipponicus had fallen in the battle of Delium about the eighty-eighth Olympiad.[1] And by this time Pericles the son of Xanthippus must have been dead more than five years, having lost his sons by the plague. And yet both his sons are said by Plato to have been present! And, moreover, the incipient beard of Alcibiades, mentioned in the beginning, which Socrates in his infatuation professes to admire, must have been sprouting for at least ten years upon a man who had already campaigned both at Delium and at Potidaea. Nor would you easily gather from Plato's story that Socrates was only about ten years younger than Protagoras. If, therefore, Plato blunders so grossly about simple facts which he might easily have ascertained, how can you trust him to report correctly the subtleties of a philosophical debate?

P. What you tell me, Antimorus, is as distressing as it is astonishing. For if the writings of Plato are not to be believed, what shall I be able to fancy that I know either about Socrates or about Protagoras or any of the old philosophers?

A. Was it not well said by Bias that "to know we know not is the beginning of knowledge"? And are there not those yet alive who can tell you the truth both about the "*Truth*" of Protagoras and the "ignorance" of Socrates?

P. I would beseech you, Antimorus, to enlighten mine before you expound that of Socrates. For at present I have no longer any reason to believe anything, not even that Protagoras declared that *Man is the measure of all*

[1] 424 B.C.

things, but shall have to suspect this too to be a wicked figment of Plato's, until you have given me the true measure of the man.

A. Because you have had the good fortune to be born the grandson of Eudora, and the boldness to search for truth in this old wine-jar, there shall be revealed to you what no one yet has grasped, the meaning of Protagoras!

P. Is that a still greater mystery? And was I wrong in thinking Plato's exposition had made this clear to me?

A. Which of them? That in which he makes Protagoras mean that one man is as good a measure as another,[1] or that in which he admits that Protagoras might justly prefer the judgment of the wise?[2] that in which the dictum is said to mean that knowledge is sensation,[3] or that in which it is too contradictory to mean anything at all?[4]

P. I have always understood these accounts to mean the same.

A. You are young, Philonous, and Aristocles has grown into a great dialectician. But the "Truth" of Protagoras he has neither understood nor tried to understand. Like all these dialecticians, he has attacked *that* in Protagoras which is in truth the merest truism; that which is truly important he has not grasped, while of that which is truly daring but delightful, novel but hazardous, he has never had a glimmering. Perhaps, however, you can tell me *how* you have understood all Plato's accounts to mean the same.

P. I feel more reluctance, Antimorus, and more doubt in arguing with you than ever before since I have concerned myself with philosophy. For though it all seemed difficult of access to the vulgar and full of subtlety, it yet seemed *certain* and to be grasped by pure intelligence. Whereas now it seems to me that you not only question all that has been received as true, but also that you are able to prove it false if in any respect it is untrue. And

[1] *Theaetetus*, 162 C. [2] *Ibid.* 166 D.
[3] *Ibid.* 160 D. [4] *Ibid.* 171 C.

so I begin to doubt even whether I correctly remember what Plato argued, and whether I have fully understood it.

A. You are young, Philonous, else you would never be ashamed to recite whatever has been received as true. When you are older you will fear to do anything else. Be of good cheer, therefore, and tell me the tradition.

P. Is it not possible (1) to take Protagoras to mean each individual man? And (2) was not his preference for a wise man as the measure the pleasing inconsistency of a surrender to fact? As for the inference (3) that *knowledge is sensation*, must not that be drawn from the assertion that what appears, *is*, to each? For is not sensation "what appears"? And, lastly (4), is it not clear that if what appears to each is true, and if things appear differently to different men, everything both is and is not at the same time? And so is not everything in contradiction with itself, and knowledge quite destroyed? And is it not the best of the joke that in destroying his own argument Protagoras has escaped his own notice? For what he maintains appears true *to him*, but not to the rest! And so is not what *they* say is truth by so much 'truer' than what *he* says it is as they are more numerous than he?

A. And so you are quite satisfied that Protagoras meant what Aristocles has said he meant?

P. To speak frankly, I have sometimes wondered, and the more so now that you question me, whether he really meant the individual man to be the universal measure. It seems so much simpler and more sensible to have meant *mankind* by "man," and I suspect that this is how you will defend Protagoras.

A. Protagoras needs not defence as yet so much as *you*. Did you not observe that even Aristocles makes Protagoras affirm that the wise man's judgment may be far *better* than that of the rest?

P. I now remember a distinction I did not then think much of. But even so, would this make the wise man's judgment *truer*?

A. Perhaps not, if you imagine the "true" to have no relation to the "good." If by "true" you mean what merely is, the opinions held by the veriest fool or madman may seem just as "true," just as much "facts," as those of Protagoras himself. And yet the latter will far surpass them in value. But perhaps you may some day be persuaded that you do not understand the "true" aright until you have seen that it is embraced in the "good," and that therefore the "better" is also the "truer."

P. I do not quite understand. Will you not explain?

A. When you have completed your defence! Did you not observe, secondly, that when Protagoras made man the measure, he did not mean any part of him, his smell or his sight, his palm or his foot, but the whole man, with *all* his powers?

P. How stupid of me not to have noticed this!

A. You would not now say, then, that man's life was wholly sensation?

P. Of course not. We reason also, and purpose, and desire.

A. Was it fair then to make Protagoras mean that knowledge is sensation?

P. I suppose not.

A. You are convicted then, Philonous, of doing an injustice to Protagoras.

P. I must confess it, and ask you to pardon me, on his behalf!

A. Again, why should you say that it is contradictory for the same to appear different in different relations or to different persons? Is it contradictory that I, for instance, should appear large to you here, but small from the top of Mount Athos, or large to a mouse and small to an elephant? And have you never in winter tried to mix warm water with cold, and after putting one hand in the one and the other in the other, found that the same mixture appeared warm to the hand which had been in the cold water, and cold to that which had been in the warm?

P. No, I have not tried, but I have no difficulty in perceiving all this.

A. Why then should it be absurd that different people should think differently about the same subjects? If it is customary among the Thracians never to speak to their mothers-in-law, and among the Hellenes to speak to them with honied words, shall we say that the notion of mother-in-law is that of something which both is and is not to be spoken to, and are mothers-in-law on this account contradictory and impossible?

P. Perhaps not, and yet I well remember my father Antinous saying that his mother-in-law, my grandmother Eudora, was both contradictory and an impossible woman.

A. Why then should Aristocles regard it as absurd that each should judge in his own way concerning what he perceives, and that nevertheless one man's judgment should be ten thousand times as good as another's?

P. I would no longer call it absurd. But though what you say seems reasonable, can you tell me how it comes about that we all perceive the same things, and live in a world which is common to us all? And how, if you admit this, does it follow from the saying of Protagoras?

A. I see, Philonous, that you have not yet thought deeply enough to ask what we mean by a "*common*" perception. If you had, you would be ripe to understand, not only Protagoras, but also far better the "common" world we live in.

P. We seem to have come to the brink of a great thought.

A. Aye, and one which Aristocles has never reached. The question you have asked is one which Protagoras alone has raised, and to which he alone gives the answer. And so, as a reward, you shall hear an argument between the Master and two philosophers of Elea. I was myself present, and my record is correcter by far than anything Aristocles has said either about him or about Socrates. Let us go within to get it, and to refresh ourselves with some of my most sacred wine.

You have heard of Parmenides, of course, Philonous?

P. The most wonderful of philosophers!

A. The boldest, certainly, in wandering farthest from the truth into the formless void. Then you may have heard, too, of his son, Morosophus?

P. Not until now. Was he too a philosopher?

A. He preferred to be, rather than to be thought, one.

P. That, I suppose, is why I have never heard of him.

A. Then you are probably ignorant, too, of his son Sophomorus?

P. Entirely. What prevented him from becoming famous?

A. He said *it was all one*, and did not care.

P. But concerning what did they discourse with Protagoras?

A. It was on the day after Protagoras had shown us how Man is the maker of Truth, and how Truth is the useful and good, and, in short, that whereby Man lives. All this he spoke of wondrously, telling us also a sacred story of the Babylonian priests concerning a garden in which Man was to live gloriously and happily for ever, if he would but eat of the fruit of the Tree of Knowledge which is the Tree of Life, and how by reason of the hardships of climbing the tree, and its thorns, and the roughness of its bark, Man would not, and was driven out by God, and has lived miserably ever since, a life dull, brutish, short, and utterly unlike that for which the goodness of God had destined him. And all were glad to listen, save only Sophomorus, who had been brought up to contend with words alone, and cared not for realities. So the next day, bringing with him his father Morosophus, a man of sad appearance and with bushy eyebrows, they attacked Protagoras with verbal puzzles they had excogitated overnight.

P. I should love to hear their discourse!

A. You shall (*reads*):—

" *Sophomorus.* Behold, Protagoras, my father, Morosophus, to whom I related last night your discourse

concerning the usefulness of truth. He is quite as wise
as his father, Parmenides, though not so famous, because
he is too proud to contend with sophists such as you.

Protagoras. Then I am honoured indeed that he
should now deign to converse with me!

S. Oh, as to that you need not be too conceited!
I had great difficulty in persuading him to come. Only
he has thought out some arguments which are invincible,
and I want to see you overthrown.

P. I am glad you have come, Morosophus, for whatever reason. Shall I begin to state my case, or will you
begin the attack in force?

Morosophus. I have not come, Protagoras, to *argue*
with you. It is as unworthy of the one and only true
philosophy to contend against upstart follies such as yours,
as it is of masters to contend with their revolted slaves.
And so, far from attacking you with an array of arguments,
I am minded rather, like the Scythians in the story of
Herodotus, to chastise you with whips, to repress you with
the sort of discipline my father used to inflict upon the
fools who thought that the Many *were.*

P. You promise great things, oh Morosophus! May
I take it that as in the Scythians' case you mention,
the attack with the more usual weapons of honourable
warfare has been beaten off? And will it surprise you to
find that a free spirit which was never childish enough
to be enslaved to your ancestral philosophy is not likely
to be slavish enough to be terrified by your 'whips'?

S. You soon will be!

P. Bring out your whips then and try!

S. Go in and smash him, father!

M. You asserted, did you not, that the true was
useful?

P. Assuredly.

M. Is that assertion true?

P. I hope so.

M. Then do you not see, most foolish one, that you
have *failed* in your endeavour to reduce truth to usefulness? Have you not admitted that here is a truth of

which your doctrine does not hold? Will you not bare your back to this whip and flee?

P. You are as kind as you are clever, Morosophus, but with your leave I should prefer to *face* your 'whip.' I do *not* admit that what you say impairs my argument. For that *the true is useful* is not only *true*, but, as being true, is also *useful*, and judged to be 'true' because it is useful. It confirms, therefore, instead of refuting, my first assertion.

M. And yet, Protagoras, you would have to admit that it was *true that it was useful that it was true that the true is useful.*

P. And likewise you, that it was *useful that it was true that it was useful that it was true that the true is useful.* Clearly, however often you choose to predicate truth, I can predicate usefulness, if the true be useful. I do not see what you gain by making me repeat that any 'truth' you can name will be admitted only if it can be shown to be also useful. So the magic by which you turn the one into the infinite is vain.

M. What I gain is to compel you to pursue the Infinite.

P. Only if my patience is infinite. But even if it were, what do you gain?

M. An argument which pursues the infinite is vain, and therefore false. Or do you not know that the Infinite is bad?

P. It seems to be both bad and good in your opinion. At least I seem to remember your father (or was it his follower Melissus?) arguing that the Whole was infinite, and also good.

M. That was the good Infinite.

P. How then do you distinguish them? Nay, how can you, if, as you say, all things are one? For if you distinguish two infinites, are they not *two*? But whether you have one infinite, or two, or twenty, they do not help you here. For all I have asserted is that of every truth I will display the use. This you do not refute by repeating that every truth is also 'true.' For this I have never denied. Moreover you yourself seem to think your view of truth useful—for refuting me !

S. Try another whip upon him, father !

M. Is it possible, Protagoras, that you deny that the One alone *is* ?

P. Concerning the One I cannot say whether it is or is not. It is one of many things for which life is too short and philosophy too long. All I can say is that I have never yet met the One, and that it is nowhere visible to the naked eye of unbesotted reason.

M. It is to be seen only with the eye of Intelligence. Perhaps it is in this that you are lacking.

P. Perhaps this lack is the reverse of loss. The Many are enough for me, and sometimes more than enough.

M. Without the One there is no Many.

P. So you have said before, and your father before you. But can you never explain how ?

M. Without the One, you could not perceive the world. Nor could you and I perceive the same world.

P. I am not so sure that we do, quite.

M. What, will you destroy the world with the ' Measure' of your folly ?

P. I hoped rather to discover how we set out to build up a world.

M. That is impossible. If each man is the measure, there can be no common measure, no common world, and no universal truth.

P. Pardon me if I hold that there can be as much (and more) of all these things as we in fact possess, and that, if you listen, I can show you how.

M. It is sad that you should talk such nonsense, and sadder that I should have to listen.

P. You have provoked me, but I will be merciful, and, therefore, brief. And, first, let me ask you whether you admit that we each perceive things in our own peculiar way ?

M. How can I admit the impossible and that which

is contrary to reason? I admit only that it is what *you* ought to mean, if you wished to be consistent.

P. I am consistent, and more concerned to find out what truly is, before I consider whether it is contrary to reason. And it does not seem to me folly to say that whatever is, is not impossible. Now that we each perceive things in our own way is what I must infer from all the evidence. For is this not why we differ in our tastes and opinions and acts? And so since what we experience is different, we reasonably act differently.

M. How would you prove that we perceive differently? And how would you discover that in some things we are different, unless in others we were the same?

P. True, Morosophus, you state the reason why I always first of all assume that you agree with me and perceive as I do, until I find out that you do not. But this seems to me a reason, not for getting angry or for inventing a One which is no explanation, but for inquiring into what is really important, namely, how we come to be alike in some things and to remain different in others, and what therefore is meant by 'perceiving the same.' For either if we all perceived all things alike, or if we all perceived all things differently, there would be no difficulty. In the one case we would not get sufficiently apart to quarrel, in the other we could not get sufficiently together, and each could dream as it were his own life-dream without hindrance from any one besides. But as it is, does it not seem to you a mixed world, compounded wondrously, of good and evil, reason and unreason, agreements and disagreements? As to your other question, did you ever meet Xanthias, the son of Glaucus?

M. Yes, but he seemed to me a very ordinary man and quite unfit to aid in such inquiries.

P. To me he seemed most wonderful, and a great proof of the truth I have maintained. For the wretch was actually unable to distinguish red from green, the colour of the grass from that of blood! You may imagine how he dressed, and how his taste was derided. But it was his eye, and not his taste, that was in fault. I

questioned him closely and am sure he could not help it.
He simply saw colours differently.   How and why I was
not able to make out.   But it was from his case and
others like it, but less startling, that I learnt that truth
and reality are to each man what appears to him.
For the differences, I am sure, exist, even though they
are not noticed unless they are very great and inconvenient.

M.   But surely Xanthias was diseased, and his judgments about colour are of no more importance than those
of a madman.

P.   You do not get rid of the difference by calling it
madness and disease.   And how would you define the
essential nature of madness and disease?

M.   I am sure I do not know.   You should ask
Asclepius.

P.   Ah, he is one of those gods I have never been
able to meet!   Let me hazard, rather, a conjecture that
madness and disease are merely two ways of showing
inability to keep up that common world in which we both
are and are not, and from which we seem to drop out
wholly when we die.[1]

M.   A strange conjecture truly for a strange case!
Would you apply it also to disease?   For in that case
the difficulty seems to be rather in conforming oneself to
things than to one's fellow-men.

P.   To both, rather.   Does not a fever drive one
madly out of the common world into a world of empty
dreams?   And is not the diseased body part of the
common world?

M.   Perhaps, but such conjectures do not interest
me.   Will you not rather give an account of your own
disease or madness, that of thinking that the common
world can be compounded out of a multitude of individual
worlds?

P.   Willingly.   Conceive then first of all a varied
multitude, each of whom perceived things in a fashion
peculiar to himself.

[1] Cp. *Humanism, s.f.* ed. 1, pp. 285-7 ; ed. 2, pp. 370-2.

M. You bid me conceive a world of madmen!

P. It does not matter what you call them, nor that our world was never in so grievous a condition. I only want you to see that such 'madmen' would in ,no wise be able to agree or act together, and that each would live shut up in himself, unintelligible to the others and with no comprehension of them.

M. Of course.

P. Would you admit also that such a life would be one of the extremest weakness?

M. So weak as to be impossible!

P. Perhaps. And now suppose that by the inter-position of some god, or as the saying is, 'by a divine chance,' some of these strange beings were to be endowed with the ability to agree and act together in some partial ways, say in respect to the red and the sweet, and the loud and the pleasant. Would this not be a great advantage? And would they not be enabled to join together and to form a community in virtue of the communion they had achieved? And would they not be stronger by far than those who did not 'perceive the same'? And so would they not profit in proportion as they could 'perceive the same'? and would not a world of 'common' perception and thought thus gradually grow up?

M. Only if they really did perceive the same: to 'agree in action' and to 'perceive the same' are not the same, and when you have reached the former you have not proved the latter.

P. As much as I need to. For by 'perceiving the same' I mean only perceiving in such a way that we can act together. Thus if we are told that a red light means 'danger' and a green light 'assistance,' then if we both flee from the red and welcome the green, we are said to 'perceive the same.' But whether what I perceive as red is in any other sense 'the same' as what you perceive as red, it is foolish even to inquire. For I cannot carry my 'red' into your soul nor you yours into mine, and so we cannot compare them, nor see how far they are alike or not. And even if I could, *my* comparing of my 'red' with yours would not be the same as *your* comparing them. Moreover, if we imagined, what to me indeed is absurd but to you should be possible, namely, that when I perceive 'red' I feel as you do when you perceive 'green,' and that your feeling when you perceive 'red' is the same as mine when I perceive 'green,' there would be no way of showing that we did not perceive alike.[1] For we should always agree in distinguishing 'red' and 'green.' The 'sameness,' therefore, is not the cause of the common action, but its effect. Or rather it is another way, less exact, but shorter, of asserting it. And so there arises the opinion that we all perceive alike, and that if any one does not, he is mad. Now this is true as *opinion*, being as it is convenient and salutary, and enough for ordinary life. But for the purposes of *science* we must be more precise, and regard 'perception of the same' not as a starting-point, but as a goal, which in some matters we have *almost*, and for some purposes we have *quite* reached. In short, we always at bottom reason from the 'common' action to the 'common' perception, and not conversely. Hence, too, when we wish to speak exactly, we must infer that no two ever quite 'perceive the same,' because their actions never quite agree. Moreover, this makes clear why we agree about some things and judge the same, and not about others, but judge differently. We agree about the things it is necessary to agree about in order to live at all ; we vary concerning the things which are not needed for bare life, even though they may conduce to a life that is beautiful and good. But it is only when we do not act at all that we are able to live our own private life apart, and to differ utterly from all others.

M. And what, pray, is this strange life in which we do not act ?

P. Do you not remember the saying of Heraclitus, " For the waking there is one common world, but of those asleep each one turns aside to his own privacy " ? And do you suppose that if we acted on our dreams, we could

---

[1] Cp. Poincaré, *La Valeur de la Science*, pp. 262-3.

with impunity do what we dream? Is it not merely
because we lie still, and do not stir, that we can indulge
our fancies?

M. All this might be true, and persuasive to one
less fixed in the true opinion than myself, Protagoras, were
it not that all along you have assumed that there is
one common world which all are bound to imitate within
them. It is only if they agree about this that they can
live, and live together, as you say.

P. I am not astonished that you should think,
Morosophus, that such was my assumption. But though
I spoke without precision, I can extend my way of
conceiving the growth, or the making, of a world also
to existences very different from men. The elements,
too, may have joined together in a world, because they
grew into the habit of taking notice of each other,
and prospered by so doing. And so the world may
be a city, and ruled by laws which are the customs
of its citizens. Only you must remember that habits
endure and form the 'nature' which we find. And so it
seems to us that we come into a world already made and
incapable of change. But this is not the truth. We
'find' a world made for us, because we are the heirs of
bygone ages, profiting by their work, and it may be suffering for their folly. But we can in part remake it, and
reform a world that has slowly formed itself. But of all
this how could we get an inkling if we had not begun
by perceiving that of all things, Man, each man, is the
measure?

M. It seems to me, Protagoras, that you have now
made him, not only the *measure*, but also the *maker*.
And this shows that your first dictum was not the greatest
absurdity that Man has ever made.

P. Even this, that Man is a maker of his world, has
a sense in which it is *not* absurd !

M. Can you not see, man, that Reality is not made
by you, but *pre-exists* your efforts, immutable, sublime,
and unconcerned, not to be fully grasped by man, even
when he *discovers* it? Do you not feel the reverential

awe which hedges round, as you approach it, the One, the Whole, which is and was and will be?

P. Frankly, I do *not*, and it is your feeling which seems to me absurd. For if the Real were really inaccessible to man, he could in no wise discover it. And if the mystery really were sacred, it would be impious even to desire its disclosure. And so I will not believe that the Real is unknowable or immutable, or pre-existent in the way you assume. The Real I deal with is a real which I acknowledge, and I know, because my action alters it. And what alone seems funny and absurd to me is that whenever we have made it different, and more to our liking, we should say that it was all along what we have with endless difficulty persuaded it to become. But surely this trick of ours does not really make it pre-existent absolutely, nor independent of our action. For though our actions mostly start from something which *we take* as pre-existent, it did not pre-exist *as that which it was altered into.* And so that which becomes real by our efforts is ever said to be *more real* than that which we started from, and altered, and thereby proved to be unreal, or real only for the purpose with which it was taken. I do not know whether you understand this, Morosophus, as our habits of speech render it difficult to grasp.

M. I understand at least that you destroy all reality by rendering it relative to human purposes. For in what way can anything be said to be absolutely real, if it is ever dependent upon the fleeting fancy of the moment? And without an absolute reality what is philosophy?

P. In one way only, and that the only philosophic way! The absolutely real will be that which fulfils our every purpose, and which therefore we do not seek to alter, but only to maintain. It will be immutable because no one will wish it otherwise, and not because no one is able to improve it. But your mistake lies in supposing that such a unity or harmony *already exists*, as something we can start from. And you are still more mistaken, if you suppose that because it does not appear to exist, what appears to exist is not real, but the outcome of some strange illusion. The absolutely real can be reached only through the apparently real, by remoulding it into a perfect harmony. And whether you or I can achieve this, I cannot tell ; but that we should attempt it is clearly fitting, and is the only thing that matters."

Philonous. I cannot help stopping you, Antimorus, to say how greatly your Protagoras delights me ! What I had always disliked about what I was taught to believe his doctrine was its preference for what is merely human, and relative, and happens in experience. For this seemed to leave me with nothing firm and fixed and certain. And so I longed for something not dependent on experience, and the Ideas of Plato and even the immutable One of Parmenides, though one felt they were far from desirable in many other respects and hardly related to most of our interests, seemed a sort of guarantee that all order would not be swept away in a chaotic flux of happenings. But now it seems that I was wrong, and that we may look hopefully to the future for the realization of all our desires, if only we will bestir ourselves to bring about what seems the best ! But I interrupted you, and am still eager to hear how the argument went on. With such dazzling prospects it must have reached a glorious conclusion. Tell me, did Protagoras persuade Morosophus, as he has persuaded me ?

Antimorus. Of course not ; in real life an argument does not conclude, like one of Plato's dialogues, at its best. You have heard the best part of my notes, and I will spare you the rest.

P. But will you not tell me how it ended ?

A. Morosophus, who to do him justice was clever enough in his way, at once began to dispute the reality of change, which, he said, Protagoras had assumed. You know how hard it is to refute these Eleatic tricksters, who will not look at the plain facts of common experience, and Protagoras had not got far into his explanation before that young ass, Sophomorus, interrupted and insisted

on bringing out some more of his "whips." And so
Protagoras, courteous as ever, was forced to reply to
further futilities about the true and the useful, of the sort
which are now being called sophistries, but might more
fitly be called philosophemes, seeing that philosophers
have invented nearly all of them.

P. What was the question about the true and the
useful?

A. The question was whether when Protagoras had
asserted that the true was useful he had also to admit
that the useful was true, and so either that any lie which
was convenient for a passing purpose was absolutely true,
or that truth was unmeaning. And so the end was that
Protagoras, after pointing out that if he admitted that the
useful was always true he would have to admit what he
had always denied, viz. that there was useless knowledge, had to give Sophomorus a lesson in elementary
logic.

P. And did you never learn from Protagoras by doing
what he thought we might attain the end which he divined,
the harmony which is absolutely real, or the absolute
reality which is a perfect harmony?

A. Not with any exactness. For Protagoras did not
suppose that he had found more than the beginnings of
the way. And the whole, he said, would be long and difficult, and fit only for the strong and brave. But though
he was ever zealous that we should trust all our powers
to help us in our quest, yet he seemed to rely most on
the increase of *knowledge*, and was wont to deny that any
knowledge was useless, because it was always a way of
mastering the real.

P. How splendid! I do not understand how you
can speak about it all so calmly! Why have you not
cried out aloud this Truth of Protagoras throughout the
cities of the Hellenes?

A. And why have I become the priest of Dionysus?
Did I not tell you why? I am old, oh grandson of
Eudora, and you are very young; but you would have to
live to be far older than ever I shall be, before you could

persuade the Hellenes or Barbarians to care about the Truth! Had I done as you bid me, I should soon have needed the hellebore of Anticyra to escape the hemlock of Athens! Can you wonder that one who had seen and suffered so much should prefer the sweet poison of Mende?

P. But in Mende at least you might have made a beginning. Nay, we might still! For in all the city who is there so well-born as you, the Asclepiad, or I, the Nelid, and as highly thought of? And who as clever? Why should we not easily persuade the Mendeans of this new "Truth," and even be honoured for teaching it?

A. I will tell you why, Philonous. Because "truth" for the Mendeans lies in wine alone, and the true is profitable only in this form. Because it was not given to the Asclepiads to cure men of their folly. Because I am the priest of Dionysus, to honour whom is to disgrace oneself, and it beseems me least of all men to introduce new worships. Because the Mendeans will elect a Nelid gladly enough as their general, if you ask them, but will never honour you, or any one, as their teacher. For what they will want of you is not truth but victory.

P. But I care not whether they honour me or not, nor value the petty prizes of their politics. I will live for truth alone, whether it benefits others, or only me.

A. If you can, Philonous. But it seems to me more likely that the Mendeans will not let you. They will force you to die the beautiful death of a patriot, in some silly skirmish with the boors of Thrace or with the stout burghers of Stagira. As for me, I am too old, and should be thinking of that last long journey to the house of Hades, to the vile inn (πανδοκεῖον) that receives us all, the best and the worst alike, and yet is never full.

P. Has your philosophy, then, no cure for the fear of death?

A. Because it has none for the love of ignorance! For knowledge is power, knowledge is life, while ignorance is death, and leads to death, and ends in death. And because the many have loved ignorance and hate the truth, I too must soon descend, together with the rest, unknowing but not unresentful.

P. You think, then, that our Vision of Truth was but a madman's dream ?

A. Let us dismiss both vain dreams and maddening realities ! * * * And yet the dreams may be truer than the realities, if the better be the truer ! Nay, this life itself may be wholly, or in part, an evil dream. But who knows, and why torment ourselves ? We two at least shall never know. We were born too early by ten thousand years. Come therefore, let us flee to the consolations of the god I serve, and pledge me copious cups of this my sovereign anodyne !

XV

A DIALOGUE CONCERNING GODS
AND PRIESTS

PHILONOUS ⎫ of Mende   PROTAGORAS of Abdera
ANTIMORUS ⎭   MELETUS of Athens

ARGUMENT

Philonous asks Antimorus whether he agrees with Protagoras's agnostic attitude towards the gods. Antimorus will not tell him, but criticizes the arguments for the existence of gods propounded by Philonous. (1) That from the existence of priests: can they serve the non-existent? It is objected that this would prove too much. (2) God as the One. But does not this reduce all human reality to illusion and separate it wholly from 'God'? The logical difficulties about predicating unity of our world. If unity is inapplicable, is it not meaningless to call the One 'God'? (3) The argument from human desire. It is an indispensable condition of the discovery of gods, but primarily proves only their psychological reality. Have then real gods been discovered thus? asks Philonous. Antimorus again excuses himself, but reads him a conversation of Protagoras with Meletus, explaining his seeming agnosticism. Philonous gives up the problem, and is consoled with an Egyptian Myth.

Philonous. I can never sufficiently make out from what you say, Antimorus, whether or not you believe in the gods, or agree with your master Protagoras that their existence lies beyond our ken. And, ever since the day when I went to see you in preference to the play, you have been so kind to me that I am sure you will pardon me when I beg you to remove my perplexity. For the matter, assuredly, is one of no slight importance, alike for public and for private affairs. For if there are gods, as nearly all men profess to believe, is it not most important that men should win their approval by worshipping them aright, it may be in ways very different from those now

in vogue among the Hellenes and among the Barbarians ?
If, again, there are no gods, why should we both publicly
and in private spend so much money on sacrifices and
costly temples, and expect vainly, as gifts from the gods,
benefits which we might perchance secure by our own
exertions ? I am sure that you must have reflected on
these things far longer and more deeply than I have yet
been able to do, and so I am in hopes that you can answer
my question.

Antimorus. You are looking very well to day, my
dear Philonous, and your question is a good one. Moreover, it touches a subject which is very nearly as important as men profess to think it, and much more important
than they really think it. But I am the last person, not
only in Mende but in the world, to answer it. You surely
cannot have forgotten that I am myself a priest ?

P. Of course not ; but what of that ? Nay, are not
priests of all men the most likely to know whether or not
the gods exist ?

A. How charming of you, Philonous, to say this !
But even if you think priests the most likely to know,
do you also think them the most likely to tell ?

P. Yes : if there are gods.

A. And if not, what ? Or if they do not know ?

P. It seems to me, Antimorus, that one might, in a
manner, argue from the existence of priests to that of
gods. For if there were no gods, would there be priests
to serve them ? How could they serve the non-existent ?

A. Very subtle, and better than most of the arguments of theologians ! And so you would say that
because I am the priest of Dionysus there must be a
Divine Drunkard, and because there are Atti, a Mother of
the Gods ? Would you argue similarly from the worships
of the Egyptians that there must be a Divine Crocodile
and a Divine Jackal and a Divine Onion ?

P. It does seem a little absurd.

A. Not a little. And are not Divine Men and
Women just as absurd ?

P. I suppose so. But nevertheless there are some

of the gods whom I should be sorry to lose. Apollo, for
example, and the Muses. But no doubt you are right,
and we should worship no god but the one who moves
and lives in all things, taking all shapes but tied to none,
and exceeding far in beauty and goodness and health and
might all notions men can frame.

A. It is Proteus, I suppose, whom you mean?

P. Never! The God I mean is no juggler. He
is the One and the All, that has made the world, and
made it a Cosmos. For surely there must be some reason
why the world is one, and all things work together for
good?

A. And you think that the Cause of this should be
deemed the Deity?

P. Yes, and a God of all gods, who must needs
exist, because his existence is revealed in all things that
exist. This is the God too whom philosophers seem
to me to hint at, though obscurely. And does he not
seem to you the offspring of a noble thought?

A. So noble that it seems to me oblivious of the
simple truth. Too noble to have a humble origin in the
facts of life. While as for the philosophers, so far from
rendering God's existence certain and necessary, they seem
rather to render it impossible!

P. How so?

A. Did you not say God was the One and the All?

P. Yes.

A. And also that he excelled in beauty and goodness
and might?

P. It is as all-good, and all-beautiful, and all-mighty
that I would conceive him.

A. Would you say, then, that because all things
are God, all things are good and beautiful? And if
the Many, though one in God, yet contend against each
other, would you say that God was divided against himself, and distracted by intestine war? And is he such as
to delight in this condition? Or is he discordant and
miserable, and unable to cure himself of this disease?
Or is he perchance wholly unaware of the plight we see

him to be in? As for his might, how would you measure
it? Can you measure it, if there is nothing to measure it
upon? If all things are but manifestations of God's
power, and his playthings, if in all conflicts God is merely
sparring with himself, how can you know whether or not
his might is irresistible? What, therefore, does almighty
power mean?

P. These are difficulties I had never thought of,
and I do not feel that I can answer you sufficiently at
present. But I am unwilling to yield to you wholly,
Antimorus. And so might one not hold that God at
heart is good and beautiful, even though many things
seem otherwise to us; that he is not really struggling
against himself, though we as parts, who cannot see the
whole, seem to see him so; and that so the disease of the
world is curable, nay cured, because it is not real?

A. One might indeed, Philonous, on one condition.

P. And what is that?

A. You can save the perfection of the One by
sacrificing all on the altar of the One, and condemning
the Many to utter unreality.

P. How?

A. It is true that the troubles of the Many and the
imperfections of appearances cannot mar the perfection
of the One, if they exist only for us, and not for it.
But then we also cannot exist for it. For our troubles
are inherent in our nature, and to get rid of them the One
would have also to get rid of us.

P. But might they not be our illusion?

A. Yet is not the illusion inevitable and existent?

P. Perhaps.

A. And if it is inevitable, is it not real?

P. Not if the One does not suffer from it. For all
things truly are as they appear to it, and not to us.

A. I am glad you said this; for it is just what I
was wishing you to see. If things truly are as they
appear to the One, then they can never appear to us
as they truly are. And conversely, the One can never
perceive things as they truly appear to us. You can

make the One perfect, but at the cost of separating it from a world which is utterly unreal, and would be abhorrent to its unpolluted calm. Consider now the consequences.

P. What?

A. You have imagined an image of divine perfection. But that image floats above our world, and nowhere touches it. The One cannot know our existence, and if it could know it, could regard it only as a disordered nightmare. It can afford us, therefore, no assistance toward the betterment of life. How then have we secured its divine aid? And is not the disease of appearance incurable, just because it is imaginary and unreal, and God takes no note of it? What then have we gained by convicting ourselves and our knowledge of illusion? And worst of all, we have not even got an answer to our question.

P. To what question?

A. To the question how our argument could climb from earth to heaven, and infer the existence of a god from the nature of the world.

P. Yet did we not find a ladder?

A. But so queer a one that we had to cast it down immediately we got to heaven. And when we got to heaven no one would take notice of us—we were treated as unreal. And to earth we cannot redescend. Or do you see a way?

P. Not from our present position. But tell me, how would it be if we gave up the notion that the One is beautiful and good—for it is this which seems to be impracticable?

A. By all means give it up. But how would you proceed?

P. After all, goodness and beauty are only human feelings, which we might as rightly hesitate to ascribe to God as human shapes and human passions. And so might we not worship him as simply great?

A. There are those, no doubt, who would be willing to do this.

P.   And why not you?

A.   I am not so ready to give up the search for beauty and goodness in the cosmos. I will not worship mere greatness, nor deem a whale more admirable than a man simply because he is many times as large.

P.   But has not the argument shown that the Divine cannot be beautiful and good?

A.   *Or* that what is not beautiful and good cannot be called divine?

P.   How do you mean?

A.   I mean that if the One is neither of these things, I will not worship it, nor call it God. If it is indifferent to our good, I am indifferent to its existence.

P.   But have you not still ground to fear it? Will it not resent your indifference?

A.   Why should it? I too am part of it, if I am at all, fashioned by it to please itself. And if it is indifferent to what seems good to man, why should it care about what seems evil to man?

P.   But how if its nature was to resent all disrespect, and while not rewarding the good, to inflict evil on the imprudent or irreverent?

A.   Why should my irreverence offend rather than amuse it? And why should it inflict evil on itself because a part of itself offended it? Besides, if this were somehow possible, you would only have turned your god into an evil demon. And even so, I should not reasonably change my conduct.

P.   Why not? Would you not be made to suffer for it?

A.   I might be made to suffer for my impiety, but not more probably than you for your piety. For, being evil, the Demon would dole out evils to all, to good and bad alike.

P.   I do not see that. Why?

A.   Because if he did not, but allowed himself to be propitiated by rites, however strange and horrible, there would be a way of making him good. For he would cease to be evil to those who propitiated him, and so would become good, and this would be contrary to our hypothesis.

P. It would seem then that the One can be neither good nor evil, but must be indifferent.

A. But if it is indifferent, does it remain an object of worship?

P. It seems not.

A. If this then be truth, shall we not be really atheists?

P. Hardly that. For do you not think that it will still be a great gain, not perhaps for purposes of public worship, but for the private communings of the soul, that we should feel that we do not live at random in a random concourse of things, but in a cosmos which is truly one?

A. You are satisfied with small gains, if you think this one. Still even small gains are not despicable, if they are sure. But who can feel sure about this gain of yours?

P. What? Do you think an error still lurks in my argument?

A. No, but that it flaunts itself over its whole surface.

P. Do you not admit, then, that the universe is *one?* I do not see how any one can doubt this.

A. Not if you define the universe amiss.

P. How?

A. As the totality of things known and unknown.

P. And is not this the right definition?

A. Only for one desiring to beg the real question.

P. I do not understand.

A. Do you suppose that what you now perceive and know is all that is and was and ever will be, the whole universe in short?

P. Of course not, nor what any man perceives and knows.

A. It is possible, therefore, that additions may be made to the known universe out of the multitude of unknown things?

P. Yes, I suppose so.

A. How would you ascertain whether these additions were really new births within the universe, or really additions from without, from what had not before formed part of it?

P. I hardly know.

A. Nor I. But see what follows.

P. I am looking eagerly.

A. The world at every moment would appear to you to be such that it might either give birth to endless novelties within itself, or come into contact with illimitable realities, which had until then existed out of connexion with it. Your conception, therefore, of the whole as *one*, could never cover all that was. There would always be a Many bursting into or out, in what you had taken to be *one*. And so in neither case could its unity ever be effectively maintained, could you ever get an assurance that you really knew all there was.

P. I suppose not.

A. Then what sense is there in calling our world the universe? The universe is the totality of things; but to this totality we do not attain, nor could we know it, if we did. We can never make certain, therefore, that we are dealing with the real universe, that we have really got all things together in a universe, and that what is true of it is true of the things we know.

P. But would not this uncertainty make it the more interesting?

A. Perhaps; but it would spoil your argument from the notion of a universe.

P. How?

A. Because you could never apply your notion to the world you lived in. That the universe was the totality of existences no one need trouble to deny. For the notion could never be applied. Nor would you, by possessing it, learn anything about the world you lived in. For that the world we know was the totality of things could never be asserted. And what we thought about the world would never justify prediction: it would always be at the mercy of the changes introduced by the new things that entered it.

P.   Would you explain this further?

A.   It is very simple.   If you don't know the whole of a thing and are in doubt about its character, may not your opinion alter as you get to know more of it?

P.   Not unreasonably.

A.   It will seem, therefore, better or worse as a whole, according as the new parts of it seem better or worse?

P.   Certainly.

A.   If, then, God is the whole, and the whole we know is not the true whole but a part, will not our reverence for an incomplete whole, of necessity be the worship of a false god?

P.   Perhaps.

A.   And, moreover, will not God for us grow with our knowledge, growing better or worse, or better and worse alternately, without ceasing?

P.   It will be very inconvenient, if he grows very different!

A.   It will.   And do you not think, therefore, that it will be very inconvenient to worship such a thing at all?

P.   It would not be as delightful as I had hoped.

A.   It would be quite as absurd as worshipping the onion.   And not nearly so useful.   For you can use the onion, and if need be eat it, ere it grows too large, but what can any man do with the universe?

P.   Is it then the desire of Antimorus the Wise that I should proclaim him priest of the Non-existent, and must we once more call ourselves atheists?

A.   By no means.   Remember that I am priest.

P.   Aye, a priest who refutes all gods!

A.   No, who refutes bad arguments.   When have I ever said there were no gods?

P.   But have you not refuted all the arguments the human mind has conceived?

A.   All, perhaps, that *your* mind has conceived.

P.   Has yours, then, conceived others?

A.   Perhaps.

P. Then lose no time in telling me.

A. They are, perhaps, not so different from yours.

P. Then why did you refute mine?

A. Perhaps they were not rightly stated, nor rightly argued from. You are ever so hasty, Philonous, and too eager to make an argument achieve more than its strength will bear. And when it does not at once do what you wish, you reject it utterly; whereas you should not make a leaping-pole out of a reed.

P. What strength is left in any of the arguments I mentioned? Have you not laid them low one by one without exception?

A. The first one, about the connexion between the existence of priests and of gods, was not a bad one.

P. You mean that there cannot be priests unless there are gods? But is it not possible that priests should be instituted by deluded men of false gods, and so exist, even though there are no gods at all?

A. Not quite that: you must look at things more subtly.

P. How then?

A. Leaving aside the gods for a time, let me ask you why you suppose that priests exist?

P. That is hard to say. I have often wondered why.

A. You would not say, I suppose, that priests exist because gods exist?

P. No; for what we are trying to prove is that gods exist because priests exist.

A. Nor yet that there are priests in order that they may have superior knowledge of divine things?

P. But surely they do! You are the first priest I have known who did not profess to have; and even as to you I am not sure.

A. The knowledge I mean is not concerning sacred stories, of which indeed they know a great abundance: it concerns such matters as we have been conversing about, the cause of being and of life and of suffering and of evil, and the things after death and in Hades. Have you ever anywhere met a priest who could give a reasonable account about such things, or answer questions such as would be asked about them by a reasonable man desirous of clear notions?

P. Not unless you are the man!

A. However much you flatter me, I fear that I shall disappoint you.

P. Not unless you break off the inquiry!

A. Then you must suggest a better reason for the existence of priests.

P. Shall we say that we must have them in order that the sacred rites may be performed aright?

A. Yes, that is a better answer. For assuredly it is for the sake of ritual rather than of philosophy that men need priests. But why do they need ritual?

P. It seems so natural. Perhaps without it many would become disorderly, and so it is beneficial to the State.

A. Do you think that our Bacchanalian festivals are conducive to good order?

P. Perhaps not, but does not the fear of Zeus, the guardian of the oath, stop men from swearing falsely?

A. How strange then that perjury is still so common! Or how weak the fear of Zeus! Or will you say perhaps that it is fear of some stronger god than Zeus which leads men to forswear themselves? And do you not fear that the fear of Zeus will lead men to imitate him in other ways as well?

P. A god may do without blame what it would be atrocious for a man to do.

A. How then is a man to know whether it is good to do as the gods, or bad?

P. I confess, Antimorus, I cannot defend the actions of the gods as they are narrated, and that the sacred stories seem to me most impious. That is just why I am so anxious to know what to think about the whole matter.

A. Well said. But you have not yet told me what need men have for priests.

P. I can perceive none, and yet I am persuaded that they need them. Perhaps it is just a desire.

A. Very good indeed! We have priests because we need them, and need them to satisfy our desire. And what do priests desire?

P. Gods, I should think.

A. Excellent! And do you think that they alone desire gods?

P. No, we all do, except perhaps a few scoundrels who dread their vengeance.

A. Good again! Are we not agreed, then, that gods are the embodiments of human desires, and exist as surely, and as long, as the desires which they gratify? Can you wonder any longer that Bacchus is a god, and Plutus, and Aphrodite, and the Onion? For are they not all objects of desire?

P. It seems to me, Antimorus, that you go too fast, and prove too much. If you could prove any god thus, you would certainly prove the existence of the Divine Lust and the Divine Onion. And was it not just by adducing these that you laughed me out of my argument that the existence of priests involved that of their gods? You have substituted the worshippers for the priests as the causes of the gods' existence, but otherwise the argument is the same.

A. Pardon me, Philonous, it was you who dropped the argument at the first touch of ridicule. You will never be a great philosopher until you consent to make yourself very ridiculous, and to laugh at your own ideas as well as at those of others. For if the truth did not seem ridiculous and paradoxical, do you suppose that errors would be so common, so commonplace, so solemn, and so reputable?

P. Even so, I think there are objections to your argument.

A. Then let us discuss them before we go further.

P. Well then, in the first place, if desire makes gods, can it not also unmake them?

A. No doubt, but desires are far more permanent than philosophies or theologies.

P. Again, I do not admit that the desire for a thing

is a reason for thinking that that thing exists, or in any way brings it into existence. The desire for food does not feed me, nor make me wealthy. Nor do the Helmet of Hades and the Elixir of Life exist because I should greatly desire them. And in this case of the gods this magic of desire is the less likely to have creative power, seeing that a god is a more difficult and precious thing for a desire to make than even an elixir of life.

A. You argue well against a doctrine I have not affirmed. For the gods I spoke of as creations of desire, I supposed to exist in the opinions of men, and not on the heights of Olympus.

P. Then they do not really exist?

A. Yes, they do really exist in the souls of men. And it is there that they are most potent, and far excel the dwellers of far-away Olympus, seeing that they are so much nearer.

P. But that is not what I meant, nor what men commonly mean when they ask about the existence of the gods. They inquire about gods who hold the shining mansions of the skies, and not about those who hold the hearts of men.

A. You admit, then, the existence of these latter?

P. Yes, but they do not answer my question, and have no connexion with the real gods.

A. That remains to be seen. For we must advance step by step, and before we try to climb the heights of Olympus, we must try to fathom the depths of human nature. For I should not wonder if the latter showed us the way to the former.

P. I do not oppose your considering them if you please.

A. That is right, my dear Philonous ; for you have escaped your own notice saying some very wrong things about the gods who are born of desire and dwell in the souls of men.

P. What, pray, are these ?

A. Did you not say that your desire for food had no

power to make you believe that food existed, or to satisfy
your hunger?

P. How can it have?   The desire has no arms and
legs!

A. No; but you have.   Have you not observed
four things?   First, that men do not usually get desirable things unless they actually desire them: next,
that if they desire them, they usually find a way of
getting them : thirdly, that when a thing is desired, there
is apt to arise a belief that it is existent and attainable :
and lastly, that when it is attained, it is often supposed to
have existed all along.

P. But it does not become existent because it is
desired.   Nor is it attained because it is desired, but
because it exists.

A. Quite right!   But you would admit, I suppose,
that it might remain unknown to all eternity, for lack
of a desire to know it?

P. Certainly.

A. And so, as no one looked for it, no one found it,
and it remained non-existent for us?

P. Certainly.

A. Desire then is the cause of our discovery of that
which exists beyond our former knowledge?

P. It may often be this.   But only if we are willing
to bestir ourselves to get what we desire.

A. Doubtless.   But does it seem to you reasonable that the man who will not act nor trouble himself
to look, should be thought deserving of truth or knowledge any more than of any other good thing?

P. Perhaps not.

A. Is he not as silly as the sophist's ass, who was
so consumed with desire that he could himself consume
neither of the two bundles of hay before his nose, and
wasted away?

P. I do not believe that any real ass would be as
stupid as Buridan's.

A. Nor any real philosopher.   Even Thales was
practical enough when put to it.   He made a fortune

by cornering the oil presses. They show "the philosopher's corner" still in the market at Miletus.

P. So I have heard, and I am sure the others, much as they profess to scorn wealth, are secretly consumed with envy, and really proud of Thales.

A. And rightly too! But I must not forget that just now I made a mistake to gratify you.

P. What was that?

A. I admitted that a desire could not make its object.

P. Why ought you not to have admitted this?

A. Because it sometimes can.

P. How?

A. Have you not observed how many desires bring about their own satisfaction and make real their own objects?

P. For example?

A. I will take one with which you doubtless are familiar. Is it not true that the lover desires his beloved to return his love, and if he loves wisely and fortunately, does not his desire awaken a responsive passion in the beloved? And so has not the desire for love impelled love, to make love real?

P. Yes, but the desire makes real what was not real before. It does not prove that what was desired existed before it was desired. It lied, therefore, in assuming this.

A. Say rather, it hoped for the best! Or if it lied, was it not the noblest lie?

P. What is that?

A. That which is prophetic of the truth, and engenders it. But I am not sure that it lied. For I never said that the object desired must exist before the desire which creates it. It is enough that it should have been created by the desire for it. And this assuredly is what the desire for gods should have done for us. Perhaps it will also some day make them good and kind and responsive to our wishes.

P. I begin to understand your gods that live in the hearts of men. They are real as the ideal responses to

real human needs, which really move us. But I do not
yet perceive their connexion with the gods that live above,
the real gods as I called them.

A. That surely is not difficult. If we must seek,
to find, desire, to know, it is clear that the inner gods
alone control the roads that lead to the gods above, and
render them propitious to our wishes. They are our
intermediaries. They hold the gates through which all
our prayers and petitions must ascend. And by them too
all the messages from above are re-worded and translated
from the language of the gods into a speech our souls can
comprehend. Nor is there any other way by which the
real gods can be reached.

P. It seems a long way, and we may not yet have
reached them.

A. Aye, and we may not have wanted to! Or,
having set out, we may have turned back in dismay.

P. At last we are getting to the point! Do you
think that we have *now* reached the point where the
gods above us and without us can communicate with
those within, and transmit their will to us?

A. I have long feared that we might reach a point
at which it would no longer be holy for me to answer
you. For by the body of my Lord Bacchus, I dare not
say *no*! And how can you ask one who has studied the
rites of many gods among the Hellenes and the barbarians
to say frankly *yes*?

P. Then you will disappoint me at the end?

A. I told you that I should. But I will treat
you to something better than my own opinions, to the
thoughts of my great master Protagoras, whose mouth was
not sealed and whose office was to teach the truth freely.

P. I shall be delighted to hear more of Protagoras.

A. You know that he was gravely suspected of
impiety and atheism?

P. Yes.

A. Unjustly indeed, but not without plausibility.
For how much satisfaction could the established rites
offer to one like Protagoras who, being deeply con-

cerned about divine things and the wonders of existence, really wanted to know, and would not content himself with ' sacred stories ' ?

P. To me also they often seem to be stories told to children, and not good even for them.

A. Well, you shall hear how Protagoras dealt with Meletus, the tragic poet, who was as a tragic poet comic, and as a theologian tragic.

P. The same who accused Socrates ?

A. Yes, but that was later. He had been reading Protagoras's new book on *Truth*, and like most men had not really understood a word. For truth was but a word to him, and he had never asked himself what it was in very deed. But of course he had been stirred up by the saying about the gods. And so he naturally taxed Protagoras with atheism. You shall hear how skilfully the master answered him.

(Gets out a roll and reads.)

" *Protagoras.* You are mistaken surely, Meletus, if you think that I have denied that there are gods. I only said that I had neither met them, nor been able to find out anything for certain about them. And so I am to be pitied rather than blamed : for surely no one is ignorant of his own will ; the fault therefore is not mine, but that of others, whether of the gods or of men, I cannot say.

Meletus. But it *is* your fault, if you have been un-willing either to inquire diligently into the stories men tell about the gods or to believe them when they were told you.

P. Once more you are mistaken, Meletus. For I have, as you know, travelled far and long throughout Hellas, and from my youth I have always asked the wisest men concerning what they knew about the gods, wherever I went. And they were always glad to tell me their sacred stories, which I noted down. I now have a large collection of them, which some might think most entertaining. But as for believing them, why not even Herodotus could compass that ! In Thessaly, for example,

they will tell you that Zeus lives on a mountain named
Olympus, but in Asia they tell you, no, the mountain is
in Mysia, and with them Homer also seems to hold.   In
Crete, again, they affirm stoutly that Zeus no longer lives
at all, in token whereof they even show his sepulchre.
In Arcadia, Artemis is the Huntress-Maid, in Ephesus she
is a mother with more breasts than any sow.   And so
forth, that I may mention nothing more unseemly.
Which, then, of these stories do you wish me to believe,
seeing that they cannot all be true?

M.   With the gods all things are possible, and it
is impious to question sacred stories.

P.   That is just what I cannot think.   For it seems
to me that the sacred stories malign the gods, if there
are gods, and were the inventions of wicked men.   Or
else they have become wicked by the lapse of time,
because they were thought too sacred to be retold in
ways befitting the greater insight of a later age.

M.   No.   The sacred stories are told by holy men,
priests, and if you would reverently listen to them, you
would know what to think.   You should honour the
priests, therefore, and believe what they tell you.

P.   But do the priests themselves know?

M.   They, if any men.   For they have preserved the
revelations made by the gods of old.

P.   It seems to me that if so, they have preserved
them very badly.   And who knows whether the stories
are now told as they happened?

M.   You will find that they tell the sacred stories
precisely as they received them from their ancestors, many
of whom were themselves children of the gods and must
surely have known their parents.   And so it is reasonable
to believe that the sacred tradition is exact, and that we
know quite as much about the gods as those did to whom
they revealed themselves.

P.   That is just what I complain of, and what leads
me to fear that the priests know no more than I!

M.   How so?

P.   You said, did you not, that the priests know

the revelations made by the gods of old, both concerning themselves and all things which it is good for
man to know?

M. I did.

P. And you said also that they have preserved this
knowledge exactly?

M. Certainly.

P. Then we know no less than the men of old?

M. So I contend.

P. Nor any more?

M. How could we, unless there had been fresh
theophanies!

P. And such there have not been?

M. Don't you believe it!

P. And yet I have met many who affirmed this
stoutly. They seemed indeed to be somewhat ecstatic
persons, but not liars.

M. They were deceived then.

P. This I am willing to believe. But is it not
possible that your friends also were deceived, and have
handed down stories similar to those now told?

M. Possible, but not likely.

P. Not unlikely, I should say. And in other
ways also it would seem either that the priests have
been bad guardians of sacred truths, or good guardians
of unholy falsehoods. For consider: is not the true,
good?

M. Certainly.

P. Then to attain truth should make us better?

M. Is not this what sacred truths do?

P. And also better able to attain more truth?

M. Perhaps.

P. Why then have we not attained better knowledge
of holy things by the aid of the theophanies of former
days?

M. I cannot say.

P. Again, is it the nature of benefactors to abandon
those to whom they have shown kindness, and of the
benefited to keep away from their benefactors?

M. It ought not to be.

P. And yet does not something of this sort seem to happen when gods benefit men?

M. In what way?

P. Why, do you not think that the gods, after bestowing on us beneficial revelations of themselves, have withdrawn themselves from our ken? And men similarly, after acquiring some little knowledge of the gods, show plainly that they desire to know no more about them.

M. Never have I heard this said by any one, Protagoras. But many have lamented over their ignorance of the gods.

P. In words, no doubt. But do not their deeds cry out louder than their words? And of those who claimed to believe in gods, have you ever found any one to act as if this belief opened out to him a way to real knowledge and more knowledge, and knowledge not to be attained by those who are not willing to believe in the gods?

M. It is not holy to desire more knowledge than the gods have granted, or to seek to pry into their secrets.

P. What god has revealed this to you, Meletus? And how else do you know that the gods do not desire you to desire more knowledge concerning themselves before they will, or can, reveal more? How again do you know that men should not pry into the secrets of the gods? Do you perchance suspect the gods of having evil secrets?

M. No, but I suspect you of undermining all established worship, and of wishing to improve on the gods of the city. For no religion could exist with new knowledge and new gods and new worships ever coming in to upset the old.

P. I wonder. And I deem it strange that in other matters which men try and suppose themselves to know, it is not so, but the more they know, the more eager they grow and the more able to learn, and the greater and stronger and more precious and more intelligible their

knowledge seems to them. Either, therefore, knowledge
about the gods is not really knowledge, or men are not
willing to treat it as really knowledge.   In either case I
am prevented from knowing, as I said.   Why then should
I be blamed?   How can I help it?   Either there is
nothing for me to know, or I am not allowed to know it.

M.   Still less, Protagoras, are you allowed to inquire.   Let me speak to you as a friend.   I liked your
rhetoric, and thought your lectures the best I ever listened
to.   But if you are wise, you will in the first place erase
from your book that terrible sentence about the gods, and
in the next place retire from Athens till the storm blows
over.

P.   I am sure your advice is kindly meant.   But
I do not at all agree with you.   I would rather that
my whole book on Truth should perish—excepting of
course what I said about man being the measure, for that
I feel assured cannot die—and that that one sentence be
preserved, than that it should perish and all the rest be
preserved.   For I greatly fear that the major part of my
Truth is too subtle for the dull sight of men such as now
are.   And as for leaving Athens, let the Athenians drive
me out if they think fit.   I am a stranger and accustomed
to wander over the face of the earth.   And so I will wait
to see whether it will be accounted a crime in me to have
spoken and written the ' Truth.'

M.   Then may the gods you doubt help you!   But
your days are numbered.

P.   Are they not that in any case, to one who has
passed his three-score years and ten?"

Antimorus.   Well, Philonous, how do you like that?

Philonous.   Wondrously, and yet it always makes me
uncomfortable, too, to listen to Protagoras or you.   You
are so different from the other philosophers, and so
disturbing.   You never seem to fear either the gods or
even men, and least of all, what is most terrible to the
prudent, to wit, what it has been customary to say.   And
you always throw out hints of something new and un-

heard of to come, that might at any time break in upon
our life and transform it beyond all recognition. And
yet you will never tell us what you think it is.

A. So long as the unknown God is undesired,
he is unknowable. Moreover, all you ever want to
hear is a pleasing tale. You Greeks are children,
like the others. You have need of priests, because
you will not trust the gods within you; and yet
you will not truly believe even your priests. You only
want them to sing you lullabies about the gods; and
whatever saves you thought and trouble you are willing
to believe—after a fashion. And whether what we
chant is true and certain, you care not, provided it is
comforting, nor what our comforting is worth. And to
please you, we humour you, and tell you what you wish
to hear, even though we know that you had much better
test the hidden oracle, and seek the lonely way that leads
to the unknown God each soul that dares and perseveres.

P. I do believe you are right, Antimorus. And so
too are the others. For these things are too high for
mortals. I˙too am afraid! I would rather trust priests
and rites and sacrifices and expiations and sacred stories,
nay chants and charms and amulets, than my naked self.
Philosophy becomes too terrible when it bids us do such
things.

A. You have not yet learnt that the most efficacious
of all expiations is to sacrifice your fears, and you fear
philosophy so soon as it ceases to be idle babble, and
requires you to think things out and act on your convictions! But never mind, my poor boy, I will comfort
you with a most sacred story, which was told me by
the oldest of the priests of Ra at Thebes in Egypt,
a man so old and holy that he had forgotten even his
own name, and become one with his god, and answered
to the name of Ra.

P. I should dearly love to hear it.

A. You have heard, perhaps, that in truth, not
Uranus, but Eros was the oldest of the gods?

P. I have heard it as a secret doctrine.

A. Consider it then to be true, if you are willing to believe the divine genealogies of my Egyptian priest.

P. I will. But what of the rest of the genealogy?

A. Many things he said which are contrary to received opinions, especially holding it to be false that older things are better, and the gods happier than mortals. For, he said, the divinest of all things is to endure suffering without dying. And the gods in the beginning suffered ineffably in their endeavours to make a cosmos. And most of all Eros, seeing that he was very eager, and yet blind, and encompassed about with darkness. And in darkness he would have remained, had he not encountered Pistis,[1] whose nature it is to bring light and brightness wherever she is. And she enlightened Eros, so that he was enabled to see, and consorting with him, she bare Praxis,[2] who again, when she was of age, mingled with Chaos. And there were born to Praxis and Chaos two sons, Pragma and Prometheus, whereof the former was very large, being a giant of a violent and intractable disposition. And he often threatened to swallow up both his mother and the other gods. Wherefore Prometheus, who was crafty, slew him by stealth, and his mother cut him up into many things,[3] and thus made the world we now inhabit. But Eros was wroth with Prometheus, and chained him for ever to the collar-bone of the brother he had slain—which is Mount Caucasus.

P. I suppose it is this story which Agathon means when he says:

"Action of old discriminated all things." [4]

A. Doubtless: but the time has come for my evening sacrifice to Dionysus. So run away, Philonous, and get yourself elected a general by the Mendeans. There may not be a war after all, and even if there is, it is easier to face the risk of death than of eternal life.

---

[1] Faith.   [2] Action.   [3] πράγματα.
[4] Πρᾶξις πάλαι διεῖλε πάντα πράγματα.

XVI

FAITH, REASON, AND RELIGION [1]

ARGUMENT

§ 1. The problem of religious philosophy that of the relations of 'faith' and 'reason.' The rationalistic criticism of religion, and the pragmatic criticism of rationalism. § 2. Faith as a specifically religious principle. Its revival as a philosophic principle, and a presupposition of reason. § 3. The Will-to-believe and to disbelieve. Humanism as a recognition of actual mental process. § 4. The analysis of 'reason.' § 5. Thought dependent on postulation, *i.e.* 'faith.' § 6. The definition of 'faith.' § 7. The pragmatic testing of faith and knowledge. § 8. The incompleteness of this process. § 9. The analogy of scientific and religious faith. § 10. Their differences. § 11. Five spurious conceptions of faith. § 12. The possibility of verifying religious postulates. § 13. Humanist conclusions as to the philosophy of religion. The pragmatic character of Christianity obscured by an intellectualist theology.

§ 1. THE nature of religion, and the extent to which what is vaguely and ambiguously called 'faith' and what is (quite as vaguely and ambiguously) called 'reason' enter into it, rank high among the problems of perennial human interest—in part, perhaps, because it seems impossible to arrive at any settlement which will appear equally cogent and satisfactory to all human minds. Of late, however, the old controversies have been rekindled into the liveliest incandescence, in consequence of two purely philosophic developments.

On the one hand, Absolutism, despite its long coquettings with theology, has revealed itself as fundamentally hostile to popular religion (see Essay xii.). In works like

[1] This essay appeared in substance in the *Hibbert Journal* for January 1906. It has been retouched in a few places to fit it more effectively for its place in this volume.

Mr. Bradley's *Appearance and Reality*, and still more formidably, because more lucidly and simply, in Dr. McTaggart's *Some Dogmas of Religion*, it has reduced Christian Theism to what seems a position of grotesque absurdity by an incisive criticism from which there is no escape so long as its victim accepts the rationalistic tests and conceptions of truth and proof with which it operates.

On the other hand, it has simultaneously happened that just these tests and conceptions have been impugned, and to a large extent condemned, by the pragmatic movement in philosophy. It threatens to deprive Rationalism [1] of its favourite weapons just as it is about to drive them home. It promises to lead to a far juster and more sympathetic, because more psychological, appreciation of the postulates of the religious consciousness, and to render possible an unprejudiced consideration of the non-' rational ' and non-rationalistic evidence on which religion has all along relied. And so rationalistic philosophers have at once taken alarm.

Hence, though this movement appears to affect immediately nothing but technicalities of the theory of knowledge, it has been extensively taken as an attempt at a revolutionary reversal of the relations of Faith and Reason. The new philosophy was promptly accused of aiming at the oppression, nay, at the subversion, of Reason, of paving the way to the vilest obscurantism and the grossest superstition with the ruins of the edifice of truth which its scepticism had exploded ; in short, of attempting to base Religion on the quicksands of irrationality. But, it was urged, the dangerous expedients which are used recoil upon their authors : the appeal to the will to-believe ends by sanctioning the arbitrary adoption of any belief any one may chance to fancy, and thus destroys all objectivity in religious systems ; religious sentiment is freed from the repressive régime of a rigid rationalism only to be ignobly dissipated in excesses of subjective licence.

---

[1] I am using the term strictly as = 'a belief in the all-sufficiency of reason,' and not in its popular sense as = ' criticism of religion.' A rationalist in the strict sense may, of course, be religious, and *per contra* a voluntarist, or a sensationalist, may be a rationalist in the popular sense.

Now, the first thing that strikes one about such denunciations is their premature violence. The opponents of the new *Humanism* should have met it on the logical, and still more on the psychological, ground whence its challenge proceeded, before they hastened to extract from it religious applications which had certainly not been made, and possibly were not even intended, by its authors, and which there is, as yet, hardly a sign, in this country at least, that the spokesmen of the religious organizations are willing to welcome. And until the leaders of the churches show more distinct symptoms of interest, both in the disputes of philosophers in general and in this dispute in particular, it seems premature to anticipate from this source the revolution which is decried in advance. Theologians, in general, have heard 'Wolf!' cried too often by philosophers anxious to invoke against their opponents more forcible arguments than those of mere reason, they have found too often how treacherous were the specious promises of philosophic support, they are too much absorbed in historical and critical researches and perplexities of their own to heed lightly outcries of this sort.

The controversy, then, has not yet descended from the study into the market-place, and it seems still time to attempt to estimate philosophically the real bearing of *Humanism* on the religious problem, and to define the functions which it actually assigns to reason and to faith. It may reasonably be anticipated that the results of the inquiry will be found to justify neither the hopes of those who expect an explicit endorsement of any sectarian form of religion (if such there are), nor the fears of those who dread a systematic demolition of the reason.

§ 2. Perhaps a brief historic retrospect will form the best approach to the points at issue. Thoughtful theologians have always perceived, what their rationalistic critics have blindly ignored, viz. that religious truths are not, like mathematical, such as directly and universally to impose themselves on all minds. They have seen, that is, that the religious attitude essentially implies the addition of what was called 'faith' for its proper appreciation. This 'faith,' moreover, was conceived as an intensely *personal* act, as an emotional reaction of a man's whole nature upon a vital issue. It followed that it was unreasonable, on the part of rationalists, to ignore this specific character of religious truth or to treat it as irrational. And it was this perception which prompted a Pascal to array the 'reasons of the heart' against the (abstract) reasons of 'the head,' a Newman to compile his *Grammar of Assent*, and a Ritschl to spurn the pseudo-demonstrations of (a Hegelian) philosophy, and to construct an impregnable citadel for the religious sentiment in the exalted sphere of 'judgments of value.'

Accordingly, when that great student of the human soul, William James, proclaimed the right of inclining the nicely-weighted equipoise of intellectual argumentation by throwing into the scales a will-to-believe whichever of the alternatives seemed most consonant with our emotional nature, it might well have seemed that he was merely reviving and re-wording a familiar theological expedient which philosophy had long ago discredited as the last desperate resource of an expiring religious instinct.

It turned out, however, that there was an important novelty in the doctrine as revived. It reappeared as a *philosophic* doctrine, firmly resting on psychological and epistemological considerations which were, intrinsically, quite independent of its religious applications, and took the field quite prepared to conduct, on purely philosophic grounds, a vigorous campaign against the intellectualist prejudices of the current rationalism. In other words, by conceiving the function of 'faith' as an example of a general principle, the religious applications, through which the principle had first been noticed and tested, were rendered derivative illustrations of a far-reaching philosophic view. It ceased, therefore, to be necessary to *oppose* the reasons of the heart to those of the head; it could be maintained that no 'reasons' could be excogitated by an anæmic brain to which no heart supplied

the life-blood ; it could be denied that the operations of
the ' illative sense ' and the sphere of value-judgments
were restricted to religious truths.   The new philosophy,
moreover, as we have seen,[1] has been taught by the
sceptical results to which the old abstractions led, that
knowledge cannot be *depersonalized*, and that the full
concreteness of personal interest is indispensable for the
attainment of truth.   Hence the theologians' insistence on
the personal character of ' faith,' which on the old assumptions had seemed a logical absurdity, was completely vindicated.   And so the indications of emotional influence, aɪ
the proofs of the ineradicability of personality, multipliec
throughout the realm of truth, until the apparently dispassionate procedure of mathematics ceased to seem typical
and became a paradox.[2]   Thus, throughout the ordinary
range of what mankind esteems as ' truth,' the function
of volition and selection, and the influence of values in
all recognition of validity and reality, have become too
clear to be ignored, and there has resulted the curious
consequence that, by the very process of working out the
claims of faith fairly to their logical conclusion, ' faith '
has ceased to be an adversary of and a substitute for
' reason,' and become an essential ingredient in its
constitution.   Reason, therefore, is incapacitated from
systematically contesting the validity of faith, because
faith is proved to be essential to its own validity.

§ 3.   The sweeping nature of this change was at first
obscured by the accident that the new philosophy was
first applied in a paper written for a theological audience,
and promulgated as a ' Will-to-believe,' without sufficient
emphasis on the corresponding attitudes of a Will-to-
disbelieve or to play with beliefs, or to suspend belief, or
to allow belief to be imposed by what had already been

---

[1] Cp. Essays ii., iii., and vi.

[2] Of course, the discrepant character of mathematical truth as ' self-evident
and ' independent' of our arbitrament, is only apparent.   It arises mainly from
the ease with which its fundamental postulates are made and rendered familiar,
from the general agreement about their sphere of application, from the complete
success of their practical working, and from the obvious coherence of truths
which are tested in whole systems rather than individually.   Cp. *Humanism*,
pp. 91, 92 ; and *Personal Idealism*, pp. 111-17, and 70 *n*.

accepted as external 'fact.' Thus it was the special character of the first application that led the less discerning to overlook the general character of the principle and the universal scope of the method. But in itself the new doctrine is perfectly general and impartial in its application to all cognitive states. It proceeds essentially from simple observations that, on the one hand, pure cognition is not an actual process in any human mind, but at best a fiction for theoretic purposes (of the most dubious character); while, on the other, all actual mental procedure is thoroughly personal and permeated through and through with purposes and aims and feelings and emotions and decisions and selections even in such cases where these features are ostensibly abstracted from.

Fundamentally, therefore, the new *Humanism* is nothing but an attempt to dismiss from psychology fictions which have been allowed to engender a brood of logical monsters, which in their turn have tyrannized over human life, and driven back the healthy human instinct to experiment, and thereby to know, from what they perniciously proclaimed forbidden ground. And as this fundamental position has never directly been impugned, does it not become an easy and inevitable inference, that the attitude of the denier, the doubter, and the believer cannot be discriminated by the 'pureness' of the thought, by the test of the presence or absence of emotion? If no thought is ever 'pure,' if it is neither 'self-evident' nor true in point of fact that the more nearly 'pure' it is the better it is for all purposes, if emotion, volition, interest, and bias impartially accompany all cognitive procedures, is it not preposterous to treat the concrete nature of the mind, the personal interests which give an impulse to knowledge and a zest to life, merely as impediments in the search for truth? What emotions, etc., must be repressed, to what extent, for what purposes, depends entirely on the character of the particular inquiry and of the particular inquirer. Thus, the anger which leaves one man speechless will add eloquence and effect to the speeches of another; and the

desire to prove a conclusion, which impairs the judgment
of one, will stimulate another to the most ingenious
experiments and the most laborious efforts.   It is useless,
therefore, to generalize at random about the cognitive
effect of these psychological influences.   They must be
admitted in principle, and evaluated in detail.   It *must*
surely be futile to protest against the normal functioning
of the mind ; it must be rational to recognize influences
which affect us, whether we approve of them or not.
For how can they be estimated and treated rationally,
unless we consent to recognize their potency?   Has it
not then become necessary to examine, patiently and in
detail, how precisely these forces act ; how, when, and to
what extent their influence may be helpful or adverse,
how they may be strengthened and guided and guarded
or controlled and disciplined?   And is it not a strange
irony that impels a purblind rationalism to denounce as
irrational so reasonable an undertaking ?

§ 4.   Let us therefore set aside such protests, and proceed with our inquiry.   Like most terms when scrutinized,
neither reason nor faith are conceived with sufficient
precision for our scientific purpose, and it would be hard
to say which of them had been misused in a more flagrant
or question-begging way.   Reason to the rationalist has
become a sort of verbal fetish, hedged round with
emotional taboos, which exempt it from all rational
criticism.   It is credited with supra-mundane powers of
cognition *a priori* ; it is sacrosanct itself ; and when its
protecting ægis is cast over any errors or absurdities, it
becomes blasphemy and ' scepticism ' to ask for their
credentials.   Hence it is only with the utmost trepidation
that we can dare to ask—What, after all, does reason
mean in actual life ?   When, however, we ask this
question, and ponder on the answer, we shall not be
slow to discover that, in the first place, *reason is not
reasoning*.   Reasoning may, of course, enter into the
' rational ' act, but it is by no means indispensable, and
even when it does occur, it only forms a small part of
the total process.   Ordinarily instinct, impulse, and habit

account for by far the greater number of our 'rational' acts. On the other hand, it is *not* rational to 'reason' three hours a day about the clothes one is going to put on ; the reasoning of the victims of such 'abulia,' so far from being taken as a mark of superior rationality, is taken as a symptom of a *loss of reason.*

In the next place, 'reason' is *not a faculty*. It stands for a group of habits which men (and to some extent some animals) have acquired, and which we find extremely useful, nay necessary, for the successful carrying on of life. Among these habits may be mentioned that of inhibiting reaction upon stimulation, *i.e.* of checking our natural and instinctive tendencies to act, until we have reflected what precisely it is we are dealing with. To determine this latter point, we have developed the habit of *analysis*, *i.e.* of breaking up the confused complex of presentations into 'things' and their 'attributes,' which are referred to and 'identified' with former similar experiences, and expressed in judgments as to what the situation 'really is.' This enables us to rearrange the presented connexions of attributions, and the whole reasoning process finds its natural issue and test in an action which modifies and beneficially innovates upon the original habit of reaction.

§ 5. In other words, thinking or judging is one of the habits that make up man's 'reason,' and thinking or judging is a highly artificial and arbitrary manipulation of experience. The 'rational' connexion of events and the 'rational' interpretation of experiences are very far removed from our immediate data, and arrived at only by complicated processes of thought. Now, thinking involves essentially the use of concepts, and depends ultimately upon a number of principles (identity, contradiction, etc.), which have long been regarded as fundamental 'axioms,' but which reveal themselves as *postulates* to a voluntarist theory of knowledge which tries to understand them.

Now, a postulate is not a self-evident 'necessary' truth —it ceases to be necessary so soon as the purpose which

called it into being is renounced.   Neither is it a passively
received imprint of experience.   It is an assumption,
which no doubt experience has suggested to an *actively
inquiring* mind, but which is not, and cannot be, proved
until after it has been assumed, and is often assumed
because we desire it, in the teeth of nearly all the apparent
'facts.'   It is therefore a product of our volitional activity,
and initially its validity is uncertain.   It is established
ex post facto by the experience of its practical success.   In
other words, it is validated in just the same way as are
the other habits that make up our 'reason.'   In so far as,
therefore, reasoning rests on postulates, and postulates are
unproved and open to doubt at the outset, our attitude in
adhering to them implies 'faith,' *i.e.* a belief in a 'verification' yet to come.   Must we not say, then, that at the
very roots of 'reason' we must recognize an element of
'faith'?   And similarly it would seem that as the fundamental truths of the sciences are attained in the same
way, they all must presuppose faith, in a twofold manner—
(1) as making use of reasoning, and (2) as resting upon
the specific postulates of each science.

§ 6.   That the principle of faith is commonly conceived
very variably and with great vagueness has already been
admitted, though its critics seem unfairly to incline
towards the schoolboy's definition that it is 'believing a
thing when you know it's not true.'   Even this definition
would not be wholly indefensible, if it were only written
'believing when you know it's not *true*,' and if thereby
proper attention were drawn to the fact that a belief
sustained by faith still stands in need of verification to
become fully 'true.'   On the whole, however, it would
seem preferable to define it as the mental attitude which,
for purposes of action, is willing to take upon trust
valuable and desirable beliefs, *before* they have been proved
'true,' but in the hope that this attitude may promote
their *verification*.   About this definition it is to be noted
(1) that it renders faith pre-eminently an attitude of will,
an affair of the whole personality and not of the (abstract)
intellect; (2) that it is expressly concerned with values,

and that the worthless and unimportant is not fitted to evoke our faith ; (3) that it involves risk, real stakes, and serious dangers, and is emphatically not a game that can be played in a casual and half-hearted way ; (4) that a reference to verification is essential to it, and that therefore it is as little to be identified with, as to be divorced from, knowledge.   Now, verification must come about by the results of its practical working, by presuming the 'truth' of our faith and by acting on its postulates ; whence it would appear that those theologians were right who contended that real faith must justify itself by works. On the other hand, we might anticipate that spurious forms of faith would fall short in one or more of these respects, and so account for the confusion into which the subject has drifted.

§ 7. Such, then, being the nature of the faith which is said to envelop and sustain reason, and to engender knowledge, can it be fairly charged with forming a principle of unbridled individualism which abrogates all distinctions between subjective fancy and objective reality ? Nothing surely could be further from the truth.   At first, no doubt, it looks as though to recognize the psychological necessity and logical value of the will to believe opened the door to a limitless host of individual postulates.   But the freedom to believe what we will is so checked by the consciousness of the responsibility and risk attaching to our choice, that this part of the doctrine becomes little more than a device for securing an open field and a fair trial to every relevant possibility.   Furthermore, all such subjective preferences have to submit to a severe sifting in consequence of the requirement that our postulates must stand the test of practical working, before their claim to truth can be admitted.   Whatever our faith, it must be confirmed by works, and so prove itself to be objectively valid.

Alike, therefore, whether it is applied to knowledge or to faith, the pragmatic test is a severe one.   It allows, indeed, the widest liberty to experiment ; but it inexorably judges such experiments by the value of their actual achievements, and sternly withholds its sanction from insincere phrasemongering, from ineffectual aspiration, from unworkable conceptions, from verbal quibblings and dead formulas. Throughout the intellectual world the pedantry of the past has heaped up so much rubbish which the application of this pragmatic test would clear away, that it is not always easy to repress a suspicion that much of the philosophic alarm at the consequences of applying our test may have been inspired, more or less unconsciously, by an unavowed dread lest it should insist on pensioning off some of the more effete veterans among philosophic traditions.

For really the pragmatic value of much that passes for philosophy is by no means easy to discern. Metaphysical systems, for instance, hardly ever seem to possess more than individual value. They satisfy their inventors, and afford congenial occupation to their critics. But they have hitherto shown no capacity to achieve a more general validity or to intervene effectively in the conduct of life. Again, it is inevitable that the pragmatic inquiry as to what difference their truth or falsehood can be supposed to make should be raised concerning many metaphysical propositions, such as that the universe is ' one ' or 'perfect,' or that truth is ' eternal,' or that ' substance ' is immutable, which, in so far as they are not taken as merely verbal (and this is all they usually profess to be when criticized), seem only very distantly and doubtfully connected with life. Their *prestige*, therefore, is seriously imperilled.

Now, similar dogmas abound in religion, and are not wholly absent even from the sciences. But their occurrence is outbalanced by that of assertions which carry practical consequences in the most direct and vital way. Hence the pragmatic importance and value of science and religion can hardly be contested. And as tested by their material results in the one case and by their spiritual results in the other, they both indisputably ' work.' It is inevitable, therefore, that we should regard them as resting on conceptions which are broadly ' true,' or ' true ' at all events until superseded by something truer. They have

nothing, consequently, to fear from our method of criticism :
if anything, its application may be expected to invigorate
their pursuit, and to relieve them of the burden of non-
functional superfluities with which an officious formalism
has encumbered them.

Selection, then, of the valuable among a plurality of
alternatives is essential to the life and progress of religious,
as of secular, truth. Truth is not *merely* 'what each man
troweth,' but (in its fulness) also what has stood its tests
and justified our trust.

§ 8. But experience would seem to show that (at least
while the winnowing process is still going on) the results
of this testing are not so decisive as to eliminate all the
competitors but one. Over an extensive range of subjects
the most various opinions appear tenable, and are successfully maintained. But why should this astonish us?
For (1) what right have we to expect final results from
an incomplete process? (2) What right have we to assume
that even ultimate 'truth' must be one and the same
for all? The assumption is no doubt convenient, and in
a rough and ready way it works ; but does it do full
justice to the variety of men and things? Is the 'sameness' we assume ever really more than agreement for
practical purposes, and do we ever really crave for more
than this? And provided we achieve this, why should
not the 'truth,' too, prove more subtly flexible, and
adjust itself to the differences of individual experience,
and result in an agreement to differ and to respect our
various idiosyncrasies? (3) It is difficult to see why a
phenomenon, which is common in the sciences and normal
in philosophy, without exciting indignation, should be
regarded as inadmissible in the religious sphere, It is a
normal feature in the progress of a science that its 'facts'
should be established by engendering a multitude of
interpretations, none of which are capable, usually, of
covering them completely, and none so clearly 'false' as
to be dismissible without a qualm. Why, then, should
we be alarmed to find that the growth of religious truth
proceeds with an analogous exuberance? (4) Anyhow,

whether we like or dislike the human habit of entertaining divergent beliefs, the plurality of the opinions which are held to be 'true' is an important fact, and forms one of the data which no adequate theory of knowledge can afford to overlook.

§ 9. It is useless, therefore, to close our eyes to the fact that faith is essentially a personal affair, an adventure, if you please, which originates in individual options, in choices on which men set their hearts and stake their lives. If these assumptions prosper, and if so by faith we live, then it may come about that by faith we may also know. For it is the essential basis of the cognitive procedure in science no less than in religion that we must start from assumptions which we have not proved, which we cannot prove, and which can only be 'verified' after we have trusted them and pledged ourselves to look upon the facts with eyes which our beliefs have fortunately biassed. Of this procedure the belief in a causal connexion of events, the belief which all natural science presupposes and works on, is perhaps the simplest example. For no evidence will go to prove it in the least degree until the belief has boldly been assumed. Moreover, as we have argued (in Essays ii., iii., and vi.), to abstract from the personal side of knowing is really impossible. Science also, properly understood, does not depersonalize herself. She too takes risks and ventures herself on postulates, hypotheses, and analogies, which seem wild, until they are tamed to our service and confirmed in their allegiance. She too must end by saying *Credo ut intelligam.* And she does this because she must. For, as Prof. Dewey has admirably shown,[1] *all values and meanings rest upon beliefs*, and "we cannot preserve significance and decline the personal attitude in which it is inscribed and operative." And the failure of intellectualist philosophy to justify science and to understand 'how knowledge is possible,' we have seen to be merely the involuntary consequence of its mistaken refusal to admit the reality and necessity of faith.

[1] In his important paper on 'Beliefs and Existences' in *The Influence of Darwin on Philosophy.*

I find it hard, therefore, to understand why a religious assumption, such as, *e.g.*, the existence of a ' God,' should require a different and austerer mode of proof, or why the theologian should be debarred from a procedure which is always reputable, and sometimes heroic, in a man of science.

We start, then, always from the postulates of faith, and transmute them, slowly, into the axioms of reason. The presuppositions of scientific knowledge and religious faith are the same. So, too, is the mode of verification by experience. The assumptions which work, *i.e.* which approve themselves by ministering to human interests, purposes, and objects of desire, are ' verified ' and accepted as ' true.' So far there is no difference. But we now come to the most difficult part of our inquiry, viz., that of applying our general doctrine to the religious sphere, and of accounting for the different complexion of science and religion. For that there exists a marked difference here will hardly be denied, nor that it (if anything) will account for the current antithesis of faith and reason. It must be, in other words, a difference in the treatment of the same principles which produces the difference in the results.

§ 10. Now, it is fairly easy to see that certain differences in treatment are necessarily conditioned by differences in the subjects in which the verification of our postulates takes place. In ordinary life we deal directly with an ' external world ' perceived through the senses ; in science with the same a little less directly : in either case our hypotheses appeal to some overt, visible, and palpable fact, by the observation of which they are adequately verified. But the data of the religious consciousness are mainly experiences of a more inward, spiritual, personal sort, and it is obvious that they can hardly receive the same sort of verification. The religious postulates can hardly be verified by a direct appeal to sense, we think ; and even if theophanies occurred, they would not nowadays be regarded as adequate proofs of the existence of God.

But this difference at once gives rise to a difficulty.

The opinion of the great majority of mankind is still so instinctively averse from introspection, that it is not yet willing to treat the psychical facts of inward experience as facts just as rightfully and in as real a way as the observations of the senses. It does not recognize the reality and power of *beliefs*. It does not see that " beliefs are themselves real without discount," " as metaphysically real as anything else can ever be," and that " belief, sheer, direct, unmitigated, personal belief," can act on reality " by modifying and shaping the reality of other real things." [1] And because it has not understood the reality of beliefs as integral constituents of the world of human experience, and their potency as the motive forces which transform it, it has disabled itself from really understanding our world.

But it has disabled itself more seriously from understanding the dynamics of the religious consciousness. It rules out as irrelevant a large and essential part of the evidence on which the religious consciousness has everywhere instinctively relied.   It hesitates to admit the historic testimony to the ' truth ' of a religious synthesis which comes from the experience of its working through the ages, even though it may not, like the old rationalism, dismiss it outright as unworthy of consideration. It suspects or disallows many of the verifications to which the religious consciousness appeals.   And this is manifestly quite unfair.   The psychological evidence is relevant, because in the end there is a psychological side to all evidence, which has been overlooked.   The historical appeal is relevant, because in the end all evidence is historical, and the truth of science also rests on the record of its services.   The controversy, therefore, about the logical value of religious experience will have henceforth to be conducted with considerably expanded notions of what evidence is relevant.   Nor must we be more severe on religion than on science.   But it is plain that we are. We ought not to be more suspicious of the religious than of the many scientific theories which are not capable of direct

---

[1] Prof. Dewey in *l.c.* pp. 192, 188, 187.

verification by sense-perception. But even though the ether, *e.g.*, is an assumption which no perception can ever verify, it is yet, in scientific theory, rendered so continuous with what is capable of perceptual verification that the discrepancy is hardly noticed. The system of religious truths is much less closely knit ; the connexion of the postulates with our spiritual needs and their fulfilling experiences is much less obvious ; the methods and possibilities of spiritual experiment are much less clearly ascertained.

The reason, no doubt, partly is that in the religious sphere the conceptions for which the support of faith is invoked are much more vaguely outlined. It would be a matter of no slight difficulty to define the conception of religion itself, so as to include everything that was essential, and to exclude everything that was not. And it would not be hard to show that at the very core of the religious sentiment there linger survivals of the fears and terrors with which primitive man was inspired by the spectacle of an uncomprehended universe.

Again, consider so central a conception of religion as, *e.g.*, ' God.' It is so vaguely and ambiguously conceived that within the same religion, nay, within the same Church, the word may stand for anything, from the cosmic principle of the most vaporous pantheism to a near neighbour of the most anthropomorphic polytheism. And it is obvious that while this is so, no completely coherent or ' rational ' account can be given of a term whose meanings extend over almost the whole gamut of philosophic possibilities. But it is also obvious that there is no intrinsic reason for this state of things, and that theologians could, if they wished, assign one sufficiently definite meaning to the word, and then devise other terms as vehicles for the other meanings. It may be noted, as a happy foretaste of such a more reasonable procedure, that already philosophers of various schools are beginning to distinguish between the conceptions of ' God ' and of ' the Absolute,' though it is clear to me that the latter ' conception ' is still too vague and will in its turn have to be either abolished or relegated to a merely honorary position.

§ 11. It must be admitted, thirdly, that a widespread distrust of faith has been, not unnaturally, provoked by the extensive misuse of the principle in its religious signification. Faith has become the generic term for whatever religious phenomena co-existed with an absence of knowledge. Under this heading we may notice the following spurious forms of faith :—(1) Faith may become a euphemism for unwillingness to think, or, at any rate, for absence of thought. In this sense faith is the favourite offspring of intellectual indolence. It is chiefly cherished as the source of a comfortable feeling that everything is all right, and that we need not trouble our heads about it further. If we ' have faith ' of this kind, no further exertion is needed to sustain our spiritual life ; it is the easiest and cheapest way of limiting and shutting off the spiritual perspective. (2) It is not uncommon to prefer faith to knowledge because of its uncertainty. The certainty about matters of knowledge is cold and cramping : the possibilities of faith are gloriously elastic. (3) Our fears for the future, our cowardly shrinkings from the responsibilities and labours of too great a destiny, nay, our very despair of knowledge itself, may all assume the garb of faith, and masquerade as such. (4) ' Faith ' may mean merely a disingenuous disavowal of a failure to know, enabling us to retain dishonestly what we have not known (or sought) to gain by valid means. To all these spurious forms of faith, of course, our Humanism can furnish no support, though it is alert to note the important part they play (and especially the first) throughout our mental life.

The fifth form of faith is not so much fraudulent as incomplete ; its fallacy consists in allowing itself to be stopped short of works, and to renounce the search for verification. This is the special temptation of the robuster forms of faith : if our faith is very strong it produces an assurance to which, psychologically, no more could be added. Why, then, demand knowledge as well? Does not this evince an unworthy distrust of faith at the very time when faith has shown its power? To which it may be replied that we also can and must distinguish psychological assurance from logical proof, even though the latter must induce the former, and the former must lay claim to logical value as it grows more nearly universal. The difference lies in the greater psychological communicability of the 'logical' assurances and their wider range of influence. At first sight emotional exhortations (sermons, etc.) may seem to produce far intenser and more assured beliefs than calmer reasonings. But they do not appeal so widely nor last so well, and even though it is hazardous to assume that 'logical' cogency is universal,[1] it is certainly, on the whole, of greater pragmatic value.

Moreover, the motives of an unreasoning faith are easily misread; the faith which is strong enough to feel no need of further proof is interpreted as too weak to dare to aspire to it. And so a properly enlightened faith should yield the strongest impetus to knowledge: the stronger it feels itself to be, the more boldly and eagerly should it seek, the more confidently should it anticipate, the more probably should it attain, the verificatory experiences that recompense its efforts.

§ 12. It must be admitted for these reasons that the mistaken uses of the principle of faith have retarded the intellectual development of the religious view of life. It has lagged so far behind the scientific in its formal development that theologians might often with advantage take lessons from the scientists in the proper use of faith. But intrinsically the religious postulates are not insusceptible of verification, nor are religious 'evidences' incapable of standing the pragmatic test of truth. And some verification in some respects many of these postulates and much of this evidence may, of course, be fairly said to have received. The question how far such verification has gone is, in strict logic, the question as to the sphere of religious 'truth.' The question as to how much further verification should be carried, and with what prospects, is

---

[1] Cp. Essay xii. § 8.

strictly the question of the sphere of the claims to truth which rest as yet only upon faith.

§ 13. To attempt to determine with scientific precision what amount of established truth must be conceded to religion as it stands, and what claims to truth should be regarded as reasonable and valuable, and what not, is a task which probably exceeds the powers, as it certainly transcends the functions, of the mere philosopher. It would in any case be fantastic, and probably illusory, to expect any philosophy to deduce *a priori* and in so many words the special doctrines of any religion which bases its claims on historic revelation, and *may*, by its working, be able to establish them.   For what would be the need and the use of revelation if it added nothing to what we might have discovered for ourselves?   Moreover, in the present condition of the religious evidence, any attempt to evaluate it could only claim subjective and personal interest.   No two philosophers probably would evaluate it just in the same way and with the same results.

It seems better, therefore, to make only very general observations, and to draw only general conclusions.   As regards the general psychology of religion, it is clear (1) that all our human methods of grasping and remoulding our experience are fundamentally one.   (2) It is clear that the religious attitude towards the facts, or seeming facts, of life is in general valid.   (3) It is clear that this attitude has imperishable foundations in the psychological nature of the human soul.   (4) It is clear that the pragmatic method is able to discriminate rigorously between valid and invalid uses of faith, and offers sufficient guarantees, on the one hand, against the wanderings of individual caprice, and, on the other, against the narrowness of a doctrinairism which would confine our postulates to a single type—those of the order falsely called 'mechanical.' [1]

---

[1] Strictly interpreted, the word *confirms* the Humanist position which it is so often used to exclude.   For a 'mechanism' is, properly, a *device*—a means to effect a purpose.   And, in point of fact, it is as a means to ordering our experience that 'mechanical' conceptions are in use.   To abstract from this teleological function of all 'mechanism' therefore, is to falsify the metaphor : a device of nobody's, for no purpose, is a means that has no meaning.

It can show that it is not 'faith' to despise the work of 'reason,' nor 'reason' to decline the aid of 'faith'; and that the field of experience is so wide and rough that we need never be ashamed to import religion into its cultivation in order to perfect the fruits of human life.

As regards the concrete religions themselves, it is clear (1) that all religions may profit by the more sympathetic attitude of Humanism towards the religious endowment of human nature, and so towards their evidences and methods. And this for them is a gain not to be despised. For it invalidates the current rationalistic attacks, and secures religions against the ordinary 'dialectical' refutations. It gives them, moreover, a chance of proving their truth in their own appropriate way. It is clear (2) that all religions work pragmatically to a greater or less extent. And this in spite of what seem, theoretically, the greatest difficulties. The obvious explanation is that these 'theoretical' difficulties are really unimportant, because they are either *non-functional* or *pragmatically equivalents*, and that the really functional parts of all religions will be found to be practically identical. It follows (3) that all religions will be greatly benefited and strengthened by getting rid of their non-functional accretions and appendages. These constitute what may, perhaps, without grave injustice be called the *theological* side of religion; and it nearly always does more harm than good. For even where 'theological' systems are not merely products of professional pedantry, and their 'rationality' is not illusory, they absorb too much energy better devoted to the more truly religious functions. The most striking and familiar illustration of this is afforded by our own Christianity, an essentially human and thoroughly pragmatic religion, hampered throughout its history, and at times almost strangled, by an alien theology, based on the intellectualistic speculations of Greek philosophers. Fortunately the Greek metaphysic embodied (mainly) in the 'Athanasian' creed is too obscure to have ever been really functional; its chief mischief has always been to give theological support to 'philosophic' criticisms, which, by identifying God with 'the One,' have aimed at eliminating the human element from the Christian religion.[1]   As against all such attempts, however, we must hold fast to the principle that the truest religion is that which issues in and fosters the best life.

---

[1] Cp. Prof. Dewey, *l.c.* pp. 178-80.

XVII

THE PROGRESS OF PSYCHICAL RESEARCH [1]

ARGUMENT

§ 1. The impotence of 'facts' to resist interpretations prompted by bias. The attempts to interpret 'psychical phenomena' systematically. § 2. The work of Frederic Myers. § 3. The conception of the Subliminal. § 4. Myers's use of it to transcend terrestrial existence. § 5. The argument of his *Human Personality*. § 6. Current criticisms of it. § 7. Replies to these. § 8. The 'proof' of immortality. § 9. The need for organized and endowed inquiry.

§ 1. IT is a popular superstition that the advancement of truth depends wholly on the discovery of facts, and that the sciences have an insatiable appetite for facts and consume them raw, like oysters ; whereas, really, the actual procedure of the sciences is almost the exact opposite of this. For the facts to be 'discovered' there is needed *the eye to see them*, and inasmuch as the most important facts do not at first obtrude themselves, it has usually to be a *trained* eye, and animated by a persevering desire to know. Radium, for example, with the revolution in our whole conception of material nature which it imports, after vainly bombarding an inattentive universe for æons, has only just succeeded in getting itself discovered, and its wonderful activity appreciated and ranked as 'fact.'

Again, the sciences are anything but heaps of crude facts. They are coherent systems of the interpretation of what they have *taken* as 'fact,' and they, very largely, *make their own facts as they proceed*. Nor are 'facts' facts for

---

[1] This essay appeared in the *Fortnightly Review* for January 1905. It is reprinted by the courtesy of the editor, with a few additions towards the end.

a science until it has prepared them for assimilation, and can swallow them without unduly straining its structure. In other words, the sciences always select and 'cook' their facts. 'Fact' is not only 'made,' but always 'faked' to some extent. Hence what is fact for one science, and from one point of view, is not so for and from another, and may be irrelevant or a fiction. If, therefore, rival theorists are determined to occupy different points of view, and to stay there without seeking common ground, they can controvert each other's 'facts' for ever. For their assertions concern what are really different facts. So there is no way of settling the dispute save by the good old method of letting both continue until harvest-time, and finding which contributes more to human welfare. Facts, in short, are far from being rigid, irresistible, triumphant forces of nature ; rather they are artificial products of our selection, of our interests, of our hopes, of our fears. The shape they assume depends on our point of view, their meaning on our purpose, their value on the use we put them to ; nay, perhaps, their very reality on our willingness to accept them. For if there lurks within them some backbone of rigidity which we cannot hope to alter, it is at least something to which we have not yet penetrated, and which it would be fatal rashly to assume, so long as the facts that face us are still such that we *want* to alter them.

Now most of this has long been known to the logicians, though for various reasons they have not yet thought fit to make it clear to the uninitiated public. Nor should I now dare to divulge these mysteries of the higher logic were it possible to discuss the history of Psychical Research without reference to the striking way in which it illustrates this, our human, treatment of fact. This history has been a tragedy (or tragi-comedy) with three main actors, Fact, Prejudice or Bias, and Interpretation ; and the greatest of these is Prejudice. For it has determined the interpretation, which in turn has selected the facts. Thus the impotence of Fact has been most clearly shown. For of facts bearing on the subject there has always been abundance : mankind has always had experience of ghosts, trances, inspirations, dreams, fancies, illusions, hallucinations, and the like. Some men have always been ill-balanced, as others stolid, some responsive to the unusual, as others indifferent. And divergent prejudices have always been strong to emphasize whatever told in their favour, and to suppress whatever did not. So ' what the facts really were ' has manifestly depended on the interpretations put upon them.

Of such interpretations the two extremes have always been conspicuous. The one is often called the superstitious and the other the scientific. The names indeed are bad, and beg the question ; for any interpretation has a right to be called scientific if it is coherent and works, while any is superstitious which rests on mere prejudice and can give no coherent account of itself. But still, the interpretation which treats all psychic phenomena as essentially pathological has hitherto been preferred by the more scientific people, and has therefore been worked out and applied more scientifically, while hardly anything has been done to elicit the latent scientific value of its rival.

Since the formation of the Society for Psychical Research, however, this situation has been changed, and its work has begun to tell both on the facts and on their interpretation. Not that as yet much progress has been made in altering the mode in which the facts appear, *i.e.* in obtaining control of them, in making them experimental, or in eliciting new ones. But the quality of the old facts has been greatly improved ; they are beginning to be received with a more discriminating hospitality, to be scrutinized with a more intelligent curiosity, to be recorded with something like precision. And what, in the light of their past history, is probably quite as important—for what is the use of collecting facts which no one understands ?—much has been done to render their interpretation more scientific, and it is upon this aspect of the progress of Psychical Research that we may enlarge.

The better understanding of the traditional phenomena has been greatly advanced by a series of notable books proceeding from the inner circles of the Society for Psychical Research. First to be mentioned is William James's profound and delightful *Varieties of Religious Experience*, which has so signally shown the psychological significance of much that from the pathological point of view would seem sheer excesses of spiritual morbidity. Secondly, Frank Podmore's *History of Modern Spiritualism* has shown how the 'facts' look to an intelligent, competent, but intensely sceptical, critic. Lastly, Frederic Myers's *Human Personality* has made a brilliant and suggestive effort to look at the same material with a constructive purpose, and to put upon it a coherent interpretation which will convert the whilom playground of the will-o'-the-wisps of superstition into a stable habitation of science. This enterprise seems important enough to warrant an attempt to estimate its outcome, now that the first rush of readers and the first clash of critics has rolled by.

Myers's conception of the function of the Society for Psychical Research differs widely from Podmore's : it is for him not an organization for the harrying of spiritual impostors, but a possible training school for the future Columbus of an ultra-terrestrial world. And so he is inspired by the spirit of research, nay, of adventure, which is the prelude to discovery.

§ 2. Perhaps, however, the first reflection he provokes is one on the waywardness of genius, on its annoying habit of *not* sticking to its last, and *not* allowing quiet folk to drowse on in their old ancestral ways, but of making unexpected incursions into fresh territories and dragging an unwilling humanity in its train. For there can be little doubt that Myers was a genius, though not at all of the kind that would (antecedently) have been suspected of attempting epoch-making contributions to science and philosophy. His gifts were clearly of a literary and poetic character, such as seemed to promise him a distinguished place and an agreeable career among the

English men of letters, but might, in the first instance, well be thought to have unfitted him for the close reasoning and laborious experimenting that are needed by the man of science. But a strong passion of his emotional nature turned his powers in quite a different direction. A wicked fairy (I suppose) afflicted him with a well-nigh unique and unequalled longing to know, before he trod it, the path all souls must travel ; and this desire formed the tragedy and glory of his life. It is usual to suppose that a passionate desire is a mere hindrance in the search for truth ; but a more observant psychology must acknowledge what strength, what perseverance, and what daring it may bestow upon the searcher. Of this power, Myers's case affords a signal example ; for by dint of his desire to know he transformed himself. He turned himself into a man of science, keenly watchful and thoroughly cognizant of every scientific fact that seemed to bear, however remotely, on his central interest, and though, I think, he never quite secured his footing on the tight - ropes of technical philosophy, he made himself sufficiently acquainted with the abstruser mysteries of metaphysics. And so he actually trained his Pegasus, as it were, to pull the ark of the covenanted immortality out of the slough of naturalism.

It then appeared to the marvel of most beholders that there is work for the imagination to accomplish in science no less than in poetry. It was the poetry in Myers that enabled him to grasp at great conceptions, whose light could not have dawned on duller souls, and to build up out of the rubbish heaps of uncomprehended and unutilized experience the impressive structure which, if it be not the temple of ultimate truth, yet for the present marks the 'furthest north' of scientific striving towards one of the great poles of human interest. And, similarly, it was his desire that gave him driving-power. For twenty years he laboured unremittingly himself, and enlisted by his enthusiasm the co-operation of others. Like other pioneers, those of psychical research will never, probably, obtain the recognition due to their courage,

endurance, and faith in an undertaking which not only
their social surroundings, but their own misgivings, pronounced futile and absurd.   It was mainly due to Myers's
tact and enthusiasm that the Society was nerved to
persist in the tedious task of observing and collecting the
erratic bits of evidence, the perplexing phantasmagoria of
experiences, which he has now so brilliantly fitted together
into his fascinating picture of the subliminal extent and
transcendent destiny of the human spirit.   True, the
picture is impressionist: in some parts it is sketchy ; in
others its completion was cut short by death ; nowhere
perhaps will it bear a pedantically microscopic scrutiny.
But it is the picture of a master none the less, and
takes the place of a mere smear of meaningless detail
and shadowy outline.   Wherefore it is an achievement,
and its scientific value is incontestable, whether or not we
are willing to accept it as a real image of the truth.

§ 3. Accordingly, it is no wonder that, whereas those
who applied strictly technical standards, and looked for
what it is vain to expect, and difficult to use, in an inchoate science, viz. a formal precision of spick and span
conceptions, have been somewhat disconcerted by the
heuristic and tentative plasticity of Myers's terms, the
greatest of psychologists, William James, himself no
mean adept in psychical researches, should thus testify to
his suggestiveness.   " I cannot but think," he says,[1] " that
the most important step forward that has occurred in
psychology since I have been a student of the science, is
the discovery, first made in 1886, that in certain subjects
at least there is not only the consciousness of the ordinary
field, with its usual centre and margin, but an addition
thereto in the shape of a set of memories, thoughts, and
feelings, which are extra-marginal and outside of the
primary consciousness altogether, but yet must be classed
as conscious facts of some sort, able to reveal their
presence by unmistakable signs."   This then is ' the
problem of Myers,' the great question as to the nature

---

[1] *Varieties of Religious Experience*, p. 233.   Cp. also his fuller appreciation
of Myers's work in the *Proceedings* of the S. P. R., Part 42, pp. 13-23.

of the subconscious or subliminal extension of what we may, perhaps, still call the self.

To Myers this conception of the *Subliminal Self* is the great clue that guides him through the labyrinth of abnormal and supernormal fact, and holds together phenomena so various as sleep, dream, memory, hypnotism, hysteria, genius, insanity (largely), automatisms, chromatic hearing, hallucinations, ghosts, telepathy and telergy, clairvoyance and the like, and even 'ectoplasy.' It is essential then for an appreciation of *Human Personality* to grasp this great conception of the Subliminal Self, and the considerations which conduct to it.

Psychological experiment has confirmed what the best philosophic speculation had previously suspected, viz. that the world of sense is limited. That is, there exist limits beyond which any particular sense-perception either ceases or is transformed. It is only within a limited range that disturbances in the air are perceived as sounds, and in the 'ether' as sights. There are ultra-violet 'rays,' and infra-red 'rays,' which are both invisible, and there are 'tones' too high and too low to be heard. There are limits of intensity also to sensation. A very slight stimulation is not felt; *e.g.* a small fly crawling across the hand arouses no sensation. Yet we cannot say that this crawling passes quite unnoticed. For, if there are half-a-dozen such flies, we feel them collectively. But does not this imply that each separately must have contributed something? For six ciphers would add up to nothing. In this way, then, we form the notion of a *limen* or 'threshold' over which a 'sensation' must pass to enter consciousness. This threshold is not, however, a *fixed* point: it may be shifted up and down, *raised* so as to contract, or *lowered*, so as to enlarge, the range of consciousness, to an unknown extent, according to the variations of attention, mental condition, etc. At present the range of variation in the *limen* is almost unexplored; but it is undeniable that both the hyper-æsthesia which results from a lowering, and the abnormal concentration, or 'abstraction,' which results from a raising, and still more from a combination of the two (as in some hypnotic states), may easily lead to abnormalities that would hitherto have been accounted miracles.

It should be noted, furthermore, that we cannot evade the paradox of unfelt 'sensations' by interpreting the *limen* in terms of physiology. At first sight it seems easy enough to assume that there is nothing *mental* out of consciousness, and to explain that the bodily disturbances (due to the crawling flies) have to attain a certain magnitude before the mind reacts upon them. We may suppose, that is, that it is not worthy of the mind to take note of the nervous excitation due to the crawling of a single fly. But this only transfers the difficulty from the sense organs to the central brain : it still remains a fact that a mind which responds to a *sum* of slight disturbances in the brain must, in summing them, have apprehended them subliminally in their separation. Nay, in the end must not this weird power of unnoticed noticing be ascribed to ' matter ' generally? For how could anything ever respond to a sum of stimulations if the constituents of the sum had not been somehow noticed? It would seem, then, that from this notion of the subliminal there is no escape.

§ 4. But instead of being a nuisance and a paradox, it may be made into a principle of far-reaching explanation. This is what Myers has done. He has extended this scientific notion of subliminal ' perception ' from the parts to the whole, and instead of recognizing it grudgingly and piecemeal, he gladly generalizes it into a principle of almost universal application. When this is done, the supraliminal and the subliminal seem to change places in our estimation, and our normal supraliminal consciousness shrinks into a mere selection of the total self, which the necessities of mortal life have stirred us to condense into actual consciousness, while behind it, embracing and sustaining all, there stretches a vast domain of the subliminal whose unexplored possibilities may be fraught with weal or woe ineffable. Who after this will question the potency of the poetic seer to evolve romance out of the disjointed data of academic science? And yet, like all great feats, it is like the egg of Columbus and very simple. At bottom it is only a shifting of standpoint, a throwing of our spirit's centre of gravity over into the subliminal. Let us for a moment cease to regard as the true centres of our being the conscious persons of a definite kind, hedged in by social restrictions and psychical and physical incapacities of all sorts, which we appear to be, and whom, in spite of philosophic warnings, we assume ourselves to know so well : let us regard them as mere efficient, though imperfect, concentrations of our being upon the practical purposes of normal life. And then, hey presto! the thing is done! We return transfigured to the surface from our dive into the subliminal. We are greater, perhaps more glorious, than our wildest dreams suspected. We have transcended the limits of terrestrial being, and flung aside the menace of materialism. Or, in more technical philosophic language, which it is a pity Myers did not in this instance use, we find ourselves contemplating the correlation of physical and psychical from the point of view of the *transmission*, not of the *production*, theory of the latter.[1] Psychic life, that is, is not engendered by the phantom dance of ' atoms,' but conversely, its veritable nature pierces in varying degrees the distorting veil of ' matter' that seems so solid, and yet, under scientific scrutiny, so soon dissolves into the fantastic fictions of ' vortex-rings ' or ethereal ' voids' and ' stresses,' or ' energy ' equations. And the beauty of this change of attitude is that whereas no facts can be discovered which will invalidate this reinterpretation, it is quite possible that new discoveries may make its materialistic rival simply unworkable.

Myers has two great similes for illustrating what he conceives to be the relation of the conscious to the subconscious personality. It is like unto the visible portion of an iceberg of whose total mass eight ninths float beneath the surface. Or it is like the visible spectrum beyond which there extend at either end infra-red and ultra-violet rays, to say nothing of yet more mysterious

---

[1] Cp. James's *Human Immortality*.

XVII   PSYCHICAL RESEARCH   379

modes of radiation, as potent, or more potent, than those
our eyes enable us to see. The latter image has indeed
this further advantage, that close inspection will reveal
dark lines and discontinuities even within the narrow
band of visible light. Just so there are abundant breaks
of continuity in our conscious life, which may be made
to spell out messages to the psychologist from the
hidden depths of the soul, much as the dark lines in a
stellar spectrum reveal to the astronomer the composition
of far-distant stars. And he believes that in the supernormal phenomena of which his book supplies a provisional codification, we have something corresponding to
the 'enhanced' lines of spectroscopy.

§ 5. Hence it is natural enough that Myers should begin
his survey by tracing the subliminal support in the normal
operations of our consciousness. Morbid disintegrations
of personality prove that at least we are not rounded-off
and self-complete souls, which must be in their integrity,
or not be at all. And yet not all the features of such
cases look like mere decay ; they are interspersed with
signs of a complete memory and of supernormal faculty,
and of connexions deep below the surface. The analysis
of genius is next attempted, in perhaps the least convincing chapter in the book, which derives genius from
'subliminal uprushes.' In the fourth chapter sleep is
dealt with, and considered as a differentiation of psychic
life parallel with waking life, preserving a more antique
complexion, and showing (in dreams) symptoms of a
closer connexion with and access to the subliminal.
Chapter V. deals with the extension of normal into
hypnotic sleep, and the enhanced control of the organism
which it often carries with it. In these first chapters the
facts to which Myers so copiously appeals throughout
are, on the whole, beyond dispute, though there still is
abundant difference of opinion about their interpretation.
But in the sixth chapter he approaches a region in which
the ordinary man and ordinary science evince a stubborn
unwillingness to admit, and even to ascertain, the facts.
Starting with an ingenious suggestion that *synæsthesiæ*,

like 'coloured hearing,' are vestiges of a primitive sensitivity not yet definitely attached to special organs of sense, he proceeds to other forms of sensory automatism, which convey messages from the subliminal to the conscious self. These may take the form of spontaneous hallucinations, or be experimentally induced by 'crystal-gazing,' and often reveal *telepathic* influence.

Of *telepathy*, Myers is not long content to retain the provisional description, officially prescribed by the Psychical Society, as 'a mode of communication not requiring any of the recognized channels of sense.' He soon takes it more positively as a law of the direct intercourse of spirit with spirit, as fundamental as gravitation in the physical world. So it becomes, not an alternative to the spiritistic interpretation, as with Podmore, but rather its presupposition, and a way of rendering it feasible and intelligible. Granting, therefore, that spirits as such are in immediate telepathic interaction in a subliminal 'metetherial' (*i.e.* spiritual) world, it becomes arbitrary to deprive them of this power on account of the mere fact of death. Telepathy from the dead becomes credible, and the seventh chapter, on 'phantasms of the dead,' revels in ghost stories. The eighth chapter, on *motor automatism*, expounds and interprets the phenomena of planchette writing, table tilting, etc., and the evidence of discarnate intelligence they often seem to involve, which seems sometimes to amount to a 'psychical invasion,' or 'possession' of the automatist. Hence there is an easy transition in the ninth chapter to the subjects of trance, possession, and ecstasy, in which the organism may be operated entirely by alien 'spirits,' while the normal owner may be enjoying a subliminal excursion into a spiritual world. As finally the action of spirit on matter is a mystery anyhow, and as the actual limitation of our power to produce movements to bodies directly touched by our organism is wholly empirical, and may result only from the unimaginative habits of the supraliminal self, and as, moreover, discarnate spirits may possess a greater and more conscious power to manipulate the molecular arrangements of matter, there is no *a priori* reason for discrediting even the stories of *telekinesis* and *ectoplasy*, which form the so-called 'physical phenomena' of spiritism.

§ 6. Such, in barest outline, and without attempt to reproduce his multitudinous references to cases, and the felicities of his phrasing, is Myers's argument for the extension of human personality beyond its habitual limits. It will be thought by many to pander to the human love of welltold fairy-tales, and to recall within the bounds of scientific possibility every aberration of savage superstition. And certainly Myers has cast his net very wide and deep, and brought into it not only a fine collection of fish, of which some are very rare and queer specimens, but also not a few of the abhorrent monsters of the abyss which common sense can hardly bear to look upon.

Moreover, in a sense criticism is easy ; in token whereof we may instance some of its more valid forms. It has been objected then : (1) That Myers deals largely in suggestions which, after all, are merely possibilities ; (2) that he never defines the nature of the personality for which he claims survival of death, and never proves that what seems to survive is truly personal ; (3) that such of his facts as would be generally admitted are capable of alternative interpretations ; while (4) for the disputed phenomena, even the copious evidence adduced is inadequate and dubious ; (5) that telepathy among the living is, as yet, assumption enough to explain everything ; (6) that his theory is a jumble of physiological materialism with the wildest spiritualism ; (7) that he is absurdly optimistic in his anticipations both as to the benefits to be derived from the study of our 'metetherial' environment ; and also (8) as to the reasonableness of incarnate and discarnate spirits in forwarding his aim.

§ 7. To these objections it might fairly be replied : as to (1), that Myers himself claims no more, and more cannot fairly be expected of him. As to (2), that while he certainly takes personality for granted, our immediate experience fully entitles us to do so. The people who decline to admit the existence of personality until it has been abstractly defined to their liking, are beyond the pale of ordinary scientific argument. On the other hand, it must be granted that the proof of personality in the subliminal, and of the persistence of a *human* person after death is, as yet, on Myers's own showing, somewhat incomplete. But the indications point that way, and it was a merit in Myers to refrain from the usual philosophers' leap to the absolute world-ground so soon as they are driven off the field of ordinary experience.

(3) It is quite true that for *most* of the admitted facts of secondary personality, hypnotism, automatism, sleep, dream, etc., there exist alternative interpretations. That is, there are *descriptions* of them in technical formulas. But these in no case amount to real explanations. Moreover, they are various and complicated, and Myers's conception of a single subliminal self would effect a great simplification. Further, it is precisely some of these comparatively normal facts that seem to need his theory most. As this point will bear more emphasis, it may be pointed out that the orthodox psychological treatment of dreams, *e.g.*, is plainly insufficient. The conscious self is in no proper sense the creator of its dreams. Even if we grant that the stuff that dreams are made of is taken from the experiences of waking life (though dreams of 'flying,' *e.g.*, show that this is not strictly true), this does not explain the *selection*. Nor does it avail to point to probabilities of peripheral stimulations as the physiological foundation of dreams. The extraordinary transmutation of the stimuli thus supplied needs explanation. Why should a mosquito bite during sleep set up a thrilling tale of battle, murder, and sudden death ? Who is the maker of these vivid plots to which the dreamer falls a victim ? It is certainly not the conscious self of the dream which may be (more or less) identified with that of waking life. Must we not assume some sort of subliminal self ? [1]

---

[1] Dr. Morton Prince's fascinating study of the tribulations of the ' Beauchamp ' family (*The Dissociation of a Personality*) warrants, perhaps, the suggestion that its heroine, 'Sally,' was such a subliminal self.

Or should we, still more bravely, argue that since dreams (while we dream them) have all the marks of an independent reality, are immersed in a space and a time of their own, and contain personages just as external to us, and as uncontrollable in their actions as those of waking life, these dream-worlds really exist, and are actually visited by us? Philosophically something might be said for this, and still more for the converse of this view, viz. that our waking life is but an incoherent dream, whose full explanation would lie in an awakening yet to come.

This, indeed, was the view taken by one of Myers's best 'spirits,' Mrs. Piper's 'G. P.,' whose communication may be cited in answer to complaints that 'spirits' have never yet revealed anything novel or worth knowing.[1] "You to us," he says (ii. 254), "are *sleeping* in the material world ; you look shut up as one in prison, and in order for us to get into communication with you, we have to enter into your sphere, as one like yourself, asleep. This is just why we make mistakes, as you call them, or get confused and muddled."

The truth is that psychologists have hitherto accepted the rough criteria of practical life, and disregarded the theoretic study of dreams, because they seemed to yield so little fit to use for the purposes of practice. Yet, what is it but an empirical observation that dream-worlds are worlds of *inferior* reality?[2] Is it not conceivable, therefore, that we should discover some of *superior* reality and value? At present, while psychology seems confronted with the choice between the Scylla of the Subliminal and the Charybdis of real dream-worlds, can one wonder that it should try to put off the evil day as long as possible?

---

[1] Cp., too, Dr. Wiltse's dream (ii. 315) for a striking account of what 'death' feels like. A genuine experience like this will always bear comparison with literary imitations even by so consummate an artist as Plato, *e.g.* in his 'vision of Er,' and will be felt to be, psychologically, more convincing. The best reproduction of the psychological quality of such genuine experiences with which I am acquainted in literature is to be found, to my thinking, in the 'dream' finale of Mr. G. L. Dickinson's *Meaning of Good*.

[2] Cp. Essay xx. § 22.

(4) It must be admitted that all over the field covered by Myers much more evidence is required, and that a critic with the knowledge and temper of, *e.g.* Podmore, could pick endless holes in nearly all of it. The possibilities of fraud and error seem inexhaustible, especially if semi-conscious cheating in abnormal mental states be common. It is true also that in default of better material Myers sometimes uses half-baked bricks, just to complete his structure. But he himself was quite aware of this, and when a man knows that he has only months before him to complete his life's work, and feels that if he does not succeed in putting together the scattered material into a synthesis (however provisional) no one else will do so, he may well be pardoned if he makes what use he can of the material that lies handy. It should · be recognized also that a synthesis which embraces such a multitude of facts does not rest solely on any one set of them, and in a sense grows independent of them all. That is, the mere coherence of the interpretation becomes a point in its favour as against a variety of unconnected alternatives. Again, the collection and correction of the evidence is the proper function of the Psychical Society, for which Myers's system provides the aid of a working theory, a provisional classification, and a technical terminology.

(5) It is possible that telepathy (in its original sense) might be stretched over all the facts which it seems too harsh to dismiss. But, then, telepathy is itself a mere description, and in no way an explanation. It has to be interpreted, either in definitely physical or in definitely spiritual terms ; it can hardly stand by itself as a fact which transcends the physical order without opening out upon another. Hence the attempt to conceive it as the ndit to a spirit-world must be pronounced legitimate.

(6) Myers no doubt might have considerably improved his statement by greater reliance on the contentions of an idealist philosophy, but the charge of confusing the physical and the spiritual seems in the main to fail. For, as we saw (p. 378), Myers has silently adopted the

'transmission' view of soul, and this entitles him to the free use of all the facts that are presented on the materialistic side.

(7) *Omne ignotum pro magnifico* may be a generous delusion, but at least it makes a good stimulus to research. Lastly, as to (8), he is well aware that his gospel will impinge on rooted prejudice and meet the bitterest hostility. He knows how "immemorial ignorance has stiffened into an unreasoning incredulity" (i. 157). He tells us (ii. 77) " that the novelties of this book are intended to work upon preconceptions which are ethical quite as much as intellectual." [1]

But still he underrates the resistance which human minds and tempers are sure to offer to his doctrine. Concerning any considerable novelty of thought the prediction may be made that hardly any one above thirty will be psychologically capable of adopting it, unless he had previously been looking for just such a solution. Myers, therefore, will no more persuade the existing generation of psychologists than Darwin persuaded the biologists of his age. It is vain to expect it. Novelty as such must always make its appeal to the more plastic minds of the young who have not yet aged into 'great authorities.'

Again, it is obvious that Myers's whole trend of thought must be utterly distasteful to the numerous people who do not believe that they have more than an illusory personality now, and (rightly or wrongly) have no desire to have it perpetuated after death. Then, again, there are many whose *a priori* sense of spiritual dignity is outraged by what they think the indecorum in which 'ghosts' have been observed to indulge, and who, as Myers observes, are the spiritual descendants of the people who would not listen to a heliocentric astronomy, on the ground that it was unworthy of heavenly bodies to move in elliptical, and not in circular, orbits. Many others will not care to look beyond the fact that the new 'psychical science' seems superficially to revive old superstitions of savage thought—though why it should *enhance* their

---

[1] Cp. also i. 185, and ii. 2, ii. 79-80.

confidence in human knowledge to find that immemorial traditions had been wholly wrong, or *destroy* it to find that from the first men had possessed some inkling of the truth, is perhaps a feeling it were hard to refine into a logical lucidity. In short, no one who has learnt from Mr. Balfour that the causes of belief are hardly ever rational, will expect an immediate revolution in habitual modes of thinking from the work of Myers.

§ 8. "However this may be, do you in point of fact believe that immortality is proved?" If I were point blank asked this question, I should probably reply that most people are still unaware of the nature of proof. They imagine that 'proofs' can be provided which appeal to 'plain facts,' and rest upon indisputable principles. Whereas we saw that really no science deals with plain facts or rests on absolutely certain principles. Its 'facts' are always relative to its principles, and the principles always really rest on their ability to provide a coherent interpretation of the facts. All proof, therefore, is a matter of degree and accumulation, and no science is more than *a coherent system of interpretations*, which, when applied, will work. In every science, therefore, there is a finite number of facts which would have to be rejected or reinterpreted, and a small number of principles which would have to be modified or withdrawn, in order to qualify as 'false' the system of that science. In a science, however, of a *high* degree of certainty, the principles are well tested and very useful, and the facts are capable of being added to at pleasure. Also, the subject is sufficiently explored to minimize the danger of discovering an anomaly. That a new fact like radium should *prima facie* threaten to derange so fundamental a principle as the Conservation of Energy, and should have to be bought off by giving up the old sense of the Indestructibility of Matter, is an incident which occurs but rarely in a respectable science like Chemistry, and it speaks well for the open-mindedness of chemists and their confidence in the stability of their system that they should have admitted its existence as soon as M. Curie had announced it.   But Psychology is not so firmly rooted, and at present shows the inhospitable temper that comes from a secret lack of self-assurance.   And so psychologists dare not be as open-minded ; they do not credit themselves or others with sanity of soul enough to encounter abnormal facts without loss of mental balance.   In Psychical Research all is still quite inchoate, and therefore plastic, and the final interpretation of its data must depend on inquiries yet to make.

One can only say, therefore, that Myers's interpretation has for the first time rendered a future life scientifically *conceivable*, and rendered much more *probable* the other considerations in its favour.   *And, above all, it has rendered it definitely provable.*   The scientific status of a hypothesis depends chiefly on the facilities for experimental verification it affords.   No matter how probable it may seem at first sight (*i.e.* how concordant with our prejudices), it is naught, if naught can verify it ; no matter how wild it seems, it is useful, and tends to be accepted, if it can suggest experiments whereby to test it, and to grapple with the facts.   Now it is one of the greatest merits of Myers's book that he throughout conceives his hypothesis in this scientific spirit.   His cry is ever for further observation, more thought, and keener experimentation.   And his conception is capable at every point of definite investigation, and at many actually appeals to definite experiment.   Whoever has a vestige of the scientific spirit must regard this as the atonement for his initial daring.

It may well be that in this way there will gradually grow up a consistent body of interpretations, embodying our most convenient way of regarding the facts, which can be adopted as a whole, even though no single member of the system taken in isolation will be sufficient to compel assent.   And then human immortality will be scientifically ' proved.'   Until then it will remain a matter of belief, however ' probable ' it grows.

§ 9. How long the ' proof' will be in coming who can say ?   If we sit down and wait, we may wait for ever. Something will depend on the activity of the Society

for Psychical Research and kindred bodies, more on
the attitude of the general world. To work out fully
all the rich suggestions of Myers's grandiose scheme
might well absorb all the available psychological
energies of hundreds, nay, at the former rate of progress, of thousands of years. But, short of this, if we
tried to verify only the main ideas, it would be a
question of whether, say, half-a-dozen first-rate minds
could be induced to take up the subject, not (as now) in
the scanty leisure of professional preoccupations, but as
their life's work. If they will, comparatively slight
discoveries might raise the subject from the observational
to the experimental plane, and so indefinitely quicken the
pulse of progress. In psychical, as in all other, science
we must get staid professionals to consolidate the work
of the enthusiastic amateurs who opened out the way.

But it is obvious that to secure them funds are needed,
and that on a generous scale. To some small extent,
perhaps, these may come from a growth in the numbers
of the Society, which has now started an Endowment Fund.
It has modestly asked for £8000 in order to subsidize
a psychologist for special work. But for anything like a
thorough investigation money will be needed on a far more
liberal scale. A vigilant literary committee to record and
probe the spontaneous evidence, and an expensive labora-
tory for experimental tests are obvious necessaries, and
instead of one, a dozen specialists. For all this £100,000
would scarcely be enough. There is nothing unreasonable
in the view of the Hon. Sec. of the Society, who assured
me that he would undertake to find permanent and profitable employment for the income of half a million.

The situation, however, is so discreditable as to warrant
a bolder suggestion. In every civilized community many
millions are annually spent by and on organizations which
profess to be the depositaries of invaluable truths concerning spiritual things, and to regard it as their most sacred
duty to teach and to sustain elaborate systems of spiritual
knowledge. It is, however, a serious drawback to their
efficacy that considerable and growing doubt exists about

the authenticity of this knowledge. The position of every church could be indefinitely strengthened, if it could obtain further verification of the evidence on which its claims are based. These claims, moreover, rest largely on allegations susceptible of verification. The spiritual truths professed, that is, are not wholly matters of direct personal experience (though these perhaps are the most distinctive features of the religious experience); they concern also what were not originally or in intention ' matters of faith ' at all, but matters of observation and experiment, and are therefore capable of continuous verification by analogy.[1]

The notion of an initially perfect revelation is, like that of an initially absolute truth, a prejudice. Even if we had it, the mere lapse of time would fatally impair its value. Even initially dubious revelations, on the other hand, would authenticate themselves by becoming progressive and increasingly valuable. Yet, strange to say, no church anywhere bestows any of its energy and its income upon substantiating in this way its claim to truth. The apologetics of all churches are merely argumentation, and wholly overlook the simplest, most scientific, and effective means of establishing their case. The ideas that the proper function of a church is to be a channel of communication between the human and the superhuman, that its knowledge should be progressive like that of secular science, that its ' talents ' should not be stowed away for safe custody, that its revelations should be employed so as to *earn* more, that its present apathy is slowly but inevitably sapping the confidence of mankind in the genuineness of religious truths, and in the belief professed in them, in short, that theology could and should be made into an experimental science, seems never to have occurred to any one of them.

And yet if the churches should awaken to the fact that religious truths need verification like any others, and that they offer to intelligent and persevering research rewards as great and probable as those of science, they could not but recognize that they should not merely tolerate psychical

---

[1] Cp. *Humanism*, ed. 1, p. 237 ; ed. 2, p. 322.

research, but even actively participate in it. For such research might make important contributions to the verification needed. The churches, therefore, would have to organize themselves, in part at least, for the purpose of psychical research, primarily, no doubt, along the lines indicated by their several creeds ; and thus the difficulty about finding the means and the workers of a systematic inquiry would to a large extent be overcome.

However this may be, the money will no doubt eventually be raised in one way or another. For our present procedure seems too irrational. It compares unfavourably with that of the ancient Egyptians who spent their declining years in learning elaborate spells, to safeguard the soul in its future journeyings. We do nothing ; or at best trust to a little oil, and a little unction. But will the human reason never realize how monstrous it is that for our last, our longest, and most momentous journey alone we make no preparation, nor seek to know the dangers or the routes, but set out blindly and stolidly like brutes, or at best like children, equipped only with the vaguely-apprehended consolations of a 'faith' we have never dared to verify ?

XVIII

FREEDOM

ARGUMENT

§ 1. Humanism must establish the reality of Freedom. § 2. Real freedom involves indetermination. § 3. The difficulty of the question due to a clash of Postulates. § 4. Determination a postulate of science. Its methodological grounds. § 5. The moral postulate of Freedom; it implies an alternative to wrong, but not to right, action. § 6. The empirical consciousness of freedom shows that moral choices are neither common nor unrestricted nor unconnected with character. § 7. The reconciliation of the scientific and the moral postulates. The methodological validity of determinism compatible with real, but limited, indetermination. § 8. Why the alternative theories make no practical difference. § 9. The positive nature of freedom and its connexion with the plasticity of habits and the incompleteness of the real. § 10. Human freedom introduces indetermination into the universe. § 11. Is human the sole freedom in the universe? It need not be supposed. The possibility of ascribing a measure of indetermination to all things. The incompleteness of the proof of mechanism. § 12. The metaphysical disadvantages and advantages of Freedom. Is predestinate perfection thinkable, and an incomplete reality unthinkable?

§ 1. IT is one of the most striking features of a new philosophy that it not only breaks fresh ground but also brings up old issues in a new form, and exhibits them in a new light. Accordingly, it is natural enough that Humanism should have something distinctive to say about the old puzzle concerning freedom and determination. It is in fact under obligation to treat this subject, because it has implicitly committed itself, as its chief exponents have of course been perfectly aware.[1] It has assumed that human

[1] See James's 'Dilemma of Determinism' in *The Will to Believe*, which is the only profitable thing written on the whole subject in English for the last thirty years. My aim in this essay is merely to carry a little further and to render a little more explicit the. consequences of James's principles. Prof. R.

action is endowed with real agency and really makes a difference alike to the system of truth and to the world of reality. Without this assumption all the talk about the ' making' of truth and reality would be meaningless absurdity. And the assumption itself would be equally absurd, if all human actions were the completely determined products of a rigidly necessary order of events.

It is obvious, therefore, that unless the selections and choices which are shown to pervade our whole cognitive function are real, the system of our science will collapse as surely as our conception of moral agency, and that there can be no real making of either truth or reality. And conversely, if a philosophy finds it necessary to recognize choices and selections *anywhere*, it must provide for their ultimate reality and collide with a theory which declares them to be ultimately illusory. Our trust in an immediate experience which presents us at least with an appearance of alternatives and choices stands in need of vindication, and if we distrusted this appearance, we should engender a scepticism about our cognitive procedure to which it would be hard to set limits. Thus our immediate experience plainly suggests the reality of an indetermination which seems irreconcilable with the assumption of determinism ; and immediate experience our Humanism dare not disavow.

Humanism, therefore, has to defend and establish the reality of this indetermination, and so to conceive it that it ceases to conflict with the postulates of science, and fits harmoniously into its own conception of existence. It has, in other words, to make good its conception of a determinable indetermination and to show that it is involved in the assertion of a really evolving, and therefore as yet incomplete, reality. This it can do by showing that the indetermination, though real, is not dangerous, because it is not unlimited, and because it is determinable, as the growth of habit fixes and renders determinate

---

F. A. Hoernle has detected the vital importance of this criticism of determinism, and gives an excellent account of the Humanist attitude towards it in *Mind*, N.S. No. 56, pp. 462-7.

reactions which were once indeterminate. But no one who is at all acquainted with the complexities of human thought will suppose that this goal of Humanist endeavour will be easily attained.

§ 2. What we must mean by 'freedom' should be clear from what has been said, and it will be unnecessary to delay the discussion by examining attempts to conceive 'freedom' in any less radical fashion. There have been of course a variety of attempts to conceive freedom as a sort of determinism, and these have been admirably classified by William James as 'soft' determinisms. But under sufficient pressure they always harden into the most adamantine fatalism, and a 'soft' determinism usually betokens only the amiable weakness of an intelligence seeking for a compromise.

Thus the notion of 'self-determination,' for example, when thought out, will be found to involve that of self-creation, and it may be doubted whether any being, actual or imagined, could completely satisfy its requirements, if we except the jocose paradoxes of a few Indian creation-myths in which the Creator first lays the World-Egg, and then hatches himself out of it. In all the ordinary exemplifications of the notion, the being which is supposed to determine itself is ultimately the necessary product of other beings with which it can no longer identify itself. We are made by a long series of ancestors, and these in their turn were inevitably generated by non-human forces—of a purely physical kind, if science is to be trusted. Nor do we escape this derivation of the 'self-determining' agent from a not-self by postulating a non-natural cosmic consciousness, and trusting to it to break through the chains of natural necessity. For such a being must be conceived either as itself the imponent of the natural necessity to which we are enslaved, or, if it escapes therefrom itself, as abrogating it so thoroughly as to invalidate our whole faith in a stable order of nature. Moreover, in neither case would such a being be our 'self' any more than is the stellar nebula, among the last and least of whose differentiations we are bidden to enrol ourselves. Any 'universal consciousness' must be common to us all, and cannot therefore be that which is peculiar to each, and the source of our unique individuality. It is better, therefore, to accept the doctrine of our 'self-determination' by identification with the Absolute as sheer dogma than to try to think it out.

We shall dismiss, therefore, from consideration any use of 'freedom' which does not primarily involve the possibility of real alternatives, between which real choices have to be made, which are not merely illusory.

§ 3. Now the difficulty of the question of freedom arises from the fact that it lies in the focus where two of the great postulates that guide our actions meet and collide. But herein also lies its interest and its instructiveness for the theory of knowledge. For nothing is better calculated to reveal the nature of our postulation than the way in which we treat such cases.

The two postulates in question are the Scientific Postulate of Determinism and the Ethical Postulate of Freedom. The first demands that all events shall be conceived as fully determined by their antecedents, in order that they may be certainly calculable once these are known; the second demands that our actions shall be so conceived that the fulfilment of duty is possible in spite of all temptations, in order that man shall be responsible and an agent in the full sense of the term.

It is clear, however, that these postulates conflict. If the course of events really conforms to the determinist postulate, no alternatives are possible. No man, therefore, can act otherwise than he does act. Nor is there any sense in bidding him do otherwise than he does or be other than he is; for good or for evil his predestined course seems to be inevitably marked out for him, down to the minutest detail, by forces that precede and transcend his individual personality. To speak of responsibility or agency in respect to such a being seems a mockery; man is but a transitory term in an infinite series of necessitated events which recedes into the past, and portends its extension into the future, without end;

so that at no point can any independence or initiative be ascribed to him.

We are confronted, then, by this dilemma, that if the course of events is wholly determined, the whole of the ideas and beliefs and phraseology which imply the contrary must rest upon illusion. There are not really in the world any alternatives, disjunctions, contingencies, possibilities ; hypotheses, doubts, conditions, choices, selections are delusions of our ignorance, which could not be harboured by a mind which saw existence as it really is, steadily and as a whole. If *per contra* the course of events is not determined, we seem to reject the sole assumption on which it can be known and calculated, and to reduce nature to a chaos. We must sacrifice either our knowledge or ourselves. For what alternative can be found to these imperious postulates ? If all things are determined, all are irredeemably swept along in one vast inhuman flow of Fate ; if anything is undetermined, we have sold ourselves to a demon of caprice who can everywhere disrupt the cosmic order.

It speaks well for the levelheadedness of humanity that it has not allowed itself to be scared to death by the appalling pretensions of these philosophic bogies ; and that on the whole mankind has exhibited an equanimity almost equal to the *sangfroid* of Descartes when he set himself to doubt methodically everything that existed, but resolved meanwhile not to change his dinner hour.

In point of fact determinists and indeterminists for all practical purposes get on quite well with each other and with uncritical common sense. They profess to think the universe a very different thing, but they all behave in very much the same way towards it.

Still it is worth while to try to account for so strange a situation. And if we have the patience to analyse precisely the nature of the conflicting postulates, and of the immediate consciousness of freedom, we shall perhaps perceive how the puzzle is constructed.

§ 4. Determinism is an indispensable Postulate of Science as such. Its sway extends, not merely over the natural sciences, in which it is nowadays often thought to originate because its somewhat discreditable ethical origin has been forgotten,[1] but quite as cogently over theology and ethics. Unpredictable miracles and incalculable choices are just as disconcerting and subversive as interruptions of the mechanical sequence of happenings.

The reason is that, always and everywhere, we are interested in predicting the future behaviour of things, because we wish to adjust our conduct accordingly. We welcome, therefore, an assumption which will constitute a general justification of our habitual procedure, and encourages us to try to predict the future of all things from their known antecedents.

The assumption of Determinism, therefore, has primarily a *moral* significance; it is an encouragement and not a revelation. It does not in itself enable us to predict how anything will behave; to discover this we have to formulate the special 'laws' of its behaviour. But it gives us a general assurance to counteract the primary impression of confusion with which the universe might otherwise afflict us. It justifies us in looking for special laws and rejecting *a priori* the attribution of events to lawless and incalculable chance. Whenever experience confronts us with 'facts' which exhibit such a character, we feel emboldened to declare them to be mere 'appearances.' The facts, we affirm, are really law-abiding, only we do not yet know their laws. And to a perfect knowledge all events would be completely calculable. In short, by making the determinist assumption we nerve human science to carry on from age to age its heroic struggle against the brute opacity, the bewildering variety, of the presented sequence of events.

But there is nothing in all this to carry the assumption

[1] This very prettily exemplifies the divergence between the origin of a belief and its validity. For as a matter of history determinism was devised as an excuse for the bad man, and arose out of Socratic intellectualism. We see from Aristotle's *Ethics* (*Eth. Nic.* iii. ch. 5) that in his time the moralist had to contend against the view that vice is involuntary while virtue is voluntary. Aristotle meets it by showing that the argument proves virtue to be as involuntary as vice. This inference has merely to be accepted to lead to full-blown determinism. Accordingly we find that in the next generation this was done, and the 'freewill' controversy was started between the Stoics and the Epicureans.

out of the realm of methodology into that of metaphysics. By conceiving Determinism as a postulate we go a very little way towards showing that determination is actual and complete and an ultimate fact. For it is quite easy to accept it as a methodological assumption without claiming for it any ontological validity. So long as we restrict ourselves to the methodological standpoint any postulate is good while it is serviceable; its ultimate validity is not required or inquired into: nay, it may continue to be serviceable even after it has been discovered to be false.

This point may be illustrated by an instructive example suggested by the late Prof. Henry Sidgwick.[1] He supposes that " we were somehow convinced that the planets were endowed with Free Will," and raises the question how far this would reasonably impair our confidence in the stability and future of the Solar System. Now, according to the ordinary account of the matter as given by a dogmatic and metaphysical rendering of Determinism, the consequences should be terrible. The fatal admission of indetermination should carry with it the death-knell of astronomy, and ultimately of all science. For of course we should always have to face the contingency that the planets might depart incalculably from their orbits, and so our most careful calculations, our most cogent inferences, could always be refuted by the event. ' What use, therefore, is it any longer,' a convinced determinist might exclaim, ' to try to know anything when the very basis of all knowing is rendered fundamentally unknowable? '

But a practical man of science would decline to concur in so alarmist an estimate of the situation. He would wait to see whether anything alarming happened. He would reflect that after all the planets might not exercise their freedom to depart from their courses, and might abstain from whirling the Solar System headlong to perdition, at least in his time. And even if they did vary their orbits, their vagaries might prove to be so limited in extent that they would not be of practical

[1] *Methods of Ethics*, bk. i. ch. v. § 3.

importance. In fact, the divergences might be so small
as to be cloaked by the discrepancies between the
calculated and the observed orbits, which until then had
been ascribed to the imperfection of our knowledge. It
would only be if *de facto* he found himself a horrified
spectator of heavenly bodies careering wildly across the
sky that he would renounce the attempt to predict their
behaviour. Until then he would continue to make his
calculations and to compile his nautical almanacs, hoping
and praying the while that the Sun's influence would
prevent Mars and Venus from going wrong. For however
much his inward confidence in the practical value of his
labours might be abated, his methods would be affected not
one jot. So long as it was worth while to calculate the
planets' orbits, he would have to assume methodologically
that they were determined according to the law of
gravitation, just as before. He would realize, that is,
that the methodological use of his deterministic principle
could survive the discovery of its metaphysical falsity.
For since the 'free' act was *ex hypothesi* incalculable, the
truth of freedom as a metaphysical fact could yield no
method by which calculations could be made and
behaviour predicted, and hence science would unavoidably ignore it.

We see, then, (1) that in whatever way the metaphysical question is decided, the methodological use of
the determinist principle is not interfered with, and
that science in consequence is safe, whatever metaphysics
may decree. And (2) the principle, and with it science,
in so far as it depends on the principle and not on
actual experience, is practically safe whatever the actual
course of events. For however irregularly and intricately
things might behave, they could not thereby force us
to renounce our postulate. We should always prefer to
ascribe to our ignorance of the law what might really be
due to inherent lawlessness. The postulate would only
be abandoned in the last resort, when it had ceased to
be of the slightest practical use to any one, even as a
merely theoretic encouragement in attempting the control

of events. (3) It should follow from this that the scientific objection to a doctrine of Freedom was strictly limited to its introduction of an unmanageable contingency into scientific calculations. It would hold against an indeterminism which rendered events incalculable, but not against a belief in Freedom as such. A conception of Freedom, therefore, which allowed us to calculate the 'free' event, would be scientifically quite permissible. And a conception of Freedom which issued in a plurality of calculable alternatives would be scientifically un-objectionable, even though it would smother meta-physical Determinism with kindness and surfeit it with an *embarras de richesses*. We should prepare ourselves, therefore, to look out for such a conception of Freedom.

§ 5. In considering the moral Postulate of Freedom we should begin by noting that the moralist has no direct objection to the calculableness of moral acts and no unreasoning prejudice in favour of indeterminism. He seems to need it merely in order to make real the apparent alternatives with which the moral life confronts him. But he would have as much reason as the determinist to deplore the irruption into moral conduct of acts of Freedom, if they had to be conceived as destructive of the continuity of moral character : he would agree that if such acts occurred, they could only be regarded as the irresponsible freaks of insanity. But he might question whether his dissatisfaction with determinism necessarily committed him to so subversive a conception of moral freedom. He would deny, in short, that rigid determination or moral chaos were the only alternatives.

The moralist, moreover, if he were prescient, would admit that he could perfectly conceive a moral life without indetermination. Nay, he might regard a moral agent as possessed of the loftiest freedom whose conduct was wholly calculable and fully determined, and there-fore absolutely to be trusted. For whether or not he regarded a course of conduct as objectionable would naturally depend on its moral character, and a good life is all the better for resting on a staunch basis of fixed habits.

As compared with such a life, it would of course have to be admitted that an indetermination in moral action which implied a possibility of wrong-doing was a stain upon the agent's character, and indicative of a defect or incomplete development of the intelligence or moral nature. The moralist, therefore, would agree with Aristotle that the divine ideal would be that of a 'necessary' being, fully determined in its actions by its own nature, and therefore 'free' to follow its promptings, and to realize without impediment its own perfections. Why then, and where, does the moralist come into conflict with determinism? It is only when we have to deal practically with the bad man that it becomes morally necessary to insist that an alternative to his bad life must be really possible. The bad man's life may be habitually bad, but his case is not hopeless, unless he is necessitated to go on in the way he is going. If alternatives are possible, his redemption is possible. But his redemption is hopeless, if there never was but one way for him and all the world. The moralist, therefore, demands an alternative to the bad man's foredoomed badness, in order to rationalize the moral universe.

He wants to be able to say to the bad man: 'You need not have become the leper you are. You might have moulded yourself otherwise. Your villainous instincts and unhappy circumstances do not exculpate you. You might have resisted your temptations. Even now your case is not quite hopeless. Your nature is not wholly rigid. In God's universe no moral lapses are wholly irretrievable. Occasions therefore will present themselves in which, even for you, there will be real alternatives to evil-doing, and if you choose to do right, you may yet redeem yourself.' But he does *not* need or desire to say analogously to the good man: 'In spite of the deeply ingrained goodness of your habits, you are still free to do evil. May I live to see the day when you commit a crime and vindicate thereby your moral freedom !'

The moralist, in short, insists on the reality of the alternative in the one case only ; he has no objection to a freedom which transcends itself and is consolidated into impeccable virtue. In other words, he does not wish to conceive all moral acts as indeterminate, but only some ; and he has no need whatever to conceive them as indeterminable. This alone suffices to constitute an essential difference between the real demand for moral freedom and the bogey of indeterminism which determinists seek to put in its place.

It should further be observed that there is no moral need to insist on an unlimited indetermination even in order to impress the bad man. A very slight degree of plasticity will suffice for all ethical demands. And in point of fact no moralist or indeterminist has ever denied the reality of habits. Any notable alteration of habit or sudden conversion is always regarded as more or less miraculous, if it tends in the right direction, or as morbid, if it does not. We see, therefore, that the moral postulate of Freedom is by no means in itself an absurd or extreme one, even though it is not yet apparent how it can scientifically be satisfied.

§ 6. We may, however, obtain light on this subject by next considering the empirical consciousness of Freedom. Consciousness certainly appears to affirm the existence of real alternatives, and of real choices between them. But it can hardly be said to testify to a freedom which is either unceasing or unrestricted.

(1) What we feel to be 'free' choices are comparatively rare events in a moral life of which the greater part seems to be determined by habits and circumstances leaving us neither a real, not even an apparent, choice. Empirically our free choices occur as disturbances in the placid flow of experiences, as distinctly upsetting to the equilibrium of our lives as the crises in which we feel 'unfree' and constrained to do what we would rather not. Both felt freedom and felt necessity, in short, are symptoms of a

crisis, and mark the turning-points of a life. They are in a sense correlative and indicative of a certain (specifically human) stage in moral development.[1]

(2) The alternatives which we empirically encounter never seem to be unlimited. We never feel ' free ' to do anything and everything. Intellectually our choice seems always to be one between alternative ways of achieving an end, of realizing a good. Morally it seems always to be a choice between ' duty ' and ' inclination,' ' right ' and ' wrong.' We feel ' free ' to choose, but not at random ; the alternatives are definitely labelled ' wrong but pleasant ' and ' right but repugnant.'

(3) These alternatives do *not* seem unconnected with our character. So far from appearing to be so, it is of the essence of our ' choice ' that *both* alternatives should appeal to us. Alike if our sense of duty had grown strong enough, and we had no inclination to do anything but what is right ; and if evil indulgences had utterly destroyed our sense of duty, and we retained no inkling of what was right, our choice would disappear, and with it the feeling that we were ' free.'

Our moral ' freedom,' therefore, seems to indicate a moral condition intermediate between that of the angel and that of the devil. It seems to lie in the indeterminateness of a character which is not yet fixed in its habits for good or evil, but still sensitive to the appeals of both. Similarly, the intellectual alternatives would disappear for intelligences either vastly more perfect or vastly less perfect than our own. A mind that could unerringly pick out the best means for the realization of its ends would not be perplexed by alternatives, any more than a mind that was too stupid to perceive any but the one most obvious course. In either case, therefore, the reality of the alternatives and the feeling of ' freedom ' which accompanies our choice seem to be relative to definite moral and intellectual states which occur at a definite stage of habituation. A mind to which the truths of arithmetic are still contingent, which sometimes judges 12×12 to

---

[1] As I pointed out long ago in *Riddles of the Sphinx*, pp. 445-6.

be 144 and sometimes not, is not yet decided in its habits
of arithmetical calculation. A will to which moral alternatives are contingent, which when entrusted with a bottle
of whisky doubts whether to get drunk or to stay sober,
is not yet established in its virtue.

In both cases, no doubt, the contingency of our reaction
betokens a defect. To a perfect knowledge the best
course would allow no inferior alternative to be entertained ; a perfect will would not be tempted by an alternative to the right course. To a combination, therefore,
of perfect will with perfect knowledge no alternatives of
any sort could exist, and no act could ever be ' contingent.'

But why should this prevent us from recognizing the
alternatives that seem to exist for us ? It only renders
them relative to the specific nature of man. It does not
render them unintelligible. They are not irruptions from
nowhere. They spring from a character in which they are
naturally rooted, because that character is still contingent.

When, therefore, the determinist attempts to represent
our freedom as incalculably upsetting the continuity of
character, he is stooping to sheer calumny. If I am
perplexed to choose between a number of possible means
to my end, it is because just my intelligence presents just
those alternatives to me under just those circumstances.
A mind whose make-up, knowledge, and training were
even slightly different might have quite different alternatives, or none at all, or be puzzled in cases when I should
not feel the slightest hesitation. So too our moral choices
are personal ; they presuppose just the characters and
circumstances they arise from.

§ 7. It is extremely important to observe the precise
character of these empirical appearances, because if this
is done, it is easy to perceive in them the real solution of
the whole crux. They directly suggest a way of reconciling the scientific and the ethical postulate ; a way so
simple that it would seem incredible that no one should
have perceived it before, had we not learnt from long and
sad experience that the simplest solutions are usually the
last which the philosophic mind is able to hit upon or

willing to accept, especially if such solutions happen also
to be empirically obvious.   And yet what could be simpler
than the inferences from the facts we have described ?   If
it is true that empirically the 'free' acts always seem to
spring from the given situation, if the alternatives always
seem to exist for a particular mind under particular
circumstances, does it not follow at once that *whichever
of the alternatives is chosen, it will appear to be rationally
connected with the antecedent circumstances*?   There will
be no break, and no difficulty of transition from the act
to its antecedents and back again.

If, therefore, the actual course of events is contemplated *ex post facto*, it will always be possible to argue
that it is intelligible because it sprang from character and
circumstances.   And if our purpose is deterministic, it
can always be maintained that no other course could
have been adopted ; that because *it* was intelligible, no
other course would have been.   But this is manifestly
false ; the alternative, had it been adopted, would have
seemed equally intelligible, just because it was such as to
be really entertained by the agent under the circumstances, and as naturally rooted in them.   After the event,
therefore, the determinist is in the position to argue
'heads I win, tails you lose' ; whatever the issue, he can
claim it as a confirmation of his view.   Before the event,
on the other hand, he was always impotent ; he could
always modestly disclaim prediction (and therewith avoid
refutation) on the ground of insufficient knowledge.   His
position, therefore, seems inexpugnable.

And yet what has happened has really utterly upset
him ; for we have come upon a sort of third alternative
to Determinism and Indeterminism.   The determinists
had argued that if the course of events was not rigidly
determined it must be wholly indeterminable ; that if it
was not uniquely calculable, it could not be calculated at
all.   But here we appear to have a case in which alternative
courses are equally calculable, and to be confronted with
a nature which is really indeterminate and really determinable in alternative ways which seem equally natural

and intelligible. The determinist, therefore, is really baffled. It no longer follows from the rejection of his theory that we must give up calculating and understanding the course of things. If their nature is such that at various points they engender real alternatives, they will engender a plurality of intelligible possibilities, and the choice between them will constitute a real 'freedom,' without entailing any of the dreadful consequences with which determinism and indeterminism both seemed to menace us. Thus we need neither overturn the altar of science, nor sacrifice ourselves upon it : the freedom, which seemed lost so long as only one course of nature seemed rational, intelligible, and calculable, is restored when we recognize that two or more may seem intelligible, because equally natural and calculable. We can satisfy, therefore, the scientific postulate of calculability, without denying the reality of the alternatives which our moral nature seems both to require and to attest. For we can confidently lay it down that no event will ever occur which will not seem intelligibly connected with its antecedents *after it has happened*. It will, therefore, be judged to have been calculable, even though this inference will contain a certain modicum of illusion. For though, no doubt, if we had known enough, we might have calculated it out as a real possibility, we could not have made sure that just this possibility and not any of its alternatives would actually be realized. But practically this is more than enough for science, and would admit of far greater success in calculation than the deficiencies of our knowledge now actually concede to us.

It must not be thought, however, that the conception of Freedom we have thus arrived at constitutes a refutation of Determinism. Methodological postulates as such cannot be refuted ; they can only be disused. And metaphysical dogmas also, that is, ultimate attitudes of thought, cannot be refuted ; they can only be chosen or rejected ; for they form the foundations on which our demonstrations rest. Determinism, then, as a scientific postulate, has not been endangered ; as a metaphysical creed it reduces itself, like all such ultimate assumptions, to a matter of free choice. And herein, in this case, lies a paradox, perhaps; for as we cannot vindicate our freedom unless we are determined to be free, so we cannot compel those to be free who are free to be determined, and prefer to think it so.[1]

§ 8. But though this paradox may be left to the careful consideration of determinists, we can now resolve another—that which was noted in § 5—as to the charming agreement which obtains between determinists, libertarians, and ordinary folk, in their practical behaviour. For if the postulates are really methodological necessities, every one in his practice will have to use them, however he may think about them metaphysically, and whether or not he thinks about them at all. The theoretic divergences, therefore, in our views will make no practical difference; both parties will use both postulates, and will have a right to do so.

(1) Every one has to take it for granted that the course of events is calculable in so far as he is interested in forecasting it. This, indeed, is merely a periphrasis of the statement that determinism is a methodological postulate. The libertarian, therefore, has the same right as any one else to treat events as calculable, to try to calculate all he can and knows. He may be conscious that this aim can never be fully realized, that things are not wholly calculable; but while he calculates he must hope that they will behave as if they were determined, and will not frustrate his efforts by exhibiting their freedom. Even if he fails, it will be his interest to attribute his lack of success, not to the real contingency he has admitted into nature, but rather to the defects of his knowledge. He will wholly agree, therefore, with the determinist that if he had known more, his calculation would have succeeded. And he would defend himself by urging that anyhow the contingency introduced into our

---

[1] As William James well says, freedom "ought to be freely espoused by men who can equally well turn their backs upon it. In other words, our first act of freedom, if we are free, ought in all inward propriety be to affirm that we are free" (*Will to Believe*, p. 146).

world by our ignorance must vastly exceed that due to
any real indetermination in the nature of things.

In dealing, on the other hand, with cases which evoke
the moral postulate of freedom, the libertarian will, of
course, recognize the reality of the freedom he has
assumed. But this will not debar him from calculating.
He will assume the indetermination in the nature he is
studying to be real, and calculate the alternative courses
to which it can be supposed to lead. And if he has a
pretty clear conception of the nature of his ' free ' fellow-
men, his success in forecasting their behaviour will not
fall sensibly short of his success in calculating that of
more remote natures which he takes to be fully
determined.

(2) The determinist regards the scientific postulate as
the expression of an ultimate truth about reality. But
in practice it reduces itself to the expression of a pious
hope. ' If I knew all the antecedents, I could calculate
all the consequences,' is an aspiration and a wish rather
than a positive achievement. This was why we treated
it in § 4 as essentially a moral encouragement to
endeavour. Even the determinist, moreover, must be
dimly conscious that his wish will never be granted him,
that the whole course of events never will be calculated
by him. Why, then, should he repine at learning that
the impossibility of his ideal rests ultimately on the
inherent nature of reality rather than on the ineradicable
weakness of his mind ? Practically it makes no difference.
He finds *de facto* that he cannot calculate all events. He
tries them all, just like the libertarian. But he is baffled
in just the same way. Both, therefore, must agree that
contingencies exist in their common world which *they*
cannot calculate. To deny their ultimate reality is no
practical assistance ; it only adds the annoyance that we
must conceive ourselves to be subject to illusion and
incapable of perceiving things as they really are.

On the other hand, in dealing with moral contingencies
the determinist has to treat them as just as real as the
libertarian. However firmly he may be convinced that

his neighbour's acts are rigidly determined, he does not always feel certain that he knows his nature sufficiently to predict them. He is fortunate if he can feel sure what alternatives are most likely to appeal to him, and calculate the consequences and adjust his own course accordingly. In practice, therefore, he will do just as the libertarian did : he will have to recognize, that is, real but calculable, alternatives which exist, at all events for him.

In other words, the pragmatic difference between the rival theories tends to be evanescent ; in practice both parties have to pocket their metaphysics and to act sensibly ; in theory the differences are such that their influence on practice is very remote, and mainly emotional. For common sense, again, there are no practical alternatives ; the whole metaphysical controversy, therefore, seems nugatory, and is regarded with the utmost equanimity. And is not this all as it should be in a universe in which thought is secondary to action ?

§ 9. We have, however, pushed forward our doctrine of Freedom somewhat rapidly, and shall do well to analyse its nature in order to secure our ground.

We should realize, in the first place, that we took a risk in declaring the immediate consciousness of Freedom to contain the solution of the puzzle. There is always a risk in taking appearances to contain ultimate truth. But it is not so serious as to take them as containing no truth at all. And to our Humanism it will naturally seem a better risk to take to trust appearances than to invalidate them for no sufficient reason. Let us therefore bravely accept the risk and pose our critics by asking, Why, after all, should the alternatives which seem to be real not be really real ? Because to regard them as real renders science impossible and life chaotic ? That allegation we have shown to be untrue. Science is in no danger from our doctrine, and for the purposes of life we all assume the reality of contingencies. Because we do not yet understand the positive nature of Freedom, beyond this that it involves indetermination ? And because a real indetermination ultimately leads to a metaphysically unthinkable view of the universe?

These latter suggestions are more deserving of consideration. And so let us first explore the positive nature of the sort of Freedom we have seemed to find, considering it empirically and psychologically, before attempting to evaluate its metaphysical significance.

There does not seem to be any reason why we should not accept the empirical reality of psychological indetermination, once we have really disabused our minds of the prejudice engendered by a misconception of the scientific postulate. Such indetermination, indeed, appears to be a natural incident in the growth of a habit, and the capacity for retaining a certain plasticity and growing new habits seems to be essential to existence in a universe which has, on the one hand, acquired a certain stability and order, and yet, on the other, is still evolving new conditions, to which novel adjustments are from time to time required. A nature, therefore, which was entirely indeterminate in its reactions, and one which was entirely rigid and determinate, would alike be inefficacious and unsuited to our world. To live in it we need a certain degree of plasticity and the intelligence to perceive when better adjustments can be effected by varying our habits of reaction. This power, indeed, seems to be the essence of our ' reason.' [1] Why then should philosophy insist on regarding this plasticity as quite illusory?

It appears, further, to be a misapprehension when this plasticity of habit is regarded as conflicting with the conception of 'law.' Law, subjectively regarded from the standpoint of a knower trying economically to conceive the universe, means regularity, and therefore calculableness and trustworthiness. Phrasing it intellectualistically, this constitutes the ' intelligibility' of the natural order. Regarded objectively, however, 'law' means nothing but habit. The 'laws of nature,' however they may be thought to originate, are *de facto* the established habits of things, and their constancy is an empirical fact of

---

[1] Cp. Essay xvi. § 4.

observation. It is from experience alone that we learn
that nature in general conforms itself to our postulate of
regularity and renders it so applicable that we can take
it to be 'true.'

But experience never fully warrants the assertion that
the habits of nature are absolutely fixed and constant.
For all we can prove to the contrary, even the most
fundamental laws may be changing — let us hope
'evolving' into something better. Over large tracts of
nature—wherever we can trace the working of intelligence
—the laws do not even appear to have an absolute
constancy. All this, however, will not interfere with our
methodological assumption of constancy unless the changes
in habits are very rapid ; as rapid, say, as the changes in
the fashions. Nor will it necessarily render the course of
things unintelligible. On the contrary, we have seen that
adaptive innovations in habits, intelligent divergences from
law, are the very essence of 'reason,' and if the changes
of fashions are irrational in their frequency, they are at
the same time rational, as satisfying the desire to display
one's credit with one's dressmaker or tailor.

There is then no real psychological difficulty about the
idea that the plasticity of habit carries with it a certain
indetermination, which, however, is intelligible and calculable and salutary. The only difficulty really involved
lies in conceiving a nature which is, as it were, divided
against itself and advancing at different rates in different
parts, in such a way that the 'desires' may engender
internal friction by persistently hankering after ingrained
habits of behaviour long after the 'reason' has condemned
their inappropriateness under the now altered circumstances. And this difficulty no doubt deserves more
attention than psychologists and moralists have yet
bestowed upon it. But in whatever way it may be
explicable, it can hardly be denied that something of the
sort actually exists ; and for our present purpose this
suffices.

Metaphysically, on the other hand, the difficulty which
the existence of indetermination involves is a very big

one. If, that is, it is admitted to exist at all, it touches the last problems of ontology. For it resolves itself into the question of the possibility of thinking a really incomplete reality, a world which is really plastic and growing and changing. And the *a priori* sort of metaphysics has always found the reality of change an insuperable stumbling-block.[1] We, on the other hand, may think the reality of change too evident to argue over, we may deem the objections raised against it silly quibbles, we may see that to deny it only leads to phantom universes having no relation to our own ; but we must recognize the reality of a formidable prejudice. It will be more prudent, therefore, to postpone the final tussle with this prejudice till we have considered (1) how far the consequences of the human Freedom we have conceived may be traced throughout the world ; (2) how far something analogous can be attributed to the other existences in the world ; and (3) how we should value a world whose nature is ultimately ' free.'

§ 10. *If human freedom is real, the world is really indeterminate.* This is easily demonstrable. For if we really have the power to choose between alternatives, the course of things will necessarily differ according as we do one thing or an other. This follows alike whether we conceive the rest of the world to be fully determined, or to have itself some power of spontaneous choice. If a single variable factor is introduced among a mass of invariable antecedents, the consequents will needs be different. If it is introduced amid a mass of antecedents which themselves are variable, the final outcome may indeed remain the same, but only if these other factors set themselves intelligently to counteract and thwart the first. Thus the intermediate course of events will yet be different, seeing that it will have been altered to encounter the first variable. In either case, therefore, there will be alternative courses of history, and a real indetermination in a universe which harbours a free agent.

Humanly speaking, the first case seems clearly to be

[1] Cp. Essay ix. § 1.

congruous with the facts. Human purposes have not all been thwarted ; they have left their mark upon the earth, and made it a very different place from what it would otherwise have been. Of course, however, we may hold that their realization has occurred only in so far as it has not thwarted an ulterior and diviner purpose which has a countermove to every human sin and error.[1]

This consequence, then, of human freedom is too clear to be denied. It can only be minimized. After all, it may be said, what does human freedom come to ? It can only effect infinitesimal changes on the surface of the earth. It cannot divert the stars in their courses, it cannot even regulate the motions of the earth, it cannot ward off the ultimate collapse of the Solar System.

To which it may be replied (1) that our agency is not necessarily negligible because it cannot control the cosmic masses ; (2) that our interests are chiefly confined to the earth's surface, and that it matters not a little whether or not we can manipulate that ; (3) that the extent to which we can alter the course of things depends on the extent to which we can render things plastic to our purposes ; (4) that with audacity and study we may find the world far more plastic than as yet we dare to think. Science is as yet only beginning, and mankind is only beginning to trust itself to science, which as yet hardly dares to speculate about all that it might possibly attempt. Lastly (5), even differences of choices which at first seem infinitesimal may lead to growing divergences, and ultimately constitute all the difference between a world in which we are saved and one in which we are damned.

On the whole, therefore, we shall do well not to think too meanly of our powers, but to reflect rather on the responsibilities involved even in our most trivial choices. If we can really make our ' fate ' and remake our world, it behoves us to make sure that they shall not be made amiss.

§ 11. It will next be politic to face an objection which has probably long been simmering in our readers' minds.

---

[1] Cp. James, *Will to Believe*, pp. 181-2.

'Is it credible,' they will incline to ask, 'that man alone should be free and form an exception to the rest of the universe? And if the rest of the universe is determined, is it not probable that man will be likewise?'

Now it cannot be admitted that our view of man should necessarily be falsified in order to accommodate it to our beliefs about the rest of the universe. But at the same time the human mind finds exceptions irksome, and is disposed to question them. We can, however, get rid of this 'exception' in another way. Instead of sacrificing our freedom to cosmic analogies, let us try to trace something analogous to our freedom throughout the universe.

It is evident, in the first place, that a higher and more perfect being than man, if the intelligent operations of such a one are traceable in the world, would be both 'freer' than man, that is more able to achieve his ends and less often thwarted, and also more determinate in his action, and more uniform and calculable in the execution of his purposes. It is clear, therefore, that a 'God' would work by 'law' rather than by 'miracle,' in proportion as he really controlled the world, and that consequently it would be very easy to misinterpret his agency, and to ascribe it to a mechanical necessity; which of course is what has usually been done.

Turning next to beings lower in the scale than ourselves, we have of course good reason to attribute to the higher animals a mental constitution very like our own. And that should carry with it something very like our sense of freedom. A dog, for example, appears to be subject to conflicting impulses, to doubt and hesitate, to attend selectively and choose, and sometimes to exhibit a spontaneity which baffles calculation almost as completely as that of his master. We can indeed imagine the great motives that broadly determine his conduct, but in some respects his motives are harder to appreciate, because his mind is remoter from our own.

As we descend the scale of life these difficulties grow more marked; our spiritual sympathy with, and inward understanding of, the conduct we observe grow less and less. The feelings which prompt, and the motives which impel, to the spontaneous acts we notice grow ever more mysterious. But externally we can still predict the lower animal's behaviour. We do not understand the why of its spontaneous, random motions. But we observe that these variations lie between certain narrow limits, which are narrowed down as intelligence is lowered. An amœba never does anything startling to shock the biologist. Hence as intelligence diminishes or grows alienated from our own, conduct becomes more uniform, and therefore in a way more calculable. Only it is in another way. We have become external spectators of acts to which we have lost the inner clue.

Nevertheless when we descend to the inanimate, and meet apparently perfect regularity, we feel that we have reached the true home of mechanical 'law' which knows no breaking, disturbed by no intelligence, and varied by no vestige of spontaneous choice. But we have no inward comprehension whatever of the processes we watch. Why should material masses gravitate inversely as the square of the distance? What satisfactions can they derive from this ratio in particular? Why should atoms dance just in the mazy rhythms they severally choose? Why should electrons carry just the 'charges' they empirically bear? All this is sheer, brute, uncomprehended fact, of which no philosophy since Hegel's has had the folly to essay an *a priori* explanation. But little we care, or scientifically need care, so long as it all happens with a 'mechanical' regularity which can be accurately calculated.

It is convenient, therefore, to assume that the inorganic is the realm of rigid mechanism and devoid of every trace of spontaneous spirit. But this is an assumption which is strictly indemonstrable. The regularity to which we trust is no adequate proof. For, taken in large masses, human actions show a similar constancy. Averages remain regular and calculable, even though their individual components may vary widely and incalculably from the mean. Under stable and normal conditions of society the statistics of births, marriages, and deaths do not vary appreciably from year to year. Yet some of these events are usually set down to individual choices.

Now in observing the inorganic we are dealing with the world's constituents in very large numbers. Physical and chemical experiments operate with many thousands and millions of millions at a time. The least speck visible under the microscope is composed of atoms by the million. Consequently the regularity we observe may very well be that of an average. If, then, a single atom here or there displayed its extraordinary intelligence or original perverseness by refusing to do as the rest, how pray should it ever be detected by us? How should we ever suspect that the process rested upon choice and was not utterly mechanical?

Thirdly, it must be borne in mind that we may fail to observe the differences in the behaviour of individual atoms or electrons merely because our experiments are too ignorant and clumsy to discriminate between them, so as to tempt some, without alluring others. Their complete qualitative identity is inferred from experiments which are as crude and barbarous as would be experiments which concluded to the non-existence of human individuality from the fact that when men were hurled over a precipice in large quantities they were all equally dashed to pieces.

How coarse our methods are we usually discover only when they are improved. Thus it long seemed inexplicable how a grain of musk could retain its fragrance for years without sensibly losing weight, if this quality really rested on the emission of particles ; but this mystery is now to a large extent solved by the discovery of radio-activity. It has turned out that the electroscope is a far more delicate instrument than the most sensitive balance, which remains unaffected by the violent propulsion of electrons which accompanies the disruption of atomic matter. And so the whole doctrine of the indestructibility of matter may be radically wrong, and its apparent proofs due merely to the roughness of our former measurements. In

experimenting with radium we have managed to select
those 'atoms' which are nearing their explosive end, and
to concentrate them until their death agonies grow visible
to us ; but concerning the generation of atoms we are still
in the dark, though we suspect a good deal, enough at
any rate to entertain the idea that the constancy of matter
may be merely the stability of an average.   Similarly it
is possible that long-continued fractionations might sift
out the chief individual differences in all the chemical
'elements.'   It is therefore quite fallacious to infer that
things have a rigid and unalterable nature, because they
show their indifference to us by reacting alike to modes
of treatment which to our eyes seem different.   In view
of our ignorance of their inner nature this may only show
that differences which seem important to us do not seem
important to them.[1]

Deficient as our observations are in delicacy, they are
still more deficient in endurance.   The evidence that the
'laws' of nature remain really constant is hardly complete
even for the last few centuries.   The discrepancies, for
example, between the historically recorded and the retro-
spectively calculated eclipses of the sun and the moon are
too great to be compatible with existence of our present
planetary orbits even a few centuries ago.[2]   To explain
them we have to choose between the assumptions that our
records are false, that the moon is slowly escaping us, that
the earth's diurnal rotation is slowing down, that the sun's
motion or attraction is altering, or that the law of gravitation is changing, or whatever combination of these and
other hypotheses we can devise to fit the facts more
nearly.   To guide that choice we have only the vague
methodological maxim that it is well to try first such
hypotheses as involve the least disturbance of the accepted
system of science.   But even the greatest readjustments
may be needed.   If now we supposed the primary laws
of nature to be changing slowly and continuously, most of

---

[1] Cp. *Humanism*, p. 11, note.
[2] See an article on "Ancient Eclipses" by Prof. P. H. Cowell in *Nature*,
No. 1905.

the evidence which is now held to imply their rigid
constancy would be seen to be inconclusive. Thus even
in the inorganic world habits might be plastic and 'laws'
might be gradually evolving.

If this be so, it is, moreover, clear that we ourselves
might take a part in determining this evolution. Our
operations might induce things to develop their habits in
one way rather than another, and so we should literally
be altering the laws of nature. It is even permissible to
surmise that we may already sometimes have accomplished this. The chemist, for example, seems often so
to play upon the acquired habits of his substances as
to bring into existence compounds which but for him
would never have existed, and never could have existed
in a state of nature. And so he may induce new
habits; for once these combinations have been formed,
they may leave permanent traces on the natures that
take part in them, and so alter their 'affinities' for the
future.

The speculations whereby we have illustrated the
possibility that individuality, plasticity, and freedom may
pervade also the inorganic world will seem wild and
unfamiliar. But they are such that science may some day
verify them, if they are looked for. At present we blind
ourselves to their possibility by making the methodological assumptions of determinism and mechanism. But
it should be clearly confessed that it is entirely possible
that the world may now be, and may always have been,
such as to contain a certain indetermination throughout
its structure, which we have only failed to discover because
we have closed our eyes to it, in order to have a more
easily calculable universe. If, however, this postulate is
modified so that 'free' acts also are conceived as calculable,
our eyes may be opened, as it were by magic, and the
evidences of 'freedom' may everywhere pop up and stare
us in the face.

§ 12. We come at last to the ultimate metaphysical
advantages and disadvantages of the belief in Freedom
which we have developed. That it has its drawbacks is

fairly obvious. Indeterminism, even when it has been tamed, *i.e.* limited, and rendered calculable and determinable, still means chance ; and chance means risk ; and risk, though it seems inseparable from life, means a possibility of failure. Our craven instincts, therefore, our indolence, our diffidence, will always demand an assurance of salvation, a universe which *cannot* go astray, but is predestined to be perfect.

The prejudices thus engendered are probably among the strongest of the secret motives which inspire the absolutist's aversion from Pragmatism. As Prof. Muirhead opportunely confesses, the admission of contingency seems to turn the universe into " a joint-stock enterprise under God and Co., Limited, *without insurance against accident*," [1] and this would be very much of a *pis aller* to predestinate perfection.

But is predestinate perfection possible or really thinkable ? And what is the ' insurance against accident ' offered us by the agents of the Absolute really and truly worth ?

If the universe as we know it is predestined to anything, it is predestined to go on as it is upon its fatal course. For the universe, we are assured, contains no free agents, human or divine, to work out beneficial transformations in its nature. It is predestined, therefore, to be an unmeaning dance of cosmic matter, diversified at intervals by catastrophes, as blind blundering suns go crashing into each other's systems and make holocausts of the values and polities which some powerless race of planetary pygmies has painfully evolved. It is predestined to a fate which nothing can avert, which no one can mitigate or improve.

And to make our ' insurance ' doubly sure, we are furthermore assured that this universe, which extorts its tribute of tears from every feeling breast, is *already perfect*, if only we could see it—which being necessarily ' finite ' we cannot ! There is not, therefore, the slightest reason why, for finite minds, the universe should ever seem, or

[1] *Hibbert Journal*, vol. iv. p. 460. Italics mine.

become, more satisfactory than now it is. The absolutist in his determinism at bottom entirely agrees with Mephistopheles—

> Glaub' unser einem dieses Ganze
> Ist *nur* für einen Gott gemacht.

The only boon which his view 'insures' us is that a world which with all its faults had seemed plastic and improvable, becomes a hopeless hell for the wanton and superfluous torture of helpless 'finite' beings, whose doom was predestined from all eternity !

For my part, I should prefer a universe marred by chance to such a certainty. For the 'chance' in this case means a chance of improvement. Of course a world that was really perfect in a simple and human way, and was incapable of declining from that perfection because it contained no indetermination, would be better still. But such a world ours plainly is not, though it has a chance of developing such perfection by becoming wholly harmonious and determinate. And is it not 'assurance' enough for all reasonable requirements that in a world wholly harmonized no one could upset its harmony nor have any motive for changing his habits and the way of the world ?

There remains to be discussed the metaphysical objection to the conception of indetermination which was postponed in § 9. It is at bottom an objection to the reality of change in ultimate reality, to the notion of its incompleteness and development. It is, however, merely a survival of Eleatic prejudice, and the simplest way to dispose of it is by a demand for its credentials. For why should it be taken as certain *a priori* that the real cannot change ? All we *know* about reality negatives this notion. And if our immediate experience is not to convince us of the reality of change, of what can anything convince us ? Or if it is claimed that the impossibility of change can be made dialectically evident by *a priori* reasoning from ideas, our reply will be that, if so, the ideas in question must be faulty. For our ideas should be formed to

understand experience, not to confute it. Ideas which
are inapplicable are invalid. Ideas which contradict
experience are either false, or in need of verification by
the altering of the reality which contradicts them. In
short, it is vain to threaten libertarians with the metaphysical terrors of what James calls 'the block-universe.'
That conception is usually mystical, when it is not a
materialistic corollary from an obsolescent physics; it
can never be really thought out in metaphysics except
into sheer, unmitigated Eleaticism. And, as in Zeno's time,
the puzzle ' *solvitur ambulando* ' by those who really wish
to know : we leave it aside and pass on.

To sum up ; our Freedom is really such as it appears ;
it consists in the determinable indetermination of a nature
which is plastic, incomplete, and still evolving. These
features pervade the universe ; but they do not make it
unintelligible. Nay, they are the basis of its perfecti-
bility.

XIX

THE MAKING OF REALITY

ARGUMENT

§ 1. Hegel's great idea of a thought process which was to be also the cosmic process spoilt by his dehumanizing of the former. The false abstractions of the 'Dialectic' from time and personality lead to its impotence to explain either process. § 2. Humanism renews Hegel's enterprise by conceiving the 'making of truth' to be also a 'making of reality.' Its epistemological validity. § 3. The problem of a metaphysical 'making of reality.' § 4. Its difficulties. (1) Can reality be wholly engendered by our operations? (2) Can the Pragmatic Method yield a metaphysic? § 5. Even epistemologically we must (1) distinguish between 'discovering' and 'making' reality. The distinction may mark the division between Pragmatism and Humanism. But it is itself pragmatic, and in some cases the difference between 'making' and 'finding' becomes arbitrary. § 6. (2) The great difference between original and final 'truth' and 'fact' in the process which validates 'claims' and makes 'realities.' The pragmatic unimportance of starting-points. Initial truth as 'sheer claim' and initial fact as mere potentiality. Their methodological worthlessness. § 7. (3) The methodological nullity and metaphysical absurdity of the notion of an 'original fact.' Ultimate reality something to be looked forward, and not back, to. § 8. The transition of metaphysics. Humanism and metaphysics. § 9. Four admitted ways in which the 'making of truth' involves a 'making of reality.' A fifth, knowing makes reality by altering the knowers, who are real. § 10. But is the object known also altered, and so 'made'? Where the object known is not aware it is known, it is treated as 'independent,' because knowing seems to make no difference. Fallaciousness of the notion of mere knowing. Knowing as a prelude to doing. § 11. The apparent absence of response to our cognitive operations on the part of 'things,' due to their lack of spiritual communion with us. But really they do respond to us as physical bodies, and are affected by us as such. § 12. Hylozoism or panpsychism as a form of Humanism. 'Catalytic action' and its human analogues. § 13. Hence there is real making of reality by us out of plastic facts. § 14. The extent of the plasticity of fact, practically and methodologically. § 15. Non-human making of reality. § 16. Two indispensable assumptions : (1) the reality of freedom or determinable indetermination, and (2) § 17, the incompleteness of reality, as contrasted with the Absolutist notion of an eternally complete whole, which renders our whole world illusory.

§ 1. It was a great thought of Hegel's [1] that truth and reality, logic and metaphysics, belonged together and must not be separated, and that, to make the world truly intelligible, the making of truth and the making of reality must be made to coincide. He tried, therefore, to conceive the cosmic process as one with the thought process, and to represent all the events which happened in the real evolution of the world in time as incidents in the self-development of a ' dialectical process ' in which the Absolute Idea arrived at a full logical comprehension of its own eternal meaning.

But, unfortunately, he spoilt this great idea (with which Dr. McTaggart alone of his English followers seems to concern himself) in the execution. He tried to conceive thought as out of time, and its ' eternity ' as higher than the time-process of reality, and as containing the ' truth ' and meaning of the latter. But this equation of the *eternal* ' logic-process ' with the *temporal* ' cosmic process ' did not work out to a real solution. The one was eternally complete, the other manifestly incomplete ; and no real correspondence could be established between their respective terms.[2] Moreover, the real events of the cosmic process stubbornly refused to be reduced to mere illustrations of a dialectical relation of ' categories,' and the desperate attempt of the ' Dialectic ' to declare the *surplus* of meaning, which the real possessed over the logical, to be really a *defect*, to be mere meaningless ' contingency ' which reason could not, and need not, account for, was really a covert confession of its fundamental failure.

This failure, moreover, was really an inevitable consequence of its own fundamental assumptions. It had begun by misconceiving the ' thought - process,' which was to be its clue to reality. It had begun by abstracting from its concrete nature, from the actual thinking of human beings. It had begun, that is, by misconceiving the function of abstraction. It had begun, in short, by *dehumanizing* thought in order to

[1] Or rather of Fichte's ; but Hegel appropriated
[2] Cp. *Humanism*, ch. vi.

XIX   THE MAKING OF REALITY   423

make it more adequate to ultimate reality. But the result was that it destroyed the real link between reality and thought. For it is only as concrete human thinking that we know thought to be a real process at all. Once this link is severed, once the human side of thought is flung aside as meaningless and worthless, thought *per se*, however 'absolute' and 'ideal' and 'eternal' we may call it, is wafted away from earth into the immense inanity of abstractions which have lost touch with a reality to which they can never again be applied.

This fate has overtaken the 'Dialectic.' The self-development of its 'categories' is not the real development of any actual thought. It is not, consequently, the real explanation of any actual process. It still bears a sort of ghostly resemblance to our concrete thinking, to the body of incarnate truth from which it was abstracted; and, therefore, it can still claim a shadowy relevance to the real events of life. But it is too abstract ever to grasp either thoughts or events in their full concreteness. Thus its claim to predict events is very like the weather prophecies in *Zadkiel's Almanac* — so vaguely worded that almost anything may be said to confirm it. But it can never suggest any definite reason why definite persons at any definite time should think just those thoughts which they think, or use just the categories which they use, rather than any other. It can never allege any reason why events should exemplify the logical relations of the categories in the precise way they are said to do, rather than in a dozen other ways which would do equally well, or why, conversely, the categories should achieve exemplification by just the events which occur, rather than by a myriad others which would perform this function no less well. All such definite questions it waves aside as concerned merely with the impenetrable 'contingency' of the phenomenal. Even, therefore, if we take the most favourable view of its claims, and admit it to be an explanation of everything in general, it still fails to satisfy the demands, either of science or of practice, by being too vague and too ambiguous to be the explanation of anything in particular. It is truly the "unearthly ballet of bloodless categories," Mr. Bradley has called it, a mere Witches' Sabbath of disembodied abstractions, from which the true seeker after the meaning of reality will no more distil spiritual satisfaction than Dr. Faustus did from the *Walpurgisnacht* on the Brocken. And even as an intellectual debauch, as a sowing of spiritual wild oats, it is better to avoid what may so seriously confuse and debilitate the mind.

It remains, however, to show that the points at which the Hegelian Dialectic's failure becomes patent are in direct connexion. It fails, practically on its own showing, to account for *the whole* of the time process, *because* it fails to account for *the whole* of the thought process. For it has in both cases made the same fatal abstraction. It has assumed that because *for the practical purposes of human knowing* it is convenient and possible and sufficient to abstract from the full concreteness ('particularity') of the Real, what we neglect, and often have to neglect, is really meaningless. But this is not the case. There is nothing 'accidental' and void of significance about the Real, nothing which a *complete* theory of events can afford to ignore. The minutest 'incident' has its meaning, every least shade of personality its importance, even though our limitations may practically force us to neglect them. Such concessions may be accorded to the humility of a pragmatic theory of knowledge : they cannot be rendered compatible with the all-embracing claims of a theory of absolute knowledge. Hence the pretensions of the Dialectic to absolute completeness do not entitle it to the arrogance of such abstractions. If it cannot or will not explain everything, it forfeits its claim to be 'concrete' and to be valid. It has misunderstood, moreover, the nature of abstraction. The abstraction which occurs in actual thinking is human, and not absolute ; it is relative to a restricted purpose, and can be rectified by altering the purpose whenever this is requisite or desirable. Abstraction, in other

words, is an instrument of thought, and not a good *per se*.
It should not be dehumanized any more than any other
feature of our thinking. And if we refrain from dehumanizing our thought, we shall not be forced to
' de-realize ' reality in order to make it ' intelligible.'

§ 2. Let us try, therefore, to renew Hegel's enterprise
of the identification of the making of truth and the
making of reality, under the better auspices of a logic
which has not disembowelled itself in its zeal to become
true. That the pragmatic theory of knowledge does
not start with any antithesis of ' truth ' and ' fact,' but
conceives ' reality ' as something which, for our knowledge
at least, grows up in the making of truth, and consequently recognizes nothing but continuous and fluid transitions from hypothesis to fact and from truth to truth,
we have already seen in Essays vii. and viii. It follows
that the ' making of truth ' is also in a very real sense a
' making of reality.' In validating our claims to ' truth '
we really ' discover ' realities. And we really *transform*
them by our cognitive efforts, thereby proving our
desires and ideas to be real forces in the shaping of
our world.

Now this is a result of immense philosophic importance. For it systematically bars the way to the
persistent but delusive notion that ' truth ' and ' reality '
somehow exist apart, and apart from us, and have to be
coaxed or coerced into a union, in the fruits of which we
can somehow participate. The making of truth, it is
plain, is anything but a passive mirroring of ready-made
fact. It is an active endeavour, in which our whole
nature is engaged, and in which our desires, interests,
and aims take a leading part. Nevermore, therefore,
can the *subjective* making of reality be denied or ignored,
whether it be in the interests of rationalism, and in
order to reserve the making of reality for an ' absolute
thought,' or whether it be in the interests of realism, and in
order to maintain the absoluteness of an ' independent '
fact. Taken strictly for what it professes to be, the
notion of ' truth ' as a ' correspondence ' between our

minds and something intrinsically foreign to them, as a mirroring of alien fact, has completely broken down. The reality to which truth was said to 'correspond,' *i.e.* which it has to know, is *not* a 'fact' in its own right, which pre-exists the cognitive functioning. It is itself a fact *within* knowing, immanently deposited or 'precipitated' by the functioning of our thought. The problem of knowledge, therefore, is *not* — 'how can thought engender truth about reality?' It is rather—'how can we best describe the continuous cognitive process which engenders our systems of 'truth' and our acceptance of 'reality' and gradually refines them into more and more adequate means for the control of our experience?' It is in this cognitive elaboration of experience that both reality and truth grow up *pari passu*. 'Reality' is reality for us, and known by us, just as 'truth' is truth for us. What we judge to be 'true,' we take to be 'real,' and accept as 'fact.' And so what was once the most vaporous hypothesis is consolidated into the hardest and most indubitable 'fact.' Epistemologically speaking, therefore, so far as our knowledge goes or can go, the making of truth and the making of reality seem to be *fundamentally one*.

§ 3. But how about metaphysics? Does this 'making of truth' supply a final answer to all the questions we can ask? This is by no means obvious. Even on the epistemological plane the making of truth seemed to recognize certain limitations, the exact nature of which, being unable to pursue the subject into the depths of metaphysics, we were not able to determine. We had to leave it doubtful, therefore, how far a coincidence of our cognitive making of truth with the real making of reality could be traced, and whether ultimately both processes could be combined in the same conception. It seemed possible that our so-called making of reality would not in the end amount to a revelation of the ultimate essence of the cosmic process, and that the analogies between the two would finally prove fallacious or insufficient.

We postponed, therefore, the further consideration of these questions, and have been rewarded since then by lighting upon a number of truths which may be distinctly helpful in a renewed attack upon our problem of the 'making of reality.'

(1) We have seen in Essay ix. § 1 that an evolutionist philosophy ought not prematurely to commit itself to a static view of Reality, and that it is not an ineluctable necessity of thought, but a metaphysical prejudice, to believe that Reality is complete and rigid and unimprovable, and that real change is therefore impossible. We have thus gained the notion of a plastic, growing, incomplete reality, and this will permit us to conceive a 'making of reality' as really cosmic.

(2) The examination of Freedom in the last essay (§§ 9-12) brought us once more into contact with this idea of a really incomplete reality. For it seemed that there might after all be a vein of indetermination running through the universe, and that the behaviour and the habits of things could still be altered. This idea cropped up as a logical consequence of the reality of human freedom, which we found it possible to maintain on other grounds. This freedom and plasticity, moreover, would explain and justify our treatment of our ideas as real forces, and our claim that the 'making of truth' was necessarily also a making of reality. For the plasticity of the real would explain how it was that our subjective choices could realize alternative developments of reality.

And (3) it appeared to be possible that this plasticity of things might involve not merely a passive acquiescence in our manipulations, but a modicum of initiative, and that thus 'freedom' might not be confined to human nature, but might in some degree pervade the universe. If so, not only would the possibilities of 'making reality' be vastly enlarged, but we should have established the existence of a very real and far-reaching identity in nature between human and non-human reality, which would justify the expectation of very considerable likeness in the processes by which they severally adjust themselves to

their environment.   Accordingly, we might feel entitled
to look for analogues also to the human making of truth
and reality, and these might help to render intelligible
the vast masses of reality, which it seemed at the end of
Essay vii. we could not humanly claim to have 'made.'

§ 4. Still it will not do to underrate the difficulties of
the situation.   The Pragmatic Method, we have always
admitted, has definitely postulated an initial basis of fact
as the condition of its getting to work at all.   And
although any particular 'fact' can always be conceived as
having been 'made' by a previous cognitive operation,
this latter in its turn will always presuppose a prior basis
of fact.   Hence, however rightly we may emphasize the
fact that *what we call reality* is bound up with our knowing
and dependent on our manipulations, there will always
seem to be an insuperable paradox in the notion that
*reality can, as such and wholly, be engendered by the con-
sequences of our dealings with it.*

Our Pragmatic Method, moreover, has so far fought
shy of metaphysics.   It has pleaded that originally it
had professed to be merely epistemological in its scope,
and has gravely doubted whether metaphysics were not
for it *ultra vires*.[1]   It may be well, therefore, to indulge
the foibles of our method, to the extent at least of considering what more can be said about the making of reality
on strictly epistemological ground, before we transform it,
by claiming for it universal application and expanding it
to cosmic dimensions, and thereby soar to metaphysics.

§ 5. In point of fact there is a good deal more to be
said.   For example, (1) the difficulty about conceiving
the acceptance of fact as the basis of the pragmatically
developed situation should be treated, not as an objection
to the Pragmatic Method, but as a means of bringing out

---

[1] I do not think that the text of *Axioms as Postulates* anywhere, even in
isolated paragraphs, entitles critics to read it in a metaphysical sense.   And
certainly the whole method and purpose of that essay should have made it unmistakable that it was nowhere intended to be taken in any but an epistemological
sense.   If so, it is beside the point to object to §§ 3-7 as not giving a
satisfactory account of the creation of the universe.   Really that would have
been too much to expect even from the untamed vigour of a new philosophy !
That the question under discussion referred only to our cognitive making of
reality was quite plainly stated in § 7.

its full significance. For it can be made to bring out the important distinction between the reality which is 'made' only for us, *i.e. subjectively*, or as we say 'discovered,' and that which we suppose to be *really* ' made,' made objectively and in itself. That we make this distinction is obvious ; but why do we make it ? If both the subjective and the objective ' making of reality' are products of the same cognitive process, of the same 'making of truth' by our subjective efforts, how can this distinction arise, or, ultimately, be maintained ?

Now it is clear, in the first place, that acceptance of the Pragmatic Method in no wise compels us to ignore this distinction. Nor does it as such compel us to assert the ' making of reality' in the *objective* sense. It seems quite feasible to conceive the making as *merely subjective*, as referring only to our *knowledge of reality*, without affecting its actual existence.[1] Nay, the existence of the distinction may itself legitimately be appealed to to show that common sense draws a clear line at this point. And so it may be denied that we ' make' reality metaphysically, though not that we ' make' it epistemologically.

The validity of this position may provisionally be admitted. Let it merely be observed that it is compatible with a full acceptance of Pragmatism *as a method*, and even with a very extensive 'making of reality' by our efforts. For these efforts are still indispensable in order that reality may be ' discovered.' It is still true that our desires and interests must anticipate our ' discoveries,' and point the way to them—and that so our conception of the world will still depend on our subjective selection of what it interested us to discover in the totality of existence. And of course the 'making of reality,' in so far as we mould things to suit us, and in so far as social institutions are real forces to be reckoned with and potent in the moulding of men, is also unaffected by the refusal to conceive the ultimate making of reality as proceeding identically, or analogously, with our ' making

[1] Hence it seems possible to be, *e.g.*, a pragmatist in epistemology, and a realist in metaphysics, like Prof. Santayana.

of truth.' So that it is quite possible to be a good pragmatist without attempting to turn one's method into a
metaphysic.

Secondly, it is clear that if the Pragmatic Method is
true, the distinction between 'discovering' and 'making'
reality must itself have a pragmatic ground. It must be
evolved out of the cognitive process, and be validated by
its practical value. And this we find to be the case.
The distinction is a practical one, and rests on the various
behaviours of things. A reality is said to be discovered,
and not made, when its behaviour is such that it is
practically inconvenient or impossible to ascribe its reality
for us entirely to our subjective activity. And as a rule
the criteria of this distinction are plain and unmistakable.
To wish for a chair and find one, and to wish for a chair
and make one, are experiences which it is not easy to
confuse, and which involve very different operations and
attitudes on our part. In the one case, we have merely
to look around, and our trusty senses present to us the
object of our desire in effortless completion : in the other
a prolonged process of construction is required.

More verbally confusing cases arise when we have
made a claim to reality which we cannot sustain, or denied
a reality which we subsequently recognize. These cases
seem to lend themselves to the belief in an 'independent'
reality, because in our dealings with them we do not
seem to alter 'reality,' but only our beliefs about it. The
confusion, however, is at bottom one between a reality (or
truth) which is claimed, and one which is verified. If a
claim is falsified, the new truth (or reality) which takes its
place may always be antedated, and conceived as having
existed independently of the claim which it refutes. But
it cannot be said to be similarly independent of the
process which has established it. The truth is that what
in such a case we have made is not a reality, but a
mistake. And a mistake is a claim to reality (or truth)
which will not work, and has to be withdrawn. But the
failure of a cognitive experiment is no proof that experimentation is a mistake. Nor does the fact that a reality

existed, which we mistakenly denied, prove that it was not 'made,' even by ourselves.

In other cases the line is not so clear, and the 'finding' seems to involve a good deal of 'making.' Our language itself often testifies to this. Thus we often 'find' that when we have 'made' mistakes, the precise amount of wilfulness involved in the 'making' is difficult to gauge. Or consider our dealings with other beings spiritually responsive to our action. Our behaviour to them may really determine their behaviour to us, and make them what we believed or wanted them to be.[1] Thus 'making love' and 'finding love' are not in general the same. But you may make love, because you find yourself in love, and making love may really produce love in both parties to the suit. Few people, moreover, would really 'find' themselves in love, if the object of their affections had done absolutely nothing to 'make' them fall in love. And every married couple has probably discovered by experience that the reality and continuance of their affection depends on the behaviour of both parties.

It is clear then (1) that, roughly and in the main, there is a real pragmatic distinction between 'discovering' and 'making' reality. But (2) we also get some suggestive hints that this distinction may not be absolute, and that in our dealings with the more kindred and responsive beings in the world our attitude towards them may be an essential factor in their behaviour towards us. If so, we shall have sufficient ground for the belief that our manipulations may really 'make,' and not merely 'find' reality, and sufficient encouragement to pursue the subject farther.

§ 6. (2) In admitting that the pragmatic making of truth always presupposed a prior basis of fact an important point was omitted. We neglected to notice also the great and essential difference between the nature of the truth and the reality as it enters the process at the beginning and as it emerges from it at the end. Both the truth and the reality have been transformed. Their originally tentative character has disappeared. The 'truth,' which

---

[1] Cp. *Humanism*, p. 12, *n.*

entered the process as a mere claim, has now been validated.
The 'reality,' which at first was a suspicion, a hope, a
desire, or a postulate, is now fully substantiated, and an
established fact.   The difference wrought by the pragmatic
verification, therefore, is as great in the case of the 'reality'
as in that of the truth, and it was surely worth the whole
labour of rethinking the traditional formulas in pragmatic
terms to have had our attention drawn to its existence.

For the pragmatic theory of knowledge initial principles
are literally ἀρχαί, mere starting-points, variously, ar-
bitrarily, casually selected, *from which we hope and try
to advance to something better*.   Little we care what their
credentials may be, provided that they are able to conduct
us to firmer ground than that from which we were fain to
start.   We need principles that work, not principles that
possess testimonials from the highest *a priori* quarters.
Even though, therefore, their value was prospective and
problematical, they were accepted for the services they
proffered.   For we knew better than to attach undue
importance to beginnings, than to seek for principles self-
evident, and realities undeniable to start with.[1]   We
divined from the first that truth and reality in the fullest
sense are not fixed foundations, but ends to be achieved.

Consequently, the question about the nature of initial
truth and reality cannot be allowed to weigh upon our
spirits.   We have not got to postpone knowing until we
have discovered them.   For actual knowing always starts
from the existing situation.[2]   Even, therefore, if we fail to
penetrate to such absolute beginnings our theory can
work.   And it is not disposed to regard initial facts or
truths as specially important, even if they could be
ascertained.   Indeed our method must treat them as
conceptual limits to which actual cognition points, but
which it never rests on.   Initial truth it will regard as
sheer claim, unconfirmed as yet by any sort of experience,
and undiscriminatingly inclusive of truth and falsehood.
A really *a priori* truth, *i.e.* a claim which really preceded
all experience, would be as likely to be false as true when

[1] Cp. Essay ix. § 9.   [2] Cp. Essay vii. § 3.

it was applied.   It has no value, therefore, for a theory of
knowledge which is wishful to discriminate between true
and false.   Initial reality, similarly, would be *sheer
potentiality*, the mere ὕλη of what was destined to develop
into true reality.   And whatever value metaphysics may
attach to them, the theory of knowledge can make
nothing of sheer claims and mere potentialities.   Methodologically we may and must assume that every truth and
every reality now recognized is to be conceived as evolved
from the cognitive process in which we now observe it,
and as destined to have a further history.

For if we declined to treat it so, we should lose much
and gain nothing.   We should gratuitously deprive ourselves of the right of improving on the imperfect and
unsatisfactory realities and truths which we *now* have.
By conceiving them as *rigid, i.e.* as fixed and unalterable
from the beginning, we should merely debar ourselves
from discovering that after all they were plastic, if such
chanced to be their nature.   If, on the other hand, they
chanced to be rigid, we should not be put to shame ; we
should merely suppose that we had not yet found the
way to bend them to our will.   The sole methodological
principle, therefore, which will serve our purpose and
minister to a desire for progressive knowledge is that
which conceives no reality as so rigid and no truth as so
valid as to be constitutionally incapable of being improved
on, when and where our purposes require it.   We may be
de facto quite unable to effect such an improvement.   But
why should that compel us to forbid effort and to close
the door to hope for all eternity ?

To sum up then : even though the Pragmatic Method
implies a truth and a reality which it does not make, yet it
does *not* conceive them as valuable.   It conceives them only
as indicating limits to our explanations, and not as reveal-
ing the solid foundations whereon they rest.   All *effective*
explanation, however, starts from the actual process of
knowing, which is pragmatic, and not from hypothetical
foundations, which are dubious.   And all effective truth
and reality result from the same pragmatic process.

§ 7 (3). It is clear, then, that we have, on methodological grounds, a certain right to demur to the demand for
an explanation of the initial basis of fact.   It is quite true
that our method logically implies a previous fact as its
datum.   But it is also true that since any determinate character in a 'fact' may be conceived, and must be assumed,
to have been derived, this original datum is reduced for us
in principle to a mere potentiality, an indeterminate
possibility of what is subsequently made of it.   And so
methodologically, as we saw in the last section, it need not
trouble us, because we are concerned, not with presuppositions, but with ends.

It is only, however, when this notion of an original
fact is translated into the language of metaphysics that
its methodological nullity is fully revealed.   When the
doctrine of the making of reality out of a relatively
indeterminate material is construed metaphysically, and
pushed back to the 'beginning,' it seems to assert the
formation of the Real out of a completely indeterminate
Chaos, of which nothing can be said save that it was
capable of developing the determinations it *has* developed
under the operations which *were* performed upon it.

But how, it is asked, with a fine show of indignation, by
philosophers who have forgotten Plato's δεξαμένη and the
creation stories of all the religious mythologies from the
book of Genesis downwards, can such a notion be
put forward as a serious explanation?   How can a
wholly indeterminate 'matter' be determined by experiment?   What would any experiment have to go upon?
By what means could it operate?   And why should the
'matter' react in one way rather than in any other?
And then, without awaiting a reply or crediting us with
any awareness of some of the oldest and least venerable
of metaphysical puzzles, they hastily jump to the conclusion that Pragmatism has no real light to throw on the
making of reality, and that they may just as well revert to
the cover of their ancient formulas.

It is, however, from their conclusion only that we
should dissent.   We may heartily agree that these

questions should be put in a metaphysical sense, if only
in order that it may be seen what their answers would
involve.   We may agree also to some of their terms.   It
is obvious, for example, that to derive reality from chaos
is not seriously to explain it.   But then we never said or
supposed it was.   On the other hand we should *not* admit,
at least not without cause alleged, that because a thing is
indeterminate it is necessarily indeterminable, or that if it
is indeterminate, it must be conceived as *infinitely* so,
merely because we are not able *before the event* to predict
in what ways it will show itself determinable.   We shall
plead, in short, the doctrine that *the accomplished fact* has
logical rights over the 'original' fact.

Still Chaos is no explanation.   This is just our reason
for the methodological scruple about the whole notion of
expecting a complete metaphysical explanation of the
universe from the pragmatic analysis of knowledge.   It
may reasonably be contended that the whole question is
invalid because it asks too much.   It demands to know
nothing less than how Reality comes to be at all, how
fact is made absolutely.   And this is more that any
philosophy can accomplish or need attempt.   In
theological language, it is to want to know how God
made the world out of nothing.   Nay it includes a
demand to know how God made himself out of nothing !
But this is not only a question to which we are never
likely to get an answer, but also one which, as Lotze
wisely remarked, is logically inadmissible.   For it ignores
the facts that something must be taken for granted in all
explanation, and that the world, just as we have it now,
is the presupposition *de facto* of every question we ask
about it, including those as to its past and its 'origin.'
Thus in a methodological sense the existing world, with
its pragmatic situation, is the necessary presupposition of
the original datum from which it is held to be derived.

Moreover, even if *per impossibile* the demand could
somehow be satisfied, and we could learn how the first
fact was made, there is no reason to think that the procedure would strike us as particularly 'rational' or

enlightening, or that this ' knowledge' would leave us any
the wiser. It would certainly appear to have been a
making of something out of nothing. And the first
' something' would probably seem something despicable
or disgusting. It would very likely look to us like the
primordial irruption into the world we now have of that
taint of corruption, evil, or imperfection, which philosophers have tried so often to *think*, and so rarely to *do*,
away.

The fact is that the conception of ultimate reality
looks forward, and not back, and must do so (like
Orpheus) if it is to rescue our life from the house of
Hades. It cannot be separated from that of ultimate
satisfaction.[1] We can conceive ourselves, therefore, as
getting an answer to the question about the beginning of
the world-process only at the end. And it will be no
wonder if by that time we should have grown too wise
and too well satisfied to want to raise the question. To
us, at least, it is no paradox that a *psychological* inability
or unwillingness to raise a problem may also be its only
logical solution. When Perfection has been attained, the
universe, having at last become harmonious and truly *one*,
will perforce forget its past in order to forget its sufferings.
For us, meanwhile, it should suffice to think that Perfection may be attained.[2]

To reject this would be to allow the validity of
von Hartmann's objection to the existence of a God on
the ground that, if he were conscious, he would go mad
over trying to understand the mystery of his own existence. Von Hartmann infers that the Absolute must
be unconscious; but even that does not apparently
prevent it from going mad, as we saw in Essay xi.

The objection, therefore, which has troubled us so
long may now finally be put aside. Methodologically an
original fact is unimportant, because it is unknowable,
and because no actual fact need be treated as original.

---

[1] Cp. *Humanism*, pp. 200-3.
[2] Cp. Essay vii. § 12, *s.f. Humanism*, ch. xi. *s.f.*, ch. xii., § 3-6, § 8 ; *Personal Idealism*, p. 109 ; *Riddles of the Sphinx*, ch. xii.

The demand to know it, moreover, is invalid, and cannot
be satisfied by any philosophy in any real way. 'Original
fact' is a metaphysical impostor. For it could be the
explanation of nothing, not even of itself. And, lastly,
we now perceive that the way to satisfy what is legitimate
in the demand is, not by conceiving an original fact, but
by conceiving a final satisfaction.

§ 8. The only obstacle, therefore, which can still
impede our progress on our projected excursion into metaphysics, is that which arises from the native reluctance of
the Pragmatic Method itself to sanction such adventures.
But at this point we may bethink ourselves that this
method itself is not final. We have conceived it from
the first as included in, and derivative from, a larger
method, which may show itself more obliging. Our
Pragmatism, after all, was but an aspect of our Humanism.[1] And Humanism, though itself only a method,
must surely be more genial. It cannot but look
favourably on an attempt thoroughly to humanize the
world and to unify the behaviour of its elements, by
tracing the occurrence of something essentially analogous
to the human making of reality throughout the universe.
Nor will it severely repress us, when we try to answer
any question of real human interest, on the ground of its
metaphysical character.

For 'metaphysics,' it will say, 'though adventures,
and so hazardous, are not unbecoming or unmanly. There
is not really much harm in them, provided that they are
not made compulsory, that no one is compelled to
advance into them farther than he likes, and that every
one perceives their real character and does not allow
them to delude him. The worst that can happen to you
is that you should find yourself unable to advance, or to
reach the summit of your hopes. If so, you can always
retire with safety, and be no worse off than if you had
never attempted an enterprise too great for your powers.
So, too, if you grow tired. What alone renders metaphysics offensive and dangerous are the preposterous

[1] Cp. *Humanism*, preface, § 3.

pretensions sometimes made on their behalf. For, so far from being the most certain of the sciences (as is their proud aspiration), they are *de facto* the most tentative, just because they ought to be the most inclusive. Every new fact and advance in knowledge, and every new variation of personality, may upset a system of metaphysics. You must not, therefore, grow fanatical about your metaphysical affirmations, but hold them with a candid and constant willingness to revise them, and to evacuate your positions when they become untenable. And after all, you have always a safe fortress to retire upon if the worst should come to the worst. If the objective " making of reality " should prove illusory, you can take refuge with the subjective making of reality which the Pragmatic Method has quite clearly established.'

Thus encouraged, let us see how far a real making of reality can be predicated of our world.

§ 9. Dare we affirm, then, that our making of truth really alters reality, that mere knowing makes a difference, that things are changed by the mere fact of being known ? Or rather, to elicit more precise responses, let us ask *in what cases* these things may be affirmed ?

For we have seen [1] that in some cases these assertions are plainly true, and refer only to facts which should have been noticed long ago, and which the Pragmatic Method has now firmly established. Thus (1) our making of truth really alters ' subjective ' reality. It first ' makes ' real objects of interest and inquiry by judicious *selection* from a larger whole. This purposive analysis of the given flux is the most indispensable condition of all knowing, and has been wholly overlooked. It is of necessity ' arbitrary ' and ' risky,' as being *selective*. (2) It so thoroughly humanizes all knowing that any ' realities ' we ' find ' to satisfy our interests and inquiries are subtly pervaded and constituted by relations to our (frequently unconscious) preferences. (3) Our knowledge, *when applied*, alters ' real reality,' and is not real knowledge, if it cannot be applied. Moreover, (4), in some cases, *e.g.* in human

[1] Essay vii. § 13.

intercourse, a subjective making is at the same time a
real making of reality.   Human beings, that is, are really
affected by the opinion of others.   They behave
differently, according as their behaviour is observed or
not, as *e.g.* in 'stage fright,' or in 'showing off.'   Even
the mere thought that their behaviour may be known
alters it.   As we saw in § 5, the difference between
'making' and 'discovering' reality tends in their case to
get shadowy.

Still none of this has amounted to what we must now
proceed to point out, viz. (5) *that mere knowing always
alters reality, so far at least as one party to the transaction
is concerned.*   Knowing always really alters the knower ;
and as the knower is real and a part of reality, *reality is
really altered.*   Even, therefore, what we call a mere
'discovery' of reality involves a *real change* in us, and a
real enlightenment of our ignorance.   And inasmuch as
this will probably induce a real difference in our subsequent behaviour, it entails a real alteration in the
course of cosmic events, the extent of which may be
considerable, whilst its importance may be enormous.

§ 10. But what about the other party to the cognitive
transaction, the 'object' known ?   Can that be conceived
as altered by being known and so as 'made' by the
process ?

Common sense, plainly, may demur to asserting this,
at least in the ordinary sense of 'knowing.'   Often the
objects known do not seem to be visibly altered by mere
knowing, and we then prefer to speak of them as 'independent' facts, which our knowing merely 'discovers.'   This is
the simple source of the notion of the 'independent reality'
which the metaphysics of absolutism and realism agree in
misinterpreting as an absence of dependence upon human
experience.   But we have already seen (§ 5) that the distinction between 'making' and 'discovering' is essentially
pragmatic, and cannot be made absolute : we must now
examine further, when, and under what conditions, it may
be alleged.

Whether a reality is called 'independent' of our

knowing, and said to be merely 'discovered' when it is known, or not, seems to depend essentially on whether it is *aware of being known* ; or rather on how far, and in what ways, it is aware of being known.

Beings who are in close spiritual communion with us, and thoroughly aware of the meaning of our operations, show great sensitiveness to our becoming aware of them. When we cognize them, and recognize their reality, they react suitably and with a more or less complete comprehension of our action.   Such awareness is shown, *e.g.* by our fellow-men and by such animals as are developed enough to take note of us, and to have their actions disturbed and altered by our knowing, or even by the thought that we may have noticed them.   It is amusing to note, for example, how a marmot will show his perturbation and whistle his shrill warning, long before the casual intruder on his Alpine solitudes has suspected his existence.

But how does this apply to the lowest animals and to inanimate things?   They surely are quite indifferent to our knowledge of them?   To them mere knowing makes no difference.

This case looks, plainly, different, and language is quite right to distinguish them.   But before we deal with it we must elucidate the notion of 'mere knowing.' Mere knowing does not seem capable of altering reality, merely because it is an intellectualistic abstraction, which, strictly speaking, does not exist.   In the pragmatic conception, however, knowing is a prelude to doing.   What is called 'mere knowing,' is conceived as a fragment of a total process, which in its unmutilated integrity always ends in an action which tests its truth.   Hence to establish the bearing on reality of the making of truth, we must not confine ourselves to this fragmentary ' mere knowing,' but must consider the whole process as completed, *i.e.* as issuing in action, and as sooner or later altering reality.

Now that this pragmatic conception of knowing is the one really operative, the one which really underlies our behaviour, is shown by the actions of beings who display sensitiveness to our observation. The actor who exhibits stage fright is not afraid of *mere* observation. He is afraid of being hissed, and perhaps of being pelted. And the marmot who whistles in alarm is not afraid of merely having his procedures noted down by a scientific observer : he is afraid of being killed. Neither the one nor the other would care about a *mere spectator* who really did nothing but observe. If such a being really existed, and Plato's intellectualistic ideal were realized, he would be the most negligible thing in the universe. But knowing is pragmatic, and 'mere' knowing is a fable. And, *therefore*, it is terrible, and potent to make and unmake reality. It was not for nothing that the gods kept Prometheus chained : it is not for nothing, though it is in vain, that Intellectualism tries to muzzle Pragmatism.

§ 11. For one being to take note of another and to show itself sensitive to that other's operations, it must be aware of that other as capable of affecting its activities (whether for good or for evil), and so, as potentially intrusive into its sphere of existence. Man is sensitive to man because man can affect the life of man in so many ways. Hence the variety of our social reactions and the wealth of our social relations. But consider the relations of man and the domestic animals. The range of mutual response is very much contracted. Newton's dog Diamond, though no doubt he loved his master, had no reverence for the discoverer of gravitation. He in return had no appreciation of the rapture of a rabbit hunt. The marmot, similarly, conceives man only as a source of danger. Hence the simplicity of his reaction, just a whistle and a scurry. Why then should we search for anything more recondite in order to account for the apparent absence of response to our operations when we come to deal with beings who are no longer capable of apprehending us as agents? This would merely mean that they were too alien to us and our interests to concern themselves about us. Their indifference would only prove that we could not interfere with anything they cared about, and so that they treated us as non-existent. We, too, treat their feelings, if they have any, as non-existent, because we cannot get at them, and they seem to make no difference in their behaviour.

But is this absence of response absolutely real? A stone, no doubt, does not apprehend us as spiritual beings, and to preach to it would be as fruitless (though not as dangerous) as preaching to deaf ears. But does this amount to saying that it does not apprehend us at all, and takes no note whatever of our existence? Not at all; it is aware of us and affected by us on the plane on which its own existence is passed, and quite capable of making us effectively aware of its existence in our transactions with it. The 'common world' shared in by us and the stone is not, perhaps, on the level of ultimate reality. It is only a physical world of 'bodies,' and 'awareness' in it can apparently be shown only by being hard and heavy and coloured and space-filling, and so forth. And all these things the stone is, and recognizes in other 'bodies.' It faithfully exercises all the physical functions, and influences us by so doing. It gravitates and resists pressure, and obstructs ether vibrations, etc., and makes itself respected as such a body. And it treats us as if of a like nature with itself, on the level of its understanding, *i.e.* as bodies to which it is attracted inversely as the square of the distance, moderately hard and capable of being hit. That we may also be *hurt* it does not know or care. But in the kind of cognitive operation which interests it, viz. that which issues in a physical manipulation of the stone, *e.g.* its use in house-building, it plays its part and responds according to the measure of its capacity. Similarly, if 'atoms' and 'electrons' are more than counters of physical calculation, they too know us, after their fashion. Not as human beings, of course, but as whirling mazes of atoms and electrons like themselves, which somehow preserve the same general pattern of their dance, influencing them and reciprocally influenced. And let it not be said that to operate upon a stone is not to *know* it. True, to throw a stone is not usually described as a cognitive operation. But it presupposes one. For to throw it, we must *know* that it is a stone we throw, and to some extent what sort of a stone it is. Throwing a pumice-stone, *e.g.* requires a different muscular adjustment from throwing a lump of lead. Thus, to use and to be used includes to know and to be known. That it should seem a paradox to insist on the knowledge involved even in the simplest manipulations of objects, merely shows how narrow is the intellectualistic notion of knowledge into which we have fallen.

§ 12. 'But is not this sheer hylozoism?' somebody will cry. What if it is, so long as it really brings out a genuine analogy? The notion that 'matter' must be denounced as 'dead' in order that 'spirit' may live, no longer commends itself to modern science. And it ought to commend itself as little to philosophy. For the analogy is helpful so long as it really renders the operations of things more comprehensible to us, and interprets facts which had seemed mysterious. We need not shrink from words like 'hylozoism,' or (better) 'panpsychism,' provided that they stand for interpretations of the lower in terms of the higher. For at bottom they are merely forms of Humanism,—attempts, that is, to make the human and the cosmic more akin, and to bring them closer to us, that we may act upon them more successfully.

And there is something in such attempts. They can translate into the humanly intelligible facts which have long been known. For example, we have seen (§ 11) that in a very real sense a stone may be said to know us and to respond to our manipulation, nay, that this sense is truer than that which represents knowing as unrelated to doing. Again, there is a common phenomenon in chemistry called 'catalytic action.' It has seemed mysterious and hard to understand that although two bodies, A and B, may have a strong affinity for each other, they should yet refuse to combine until a mere trace of an 'impurity,' C, is introduced, and sets up an interaction between A and B, which yet leaves C unaltered. But is not this strangely suggestive of the idea that A and B did not know each other until they were introduced by C, and then liked each other so well that poor C was left out in the cold? More such analogies and possibilities will probably be found if they are looked for, and in any case we should remember that *all* our physical conceptions rest ultimately on human analogies suggested by our immediate experience.

It is hardly true, then, that inanimate 'things' take no notice of our 'knowing,' and are unaltered by it. They respond to our cognitive operations on the level on which they apprehend them. That they do not respond more intelligently, and so are condemned by us as 'inanimate,' is due to their immense spiritual remoteness from us, or perhaps to our inability to understand them, and the clumsiness and lack of insight of our manipulations, which afford them no opportunity to display their spiritual nature.

§ 13. Even, however, on the purely physical plane on which our transactions with other bodies are conducted, there is response to our cognitive manipulation *which varies with our operation*, and therefore *there is real making of reality by us*.

Even physically, therefore, 'facts' are not rigid and immutable. Indeed, they are never quite the same for any two experiments. The facts we accept and act on are continually transformed by our very action, and so the results of our efforts can slowly be embodied in the world we mould. The key to the puzzle is found in principle, once we abandon intellectualism and grasp the true function of knowledge. For the alien world, which seemed so remote and so rigid to an inert contemplation, the reality which seemed so intractable to an aimless and fruitless speculation, grows plastic in this way to our intelligent manipulations.

§ 14. The extent of this plasticity it is, of course, most important for us to appreciate. Practically, for most people at most times, it falls far short of our wishes.

Nay, we often feel that if reality is to be remade, it must first be unmade, that if we could only grasp the sorry scheme of things we should shatter it to bits before remoulding it nearer to .the heart's desire. Still, this is not the normal attitude of man. There is usually an enormous mass of accepted fact which we do not desire to have remade, and which so has the sanction of our will. Other facts it has never occurred to us to desire to remake. In other cases, we do, indeed regard an alteration as desirable in the abstract, but for some reason or other, perhaps merely because we are too lazy, or too faintly interested, or too much engrossed by more pressing needs, we do not actually attempt to affect an alteration. The amount of 'fact,' therefore, which it is ordinarily felt to be imperatively necessary to alter is comparatively small, and this is why most people find (or 'make'?) life tolerable.

But whatever our actual desire and power to alter our experience, it is an obvious methodological principle that we must regard the plasticity of fact as adequate for every purpose, *i.e.* as sufficient for the attainment of the harmonious experience to which we should ascribe ultimate reality. For (*a*) if we do not assume it, we may by that very act, and by that act alone, as William James has so eloquently shown, shut ourselves out from countless goods which faith in their possibility might realize. (*b*) Some facts, at least, are plastic, and others look plastic, at least to common sense. And even though some 'facts' do not look as if they would speedily yield to human treatment, there is (*c*) no reason in this for abandoning our methodological principle of complete plasticity. For a *partial* plasticity would be nugatory and unworkable. If we had assumed it, it might always be declared to be inapplicable to the case to which it was applied. And conversely, even if we could somehow know, non-empirically and *a priori*, that on *some* points the world was quite inflexible, we could not use this knowledge, because we should not know *what* these points were. Nor should we be entitled to infer that we had found them out, even from our failures. For a failure, if it does not discourage us, warrants nothing but the inference that we cannot get what we want in just the way we tried. Hence for the purposes of any particular experiment it would still be necessary to assume that the world was plastic. Whatever 'theoretic' views, therefore, we may privately cherish as to the unalterable rigidity of facts, we must *act as if* 'fact' were as flexible as ever is needed, if we would act effectively. And as the principle is methodological, it would *not* affect or undermine the *stability* of fact, wherever *that* was needed for our action.

§ 15. Our position, then, as genuine makers of reality seems to be pretty well established. We do not make reality out of nothing, of course, *i.e.* we are not 'creators,' and our powers are limited. But as yet we are only beginning to realize them, and hardly know their full extent ; we are only beginning cautiously to try to remake reality, and so far (with the exception of some improvement in domesticated plants and animals) our activities have been mainly destructive : in every direction, however, there seems to extend a wide field of experiments which might be tried with a fair prospect of success. Nor do we yet know the full extent of the *co-operation* which our aims might find, or obtain, from other agents in the universe.

For it seems clear that we are *not* the *sole* agents in the world, and that herein lies the best explanation of those aspects of the world, which we, the present agents, *i.e.* our empirical selves, cannot claim to have made. There is no reason to conceive these features as original and rigid. Why should we not conceive them as having been made by processes analogous to those whereby we ourselves make reality and watch its making ? For, as we have seen, all the agents in the universe are in continuous interaction, adjusting and readjusting themselves according to the influences brought to bear upon them. The precise nature of these influences varies according to the character and capacity which the various agents have acquired. There is no need to assume *any* character to be original.

All the ' laws of nature,' in so far as they are really objective and not merely conveniences of calculation, may be regarded as the habits of things, and these habits as behaviours which have grown determinate, and more or less stable, by persistent action, but as still capable of further determinations under the proper manipulation.[1]

And lest we should be thought to limit our outlook too narrowly to the agents which our science at present consents to recognize, it ought also definitely to be realized that among the agencies which we have not yet found, because we have not yet looked, or looked only in a half-hearted and distrustful manner, there may be a being (or perhaps more than one) so vastly more potent than ourselves that his part in the shaping of reality may have been so preponderant as almost to warrant our hailing him as a ' creator.' And again, it is possible that our own careers, and so our own agency, may extend much farther back into the past than now we are aware.

But these suggestions will seem wild to many, and need not be emphasized or enlarged on. They do not affect the conceivability of the making of reality, nor the conceptual unity of a cosmic process in which there may always be distinguished an aspect of what may be called ' cognition,' and another of ' action,' but in which the thought should be conceived as subsidiary, as included, tested and completed by the act.

§ 16. What may, however, more plausibly be thought to affect the conception of the making of reality are two closely connected metaphysical assumptions which we have implied throughout. They may be called (1) the reality of freedom or the determinable indetermination of reality, and (2) the incompleteness of reality. Both of these conceptions we discovered, and to some extent justified, towards the end of the last essay (§§ 10-12). But it may not be amiss to add a few words in justification and confirmation of our choice.

It is evident, in the first place, that if *we* have no

[1] Essay xviii. § 11. *Formal Logic*, ch. xxi. §§ 9-10.

freedom, and cannot choose between alternative manipulations and reactions, we are not *agents*, and, therefore, cannot 'make reality.' Freedom, therefore, is a postulate of the Humanist making of reality. Strictly speaking, however, *human* freedom would suffice to validate the notion. For if we can operate alternatively, we can initiate alternative courses of reality.

But there are no stringent reasons for confining freedom, and the plastic indetermination of habit on which it rests, to man alone.[1] It may well be a feature which really pervades the universe. All beings in the world may be essentially determinable, but still partly indeterminate, in their habits and actions. That such is the nature of the universe may indeed be argued from the fact that it responds variously to various modes of handling. And once it is admitted to be partly undetermined, it is not a question of principle how far the indetermination goes. Many or all of the other agents beside ourselves may be capable of more or less varying their responses to stimulation, of acquiring and modifying their habits. Thus the whole universe will appear to us as literally the creature of habit, but not its slave. And the more of this 'freedom' we can attribute to the universe, the more plastic to good purposes we may expect to find it. For we shall expect to find habit more rigid where intelligence is lacking to suggest readjustment and amendment, more plastic where there is more striving towards a better state ; and yet, on the other hand, more stable where there is less impediment to perfect functioning ; but everywhere, let us hope, latently plastic enough to render the notion of a perfect, and therefore universal, harmony that of an attainable ideal.[2]

§ 17. If there is freedom in the world, and reality is really being made, it is clear that reality is not fixed and finished, but that the world-process is real and is still proceeding. And so we come once more upon the metaphysical objection to the growing, incomplete, reality which seems to be demanded by a philosophy of Evolution.

---

[1] Cp. Essay xviii. § 9. [2] Cp. *Humanism*, p. 181.

We have already twice challenged or defied this prejudice,[1] and may this time try to vanquish it by explaining how it comes about.

This objection springs, we may frankly admit, from a sound methodological principle which has great pragmatic value. When we can allege no reason why a thing should change, we may assume that it remains the same. Applying this maxim to the *quantum* of existence, we conclude that *the amount of being is constant*. Applying it to the *totality* of existence, we conclude that *the universe as a whole cannot change* in any real way, but must be complete and rigid.

These two applications, however, are neither on the same footing nor of equal value. The first yields the sound working assumptions of the indestructibility of 'matter' and the conservation of 'energy,' which are of the utmost pragmatic value in physics. They are, in the first place, the easiest assumptions to work with. For it is far easier to make calculations with constant factors than with variable. They are, in the second place, applicable ; for although these principles, like all postulates, are not susceptible of complete experimental proof, experience does not confute them by discrepancies so great or so inexplicable as seriously to impair their usefulness.[2] In the third place, they are applied only to those abstract aspects of physics which have shown themselves amenable to quantitative treatment, and in regard to which, therefore, such treatment seems valid. The scientific use, therefore, of the principle of constancy is pragmatically justified by the peculiar nature of the subject-matter to which it is applied.

But can as much be claimed for its metaphysical double? It is not self-evident that the quantitative aspect of reality is of paramount authority. It is not

---

[1] Cp. Essays ix. § 1, xviii. § 12.

[2] Of course, however, it should be remembered that the leakage of energy, which takes place *de facto* in its transformations, is only *theoretically* stopped by the notion of its 'degradation' or 'dissipation.' Moreover, to conceive the universe as 'infinite' is really to render the postulate of conservation inapplicable to it. For by what test can it be known whether an infinite quantity of matter or energy is, or is not, 'conserved'?

easy to apply the quantitative notion to the spiritual aspects of existence. It is very difficult to conceive a 'conservation' of spiritual values. It is still more difficult to obtain empirical confirmation of this notion. It is almost absurd to deny the reality of our continual experience of change, out of deference to a metaphysical postulate. And, lastly, every human motive urges us to deny the completeness of Reality.

For, humanly speaking, this atrocious dogma reduces us and our whole experience to illusion. If we think out its demands, we must concede that nothing is really happening; there is no world-process, no history, no time; motion and change are impossible; all our struggles and strivings are vain. They can accomplish nothing, because everything that truly *is* is *already* accomplished. The sum total of Reality has been reckoned up, and there is lacking not a single cipher. So all our hopes and our fears, our aspirations and our desperations, *do not count.* For we ourselves are illusions, we, and all our acts and thought and troubles—all, save only, I suppose, the thought of the rigid, timeless, motionless, changeless One, which we have weakly postulated to redeem our experience, and which rewards us and resolves our problems by annihilating us! It is a pity only that it does not make a clean job of its deadly work, that it does not *wholly* absorb us in its all-embracing unity. For after all ought it not to annihilate the illusion as well as its claim to reality? If we, and the time-process, and the making of reality, are all fundamentally unreal, we ought not to be able to seem real even to ourselves. And still less should we be able to devise such blasphemous objections against the One! Somehow, not even the One knows how, the 'Illusion' falls outside the 'Reality'![1]

---

[1] Monism always ends thus. It begins by professing to include everything, but ends by excluding everything. It can make nothing of any part of human experience. Change, time, becoming, imperfection, plurality, personality, all turn out to be for it surds incompatible with the One; but in reducing them to nought it disembowels itself of its whole content, and reduces itself to nothing. The logical source of the paradox that in metaphysics $1=0$ is that all significant predication proceeds by *analysing* a given, and that so any 'real' it extracts is always a selection, and never the whole. A 'One,' therefore, which is not thus contrasted with an 'other' cannot be thought as real.

And for us, at all events, it *is* reality.   For us Reality is really incomplete ; and that it is so is our fondest hope. For what this means is that Reality can still be remade, *and made perfect* !

It is this genuine possibility, no assured promise, it is true, nor a prophecy of smooth things, but still less a proffer of false coin, which our Humanist metaphysic secures to us.   It does not profess to know how the Making of Reality will end.   For in a world which contains real efforts, real choices, real conflicts, and real evils, to the extent our world appears to do, there must be grounds for a real doubt about the issue.   We hardly know as yet how the battle of the Giants and the Gods is going ; we hardly know under what leader, and with what strategy, we are contending ; we do not even know that we shall not be sacrificed to win the day.   But is this a reason for refusing to carry on the fight, or for denying that Truth is great and must prevail, because it has the making of Reality ?

XX

DREAMS AND IDEALISM[1]

ARGUMENT

§ 1. The popularity and ambiguity of Idealism. Can Humanism be the higher synthesis of it and realism? § 2. A degenerate 'idealism' which pragmatically = a monistic realism. § 3. The drift in 'absolute idealism' towards realism. An objection both to absolutism and realism, and the coincidence of their standpoints humanistically. Realism as a shelter for absolutism. § 4. Realistic velleities in absolutism in order to meet the alleged subjectivism of Humanism. Their futility. § 5. The cry 'back to Plato.' Platonism as either realism or idealism. But realism is pluralistic, and if the Absolute also is sacrificed, only the intellectualism remains in 'absolute idealism.' § 6. Common - sense realism is *pragmatic*; but its working has limits. (1) Religiously; 'Heaven' is a *second* 'real world.' (2) Philosophically; the real world is a construction, individual and social. (3) Pragmatic realism does not transcend the experience-process. § 7. Philosophic realism has overlooked the Humanist alternative. § 8. Other idealisms, personal, subjective, absolute. § 9. An attempt to prove absolute idealism. § 10. The inadequacies and fallacies of this proof. (1) The ambiguity of 'reality is experience.' (2) The 'subject' depends on the 'object' as much as *vice versa.* (3) The Absolute does not explain *human* experiences, and vainly complicates the problem of a common world. § 11. (4) Kant's argument from the 'making of reality' criticized. § 12. (5) The psychological subjectivity of experiences presupposes a 'real' world. § 13. Can Idealism be proved pragmatically? § 14. Its fundamental dictum is *reality is 'my' experience*. Why this is not necessarily solipsistic. Why it is idealistic. § 15. The extrusion of the 'objective' world, and its volitional character. § 16. The case for solipsism. § 17. The solipsistic interpretation of dreams has a pragmatic motive, but § 18 so has the realistic interpretation of waking life, which remains immanent in experience, and cannot be more real than that. § 19. Dreams prove that this reality need not be absolute. § 20. The philosophic import of dreams. § 21. A simple argument for idealism. § 22. Seven objections to it and their refutation. § 23. Is Idealism, then, proved? A paradoxical form of Realism. § 24. The final confutation of Realism. § 25. The final confutation of Idealism. § 26. The Humanist solution, which combines the objective and subjective factors harmoniously. The Humanist Ideal.

---

[1] This essay appeared in the *Hibbert Journal* for October 1904. It has been extensively recast and added to, in order to make more explicit its connexion with the general thought of these *Studies*, and to clinch their argument.

§ 1. FOR some reason, which it is not difficult to guess at, and is probably not unconnected with the convenient ambiguities of the word, it has become more reputable for philosophers to call themselves 'idealists' than 'realists.' But it is merely a popular misapprehension, which no serious student of philosophy should countenance, to suppose on this account that any doctrine called 'idealism' must specially concern itself with the vindication of ideals.   In point of fact the term 'idealism' is very variously and vaguely used, the line between it and 'realism' is by no means an easy one to draw in practice, and the classification of many doctrines is somewhat arbitrary.   Moreover, it seems hard to say whether the new pragmatic doctrines are more akin to 'realism' or to 'idealism,' or supersede this controversy also.

It seems, therefore, that we can most fitly conclude these *Studies* by devoting ourselves to an examination of the present condition of the controversy between 'realism' and 'idealism,' with a view to determining to which of them Humanism has more affinity, and how completely it can assimilate the truths they severally contain.   For it is probable that here too, in dealing with what is perhaps the ultimate antithesis of intellectualist metaphysics, Humanism is enabled to play the part of a mediator who transcends their strife, and incorporates in a higher synthesis all that is really valuable in both.

§ 2. We begin, then, with Idealism, which, as we noted, has attained a certain primacy over Realism, and developed into a perplexing multitude of forms.   The more degenerate of these come to very little, and are significant only as illustrating the tendency of more highly differentiated philosophic thought to revert to the simpler and more convenient theories of ordinary life. To many 'idealists' their 'idealism' hardly seems to mean more than this, that they conceive themselves to be entitled to speak of the universe as somehow and in some sense 'spiritual'; as for the rest they think and act exactly like naïve realists.   But *how* and in *what* sense

the world is 'spiritual' it is impossible to extract from
their ambiguous dicta; often one suspects that all they
can really mean is that the spiritual is included in the
universe. At any rate they are careful to leave undefined
the meaning of 'spiritual,' and unelucidated the problem
of the exact relation and analogy between the spiritual
character ascribed to the universe and our human
spirits. It is useless, again, to ask them for a proof, or
derivation, of their standpoint: they are too prudent to
attempt it.

It is clear that such flabby 'idealism' cannot commend
itself to pragmatic thinkers, who will want to know why
that should be called idealism which, both in its practical
consequences and in the efficacious part of its theory,
coincides with realism. It is, accordingly, no wonder
that when the slightest logical pressure is put upon it,
this sort of idealism tends to disappear, or rather to
transform itself into a monistic realism, or realistic
absolutism.

§ 3. All forms of absolutist 'idealism,' moreover, have
recently been subjected to very severe pressure in consequence of pragmatist attacks. They have not only
been asked a number of awkward questions which they
have never been able to answer, but the functional value
and logical validity of their answers to the questions
which they always thought they could answer, and on which
they most prided themselves, have been systematically
impugned. For this transformation of the logical situation
Prof. Dewey's *Studies in Logical Theory* have been largely
responsible, and the effect upon many idealisms has been
highly paradoxical. For it has apparently driven them
in the direction of realism !

And yet at bottom nothing was more natural. There
is nothing like community in misfortune to awaken
philosophic sympathy. And Prof. Dewey had put
absolute idealism in the same box, or rather in the same
hole, with realism. He had shown, that is, quite clearly,
and in a manner which has not yet been disputed, that
the favourite weapon of idealists in their debates with

realism might be turned against them. They had for
years been accustomed to condemn the fatuity of realism
in assuming that knowledge could be accounted for by a
'transcendent' real which could not be known. And then
suddenly it turned out that their own theory involved this
same fatuity in an aggravated form! For it appeared
that absolute knowledge, as they had conceived it, failed
at every point to account for human knowledge, and that
between the two there lay what we have named in
honour of its first discoverer (or maker?) 'Plato's Chasm,'
to the brink of which their theories could approach, but
which they could never cross.

Fundamentally, therefore, as regards the theory of
knowledge, the position of absolute idealism coincides, in
all the epistemologically important points, with that of
realism. Both have tried to conceive ultimate reality as
essentially 'independent' of our knowing, as intrinsically
unrelated to our life. In order to satisfy this postulate
both have postulated that our knowing must somehow
transcend itself, and be able to bring us tidings of something which is unaffected by our process of cognition.
Both involve the fundamental self-contradiction that this
something is conceived both as related to us, and as not
related, in and by the same process. Both have failed to
perceive that there is a much simpler solution of the
problem which involves no such difficulties, that they
have misinterpreted the postulates on which they try to
build the self-contradictory structures of their theories of
knowledge, and that the 'transcendent' and the 'independent' and the 'absolute' can far better be conceived
as staying comfortably *within* the experience process.
Both, in short, have failed to reckon with a Humanist
epistemology.

In comparison with these fundamental points of agreement, the differences between 'realism' and 'absolute
idealism' are really negligible. What does it matter
whether the reality to which our knowing has to 'correspond' is called an absolute 'fact' or an absolute 'thought'?
In neither case can it be reached from the human stand-

point : in either case it would abolish our thought or render it nugatory, if it could be reached. Still, as we saw in Essays iv. § 7 and vii. § 1, though these difficulties are all insuperable, yet realism really involves a few less of them. Absolute idealism has involved itself in some additional complications, owing to the way in which absolute thought reduces our thought to an unreal 'appearance,' which can yet somehow persist in asserting its reality. There is, therefore, a sort of gain for it in becoming realistic ; and this, together with the perception of their common entanglement, would amply suffice to account for the recent drift of 'idealists' towards realism, if one could credit them with a full perception of the difficulties of their theory. But as yet this is hardly the case. They still conceive them as 'difficulties' incidental to a fundamentally sound theory : they have not yet realized its utter rottenness.

§ 4. They have, moreover, further motives for their aspirations towards 'a more objective' view of reality. They have, in the first place, committed themselves to an interpretation of the pragmatic theory of knowledge which renders it controversially desirable to give a more realistic turn or tone to absolutism. This interpretation is one which their preconceptions, no doubt, rendered natural, and perhaps inevitable, but which is nevertheless wholly mistaken. They have interpreted Pragmatism as sheer subjectivism, identified it with Protagoreanism, adopted Plato's identification of the latter with scepticism, admitted his claim to have refuted it, and added that this has been done for all time, and that there is nothing new under the sun.

But all these assertions happen to be false, as we have fully shown. What is true about them is merely that Pragmatism has tried to recall philosophy to the consideration of actual human thinking, and that this is always personal and individual. Hence the absolutist misinterpretation of this undertaking only proves how the continued contemplation of 'ideal' abstractions can vitiate a human mind. The absolutists who argue as above have evidently so disaccustomed themselves to observe the concrete facts of human existence that all actual thinking seems to them to be of necessity 'merely subjective.' That actual thinking should necessarily start with the 'subjective,' and naturally reach the 'objective' by an immanent development which engenders all distinctions, 'transcends' them because it includes them, and reconciles them because it never misconceives them as absolute, sounds to their ears incredible. They will not believe it even when they see it set down plainly in cold print. Yet such is nevertheless the case, and probably was the case from the first, and implied in the first sketch of a Humanist theory of knowledge by Protagoras.[1]

Hence the attempt to refute Humanism and to baffle its attack by growing more 'realistic' seems unlikely to succeed. For the Humanist account of the cognitive process really transcends both 'realism' and 'idealism' as hitherto maintained. It explains *both*, by tracing their genesis and pointing out exactly where they have severally drawn unwarrantable inferences. It can afford, therefore, to remain on excellent terms with Realism, more particularly with what is really the most practically important and efficient form of it, viz. the common-sense theory of ordinary life, of the pragmatic value of which it is keenly appreciative. It does not profess to despise it, to 'criticize' or 'overcome' it ; it simply *includes* it. It simply points out that, good as it is so far as it goes, it does not go the whole way, and must be supplemented.[2]

It hardly seems worth while, therefore, for 'absolute idealism' to take the trouble of becoming realistic, in order to differ from and to confute a 'subjectivism' its critics are *not* committed to.

§ 5. Still, once the cry 'back to Plato' has been raised, it cannot readily be hushed. We have ourselves joined in it heartily, and insisted that the lesson which Platonism has for all attempts to separate the ideal from the human should never be forgotten. But this cry must render an idealism which adopts it in a manner realistic. For (in

[1] Cp. Essay ii. § 5.   [2] Cp. § 6.

a sense) the Platonic philosophy seems capable of forming a common meeting-ground for realistic and idealistic intellectualisms, so much so that it may alternatively be called a realism or an idealism. Hitherto 'idealists' have preferred to call Plato 'the great idealist'; in future they may, as justly or unjustly, call him the great realist. It really does not matter. For, on the one hand, his Theory of Ideas is surely 'idealism,' and on the other, the Ideas are objective entities, and independent and free from all subjective taint. And it seems to be little more than an accident that the champion 'realists' of the day, Messrs. Bertrand Russell and G. E. Moore, have entitled their ultra-Platonic hypostasization of predicates 'realism' rather than 'idealism.' If, then, these tendencies are worked out to their logical conclusions, it may well be confessed before long that 'absolute idealism' is really *obsolete idealism*, at least so far as its substantive part is concerned.

A promising career might thus be predicted for an absolutism calling itself a realistic idealism or an idealistic realism, which Janus-like could always smile triumphantly with one face, however much the other was smitten, were it not for two sad circumstances. The first of these is the existence of Plato's Chasm, across which neither Platonism nor Realism can help it. The second is Prof. Dewey's proof that in the end all forms, both of metaphysical realism and of metaphysical absolutism, must fall into this chasm, and that neither can exonerate the other from objections which press equally on both. It seems more likely, therefore, that upon further reflection, and when the nature of the situation is clearly perceived, this attempt of absolutism to array itself in the serviceable sheepskin of an honest realism will be seen to be cankered in the bud, and will be nipped off quietly.

After all, the enterprise was always paradoxical and never really safe, and it may mitigate regrets to point out that in any case 'absolute idealism' could hardly have really paid the price of an alliance with Realism. In all but its materialistic forms, Realism seems *profoundly*

pluralistic; in its most modern philosophic form it is unmitigated pluralism. Platonism itself would be pluralistic,
but for the Idea of the Good ;[1] and even this unifying
principle *de facto* remains an aspiration, which avowedly
cannot be applied to the actual systems of the sciences.
To purchase, therefore, the support of Realism, 'absolute
idealism' would have to surrender its adjective as well as
its substantive, and to evaporate into mere general intellectualism. But this, perhaps, is what 'absolute idealists'
have at bottom cared for most.

§ 6. As the 'idealisms' we have considered have
brought up the subject of Realism, we may now improve
the occasion to have a preliminary explanation with this
doctrine. And to begin with, we must draw a sharp
distinction between (1) the common-sense or naïve realism
of ordinary life, and (2) philosophic realism.

With the first of these our Humanism will be loth to
quarrel or part company. For it manifestly is a theory
of very great pragmatic value. In ordinary life we all
assume that we live in an 'external' world, which is
'independent' of us, and peopled by other persons as real
and as good, or better, than ourselves. And it would be
a great calamity if any philosophy should feel it its duty
to upset this assumption. For it works splendidly, and
the philosophy which attacked it would only hurt itself.

Common sense, or as we may now also call it,
pragmatic realism, works for *almost every* purpose. It is
only when he tries to satisfy therewith his religious
cravings that the ordinary man discovers that it has its
limitations. For the real world he lives in is *not* an ideal
world, and he can find no room in it for his ideals.
'Heaven' cannot be found in the heavens. He is driven,
accordingly, to the thought of 'another world,' which is
not wholly continuous with the real world. Yet it must
be real too, nay, more truly real than our world. He gets,
therefore, *two* worlds, the 'reality' of each of which has
somehow to be accommodated to that of the other. The
puzzles involved in this relation the ordinary man, very

[1] Essay ii. § 13.

naturally, declines to think out.   But he must admit that they form a legitimate starting-point for a philosophic elaboration of his working assumption.

The philosopher, for his part, may discover further limits to the pragmatic sufficiency of ordinary realism. A few odds and ends of experience, which are usually put aside as ' unreal,' come under his notice.   By investigating them he slowly comes to realize that the pragmatically real world is *not* an original datum of experience at all, but an elaborate construction, made by us, individually, and socially, by a purposive selection of the more efficacious, and a rejection of the less efficacious portions of a ' primary reality' which seems chaotic to begin with, but contains a great deal more than the ' external world' extracted from it.[1]   The exact nature of the process by which the ' real world' is constructed by us, remains, indeed, in some respects obscure.   It is clear, however, that the child, from the first day of its individual life, sets to work to organize the chaos of its primary experience in ways which are certainly as far as possible removed from a ' disinterested' interest in pure knowing, and are almost certainly volitional.   But the baby is not much of a psychologist, and by the time it has organized its experience enough to be able to watch its own procedures and to tell us about them, it has long ago forgotten the details of its world-ordering achievements.   The nearest approximation we can get to an account of the process from inside is probably to be found in the fascinating and unique account by the Rev. ' Mr. Hanna' of how he *recovered* from total amnesia produced by a fall from a cart.[2]   But even here ' Mr. Hanna' had, all unwittingly, a previous existence to fall back upon, which helped him greatly in giving him cues and suggesting the interpretation of his ' chaos.'   And this suggests that even if the baby has not similarly got dim memories of previous existences to aid it in getting a world to know and know-

---

[1] Cp. Essay vii. § 5, § 14 ; Essay xix. § 7.
[2] The narrative forms Part ii. in Drs. Sidis and Goodhart's *Multiple Personality*.

ing it (a view which Plato of yore and many hundreds of millions of men at present have professed to hold), it is equipped with a bodily structure which instigates it to a multitude of traditional modes of selective functioning. Thus the individual's procedure points back (for us at least) to a human past, and this again to a non-human past, until our thought is cast back to the apparently invalid notion of a beginning in absolute chaos.[1]

It is clear, then, that, taken metaphysically, ordinary realism develops difficulties which preclude our conceiving it as ultimately and completely true, even on pragmatic grounds. It evidently contains much truth, but that truth will have to be re-interpreted.

The root error of the philosophic treatment of 'pragmatic realism' is perhaps to take pragmatic assertions as metaphysical dogmas, which they cannot be, and which they were never really meant to be. The pragmatic realism which works is *not* concerned with ultimate realities. It is relative to life and to the facts of life. When, therefore, it speaks of 'absolute facts' and 'independent realities,' it must not be understood too literally. It does not mean anything that exists out of relation to us. For such things would have no pragmatic interest or value. These terms, too, must be interpreted pragmatically. "There is none but a pragmatic transcendency even about the more absolute of the realities thus conjectured or believed in" as William James declares.[2] And we have ourselves seen that the 'independence' ascribed to certain realities does not really transcend the cognitive process.[3] It only means that *in* our experience there are certain features which it is convenient to describe as 'independent' facts, powers, persons, etc., by reason of the peculiarities of their behaviour. In the sense, therefore, in which the term is intended it is quite legitimate. But the whole is "an intra-experiential affair."[4] It becomes false only when it is misinterpreted into a metaphysical dogma, and credited

---

[1] Essay xix. § 7. [2] *Journal of Philosophy*, ii. 5, p. 117.
[3] Essays vii. § 14, and xix. § 10. [4] James, *l.c.* p. 118.

with a miraculous capacity to jump out of the universe of experience and back again as its pleases, without anybody's being a bit the better (or the worse) for it. Such acrobatic feats, of course, are pragmatically quite uncalled for. They are also humanly quite unnecessary. In short, they are a mistake, and with them vanishes all ground for a conflict between Humanism and the common-sense realism which is pragmatically valid, and which the former merely cleanses of an unessential admixture of erroneous metaphysics.

§ 7. Towards the philosophic realism, which attempts to construct a metaphysical theory of a strictly independent reality which can nevertheless be known, Humanism cannot assume an equally indulgent attitude. We have already more than once rehearsed the insoluble puzzles which this theory involves,[1] and need therefore dwell on them no further. But it must still be pointed out that even if this sort of realism involved itself in no intrinsic difficulties, it would yet be lacking in conclusiveness, because it has overlooked an alternative to the idealism which it combats. Humanism forms a third alternative to Realism and Idealism, and can give alternative interpretations of the conceptions on which they severally rely. As regards Realism, for example, it is possible to conceive of a 'truth' and a 'reality' which are valid, not because they are 'independent' of us, but because we have 'made' them, and they are *so completely dependent on us that we can depend on them to stay 'true' and 'real' independently of us.* It is possible, in other words, to conceive all the terms of the realist epistemology humanistically, as *values* selectively attached by us to phenomena *within* the knowledge-process, which is both 'objective' and 'subjective,' and 'makes,' as incidents in its development, all the terms used by the other theories of knowledge.

It would seem, therefore, that the relations of Humanism to Realism are comparatively simple. Pragmatic realism it incorporates ; philosophic realism it convicts of a misconception of its own epistemological terminology.

---

[1] § 3. Essays iv. § 7, and vii. § 1.

§ 8. Humanism, however, is as yet far from having concluded its discussion of Idealism, and here the situation is far more complicated. For there exist, in the first place, a number of idealisms which more or less obviously escape from the objection we have urged against the realisms and absolutisms we have mentioned. 'Personal idealism,' for example, in all its forms, clearly abstains from making the fatal abstraction from personality which is so ruinous to knowledge ; and it is, at least, a moot point whether Berkeleianism also may not claim exemption from condemnation on account of the personalistic element which it contains alongside of its sensationalist epistemology. Subjective idealisms, again, which culminate in outright solipsism, cannot be accused of ignoring the subjective aspects of cognition. All these idealisms, therefore, if they fail at all, fail at other points and for other reasons than those which have been mentioned.

And we have not yet done even with ' absolute idealism.' For we have not yet examined the most stalwart form of it, which is a genuine idealism and unwilling to compromise itself with realism. It makes, moreover, a real attempt to prove its standpoint, and instead of merely abusing Berkeley's ' subjectivism,' without supplying any other basis for idealism, it builds on him, and tries to exploit his argument for its own purposes. Lastly, it really tries to mediate between the human and the ' divine.' Its undertaking, therefore, is instructive and deserving of detailed examination, though undoubtedly beset with perils. For it aims at steering a safe and rational course between the Scylla of subjective idealism and the Charybdis of realism. Actually, however, it would seem rather to sacrifice part of its crew to Scylla and the rest to Charybdis, and finally to founder in an abyss of fallacy.

§ 9. (1) It sets out from what may stand as the fundamental tenet of all genuine idealism, to which, in its own sense, Humanism willingly assents, viz. the assertion that *reality is experience*. But, as thus baldly stated, this proposition needs expansion if it is to account for the facts, and idealistic absolutism also has to develop it. It proceeds, therefore, to add, on the one hand, that the experience which is co-extensive with reality is not to be identified with *our* experience—as the subjective idealists falsely suppose—while yet, on the other, the assertion that reality is independent of *our* experience is not to involve a lapse into realism.

It protests, therefore, (2) that subjective idealism is absurd. The subjectivist cannot really suppose that things cease to exist when he is not perceiving them, nor that his fellow-men are but phantoms of his own creation. But this very sensible contention at once raises a difficulty. For does not this concession block the original road to Idealism, and bring us back to Realism? (3) The absolutist, therefore, tries to save his idealism by adding to the assertion that reality is experience—'*yes, but the Absolute's, not ours.*' The Absolute is an infinite experience which includes all our finite experiences, and eternally perceives the system of the universe, thus providing a habitation for realities (ideas) which have lapsed from the minds of individual thinkers. (4) The finite subject's self-elation is thus put down, but the qualities of the absolute experience remain to be determined. And this might be difficult if the finite spirit, of which alone we seem to have direct knowledge, were *wholly* worthless. But it can be declared an imperfect reflexion of the Absolute, and then observations of finite experience may once more be appealed to to give a content to the notion of 'experience.' By their propitious aid the void and formless Absolute gets itself determined as *individual, purposive,* and *spiritual,* sometimes even as *conscious* and *personal,* while any doubts as to whether these human qualities will stand a transfer to the Absolute are silently evaded.

It is, I think, apparent that, when thus reduced to its bare essentials, this absolutist proof of Idealism seems by no means satisfactory. Nor would so many philosophers have felt bound to accept it *faute de mieux* had they not come upon it with two settled convictions—the one, derived

from their studies, that Realism is impossible, and the
other from their natural instincts, that subjective idealism
is practically absurd.

A little reflection, however, will show that if the
above argument be the best Idealism can do, then no form
of Idealism is tenable. But this as yet it would be
premature to assert. A strictly logical idealism must
certainly steer nearer to subjectivism than to absolutism,
and avoid the assumption of an absolute experience
as self-defeating and as accounting for the 'independent'
existence of the 'real' world as little as the wildest
solipsism. But, even so, it would be exposed to grave
objections.

§ 10. For it must at length be noted that all the stock
arguments for Idealism are fallacious or inadequate. Thus
(1) the mere experiencing of a world cannot be taken as
an adequate proof of Idealism, because it would occur
equally if Realism were right. For, however 'independent'
the reality might be in itself, it would be real for us only
as experienced. Still less could it validly be urged
against a view which conceives the reality and the
experiencing as evolving *pari passu.*

(2) It seems vain merely to show that without an
experiencing subject there can be no object, and that,
therefore, reality is spiritual. For this fails to show that
reality is *wholly* spiritual, if spiritual means subjective.
For the 'subject' in this argument is just as much conditioned by the 'object' as *vice versa.* Each is implied in
the other, and neither can claim the priority. Experience
is a process which plays between two poles, *both* of which
are necessary to its reality. The idealistic interpretation,
therefore, is, at most, a half truth.

(3) The argument that as the world is plainly *not*
dependent on '*my*' experience, it must be on the Absolute's, succumbs to the slightest criticism. It is traceable,
of course, to the old Berkeleian doctrine that the *esse*
of things is their *percipi,* whence it infers that as there is
a permanent world-order there must also be a continuous
divine percipient. In this, however, some serious sub-

reptions have already been committed. Thus it has been taken for granted (1) that there already is what as yet we are only struggling towards, viz. a world-order strictly 'common' to a plurality of percipients ;[1] and (2) that the alleged permanence of the world as it appears to the postulated non-human mind is available as an explanation of 'my' intermittent experience, and yields a common ground for individual experiences to meet on. The Absolute, in short, is used as an *asylum ignorantiae*, which hides from view the real difficulties, both of the practical and of the metaphysical problem of a 'common' world.

The absolutist form of this argument, moreover, is greatly inferior to the Berkeleian. For Berkeley had at least claimed the right to conceive the divine mind in a sufficiently human fashion to render plausible, if not unexceptionable, the analogy between it and the human mind. But all such analogies utterly break down when an impersonal, inhuman Absolute, is substituted for God. For then the world is not '*in*' my consciousness *in the same way* as it is in the Absolute's, nor does it exist '*for*' my mind in the same way as it is supposed to do for the Absolute's. Indeed, it is only in a different and quite improper sense that mind and consciousness can be attributed to the totality of things — the Absolute. Moreover, its experience 'includes' other experiences in a way 'mine' does not. Nor does their inclusion in an absolute 'mind' render things any the less extra-mental to me, or alleviate the pressure of an alien reality. From our human point of view, therefore, this absolute idealism is the crassest realism : it has wholly lost also the chief emotional advantage of idealism, the power, to wit, of fostering a feeling of kinship with the universe.[2]

And, finally, it is merely an illusion that the existence of an Absolute at all accounts for the common world of individual percipients. For (1) it is practically useless ; it does nothing to alleviate our practical difficulties of understanding one another—of communicating ideas and experiences. (2) It leaves the individual variations just

---

[1] Cp. pp. 4 *n*., 110, 315-20.   [2] Cp. *Humanism*, pp. 197-8.

the same. But (3) it renders their existence theoretically incomprehensible. For even when we have hastily taken it to solve the question of the possibility of a common world (by begging it), we find ourselves involved instead in a still more puzzling problem, viz. that of accounting for an indefinite plurality of fragmentary distortions of the absolute world-image. To dismiss these cavalierly as 'appearances' is to exhibit temper, not to solve the problem. For, after all, it was these human experiences which the Absolute was invoked to explain. Not only does it refuse to do this, but it leaves us (4) with our difficulty doubled. We had to explain how the many individual perceptions could correspond with one another and coalesce into a common world. We have now to explain, in addition, how each of them can correspond with an absolute perception as well !

Is it too much, therefore, to conclude that the argument from the human to the 'absolute' mind does not hold because there is no analogy between them ? An Absolute, of course, may still be conceived to 'include' us and all things, but there is no reason whatsoever to regard it as 'spiritual' or as spiritually valuable. The Absolute will help us neither to regard Reality as spiritual, nor to escape from the difficulties of Idealism.

§ 11. (4) We may consider next the idealistic argument which goes back to Kant, and forms the core of his 'transcendental idealism,' namely, the important and indispensable part played by human activity in the constitution of 'reality.' To accept from Kant the details of the operations of thought in building up reality is a feat which none of his disciples have so far achieved, and which is no doubt impossible. But his main principle is sound ; reality for us is largely of our making. Indeed, so far from disputing this, our Humanist theory of knowledge has only made it clearer. It has become manifest that selective attention and purposive manipulation are essential and all-pervasive influences in the construction of the 'real' world, and even the fundamental axioms, which (like Causation) long seemed objective and 'independent' facts, and by Kant were still regarded as facts of mental structure, are now shown to originate in subjective demands.[1] A Humanist philosopher, therefore, is not likely to undervalue whatever testimony to Idealism may be derivable from the moulding of our experience of reality by our activity. But candour compels him to avow that no proof of *complete* Idealism seems attainable in this fashion. For it cannot be proved that reality is *wholly* of subjective manufacture. Kant himself found that the 'forms of thought' must be supplied with 'matter' from 'sensation,' to render possible the construction of an 'objective' nature: nor is a disavowal of his antithesis a solution of his problem. A second factor, therefore, *not* of our making, must be admitted into our 'reality.' This *we* may (and must) attenuate into a mere indeterminate potentiality,[2] or disparage by protesting that the true reality of things is never to be sought in what they originally were, but rather in what they have been enabled to become:[3] but such pragmatic ways of dealing with the difficulty are not open to the Kantian idealist. He is still intellectualist enough to shrink from the assertion that what is methodologically null and practically valueless may be ignored by a theory of knowledge. And so *for him* there still remains a given material for his constructive manipulation —an objective condition of his activity. However much, therefore, he emphasizes the function of constructive activity in the cognition of reality, he still falls short of a proof that reality is wholly psychical.

§ 12. (5) Psychology has supplied an interesting argument to the subjectivity of all experiences from the variations of individual perceptions. But it too is insufficient to prove Idealism. For it has already presupposed a 'real' world in the very experiments which establish the existence of these subjective differences in perception. Hence, though their significance has been unduly overlooked by philosophers, and their proper

---

[1] Cp. *Axioms as Postulates*, §§ 38-9 ; *Formal Logic*, ch. xx. § 6.
[2] Essay xix. § 6.   [3] Essay xix. § 7.

observation may be scientifically most important, and throws much light on the *de facto* ways in which the 'common' world of social intercourse is established and extended, the proof that reality is psychical is *ultra vires* also for this argument. It can be appealed to only *after* it has been shown that the 'real' world which it presupposes is already 'ideal.'

§ 13. Shall it be admitted, then, that the 'proofs' of Idealism one and all break down? Certainly, if what we required was an *a priori* proof independent of experience. Our ultimate assumptions cannot be proved *a priori*; they can only be assumed and tried. And Idealism also may claim to be too fundamental to be derivable from anything more ultimate. It too may appeal to the pragmatic test, and thereby win our sympathies. Let it be assumed, then, tentatively, and to see how it works. If it is content to be proved in this way, it may claim, and perhaps substantiate its claim, to yield a successful and adequate interpretation of experience. And, moreover, by conceiving and assuming it thus, we may come upon one real, though empirical, argument in its favour, which seems to go a long way towards confirming its contention.

§ 14. In attempting such a proof we must be bold as well as sympathetic. We must not fear to follow our assumptions into their most incisive and instructive consequences. It will be futile, therefore, to shrink from the proposition that the fundamental dictum of Idealism must be formulated as being that *Reality is 'my' experience.* This dictum has a subjective tinge, which has terrified most of the *soi-disant* 'idealists,' and driven them blindly into the nearest refuge for the intellectually destitute. But there is no great harm in it, if we do not allow it to harden into solipsism, and are careful to conceive a sufficiently intimate and plastic correlation between the world or reality and the self or experient. We must especially avoid the fatal blunder of imagining that when we have pronounced our dictum, we know all about the self and the world, and have nothing more to learn from experience.

We still have almost everything to learn. For we have really still to learn both what we are and what the world is, and what precisely we mean by calling it ours. We may not, therefore, so far treat our knowledge of the self as primary and our knowledge of the world as secondary, as solipsism tries to do. It is truer to treat the knowledge of each as defining the other, and to say that the world cannot be known without knowing the self, nor the self without knowing the world.

This relation of mutual implication of self and world, therefore, might just as well be denominated realism as idealism. What alone gives superior plausibility to its idealistic interpretation is the empirical fact that the interpenetration of the self and the world is not complete. The self is not *exclusively* implicated in our ' real ' world. It has experience also of the ' primary reality '[1] out of which the real world is constructed, and it extends also, as we shall see (§§ 23, 26), into ' unreal ' worlds of experience. It is not, therefore, tied to the one pragmatically real world, and this enables it to conceive itself as transcending it, and gives it a certain primacy.

§ 15. Still the proposition that *reality is ' my ' experience* is not pragmatically workable. The initial statement, therefore, of Idealism must at once be expanded, and subjected to a modification which amounts to a correction. I have to realize that, though the reality may be really mine, it has yet been largely ' ejected ' or extruded from my consciousness, and endowed with an ' independent ' existence or ' transcendent ' reality. And the motives for this procedure need analysis.

Looking into this question, we soon perceive that our motives were *volitional*. We were not constrained by any logical compulsion, but impelled by our emotions and desires. We *refused* to accept as *ours* the whole of our experience ; and that on grounds as emotional as they are empirical. This is once more illustrated by the strange case of ' Mr. Hanna,' who, in consequence of being pitched out of a carriage on to his head, became as

[1] § 6.

a new-born babe with an adult intelligence. He subsequently described how he surrendered his natural solipsism on being restrained by the doctors, who thought him delirious. " The first that I was really sure that there was something beside me was when Dr. O. jumped on me. Then I was sure there was something against me." " But before you thought it was yourself ? " " Yes, but I thought I didn't know it all." " Did you know why he jumped on you ? " " No ; I knew I was trying to reach out, and he was trying to push me back, and I saw that Dr. O. was the only one, and I could not really make out that there were many of them in the room. It seemed to me that, after all, it was *all one* thing that was against me, and *that they were all like a part of me.*" [1] Our experience, it is clear, happens to be of such a sort that we will not accept the entire responsibility for it. So we postulate an external extramental reality, to which we can attribute, without loss of self-esteem, most of its offensive features. [2]

It is, however, quite conceivable that experience might be, or become, such that our objection to owning it would disappear. If, *e.g.* events invariably took the course we desired, should we not succumb to the temptation of fancying ourselves the omnipotent creators of the cosmic history ? Or, again, if pleasure and pain (or even pain alone) were eliminated from our experience, should we retain self-consciousness enough to frame the antithesis of ' self' and ' world' ? And what motive would remain for ascribing any feature in the course of events to an ' independent' world ?

§ 16. That there was no logical necessity about the conception of an external world follows also from the possibility of solipsism. It is unfortunate that the mere mention of this theory annoys philosophers, especially those who plume themselves on being ' idealists,' to the very verge of aphasia, and that in consequence they

---

[1] Sidis and Goodhart, *Multiple Personality*, p. 109, cp. p. 205.

[2] The primitive instinct is to assign to an external cause even the most clearly subjective disorders. Hence diseases of body and mind are ascribed to possession by demons.

rarely produce an articulate refutation of it. For solipsism is intellectually quite an entertaining doctrine, and not *logically* untenable; it is only practically uncomfortable. We might, had we willed it, have taken a solipsist view of the situation, if we were willing to take the consequences. Any one madly logical enough might always insist that he was the sole and uncontrolled creator of his whole experience. When he fell into a ditch he might applaud his subtle sense of humour in hoaxing himself. When, touching fire, he was burned, he might still proudly claim the authorship of the fire. And when, annoyed at his fatuity, you went up and boxed his ears, he might still ascribe the indignity to the bad regulation of his creative fancy! In short, no logic could refute him, so long as he himself did not *refuse to own* whatever incidents befell him, and was willing to accept them as characteristic of his nature. It might be demonstrated, of course, that such a nature must be inherently absurd and perverse, self-contradictory and self-tormenting, and even self-destroying, as, *e.g.* if he declined to manipulate that idea of his which he calls his legs in such a way as to avoid a contact between it and that idea of his which he calls an angry bull. But if he were blandly willing to admit all this, what then? However you maltreated him, you could not force him to admit your ' independent ' reality.

But, you will say, the solipsist is *mad*, and no sane person can entertain such fancies. Even about this it is not safe to dogmatize. The point whether a being, to which there must be attributed an inherently discordant and conflicting nature, is mad, would have to be settled with the philosophers of the Absolute. For must not their idol, which ' includes,' ' is ', and ' owns ' the weltering mass of suffering, struggling, and conflicting experiences that make up our world, have very much the constitution of our imaginary solipsist? And does not this philosophy come to the queer conclusion that solipsism is absolutely true and yet for us unthinkable? [1]

[1] Cp. Essay x.

§ 17. And, further, before we condemn the solipsist as an outrageous fool, should we not reflect whether we do not ourselves agree with him? Are we not in the habit of claiming as of our own fabrication large portions of our experience which are just as absurd and incoherent as those of the poor solipsist? Do we not, that is, regard ourselves as the authors and inventors of our own nightmares? And so is it not a flagrant inconsistency to adopt a solipsistic interpretation for our 'dreams' and a realist interpretation for our 'waking' experiences?

What makes this worse is that it is quite hard at times to know to which portion of life an experience ought to be assigned, and that *no fundamental differences in character between the two can be established.* For a dream-world, like that of waking life, runs its course in time and extends itself in space, and contains persons and things that seem 'independent,' and sometimes are pleasing, and sometimes the reverse. There is therefore no theoretic reason for the difference in our attitude. The reason is purely practical, and excellent so far as it goes. *Dream-worlds are of inferior value for our purposes, and are therefore judged 'unreal.'* What precisely is their philosophic value remains to be elucidated; but at any rate they show that the solipsistic interpretation of experience is neither impossible nor theoretically wrong.

§ 18. The realistic interpretation, therefore, of our waking life and the 'independent reality' of the world we experience is not an inevitable, but a pragmatic inference, and involves no real inconsistency. It is the result of an extrusion by which we resent the intrusion of unwelcome incidents. It need not, therefore, ever have suggested itself; we might all have lived and died as chaotic solipsists to all eternity. But once the happy thought occurred to any one, that he might postulate an independent reality to account for the incoherencies in his experience, the foundations of realism were laid. The procedure was a great and instant success.[1] The notion

---

[1] Cp. § 6, and *Axioms as Postulates*, § 35.

of an independent external world and independent other persons has indisputably worked, and philosophic arguments are impotent against it. If philosophy disputes it, it will only earn contempt. For common sense is always ready to suppose that whatever works is true, and, fortunately, philosophy is now tending to admit that common sense is, mainly, right.

But though the Realism of ordinary life and science is right so far as it goes, it is not a complete proof of absolute Realism. The 'independent reality' which has been postulated is not after all independent of experience, but relative to the experience which it serves to harmonize. It is nothing absolute ; it means 'real' *in* and *for* that experience. It may be, therefore, *as real* as that experience, but can never be *more real*. The external world and my fellow-creatures therein are real 'independently' of me, because this assumption is essential to my action, and therefore as real as the experience I am thereby trying to control, *provided always that the situation which evoked the postulate continues*. Thus the 'independence' of the real world is limited by the very postulate which constructed it ; it is an independence subject to the one condition that its postulation should not cease. If, therefore, anything should happen in my experience leading me to doubt its ultimateness, the reality of the 'independent' external world would be at once affected.

§ 19. Now, curiously enough, it is a fact that our experience as a whole is such as to suggest doubts of its own finality. It is not wholly real ; we predicate unreality and illusion of large tracts of it : 'real reality' is only a species, with 'unreality,' in the larger genus of primary reality. Thus it is these discontinuities in our experience which familiarize us with the notion of different orders of reality. We experience abrupt transitions from one plane to another of reality, and in consequence we often find ourselves revising our belief in the independent reality of much that at first was accepted without qualms. Our dream-experiences, of course, are a signal illustration of all this. They are facts which incontestably show that a claim to reality is no proof of it, and that our pragmatic realities need not be ultimate.

This only shows, it may be said, that philosophers are dreamers, and that you are no better than the rest. I can swallow the insult if I am allowed to exculpate the other philosophers. For really there are few subjects which philosophers have more persistently forborne to work out, not to say neglected, than the philosophic import of dreams. And yet reflection on their existence might have led to corollaries of the greatest value for the proper understanding of experience.

§ 20. (1) The fact of dream-experience, in principle, involves an immense extension of the possibilities of existence. It supplies a concrete, easy, and indisputable illustration of how to understand the notion of other worlds that are really ' other,' and the manner of a transition from one world to another. It shows us that Paradise cannot be found by travelling north, south, east, or west, however far—that it is vain to search the satellites of more resplendent suns for more harmonious conditions of existence. We must pass out of our ' real ' space altogether, even as we pass out of a dream-space on awaking. In short, we may confidently claim that to pass from a world of lower into one of higher reality would be like waking from an evil dream ; to pass from a higher into a lower world would be like lapsing into nightmare.[1]

(2) More than this, dream - experience suggests a definite doubt of the ultimateness of our present waking life, and a definite possibility of worlds of higher reality ('heavens') related to our present waking life just as the latter is to dream-life. Thus a thought which Religion long ago divined, dimly and with incrustations of mythopœic fancy, Philosophy expounds as a reasoned and reasonable possibility, and urges Science to verify in actual fact.[2] And already this unverified conception may sanction the consoling hope that of the evil and irrationality that oppress us not a little may be

---

[1] Cp. *Humanism*, p. 282, 2nd ed. p. 367.   [2] Cp. *ibid.* p. 283.

due to our not yet having found a way to dissipate the spell of a cosmic nightmare which besets us.

§ 21. (3) Do not dreams yield the simplest and most cogent of all pleas for Idealism? Do they not afford a brilliant vindication to the idealist's contention that whole worlds of vast complexity may be subjective in their origin, and that their seeming reality is no sufficient warrant for their extra-mental nature? Do they not triumphantly enforce our warning that the ascription of reality to the contents of experience must not be made more absolute than need be? For while we dream them, our dream-experiences may seem as 'independent' of our wishes and expectations as any incident in our waking life; but that this independence was deceptive, and conditional upon the dream's continuance, we mostly realize on waking up.

We seem to derive, therefore, from the empirical, but incontestable, fact of dreaming a striking confirmation of the original idealist assertion, viz. that as reality is experience, the psychic factor in it is essential to its existence, and also a proof that *apparent need not be real 'reality.'* And this is proved, not of 'dreams' alone, but of 'waking' life no less. For the existence of the former enables us to grasp the thought of a fuller reality transcending waking life, as the latter transcends dreams.[1]

Just how far these propositions go to prove Idealism and to disprove Realism of any kind, may fitly be considered when the doctrine has encountered a few of the objections which are easily suggested, and as easily refuted.

§ 22. (1) Thus it is clear that our view provides for the fullest recognition of empirical reality. Such recognition is usually just as full in dreams as in waking life. I run away from a dream-crocodile on a dream-river with the same unhesitating alacrity as I should display if I met a real crocodile on the banks of the Nile.

(2) 'But,' it may be objected, 'do you not in your

---

[1] Cp. *Riddles of the Sphinx*, ch. ix. §§ 24-5.

dreams see through the illusion and detect the unreality? Do you not *know* that you are dreaming?' Sometimes, I reply; but then I sometimes also suspect the reality of my waking life. In fact, that is what I am disputing just now. And in support of my suspicions I am able to quote a whole host of religious, scientific, and philosophic doctrines concerning the 'true reality' of worlds other than that of sense-appearance.

(3) 'But is not dream-life merely a parody of real life, a grotesque rehash of past experiences containing nothing novel or original? Why question the conventional explanation of science, which assumes the primary reality of waking life and treats all other modes of experiencing as aberrations from it?'

We are, of course, aware that the philosophic claim we are making for dreams is from the standpoint of common science, a giant paradox. Nor should we dispute that for the ordinary purposes of practice that standpoint will suffice. But with the wider outlook of philosophy one must remember (1) that the exclusive reality of 'waking' experience is not a primary fact, but the outcome of a long process of differentiation and selection (§ 6) which is not yet quite complete, as is shown by the survival of the belief in the prophetic significance of dreams. The process can be traced and practically justified, but it can never subvert the immediate reality of 'unreal' experience. (2) It is not quite true that there is no originality in dreams. There do occur in them, though rarely, experiences which cannot *as such* be directly paralleled from waking life. Do we not fly in dreams, and glide, and fall down precipices without hurt? Yet these are achievements we have never accomplished while awake. Nor can I imagine what justified me once in dreaming that I was a beautiful woman well over eight feet high! I remember that it felt most uncomfortable. (3) Whatever may be the extent and meaning of this originality in dreams, it is not essential to our answer. For the 'scientific' objection to dreams is in any case unable to rebut the suggestion that, instead of imitating 'waking' life, it and dream-life may *both* be imitating *a higher and more real* experience of which for the moment we have grown oblivious, that this is the real source of the similarity between them, and that on awaking from our 'waking' life we should discover this, and then only really understand both our earth-life and our dream-life.

(4) 'But is it not an essential difference that "dreams" are short and fleeting, while waking reality abides?' No, I reply, the difference in duration does not matter. Our subjective time-estimation is enormously elastic ; some dreams, *as experienced*, may teem with the events of a lifetime. That, on awakening, they should shrivel *ex post facto* into a few moments of 'waking' time is irrelevant. In the time of a more real world might not a similar condensation and condemnation overtake our waking life? It is as possible to have a time within a time, and a dream within a dream, as to have a play within a play, and the fact that we criticize a dream-time and a dream-reality within another of the same kind no more proves the latter's absolute reality than the fact that Hamlet can discourse about the players' play to Ophelia proves that Shakespeare did not write both the plays.

(5) ' But is it not an important difference that whereas the breaks in waking life are yet bridged so that it can continue coherently from day to day, each dream-experience forms a unique and isolated world to which we never can return?' There is a difference here, but too much must not be made of it. For it seems to be merely an empirical accident that we do not usually resume our dreams as we do our waking life. And that the fact has not imposed on our writers is attested, *e.g.*, by the tales of *Peter Ibbetson*, the *Brush-wood Boy*, and *The Pilgrims of the Rhine*. Moreover, cases of dreams continued from night to night are on record.[1] The trance - personalities, too, of many mediums are often best interpreted as continuous dreams ; as, for instance, the strange

---

[1] Cp. *Journal of the Society for Psychical Research*, i. pp. 353-77.

trance lives of Mlle. 'Helene Smith,' studied by Prof. Flournoy.[1]

Again, there are on this point assertions implied in all the great religions which should be most embarrassing to the common-sense confidence in the unreality of dreams. 'Visions' and 'revelations' of more real worlds, and experiences of spiritual ecstasies, are not merely the central reality of all mysticism, but permeate the Scriptures and the lives of the founders of religions which count their adherents by the million. Is not every good Mohammedan bound to believe that his Prophet was carried up to 'heaven' on the celestial camel Borak, and there copied the sacred text of the eternal Koran? Must not good Jews and good Christians similarly concede the authenticity of the theophanies to Moses and St. Paul? Yet from the standpoint of waking life all these experiences were indubitably of the 'unreal' order. No doctor, e.g., would hesitate for an instant to ascribe the experiences of Jesus at the Temptation to hallucinations engendered by the forty days' fast on which they followed. We have learnt, indeed, from William James that this 'medical materialism' does not dispose of the spiritual value of such 'abnormal' experiences.[2] But the fact remains that if the religions are to stand, *they must contend that phenomena which would ordinarily be classified as unreal may, properly, belong to a world of higher reality.* The ordinary man, therefore, must choose between abandoning his religion, and admitting that experiences on a different level from that of waking life are in some way real, and that it is not their discrepancy from ordinary life, but their own contents, which decide *in what way.* They are not necessarily discontinuous, incoherent, and unimportant because they diverge from the ordinary level : they may claim, and possess, greater spiritual value and a superior reality.

And so, lastly, it may be pointed out that the unreality we allege against ordinary dreams rests really on their

[1] *Des Indes à la planète Mars.*
[2] *The Varieties of Religious Experience,* ch. i.

intrinsic shortcomings. 'Real' and 'unreal' are really *distinctions of value within experience* ; the 'unreal' is what may safely be ignored, the 'real' what it is better to recognize. If in our sleep we habitually 'dreamt' a coherent experience from night to night, such a dream-life would soon become a 'real' life, of which account would be taken, and to which, as in Bulwer Lytton's story, waking life might even be sacrificed. We should have to regard ourselves as living in *two* worlds, and which of them was more 'real' would depend largely on the interest we took in our several careers.

(6) Leaving such psychological complexities, our objector might take simpler and more practical ground. 'Dwelling on dreams,' he might say, 'is pernicious. It undermines our faith in the reality of waking life; it impairs the vigour of the action which presupposes such reality.' And, of course, if this were true, if our doctrine were practically paralysing and calculated to unnerve us, no more serious objection could be brought against it in pragmatic eyes. But there is no reason to anticipate any such debilitating consequences. *Logically* there is nothing in the thought of a higher reality that should lead us to neglect the highest reality with which we are in contact, or lead us to suppose that the right principles of action in our world would be wholly abrogated in a higher. Once more we might appeal to the religious conceptions of 'higher' worlds for confirmation. The 'other' worlds they postulate are not intended as reductions of the earthly life to unimportance, but as enhancements of its significance.

Psychologically, also, it does not seem true that we do not take our dream-worlds seriously while they last, or are more careless about our actions in them ; the terrors of a nightmare are surely often among the most real and intense feelings of a lifetime, and a man who could discover a way of controlling the dreams of others would speedily master the 'real' world.

(7) Lastly, a still more personal objection may be taken. If waking life may be as unreal as a 'dream,'

may not those for whom we have cared in it turn out to
be as unreal as the personages of our dreams ?   And will
not this atrocious, but inevitable, inference rob life of most
of its personal interest ?

This argument, in the first place, cuts both ways. Not
all persons are pleasant, and it might be quite a relief to
find that some of the bad characters in our experience
were but the monsters of a dream.   Secondly, it does not
follow that because persons (and things) belong to a
dream-life they do not belong *also* to a world of higher
reality.   Our dreams, that is, may be *veridical* and
reminiscent of past terrors ; and they may refer to, or
foreshadow true reality,[1] even as already we may dream
of the persons and events of our ‘ waking ’ lives.

§ 23. All these objections, then, are capable of being
met, and the doctrine that dreams emancipate us from
too absolute a subservience to the realities of waking life
cannot be shown to deprive our life of any element of
value, while it opens out possibilities of an indefinite
enhancement of that value.   But we have still to ask how
far we may take this as meaning that Idealism has been
established, and Realism confuted, beyond doubt.

Taking the latter question first, it would seem that, so
far as this argument goes, uncompromising Realism, viz.
the assertion that existence is quite independent of experience, is still tenable.   If, that is, it is ever really true
that the real world is independent of us, then the existence
of dream-worlds does not render the belief untenable.
But it remains tenable only at the cost of a paradox
which most realists, perhaps, would shrink from.   For
inasmuch as it has been shown that a complete parallelism
exists between ‘ dream ’ worlds and ‘ real ’ worlds, the
resolute realist must take the bull by the horns, and
boldly allege that *all experiences are cognitions of real
worlds, and the dream-worlds are real too*! He might
explain further that the coexistence of an indefinite
plurality of real worlds, of infinitely various kinds and
degrees of completeness, complexity, extent, coherence,

---

[1] Cp. *Humanism*, p. 284, ed. 2, p. 369.

pleasantness, rationality, etc., was quite conceivable. Habitually, no doubt, we were confined to *one* of these, but occasionally, as in dreams, we (or our ' souls ') were enabled, we knew not by what magic, to make fleeting incursions into these other, equally real, worlds, and there to make new acquaintances or to meet old ones, to act and suffer, and finally to return and say (falsely) that ' it was all a dream.' Such is the sole interpretation of the facts a consistent Realism could come to, and though it has not yet been advocated with full philosophic consciousness, it is not very far removed from some early speculations about dreams which are still entertained by savages.

And, like most consistent views in metaphysics, it would not be quite easy to refute. It would seem like an appeal to taste rather than to principle, *e.g.* to urge that to assume such a plurality of worlds was needlessly to complicate existence, or that more idealistic interpretations of dream-worlds were to us personally more attractive.

§ 24. So it is better, perhaps, to fall back upon our general objections to metaphysical Realism, which we have meanwhile held in abeyance, and to improve them into a final confutation of this theory.

Let us then, once more, emphatically affirm that the entire independence of experience which it attributes to the real is in every way impossible and incredible. It is, moreover, an unwarranted misinterpretation. For (1) the fact we start from, and must continue to start from, is *not* a ' reality ' which is ' independent,' but one which is *experienced*. The mutual implication of ' experience ' and ' reality,' in other words, forbids their divorce (§ 14). And (2) the ' independent. ically ' attributed to some of the objects of our experience does not *mean* what the metaphysical realist supposes. It does *not* assert an absolute independence, but is relative to, and rightly understood, *means to be relative to* the experiencing mind which asserts it. The reality we predicate, therefore, is never ' extra-mental '; it has at its heart a reference to the experience which it serves to explain. If, therefore, Realism is taken to mean a denial that experience and reality *belong* together, it becomes a metaphysic for which there neither is, nor can be, any positive evidence.

§ 25. But the same considerations will confute also any idealism which asserts existence to be *merely* mental, and *a fortiori* if mental is taken solipsistically. If, as we have seen, 'reality' and 'experience' are correlated terms, it is false in principle to reduce the former to the latter. The mind can no more be real without a 'real world' *of some sort* to recognize and know, than the real world known can be real without a mind to know it. There is nothing, either in the logical situation or in our actual experience, which warrants either the 'idealist' or the 'realist' assertion. This was why we were so cautious never to admit that reality was *only* 'my' experience, or *wholly* psychic. In so far, therefore, as this claim is implied in the fundamental position of Idealism, Idealism is finally false, and as false as Realism. But is it? One can hardly answer, because so much depends upon usage. Moreover, though it matters a great deal whether or not we grasp a doctrine clearly, it matters far less whether we label it in one way or another. The old labels, however, have grown so worn and dirty, and have had so many conflicting directions inscribed upon them, they have suffered so many erasures and corrections, that even the most optimistic philosopher may well doubt whether they can convey the treasures of our truth safely to our destination, and the most conservative, whether we had not better start afresh with new ones. Humanists, at all events, will have a special motive for discarding *both* the old labels. For some of them hitherto had been accustomed to describe their doctrines as realistic, others as idealistic ; others have varied their descriptions as the exigencies of exposition seemed to require. For them, at all events, it will be simpler to regard the doctrine we have developed as neither realistic nor idealistic, but as humanistic.

§ 26. They will be confirmed in this view by observing

that the illustration from dreams, though it seemed to arise from a defence of Idealism, did not fail to bring out this most important point, that a recognition of reality was always involved. For the appeal to dreams showed the ideal character of the real only by referring to *a higher reality* in which the unreality of the 'dream' could be revealed. The notion of reality, therefore, was *not abolished, but reaffirmed.* We merely abandoned a less for a more satisfactory form of reality. For we were led to the thought of a higher reality which, so far from being merely subjective appearance, was needed for its detection. Thus a recognition of reality was the condition of the condemnation of appearance, nor could anything be condemned as a 'dream' until we had already awakened to something more truly 'real.'

Thus an 'objective' factor and a recognition of 'reality' were always essential. But so was their relation to our experience, nay to 'my' experience. For ultimately to every 'me' the recognition of reality depends on its pragmatic efficacy in harmonizing and organizing 'my' experience. If and when it comes about that 'my' experience changes, 'my' reality must change accordingly.

Thus full justice is done also to the 'subjective' factor, and both are harmoniously combined in the Humanist theory. If, nevertheless, it may seem that the balance finally inclines somewhat to the 'subjective' side, because, after all, it is still held to be possible that every individual soul may some day 'awake' to find the reality of its world with all its works abolished for it overnight, the fault lies, not in our theory, but in the actual facts. For, as we saw at the end of § 14, the real world is not yet coextensive with the totality of existence, with the whole of the self's experience. It is a selection, the arbitrariness and inadequacy of which engender doubts which mere 'faith' cannot fully cure. But these doubts would vanish with an alteration in the character of our experience. As the 'reality' we 'recognized' became more harmonious and more adequately assimilative of our whole experience, we should trust it more. And, even as it is, we can draw a certain comfort from these doubts. So long as 'the real world,' for so many and so often, is so like a hideous nightmare, it is consoling to think that it can wholly be transfigured, that it can wholly be escaped from. And so, though as pragmatists we must insist that it is our primary duty to alter and improve our present world, and to remake it into greater conformity with our ideals, we cannot humanly blame those who have at all times sighed religiously for 'heavens,' in which all wrongs should be righted and all evils overcome. We should teach them merely that the celestial and the earthly aspirations are not incompatible, that the kingdom of heaven does not come by observation, that to remake earth is to build up heaven, that there is continuity enough in the world to warrant the belief that the same forces and efforts are needed and operative and efficacious in both spheres, and that whatever is to be perfected in heaven must have been begun on earth.

But at this point apprehension may be felt by some lest this series of realities embracing and annulling dreams should be infinite, so that nothing we could ever experience could ever be real enough to be final and to assure us that it could never turn out to have been a dream. This fear, however, would rest upon a misconception. Our procedure has throughout assumed that the reality of every experience is accepted until grounds for doubting it arise. This, indeed, is why 'dreams' at first deceive us. The grounds for doubt, moreover, we have seen, are in the last resort *intrinsic*; they consist either in some breach with the continuity of the rest of experience, or in some disharmony which shocks us into a denial of its ultimate reality. Perhaps, indeed, the first case is really resolvable into the second; for a breach of continuity as such involves an unpleasant jar. And if our experience were always wholly pleasant, and its smooth flow never jarred with our ideals, should we not pay scant heed to any incoherencies it might involve?

If life were one great glorious pageant, should we dream of questioning its incidents? Should we not accept them all in the spirit of little children watching the gorgeous transformation of a pantomime? Perhaps such a childlike attitude is feasible in heaven, but on earth it is out of place. For we as yet experience discordant planes of reality, and so can and must conceive ideals of a *more* harmonious universe. We can and must doubt, too, the ultimateness of our present order : but we could not and should not doubt the absolute reality of an experience which had become intellectually transparent and emotionally harmonious. For then we should not need to postulate anything beyond our experience to account for it. Our immediate experience would cease to hint that it was the symbol of an unmanifest reality.

Is such a situation better described in terms of Idealism or of Realism? Assuredly it can be described in either way. For in such an experience everything would be absolutely real ; and yet ' I ' should disown no part of it. It is, therefore, merely a verbal question whether ' heaven ' is better defined idealistically as a condition in which whatever is desired is *realized*, or realistically as one in which whatever is *real* is approved of. But why not simply say that Humanism is alike the true Idealism and the true Realism, and has conceived the true Ideal, in which experience has become divine without ceasing to be human, because it has wholly harmonized itself, and achieved a perfect and eternal union with a perfected Reality?

INDEX

THE END